After reading chapt[...] [sp]irits of our
loved ones come back to comfort us, I cried for joy.

I was thrilled that Dr. [...]
another book. It gives [...]
what we learned in his f[...]

Destiny of Souls is going [...]
wanted more after Journey of Souls.

Jerry, Albany, NY

I never understood my flashback memories about the afterlife
until I read your work.

Dave, Atlanta, GA

The quality and comprehension of your writing about spirituality is so profound and yet you are able to convey complex
ideas so simply. Thank you from the bottom of my heart for
your inspiration.

Doris, Riverside, CA

I applaud your courage in being able to confront the mainstream of negative religious thinking in this country.

Marcia, Topeka, KS

Your analysis of the structure of the spirit world as a place of
order and love is inspiring.

Tracy, Jasper, IN

Your book brings me a lot of comfort and helps diminish my
fear of the great unknown.

René, Paris, France

The enlightening messages from your case interviews are price-
less.

Holtz, Bonn, Germany

I have often felt a deep loneliness and sense of not belonging to
this present life. You have made me see where those feelings
come from and who I really am.

Rachel, London, UK

About the Author

Michael Duff Newton holds a doctorate in Counseling Psychology, is a certified Master Hypnotherapist and a member of the American Counseling Association. He has been on the faculty of higher educational institutions as a teacher while active in private practice in Los Angeles. Dr. Newton developed his own age regression techniques in order to effectively take hypnosis subjects beyond their past life memories to a more meaningful soul experience between lives. The author is considered to be a pioneer in uncovering the mysteries about our life in the spirit world, first reported in his best-selling book *Journey of Souls* (1994), which has been translated into ten languages. Dr. Newton has an international reputation as a spiritual regressionist, appearing on numerous radio and TV talk shows and as a lecturer at New Age expositions. In 1998, he received the annual award for the "Most Unique Contribution" in bridging mind, body and spirit from the National Association of Transpersonal Hypnotherapists. He was honored for his years of clinical soul memory research and discoveries into the cosmology of the afterlife. In 2001 he was a winner of the annual Independent Publishers Book Award for *Destiny of Souls*. The author is a historian, amateur astronomer and world traveler. He and his wife, Peggy, now make their home in the Sierra Nevada Mountains of northern California.

To Write to the Author

If you wish to contact the author or would like more information about this book, please write to the author in care of Llewellyn Worldwide and we will forward your request. Both the author and publisher appreciate hearing from you and learning of your enjoyment of this book and how it has helped you. Llewellyn Worldwide cannot guarantee that every letter written to the author can be answered, but all will be forwarded. Please write to:

Michael Newton, Ph.D.
℅ Llewellyn Worldwide
P.O. Box 64383, Dept. K499-5
St. Paul, MN 55164-0383, U.S.A.

Please enclose a self-addressed stamped envelope for reply, or $1.00 to cover costs. If outside U.S.A., enclose international postal reply coupon.

MICHAEL NEWTON, Ph.D.

DESTINY
OF
SOULS

New Case Studies
of Life Between Lives

2004
Llewellyn Publications
St. Paul, Minnesota 55164-0383, U.S.A.

First Edition
Seventh Printing, 2004

Book design and editing by Rebecca Zins
Cover design by Anne Marie Garrison

Library of Congress Cataloging-in-Publication Data
Newton, Michael, 1931-
    Destiny of souls: new case studies of life between lives / Michael Newton.
        —1st ed.
        p.   cm.
    Includes index.
    ISBN 1-56718-499-5
    1. Spiritualism.   2. Death—Miscellanea.   3. Reincarnation—case
    studies.   I. Title.
    BF1275.D2 N47 2000
    133.9'01'3—dc21

                                                                        00-028270

Llewellyn Publications
A Division of Llewellyn Worldwide, Ltd.
P.O. Box 64383, Dept. K499-5
St. Paul, MN 55164-0383, U.S.A.
www.llewellyn.com

♻ Printed in the United States of America on recycled paper

Acknowledgments

This book is dedicated to my father, John H. Newton, for instilling his love of journalistic writing early in my life and to my son, Paul, for his humor and encouragement during the later years.

In gratitude to my wife, Peggy, who assisted me in reviewing hundreds of client cases in the preparation of this book. Special thanks to manuscript readers Norah Newton Mayper, John Fahey, Jacqueline Nash, Gary and Susan Aanes and my editor, Rebecca Zins.

I also wish to express my appreciation to the many people who have connected with me since the 1994 publication of *Journey of Souls* to say how much knowing about our afterlife has meant to them. Eventually, they persuaded me to take them once again to the other side of time.

Other Books by the Author

Journey of Souls (Llewellyn, 1994)
Life Between Lives (Llewellyn, 2004)

Contents

Introduction

Who are we? Why are we here? Where are we going? I endeavored to answer these age-old questions with my first book, *Journey of Souls*, published in 1994 by Llewellyn. Many people told me the book provided a spiritual awakening of their inner selves because they had never before been able to read in such detail about what life is like in the spirit world. They also said the information validated deep-seated feelings about their soul living on after physical death and the purpose of returning to Earth.

Once the book was in print, and later translated into other languages, I received inquiries from readers around the world asking me if there was going to be a second book. For a long while I resisted these suggestions. All my years of original research had been difficult to collect, organize and finally write as a comprehensive study of our immortal life. I felt I had done enough.

In the introduction to *Journey of Souls*, I explained my background as a traditional hypnotherapist and how skeptical I had been about the use of hypnosis for metaphysical regression. In 1947, at age fifteen, I placed my first subject in hypnosis, so I was definitely old school and not a New Ager. Thus, when I unintentionally opened the gateway to the spirit world with a client, I was stunned. It seemed to me that most past life regressionists thought our life between lives was just a hazy limbo that only served as a bridge from one past life to the next. It was soon evident I had to find out for myself the steps necessary to reach and unlock a subject's memory of their existence in this mysterious place. After more years of quiet research, I was finally able to construct a working model of spirit world structure and realized how therapeutic this process could be for a client. I also found that it did not matter if a person was an atheist, deeply religious, or believed in any philosophical persuasion in between—once they were in the proper superconscious state of hypnosis, all were consistent in their reports. It was for this reason that I became what I have come to call a spiritual regressionist. This is a hypnotherapist specializing in life after death.

I wrote *Journey of Souls* to give the public a foundation of information, presented in a tight, orderly progression of events, of what it is like to die and cross over—who meets us, where we go, and what we do as souls in the spirit world before choosing our next body for reincarnation. This format was designed as a travelogue through time using actual case histories from clients who told me of their past experiences between former lives. Thus, *Journey of Souls* was not another past life book about reincarnation but rather broke new ground in metaphysical research which had been virtually unexplored by the use of hypnosis.

During the decade of the 1980s, while I was formulating a working model of the world between lives, I closed my practice to all other types of hypnotherapy. I became obsessed with unraveling the secrets of the spirit world as I built up a high volume of cases. This made me more comfortable with the validity and reliability of my earlier findings. While these years of specialized research into the spirit world rolled on, I worked practically in seclusion with only my clients knowing about this work and only as it pertained to them and their friends. I even stayed out of metaphysical bookstores because I wanted absolute freedom from outside bias. Today, I still believe my self-imposed isolation and not speaking out publicly was the right decision.

When I left Los Angeles to retire in the Sierra Nevada Mountains and write *Journey of Souls*, I expected to slip into quiet anonymity. This proved to be a delusion. Most of the material presented in the book had never been published before and I began receiving a great deal of mail through my publisher. I owe Llewellyn a debt of gratitude for having the insight and courage to introduce my research to the public. Soon after publication I was sent out on road trips to give lectures and engage in radio and TV interviews.

People wanted more details of the spirit world and continued to ask if I had additional research material. I had to answer, yes. Actually, I still had a wide variety of unreported information that I assumed would be too much for the public to accept from an unknown author. Despite the fact people found *Journey of Souls* very inspirational, I resisted the idea of writing a sequel. I decided on a compromise. With the printing of the fifth edition, an index was added to *Journey of Souls* along with a new cover and some added paragraphs to meet requests for greater clarification about specific issues. This was not enough. The volume of mail I was receiving each week continued to increase dramatically with queries about life after death.

People now began to seek me out and I decided to practice again on a limited basis. I noticed a higher percentage of more developed souls. Clients must wait a long time to see me due to my semi-retirement and greatly reduced client load. As a result, I have fewer young souls in psychological crises and more cases with clients who are able to be patient. These people wish to unlock the meaning behind certain issues by tapping into their spiritual memories in order to fine-tune specific goals in life. Many are healers and teachers themselves who feel comfortable entrusting me with added information about their soul life between lives. In turn, I hope I have helped them on their paths.

During all this time the public perception remained that I had not let go of all my secrets. Eventually, my mind began to turn on how I should approach a second book. The effect of all I have described has brought about the birth of *Destiny of Souls*. I consider my first book to have been a pilgrimage through the spirit world on a great river of eternity. The voyage began at the mouth of the river with the moment of physical death and ended at the place where we return into a new body. I had gone upriver toward the Source as far as I was able in *Journey of Souls*. This has not changed. Although the memory of making this trip countless times is in the mind of every person, no one who is still incarnating seems to have the capacity to take me further.

Destiny of Souls is intended to convey travelers on a second expedition along the river with side trips up major tributaries for more detailed exploration. During our travels together on this second trip, I want to uncover more of the hidden aspects of the route to give people a greater perspective of the whole. I have designed this book by topical categories rather than by progressive time and location. Thus, I have overlapped the time frames of normal soul movement between spiritual locations to fully analyze these experiences. I have also tried to offer readers a look at the same elements of soul life from different case perspectives. *Destiny of Souls* is intended to expand our understanding of the incredible sense of order and planning which exists for the benefit of human beings.

At the same time, it is my intention that this second tour into the wonders of the spirit world be fresh and enjoyable for the unseasoned traveler as well. For first-time readers of my work, the opening chapter will give a condensed overview of what I have discovered about our life between lives. I hope this summary will add to your understanding of what follows and perhaps encourage you to eventually read my foundational book.

So, as we begin this second journey together, I want to thank all of you who have given me so much support for the hard work necessary to unlock the spiritual doorways of the mind. These associations, combined with the indulgence of many guides, particularly my own, have given me the energy to continue the task. I feel truly blessed to have been chosen as one of the messengers for this significant work.

~1

The Spirit World

At the moment of death, our soul rises out of its host body. If the soul is older and has experience from many former lives, it knows immediately it has been set free and is going home. These advanced souls need no one to greet them. However, most souls I work with are met by guides just outside Earth's astral plane. A young soul, or a child who has died, may be a little disoriented until someone comes closer to ground level for them. There are souls who choose to remain at the scene of their death for a while. Most wish to leave at once. Time has no meaning in the spirit world. Discarnates who choose to comfort someone who is grieving, or have other reasons to stay near the place of their death for a while, experience no sense of time loss. This becomes *now* time for the soul as opposed to linear time.

As they move further away from Earth, souls experience an increasingly brilliant light around them. Some will briefly see a grayish darkness and will sense passing through a tunnel or portal. The differences between these two phenomena depend upon the exit speed of the soul, which in turn relates to their experience. The pulling sensation from our guides may be gentle or forceful depending upon the soul's maturity and capacity for rapid change. In the early stages of their exit all souls encounter a "wispy cloudiness" around them that soon becomes clear, enabling them to look off into a vast distance. This is the moment when the average soul sees a ghostly form of energy coming toward them. This figure may be a loving soulmate or two, but more often than not it is our guide. In circumstances where we are met by a spouse or friend who has passed on before us, our guide is also close by so they can take over the transition process. In all my years of research, I have never had a single subject who was met by a major religious figure such as Jesus or Buddha. Still, the loving essence of the great teachers from Earth is within the personal guides who are assigned to us.

By the time souls become reoriented again to the place they call home, their earthliness has changed. They are no longer quite human in the way we think of a human being with a particular emotional, temperamental and physical makeup. For instance, they don't grieve about their recent physical death in the way their loved ones will. It is our souls that make us human on Earth, but without our bodies we are no longer *Homo sapiens*. The soul has such majesty that it is beyond description. I tend to think of souls as intelligent light forms of energy. Right after death, souls suddenly feel different because they are no longer encumbered by a temporary host body with a brain and central nervous system. Some take longer to adjust than others.

The energy of the soul is able to divide into identical parts, similar to a hologram. It may live parallel lives in other bodies although this is much less common than we read about. However, because of the dual capability of all souls, part of our light energy always remains behind in the spirit world. Thus, it is possible to see your mother upon returning from a life even though she may have died thirty Earth years before and reincarnated again.

Orientation periods with our guides, which take place before joining our cluster group, vary between souls and between different lives for the same soul. This is a quiet time for counseling, with the opportunity to vent any frustrations we have about the life just ended. Orientation is intended to be an initial debriefing session with gentle probing by perceptive, caring teacher-guides.

The meeting may be long or short depending upon the circumstances of what we did or did not accomplish with regard to our life contract. Special karmic issues are also reviewed, although they will be discussed later in minute detail within our soul cluster group. The returning energy of some souls will not be sent back into their soul group right away. These are the souls who were contaminated by their physical bodies and became involved with evil acts. There is a difference between wrongdoing with no premeditated desire to hurt someone and intentional evil. The degrees of harm to others from mischief to malevolence are carefully evaluated.

Those souls who have been associated with evil are taken to special centers which some clients call "intensive care units." Here, I am told, their energy is remodeled to make it whole again. Depending upon the nature of their transgressions, these souls could be rather quickly returned to Earth. They might well choose to serve as the victims of others' evil acts in the next life. Still, if their actions were prolonged and especially cruel over a number of lives, this would denote a pattern of wrongful behavior. Such souls could spend a long while in a solitary spiritual existence, possibly over a thousand Earth years. A guiding principle in the spirit world is that wrongdoing, intentional or unintentional, on the part of all souls will need to be redressed in some form in a future life. This is not considered punishment or even penance as much as an opportunity for karmic growth. There is no hell for souls, except perhaps on Earth.

Some lives are so difficult that the soul arrives home very tired. Despite the energy rejuvenation process initiated by our guides who combine their energy with ours at the gateway, we may still have a depleted energy flow. In these cases, more rest and solitude may be called for rather than celebrations. Indeed, many souls who desire rest receive it before reunification with their groups. Our soul groups may be boisterous or subdued, but they are respectful of what we have gone through during an incarnation. All groups welcome back their friends in their own way with deep love and camaraderie.

Homecoming is a joyous interlude, especially following a physical life where there might not have been much karmic contact with our intimate soulmates. Most of my subjects tell me they are welcomed back with hugs, laughter and much humor, which I find to be a hallmark of life in the spirit world. The really effusive groups who have planned elaborate celebrations for the returning soul may suspend all their other activities. One subject of mine had this to say about his homecoming welcome:

> After my last life, my group organized one hell of a party with music, wine, dancing and singing. They arranged everything to look like a classical Roman festival with marble halls, togas and all the exotic furnishings prevalent in our many lives together in the ancient world. Melissa (a primary soulmate) was waiting for me right up front, re-creating the age that I remember her best and looking as radiant as ever.

Soul groups range between three and twenty-five members, with the average having about fifteen. There are times when souls from nearby cluster groups may want to connect with each other. Often this activity involves older souls who have made many friends from other groups with whom they have been associated over hundreds of past lives. Some ten million viewers in the U.S. saw the TV show *Sightings,* produced by Paramount in 1995, which aired a segment about my work. Those who watched this show about life after death may remember one of my clients, by the name of Colleen, who spoke about a session we had together. She described returning to the spirit world after a former life to find a spectacular seventeenth-century full dress ball in progress. My subject saw over a hundred people who came to celebrate her return. A time and place she had loved was lavishly reproduced so Colleen could begin the process of renewal in style.

Thus, homecoming can take place in two types of settings. A few souls might briefly meet a returning soul at the gateway and then leave in favor of a guide who takes them through some preliminary orientation. More commonly, the welcoming committee waits until the soul actually returns to their spirit group. This group may be isolated in a classroom, gathered around the steps of a temple, sitting in a garden, or the returning soul could encounter many groups in a study hall atmosphere. Souls who pass by other clusters on the way to their own berth often remark that other souls with whom they have been associated in past lives will look up and acknowledge their return with a smile or wave.

How a subject views their group cluster setting is based upon the soul's state of advancement, although memories of a schoolroom atmosphere are always very clear. In the spirit world, educational placement depends on the level of soul development. Simply because a soul has been incarnating on Earth since the Stone Age is no guarantee of high attainment. In my lectures I often remark about a client who took 4,000 years of past lives finally to conquer jealousy. I can report he is not a jealous person today, yet he has made little progress with fighting his own intolerance. It takes some students longer to get through certain lessons, just as in earthly classrooms. On the other hand, all highly advanced souls are old souls in terms of both knowledge and experience.

In *Journey of Souls*, I broadly classified souls as beginner, intermediate and advanced and gave case examples of each while explaining there are fine nuances of development among these categories. Generally, the composition of a group of souls is made up of beings at about the same level of advancement, although they have their individual strengths and shortcomings. These attributes give the group balance. Souls assist one another with the cognitive aspects of absorbing information from life experiences as well as reviewing the way they handled the feelings and emotions of their host bodies directly related to those experiences. Every aspect of a life is dissected, even to the extent of reverse role playing in the group, to bring greater awareness. By the time souls reach the intermediate levels they begin to specialize in those major areas of interest where certain skills have been demonstrated. I will discuss these in more depth as we get further along in other chapters.

One very meaningful aspect of my research has been the discovery of energy colors displayed by souls in the spirit world. These colors relate to a soul's state of advancement. This information, gathered slowly over many years, has been one indicator of progress during client assessments and also serves to identify other souls my subjects see around them while in a trance state. I found that typically, pure white denotes a younger soul and with advancement soul energy becomes more dense, moving into orange, yellow, green and finally the blue ranges. In addition to these center core auras, there are subtle mixtures of halo colors within every group that relate to the character aspects of each soul.

For want of a better system, I have classified soul development as moving from a level I beginner through various learning stages to that of a master at level VI. These greatly advanced souls are seen as having a deep indigo color. I have no doubt even higher levels exist, but my knowledge of them is restricted because I only receive reports from people who are still incarnating. Frankly, I am not fond of the term "level" to identify soul placement because this label clouds the diversity of development attained by souls at any particular stage. Despite these misgivings, it is my subjects who use "level" to describe where they are on the ladder of learning. They are also quite modest about accomplishments. Regardless of my assessment, no client is inclined to state they are an advanced soul. Once out of hypnosis, with a fully conscious self-gratifying mind in control, they are less reticent.

While in a superconscious state during deep hypnosis, my subjects tell me that in the spirit world no soul is looked down upon as having less value than any other soul. We are all in a process of transformation to something greater than our current state of enlightenment. Each of us is considered uniquely qualified to make some contribution toward the whole, no matter how hard we are struggling with our lessons. If this were not true we would not have been created in the first place.

In my discussions of colors of advancement, levels of development, classrooms, teachers and students it would be easy to assume the ambiance of the spirit world is one of hierarchy. This conclusion would be quite wrong, according to all my clients. If anything, the spirit world is hierarchical in mental awareness. We tend to think of organizational authority on Earth as represented by power struggles, turf wars and the controlling use of a rigid set of rules within structure. There certainly is structure in the spirit world, but it exists within a sublime matrix of compassion, harmony, ethics and morality far beyond what we practice on Earth. In my experience the spirit world also has a far-reaching centralized personnel department for soul assignments. Yet there is a value system here of overwhelming kindness, tolerance, patience and absolute love. When reporting to me about such things, my subjects are humbled by the process.

I have an old college friend in Tucson who is an iconoclast and has resisted authority all his life, which is an attitude I can empathize with myself. My friend suspects the souls of my clients have been "brainwashed" into believing they have control over their destiny. He believes authority of any kind—even spiritual authority—cannot exist without corruption and the abuse of privilege. My research reveals too much order upstairs, which is not to his liking.

Nevertheless, all my subjects believe they have had a multitude of choices in their past and that this will continue into the future. Advancement through the taking of personal responsibility does not involve dominance or status ranking but rather a recognition of potential. They see integrity and personal freedom everywhere in their life between lives.

In the spirit world we are not forced to reincarnate or participate in group projects. If souls want solitude they can have it. If they don't want to advance in their assignments, this too is honored. One subject told me, "I have skated through many easy lives and I like it that way because I haven't really wanted to work hard. Now that's going to change. My guide says, 'we are ready when you are.'" In fact, there is so much free will that if we are not ready to leave Earth's astral plane after death, for a variety of personal reasons, our guides will allow us to stay around until such time as we are prepared to go home.

I hope this book will show that we have many choices both in and out of the spirit world. What is very evident to me about these choices is the intense desire of most souls to prove themselves worthy of the trust placed in them. We are expected to make mistakes in this process. The effort of moving toward a greater goodness and a conjunction with the Source that created us is the prime motivator of souls. Souls have feelings of humility at having been given the opportunity to incarnate in physical form.

I have been asked many times if my subjects see the Source of Creation during their sessions. In my introduction I said I could go only so far upriver toward the Source because of the limitations of working with people who are still incarnating. Advanced subjects talk about the time of conjunction when they will join the "Most Sacred Ones." In this sphere of dense purple light there is an all-knowing Presence. What all this means I cannot say, but I do know a Presence is felt when we go before our council of Elders. Once or twice between lives we visit this group of higher beings who are a step or two above our teacher-guides. In my first book, I gave a couple of case examples of these meetings. With this book, I will go into greater detail about our visitations with these masters who are as close as I can come to the Creator. This is because it is here where an even higher source of divine knowledge is experienced by the soul. My clients call this energy force "the Presence."

The council is not a tribunal of judges nor a courtroom where souls appear to be tried and sentenced for wrongdoing, although I must admit that once in a while someone will tell me they feel going in front of the council is like being sent to the principal's office in school. Members of the council want to talk to us about our mistakes and what we can do to correct negative behavior in the next life.

This is the place where considerations for the right body in our next life begin. As the time approaches for rebirth, we go to a space where a number of bodies are reviewed that might meet our goals. We have a chance to look into the future here and actually test out different bodies before making a choice. Souls voluntarily select less than perfect bodies and difficult lives to address karmic debts or to work on different aspects of a lesson they have had trouble with in the past. Most souls accept the bodies offered to them in the selection room but a soul can reject what is offered and even delay reincarnating. Then, too, a soul might ask to go to a physical planet other than Earth for awhile. If we accept the new assignment, we are often sent to a preparation class to remind us of certain signposts and clues in the life to come, especially at those moments when primary soulmates come into our lives.

Finally, when the time comes for our return, we say a temporary goodbye to our friends and are escorted to the space of embarkation for the trip to Earth. Souls join their assigned hosts in the womb of the baby's mother sometime after the third month of pregnancy so they will have a sufficiently evolved brain to work with before term. As part of the fetal state they are still able to think as immortal souls while they get used to brain circuitry and the alter ego of their host. After birth, an amnesiac memory block sets in and souls meld their immortal character with the temporary human mind to produce a combination of traits for a new personality.

I use a systematic approach to reach the soul mind by employing a series of exercises for people in the early stages of hypnotic regression. This procedure is designed to gradually sharpen my subject's memories of their past and prepare them to analyze critically the images they will see of life in the spirit world. After the usual intake interview, I place the client in hypnosis very quickly. It is the deepening that is my secret. Over long periods of experimentation, I have come to realize that having a client in the normal alpha state of hypnosis is not adequate enough to reach the superconscious state of the soul mind. For this I must take the subject into the deeper theta ranges of hypnosis.

In terms of methodology, I may spend up to an hour with long visualizations of forest or seashore images, then I take the subject into their childhood years. I ask detailed questions about such things as the furniture in their house at age twelve, their favorite article of clothing at age ten, the toy they loved most at age seven and their earliest memories as a child between ages three and two. We do all this before I take the client down into their mother's womb for more questions and then into the most immediate past life for a short review. By the time the client has passed through the death scene of that life and reached the gateway to the spirit world, my bridge is complete. Continual hypnosis, deepening over the first hour, enhances the subject's disengagement from their earthly environment. They have also been conditioned to respond in detail to an intensive question and answer interview of their spiritual life. This will take us another two hours.

Subjects who come out of trance after mentally returning home have a look of awe on their faces that is far more profound than if they had just experienced a straight past life regression. For example, a client told me, "The spirit has a diversity and complex fluid quality beyond my ability adequately to interpret." Many former clients write me about how viewing their immortality changed their lives. Here is a sample of one letter:

> I have gained an indescribable sense of joy and freedom from learning my true identity. The amazing thing is that this knowledge was in my mind all the time. Seeing my nonjudgmental master teachers left me in a glowing state. The insight that came to me was that the only thing of true importance in this material life is the way we live and how we treat other people. The circumstances of our life mean nothing compared to our compassion and acceptance of others. I now have a knowing rather than a feeling about why I am here and where I am going after death.

I present my findings involving the sixty-seven cases and numerous quotes in this book as a reporter and a messenger. Before I begin every lecture to the public, I explain to my audiences that what I have to say are *my* truths about our spiritual life. There are many doorways to the truth. My truths come from a cumulation of great wisdom from multitudes of people who have graced my life as clients over many years. If I make statements that go against your preconceptions, faith, or personal philosophy, please take what fits well for you and discard the rest.

~2

Death, Grief and Comfort

Denial and Acceptance

Surviving the loss of a love is one of life's hardest trials. It is well known that the process of grief survival involves going through the initial shock, then coping with denial, anger, depression and finally arriving at some sort of acceptance. Each one of these stages of emotional turmoil varies in length of time and intensity from months up to years. Losing someone with whom we had a deep bond can bring such despair that it feels as though we are in a bottomless pit where escape is impossible because death seems so final.

In Western society, the belief in the finality of death is an obstacle to healing. We have a dynamic culture where the possibility of our loss of personhood is unthinkable. The dynamics of death in a loving family is akin to a successful stage play that is thrown into disarray due to the loss of one of its stars. The supporting cast flounders around over the need for script changes. Dealing with this huge hole in the story left by the departed affects the future roles of the remaining players. There is a dichotomy here because when souls are in the spirit world preparing for a new life, they laugh about being in rehearsals for their next big stage play on Earth. They know all roles are temporary.

In our culture, we do not prepare properly for death during life because it is something we cannot fix or change. The apprehension about death begins to gnaw at us as we get older. It is always there, lurking in the shadows, regardless of our beliefs about what happens after death. In discussing life after death on my lecture tours, I was surprised to find that many people who held very traditional religious views seemed to be the most fearful of death.

The fear for most of us comes from the unknown. Unless we have had a near-death experience or undergone a past life regression where we remember what death felt like in a former life, death is a mystery. When we must face death either as a participant or as an observer it can be painful, sad and frightening. The healthy don't want to talk about it and frequently neither do the seriously ill. Thus, our culture views death as an abhorrence.

In the twentieth century there were many changes in public attitudes about life after death. During the early decades of the century most people held traditional views that they had only one life to live. In the last third of the twentieth century in the U.S. it was estimated some 40 percent believed in reincarnation. This change in attitude has made acceptance of death a little easier for those people who have become more spiritual and are pulling away from a belief in oblivion after life.

One of the most meaningful aspects of my work in the spirit world is learning from the perspective of the departed soul what it feels like to die and how souls try to reach back and comfort those left behind. In this chapter I hope to validate that what you sense deep inside after a loss is not just wishful thinking. The person you love is not really gone. Consider, too, what I said in the last chapter about soul duality. Part of your energy was left behind in the spirit world at the time of incarnation. When your love arrives back home again, you will already be there waiting with that portion of your energy which was left behind. This same energy is held in reserve for unification with the returning soul. One of the significant revelations of my research was to learn that soulmates are never truly apart from each other.

The sections that follow illustrate certain methods used by souls to communicate with those they love. These techniques may begin right after physical death and can be very intense. Nevertheless, the departing soul is anxious to get moving on their way home, as the density of Earth does drain energy. In death, suddenly the soul is released and given freedom. Yet if we have the need, souls are able to contact us on a regular basis from the spirit world.

Quiet contemplation and meditation should bring a greater receptivity to the departed and provide your consciousness with a heightened sense of awareness. No verbal messages from the other side are necessary. Just removing the blocks of self-doubt and opening your mind to even the possible presence of someone you love will assist the process of grief recovery.

Therapeutic Techniques of Souls

My opening case is that of an advanced soul named Tammano who is in training to be a student guide. He said to me, "I have been incarnating and dying on Earth for thousands of years and only in the last few centuries am I really getting the hang of how to alter negative thought patterns and calm people." This case begins at the point in our session where Tammano is describing the moments following his sudden death after a former life.

Case 1

S (Subject): My wife is not feeling my presence. I'm just not getting through to her at all right now.

Dr. N: What is the matter?

S: Too much grief. It is so overpowering. Alice is in such a state of shock over my being killed that she is too numb to feel my energy.

Dr. N: Tammano, has this been a recurring problem for you after your former lives, or is it just Alice?

S: Right after death the people who love you are either very agitated or completely numb. In either situation their minds can shut down. My task is to attempt a balancing of mind and body.

Dr. N: Where is your soul at this moment?

S: On the ceiling of our bedroom.

Dr. N: What do you want her to do?

S: Stop crying and focus her thoughts. She doesn't believe I could still be alive so all her energy patterns are in a terrible tangled mass. It's so frustrating. I'm right next to her and she doesn't know it!

Dr. N: Are you going to give up for the moment and leave for the spirit world because her mind is closed down?

S: That would be the easy way for me but not for her. I care for her too much to give up now. I won't go until she at least senses that someone is in this room with her. That is my first step. Then I will be able to do more.

Dr. N: How long has it been since your death?

S: A couple of days. The funeral is over and that is when I settle down to try and comfort Alice.

Dr. N: I suppose your own guide is waiting to escort you home?

S: (laughs) I have informed my guide Eaan that she would have to wait for me a while . . . which was unnecessary. She knows about all this—Eaan was the one who taught me!

This case demonstrates a common complaint I hear from newly released souls. Many are not as proficient or determined as Tammano. Even so, most souls who are anxious to depart for the spirit world will not leave Earth's astral plane until they take some sort of action to comfort those in distress who care about them. I have condensed this client's narrative of how he assisted Alice in her grief recovery in order to focus on the soothing effects of soul energy patterns on disrupted human energy.

Dr. N: Tammano, I would appreciate your taking me through the techniques you use to help your wife Alice with her grief.

S: Well, I'll start by telling you Alice has not lost me. (takes a deep breath) I began by throwing out a shower of my energy as an umbrella from Alice's waist to her head.

Dr. N: If I were a spirit standing next to you, what would this look like?

S: (smiles) A cloud of cotton candy.

Dr. N: What does this do?

S: It gives Alice a blanket of mental warmth which is calming. I must tell you I'm not fully proficient with this cloaking yet, but I have placed a protective cloud of energy over Alice the past three days since my death to make her more receptive.

Dr. N: Oh, I see, you have already begun your work with Alice. Okay, Tammano, what do you do now?

S: I begin to filter certain aspects of myself through the cloud of energy around her until I can feel the point where there is the least amount of blockage. (pause) I find it on the left side of her head behind her ear.

Dr. N: Does this spot have some significance?

S: Alice used to love to have me kiss her ears. (memories of caressing points are meaningful) When I see the opening on the left side of her head I convert my energy to a solid beam and train it on that place.

Dr. N: Does your wife feel this right away?

S: Alice is aware of a gentle touch in the beginning but the awareness is fragmented by grief. Then I increase the power of my beam—sending her thoughts of love.

Dr. N: Do you see this working?

S: (happily) Yes, I detect new energy patterns that are no longer dark coming from Alice. There are shifts in her emotions . . . her crying stops . . . she is looking around . . . sensing me. She smiles. Now, I've got her.

Dr. N: Are you finished?

S: She is going to be all right. It's time for me to go. I'll watch over her, but I know she is going to make it through this—and that's good because I'm going to be busy myself for a while.

Dr. N: Does this mean you won't contact Alice further?

S: (offended) Certainly not! I will remain in contact whenever she needs me. She is my love.

The average soul is much less skillful than even the most junior of student guides. I will discuss these elements further in chapter 4 under the sections of energy rehabilitation. Still, most souls I work with perform rather well from the spirit world on a physical body. Typically, they choose to work in concentrated areas using the beam effect described by Tammano. These loving energy projections can be very potent, even from the inexperienced soul, to people who have sustained emotional and physical trauma.

Eastern practices of yoga and meditation include the use of chakra body points in ways that resemble how souls partition the human body with healing energy. People who practice the art of chakra healing say that since we have an etheric body that exists in conjunction with the physical, healing must take into account both these elements. Chakra work includes unblocking our emotional and spiritual energy through various points of the body from the spine, heart, throat, forehead and so forth, to open and harmonize the body.

Ways Spirits Connect with the Living

Somatic Touch

I have taken the clinical terms of "somatic bridging" and "therapeutic touch" and combined them to describe the method by which discarnate souls use directed energy beams to touch various parts of an incarnated body. Healing is not limited to the chakra body points I spoke about earlier. Souls who are reaching back to comfort the living look for areas that are most receptive to their energy. We saw this in case 1 (behind the left ear). The energy pattern becomes therapeutic when bridges are established to connect the two minds of the sender and receiver in telepathic transmission.

Bridging by thought transmissions to a body which is hurting is somatic when the methods are physiological. It involves the subtle touching of body organs while eliciting certain emotional reactions which can include the use of the senses. Skillfully applied energy beams can evoke recognition by sight, sound, taste and smell. The whole idea with recognition is to convince the person grieving that the individual they love is still alive. The purpose of somatic touch is to allow the grief-stricken person to come to terms with their loss by acquiring an awareness that absence is only a change of reality and not final. Hopefully, this will allow the bereaved to move on and complete their own life constructively.

Souls are also quite capable of falling into habit patterns with somatic touch. The next case is an example of a forty-nine-year-old man who had died of cancer. While the soul of this man does not demonstrate much skill, his intentions are good.

Case 2

Dr. N: What technique do you use to reach out to your wife?

S: Oh, my old standby—the center of the chest.

Dr. N: Where exactly on the chest?

S: I direct my energy beam right at the heart. If I'm a little off, it doesn't matter.

Dr. N: And why is this method successful for you?

S: I am on the ceiling and she is bent over, crying. My first shot causes her to straighten up. She sighs deeply and senses something and looks upward. Then I use my scatter technique.

Dr. N: What is that?

S: (smiles) Oh, you know, throwing energy in all directions from a central point on the ceiling. Usually one of those bolts reaches the right place—the head—anywhere.

Dr. N: But what determines the right place?

S: That which is not blocked by negative energy, of course.

Compare the difference between case 2 and the next client who carefully spreads her energy in a focused area as if she was applying icing on a cake.

Case 3

Dr. N: Please describe the manner in which you are going to help your husband with your energy.

S: I'm going to work the base of the head just above the spine. God, Kevin is suffering so much. I just won't leave until he feels better.

Dr. N: Why this particular spot?

S: Because I know he enjoyed having the back of his neck rubbed by me, so it is an area where he is more receptive to my vibrational imprint. Then I play this area as if I was doing body massage—which I am, actually.

Dr. N: Play the area?

S: (my subject giggles and holds her hand out in front of her, opening up five fingers wide) Yes, I spread my energy and resonate myself by touch. Then, I use both hands cupped around each side of Kevin's head for maximum effect.

Dr. N: Does he know it is you?

S: (with a wicked smile) Oh, he realizes it must be me all right. No one else can do what I do to him and it only takes me a minute.

Dr. N: Isn't he going to miss this after you return to the spirit world?

S: I thought you knew about such things. I can come back whenever he really gets down in the dumps and yearns for me.

Dr. N: Just asking. I don't mean to be insensitive, but what if Kevin eventually meets another woman in this life?

S: I'll be delighted if he finds happiness again. That is a testimony as to how good we were together. Our life with each other—every scene—is never lost, and can be recaptured and played again in the spirit world.

Just about the time I think I am getting a complete grasp of soul capabilities and their limitations, a client will come along to dispel these faulty notions. For a long while I told people that all souls seemed to have difficulties getting past the uncontrolled sobs of the grieving before they could go to work with healing energy. Here is a short quote from a level III whose tactical approach during the peak of the grief process proved me wrong:

> I am not delayed by people who are crying hard. My technique is to coordinate my vibrational resonance with the tonal variations of their vocal chords and then springboard to the brain. In this way I can align my energy to effect a more rapid melding of my essence with their body. Quite soon they stop crying without knowing why.

Personification with Objects

I have heard some fascinating stories about the use of familiar objects, such as with the man in my next case. Since husbands usually die ahead of their wives I do hear more about energy techniques from their perspective. This does not mean male-oriented souls are more proficient with healing because they get more practice at comforting. The soul in case 4 has been just as effective in former lives—as a woman who preceded her husband in death—as a husband in this life.

Case 4

Dr. N: What do you do if your efforts right after death are not having the desired results anywhere on the body?

S: When I found that my wife, Helen, was not receiving me by a direct approach, I finally resorted to working with a household familiar.

Dr. N: You mean with an animal—a cat or dog?

S: I have used them before, but no . . . not this time. I decided to pick out some object of value to me that my wife would know was very personal. I chose my ring.

At this point my subject explained to me that during this past life he always wore a large ring of Indian design with a raised turquoise stone in the center. He and his wife often sat by the fire talking about their day. He had a habit of rubbing the stone while talking to Helen. His wife often kidded him about polishing the turquoise down to the metal base of the ring. Helen had once reminded him that she had noticed this nervous mannerism the night they met.

Dr. N: I think I understand about the ring, so what did you do with it as a spirit?

S: When I work with objects and people I have to wait until the scene is very tranquil. Three weeks after my death, Helen lit a fire and was looking into it with tears in her eyes. I began by wrapping my energy within the fire itself, using the fire as a conduit of warmth and elasticity.

Dr. N: Excuse my interruption, but what does "elasticity" mean?

S: It took me centuries to learn this. Elastic energy is fluid. To make my soul energy fluid requires intense concentration and practice because it must be thin and fleecy. The fire serves as a catalyst in this maneuver.

Dr. N: Which is just the opposite from a strong, narrow beam of energy?

S: Exactly. I can be very effective by rapidly shifting my energy from a fluid to a solid state and back again. The shifting is subtle but it awakens the human mind.

Note: Others have also told me this technique of energy shape shifting "tickles the human brain."

Dr. N: Interesting, please continue.

S: Helen was connecting with the fire and thus with me. For a moment the grief was less oppressive, and I moved straight into the top of her head. She felt my presence . . . slightly. It was not enough. Then I began shifting my energy as I told you, from hard to soft in fork fashion.

Dr. N: What do you do when you "fork" energy?

S: I split it. While keeping a soft fluid energy on Helen's head to maintain contact, I fork a hard beam at the box which holds my ring in a table drawer. My intent is to open up a smooth pathway from her mind to the ring. This is why I am using a hard steady beam, to direct her to the ring.

Dr. N: What does Helen do next?

S: With my guidance, she slowly gets up without knowing why. She moves, as if sleepwalking, to the table and hesitates. Then she opens the drawer. Since my ring is in the box I continue to shift back and forth from her mind to the lid of the box. Helen opens it and takes out my ring, holding it in her left hand. (with a deep sigh) Then I know I have her!

Dr. N: Because . . . ?

S: Because the ring still retains some of my energy. Don't you see? She is feeling my energy on both ends of the fork. This is a two-directional signal. Very effective.

Dr. N: Oh, I do see—then what do you do with Helen?

S: Now, I move into overdrive with a full-power bridge between myself standing on her right side and the ring on the left. She turns in my direction and smiles. Helen then kisses my ring and says, "Thanks, darling, I know you are with me now. I'll try and be more brave."

I want to encourage anyone who is in a terrible state of grief over the loss of a love to do what the gifted psychics do when they want to find missing persons. Take a piece of jewelry, an article of clothing—anything that belonged to the departed person—and hold it for a while in a mutually familiar place and quietly open your mind, while blanking out all other irrelevant thoughts.

Before leaving this section, I want to relate my favorite story about energy contact through objects from a discarnate being.

My wife, Peggy, is an oncology nurse with a graduate degree in counseling, so she involves herself a great deal with grieving cancer patients and their families. Because she administers chemotherapy at a hospital, this puts her in touch with hospice personnel. A few of these women and my wife are close friends who meet regularly as a support group. One of the members of the group is a recent widow whose husband,

Clay, died of cancer. Clay loved big band dancing and he and his wife would often go on road trips to where the best bands were playing.

One night after Clay's death, his widow, my wife and the rest of the support group were in a circle in the middle of this lady's living room floor talking about my theories of how souls reach back to comfort the people they love. The widow exclaimed in frustration, "Why hasn't Clay made himself known in a way that would comfort me?" There was a moment of silence and suddenly a music box on top of a book shelf began to play Glenn Miller's song *In the Mood*. From what I understand, there was a stunned silence followed by nervous laughter from the group. All the widow could say was, "That music box hasn't been touched in two years!" It didn't matter. I think she got Clay's message.

Light energy has some properties of electromagnetic force, and thus can work in mysterious ways with objects. JoAnn and Jim are two former clients of mine whose marriage is a very close one. After their sessions, we got into a discussion of the use of energy beams by the living. Sheepishly, they told me they combine their energy on the California freeways to push cars out of the fast lane in front of them when they are in a hurry. When I asked if they tailgate, they said, "No, we just direct a combined beam to the back of the driver's head and then fork the beam to the right (middle lane) and back again." They claim that over 50 percent of the time they are successful. I told JoAnn and Jim, half seriously, that pushing cars out of their way was clearly a misuse of power and they had better mend their ways. I think they both know that using their gift more constructively will be much better received upstairs, although it will be a hard habit to break.

Dream Recognition

One of the primary ways the newly departed soul uses to reach people who love them is through the dream state. The grief that has overwhelmed the conscious mind is temporarily pushed out of a frontal position in our thoughts when we are asleep. Even if we are in a fitful state of sleep, the unconscious mind is now more open for reception. Unfortunately, the person who is grieving will all too often wake up from a dream that could have contained a message and allow it to slip away from memory without writing anything down. Either the images and symbols they saw while asleep didn't mean anything at the time, or the dream sequence was chalked off as wishful thinking if, for example, the dreamer saw themselves with the deceased.

Before proceeding further, I want to offer an assessment about the general nature of dreams. My professional experience with dreams stems from listening to subjects in hypnosis explain how—as discarnates—they use the dream state to reach the living. Spirits are very selective in their use of our dream sequences. I have come to the conclusion that most dreams are not profound. In reviewing various texts about dreaming, I find even specialists in the field believe many dreams during the night are simply jumbled up absurdities caused by our circuits being on overload throughout the day. If the mind is venting during certain sleep cycles, then the nerve transmissions across our synaptic clefts are letting off steam to relax the brain.

I classify dreams in three ways and one of them is the cleaning house state. At times in the night many stray thoughts from the day are scrambled and swept out of the mind as gobbledygook. We can't make sense of it because there is none. On the other hand, we all know there is a more cognitive side to dreaming. I divide this state into two parts, problem solving and spiritual, with only a fine line between them. There are people who have been given a premonition about some future event as an outgrowth of dreams. Our state of mind may be altered by dreams.

One of the most stressful periods of our lives occurs during the period of mourning when the affections of someone we love are taken away from us—we think forever. About the only relief we get from oppressive grief is during sleep. We go to bed with anguish and wake up with the pain still there, yet there is enigma in between. Some mornings bring us a better idea of the initial steps to take toward coping with our loss. Problem solving through dream sequences is a process of mental incubation which has been called procedural because images appear that teach us ways to move forward. Does this insight come from somewhere other than ourselves? If the dream spills over into the spirit mode, then the Dreamweavers have probably paid us a call as prompters to assist us through our emotional distress.

Spiritual dreams involve our guides, teaching souls and soulmates who come as messengers to assist us with solutions. We do not need to be grieving to receive help in this way. Into this spiritual dream mixture we also have memory recall of our experiences on other physical and mental worlds, including the spirit world. How many of you have dreamed you could fly or swim easily underwater? I have found with some clients that these mythic memories contain information about the lives they led as intelligent flying or water creatures on other planets. Frequently, these kinds of dream sequences provide us with metaphoric clues which open the door to comparisons of former lives with our current one. Our immortal soul character does not change much between host bodies, so these comparisons are not all that bizarre. Some of our greatest revelations come from the episodic dreams of events, places and behavior patterns emanating from experiences before we acquired our present body.

In chapter 1, I briefly touched on the preparation class we attend in the spirit world before returning to a new life. This soul exercise is covered more thoroughly in my first book, but I mention it here because this experience is relevant to our dreams. The class is designed for recognition of future people and events. While we prepare to incarnate, a teacher reinforces the important aspects of our new life contract. Meeting and interacting with souls from our group and other clusters who are to share parts of our new life form an integral part of the class.

Memories of this prep class might well be triggered in our dreams to light a lamp in the darkness of despair, particularly when a primary soulmate is lost in life. Jung said, "Dreams embody suppressed wishes and fears but may also give expression to inescapable truths which are not illusions or wild fantasies." Sometimes these truths are couched in metaphoric puzzles and represented as archetypal images during our dreams. Dream symbols are culturally generalized and dream glossaries are not immune to this prejudice. Each person should use their own intuition to delineate the meaning of a dream.

The Australian Aborigines, a culture with over 10,000 years of unbroken history, believe that dream time is actually real time in terms of objective reality. A dream perception is often as real as an awake experience. To souls in the spirit world time is always in the present, so regardless of how long they have been physically gone from your life, the person you love wants you to be aware they are still in *now* reality. How does a loving spirit go about helping you gain insight and acceptance of these things in your dreams?

Case 5

My subject in this case has just died of pneumonia in New York City in 1935. She was a young woman in her early thirties who came to New York after growing up in a small midwestern town. Sylvia's death was sudden and she wanted to provide some comfort to her widowed mother.

Dr. N: Do you leave immediately for the spirit world after death?

S: No, I do not. I must say goodbye to my mother so I want to stay around Earth for a while until she gets the news.

Dr. N: Is there anyone else you care to see before going to your mother?

S: (with hesitation, then in a husky voice) Yes . . . I have an old boyfriend . . . his name is Phil . . . I go to his house first . . .

Dr. N: (gently) I see; were you in love with Phil?

S: (pause) Yes, but we never married . . . I . . . just want to touch him once more. I don't really make contact with him because he is sound asleep and not dreaming. I can't stay long because I want to reach my mother before she hears the news about me.

Dr. N: Aren't you being a little too rushed with Phil? Why don't you wait for a proper dream cycle and leave a message?

S: (firmly) Phil hasn't been part of my life for years. I gave myself to him when we were both young. He hardly thinks about me anymore . . . and . . . well . . . to pick up on me through a dream . . . he could miss the message anyway. My leaving traces of my energy is enough for now because we will be together again in the spirit world.

Dr. N: After leaving Phil, do you go to your mother?

S: Yes. I begin with more conventional thought communication while she is awake but I am getting nowhere. She is so sad. My mother's grief at not being at my bedside is overpowering her.

Dr. N: What methods have you tried so far?

S: I project my thoughts with an orange-yellow light, like the flame of a candle, and place my light around her head, sending loving thoughts. I'm not effective. She doesn't realize I am with her. I am going for a dream.

Dr. N: All right, Sylvia, take me through this slowly. Please start by telling me if you pick out one of your mother's dreams or if you can create one of your own.

S: I don't create dreams well yet. It is much easier for me to take one of hers so I can enter the dream to effect a more natural contact and then participate. I want her to know it is clearly me in the dream.

Dr. N: Fine, now take me through this process with you.

S: The first couple of dreams are unsuitable. One is a muddle of absurdity. Another is a past life fragment, but without me in it. Finally, she has a dream where she is walking alone in the fields around my house. You should know she has no grief in this dream. I am not dead yet.

Dr. N: What good is this dream, Sylvia, if you are not in it?

S: (laughing at me) Listen, aren't you seeing—I'm going to smoothly place myself in the dream.

Dr. N: You can alter the sequence of the dream to include yourself?

S: Sure, I enter the dream from the other end of the field by matching my energy patterns to my mother's thoughts. I project an image of myself as I was the last time she saw me. I come slowly across the field to let her get used to my presence. I wave and smile and then come to her. We hug each other and now I send waves of rejuvenating energy into her sleeping body.

Dr. N: And what will this do for your mother?

S: This picture is raised to a higher level of consciousness for my mother. I want to insure the dream will stay with her after she wakes up.

Dr. N: How can you be sure she won't think this is all a projection of her desire for you and discount the dream as not being real?

S: The influence of a vivid dream like this is very great. When my mother wakes up, her mind has a vivid impression of this landscape with me and suspects I am with her. In time the memory is so real she is sure of it.

Dr. N: Sylvia, does the image of the dream move from the unconscious to a conscious reality because of your energy transfer?

S: Yes, it is a filtering process where I continue to send waves of energy into her over the next few days until she begins to accept my passing. I want her to believe I am still part of her and always will be.

Turning back to Phil's sleep state, it was evident Sylvia did not intend to stay long to manifest her feelings within his unconscious mind. Dreams do not appear to occur in the deep delta stages of brain-wave activity where there is no rapid eye movement. REM sleep, also known as paradoxical sleep, is a much lighter and therefore more active dream state occurring mostly in the early and late stages of sleep. In my next case, the dreamer will be reached between dreams presumably because he is still in REM sleep.

The Dreamweaver souls I have come in contact with all engage in dream implanting, with two prominent differences.

1. **Dream Alteration.** Here a skillful discarnate enters the mind of a sleeper and partially alters an existing dream already in progress. This technique I would call one of interlineation, where spirits place themselves as actors between the lines of an unfolding play so the dreamer is not aware of script tampering with the sequences. This is what Sylvia was doing with her mother. She was waiting for the right sort of ongoing dream to enter and initiate a smooth fit. As difficult as this approach seems, it is evident to me the second procedure is more complex.

2. **Dream Origination.** In these cases the soul must create and fully implant a new dream from scratch and weave the tapestry of these images into a meaningful presentation to suit their purpose. Creating or altering scenes in the mind of a dreamer is intended to convey a message. I see as this an act of service and love. If the dream implantation is not performed skillfully to make the dream meaningful, the sleeper moves on and wakes up in the morning remembering only disjointed fragments or nothing at all about the dream.

To illustrate the therapeutic use of Dream Origination, I will cite the case of a level V subject whose name was Bud in his last life. Bud was killed in a 1942 battle during World War II. The case involves a dreamer called Walt, who was Bud's surviving brother. Bud is adept at dream-weaving, so after his battlefield death he returned home to the spirit world and made preparations for an effective method to comfort Walt. This is one of those cases that gave me greater perspective of the subtle integration methods Dreamweaver Souls are able to use with sleeping people. During this condensed case, my subject will describe the dream techniques taught to him by his guide, Axinar.

Case 6

Dr. N: How do you plan to alleviate your brother's grief after returning to the spirit world?

S: Axinar has been working with me on an effective strategy. It's very delicate because we are with Walt's duplicate.

Dr. N: You mean that dual part of Walt's energy mass that remained behind during his incarnation to Earth?

S: Yes, Walt and I are in the same soul group. I begin by connecting myself to his divided nature here to more closely communicate with Walt's light on Earth.

Dr. N: Please explain this procedure.

S: I float next to the cache where his remaining energy is anchored and meld with it briefly. This allows for a perfect recording of

Walt's energy imprint. There is already a telepathic bonding between us but I want to have a tighter vibrational alliance when I reach his bedside.

Dr. N: Why do you wish to carry an absolutely accurate print of Walt's energy pattern with you on your return to Earth?

S: For a stronger connection to the dreams I will create.

Dr. N: But why can't Walt's other half communicate with himself on Earth instead of you?

S: (sharply) This does not work well. It is nothing more than talking to oneself. There is no impact, especially during sleep. It's a washout.

Dr. N: All right, since Walt's exact energy print is with you, what happens when you go to his sleeping body?

S: He is tossing and turning at night and really suffering a lot over my being killed. Axinar trained me to work between dreams because he does these energy transfers so well himself.

Dr. N: You work between dreams?

S: Yes, so I can leave messages on either side of two different dreams and then link them for greater receptivity. Because I have Walt's exact energy imprint, I slip into his mind quite easily to deploy my energy. After my visit, a third dream about the first two unfolds as a delayed reaction and Walt sees us together again in an out-of-body setting, which he won't recognize as the spirit world but the activation of these inviting memories will sustain him.

Note: Some cultures, such as the Tibetan mystics, believe they do recognize the spirit world as an almost physical paradise to be a natural part of dreaming.

Dr. N: What were the dreams you created?

S: Walt was three years older, yet we played a lot together as boys. This changed when he was thirteen, not because we weren't still close as brothers, he just became attached to guys his own age and I was excluded. One day Walt and his friends were swinging on a rope tied over the branch of a big tree high above a pond near our farm. I was nearby, watching. The other boys went first and were engaged in a water fight when Walt swung too high and hit his head hard on another branch and was almost knocked out as he fell into the water. They did not see him fall. I dove into the pond and held up his head screaming for help. Later, on the bank, Walt looked up at me with a dazed expression and said, "Thanks for saving me, Buddy." I thought this act would admit me to their club but a few weeks afterwards Walt and his friends would not let me play a game of softball with them. I felt betrayed that Walt would not stand up for us. During the game the ball was hit into some bushes and they couldn't locate it. That evening I found their ball and hid it inside our barn. We were poor kids and this ruined their game for a while until one of the boys got another ball on his birthday.

Dr. N: Tell me the message you wanted to convey to Walt?

S: To show two things. I wanted my brother to see me crying and holding his bleeding head in my lap on the bank of the pond and remember what we said to each other after he stopped choking. The second dream about the softball game ended when I added a trailer to the dream and took him to the barn where the softball was still hidden. I told Walt I forgave him for every slight in our lives together. I want him to know I am always with him and the devotion we have for each other can't die. He will know this when he returns to the old barn to look for the ball.

Dr. N: Does Walt need to dream again about all this after your visit?

S: (laughs) It's not necessary as long as he recalled the location of the ball after he woke. Walt did remember what I had implanted. Going back to our old barn and finding the ball made the message come together. This gave Walt some serenity about my death.

Dream symbolism moves on many levels in the mind, some of which are abstract while others are emotional. The dreams of this case, involving experiential imagery, reinforced poignant memories of two brothers in a slice of recorded time. Future unification was pictured for Walt in a third, rather wispy dream of both souls happily together once again in the spirit world.

It took me quite a long while before I found an advanced subject apprenticed to a Dreammaster, a title I feel is appropriate for Axinar in case 6. As with any spiritual technique, some souls show more inclination than others toward acquiring advanced skills. In case 6, Bud not only originated a sequence of dreams in Walt's mind but then engaged in the more complex technique of linking them into a central theme of love and support for his brother. Finally, Bud provided physical evidence that he was there through the use of a hidden baseball. I take nothing away from Sylvia in case 5, because she was very effective entering her mother's dream to give her peace without disruption to the dreamer. It's just that case 6 demonstrated more spiritual artistry.

Transference Through Children

When souls have difficulty reaching the mind of a troubled adult they might resort to using children as conduits for their messages. Children are more receptive to spirits because they have not been conditioned to doubt or resist the supernatural. Frequently the young person chosen as a conduit is a family member of the departed. This situation is helpful to the spirit who is trying to reach a surviving relative, especially in the same household. The next case is that of a man who died of a heart attack in his back yard at age forty-two.

Case 7

Dr. N: What do you do to comfort your wife at the moment of death?

S: At first I try to hug Irene with my energy but I don't have the hang of it yet. (subject is a level II) I can relate to her sorrow but nothing I'm doing is working. I'm worried because I don't want to leave without saying goodbye.

Dr. N: Just relax now and move slowly forward. I want you to explain to me how you work through this dilemma.

S: I soon realize that I ought to be able to console Irene a little by reaching her through Sarah, our ten-year-old.

Dr. N: Why do you think Sarah might be receptive to you?

S: My daughter and I have a special bond. She also has great sorrow over my passing but much of this is mixed with fear over what happened to me so suddenly. Sarah doesn't comprehend it all yet. There are too many neighbors crowding around trying to sustain my wife. No one is paying much attention to Sarah, sitting alone in our bedroom.

Dr. N: Do you look upon this as an opportunity?

S: Yes, I do, in fact Sarah senses I am still alive and so she is more open to accepting my vibrations as I move into the bedroom.

Dr. N: Good—what happens next between you and your daughter?

S: (takes a deep breath) I've got it! Sarah is holding a set of her mother's knitting needles. I send warmth through them into her hands and she feels this right away. Then I use the needles as a springboard to reach her spine at the base of the neck and work around to her chin. (subject stops and begins laughing)

Dr. N: What is making you happy?

S: Sarah is giggling because I'm tickling her chin like I did before she went to sleep every night.

Dr. N: Now what do you do?

S: The crowd is breaking up and leaving because I have been taken out to the street and placed into an ambulance. Irene comes alone into the bedroom to get ready for a neighbor who will drive her to the hospital. She also wants to check on our daughter. Sarah looks up at my wife and says, "Mommy, you don't have to leave, Daddy is here with me—I know 'cause I can feel him tickling my chin!"

Dr. N: And then what does your wife do?

S: Irene is tearful but not crying as hard as before because she doesn't want to scare Sarah. So she hugs our daughter.

Dr. N: Irene does not want to indulge in what she believes to be Sarah's fantasy about your being with her?

S: Not yet—but I'm ready for Irene now. As soon as my wife holds our daughter I jump the gap between them, sending energy flowing over both. Irene feels me too, although not as much as Sarah. They sit down on the bed and hold on to each other with their eyes closed. For a while all three of us are alone together.

Dr. N: Do you feel you have accomplished what you set out to do on this day?

S: Yes, it's enough. It is time for me to leave and I pull back away from them and float out of the house. Then I am high over the countryside and sucked up into the sky. Soon I move into bright light, where my guide comes to meet me.

Contact in Familiar Settings

It may seem from the last case that once the departing soul has reached out and touched those who care about them, they go off to the spirit world without bothering to be near us again. There are people who don't feel a soul's presence right after death but will in the future. Survivors who have reached the acceptance stage in their grief process would find solace in knowing those they have loved are still watching over them. Yet there are those who never pick up anything.

Souls don't give up easily on us. Another way spirits touch people is through environmental settings associated with their memory. These contacts are effective to minds which may be closed to all other forms of spiritual communication. The following case illustrates this method. My subject, a woman called Nancy in her last life, died of a sudden stroke after thirty-eight years of marriage to Charles. Her husband was stuck between the denial and anger stages of grief and his emotions were so pent up that he could not accept help from their friends or seek outside professional counseling. As an engineer, his predominately analytical mind rejected any spiritual approach to his loss as being unscientific.

Nancy's soul had tried reaching her husband in several ways for months after the funeral. His stoic nature created such a wall around himself that Charles had not really cried since his wife's death. To overcome this obstacle, Nancy decided she could reach his inner mind through his sense of smell by connecting with an environmental setting familiar to both of them. The use of sense organs by souls complements communication with the subconscious mind. Nancy decided to use her garden, specifically a rose bush, to reach Charles.

Case 8

Dr. N: Why do you think Charles is going to react to your presence through a garden?

S: Because he knows I loved my garden. For him my plants were a take it or leave it situation. He knew it gave me pleasure but to Charles gardening was just a lot of hard work. Frankly, he helped very little in our yard. He was too busy with his mechanical projects.

Dr. N: He paid no attention, then, to your yard work?

S: Not unless I drew his attention to something. I had a favorite white rose bush by our front door and whenever I cut these flowers I would wave them in front of his nose and tell Charles that if this sweet scent did not affect him, then he had no romance in his soul. We used to laugh about this a lot because Charles was actually a tender lover but outwardly you would never know it. To avoid the issue, he would tease me by saying gruffly, "These are white roses, I like red."

Dr. N: So, how did you implement a plan with roses to let Charles know you are still alive and with him?

S: My rose bush died from lack of attention after my death. In fact, my whole yard was in bad shape because Charles was not functioning well at all. One weekend he was walking around the garden in a daze and came near some roses belonging to our next-door neighbor. He caught the smell. This is what I was waiting for and I moved quickly into his mind. He thought of me and looked at my dead rose bush.

Dr. N: You created an image of your rose bush in his mind?

S: (sighs) No, he would have missed that in the beginning. Charles understands tools. I started out by getting him to picture a shovel in his mind and digging. Then we made the transition to my rose bush and the garden center in town where it could be purchased. Charles pulled out his car keys.

Dr. N: You got him to walk to the car and then drive over to this nursery?

S: (grinning) It took persistence, but yes, I did.

Dr. N: Then what did you do?

S: At the nursery Charles wandered around for a bit until I was able to draw him to the roses. They were only red varieties, and that suited him. I was projecting a white color in his mind so he asked a clerk why there were no white roses. He was told red was all they had left in stock. Charles overrode my thoughts and bought a big pot of red roses, telling the clerk to deliver them to our house because he didn't want to get his car dirty.

Dr. N: What do "overriding thoughts" mean to you?

S: People under stress get impatient and fall back on established thought patterns. To Charles, the standard rose is red. That's his mindset. Since the store didn't have white roses at the moment, my husband would not deal with it further.

Dr. N: So, in a sense, Charles was blocking the conflicting images between his conscious thoughts and what you were projecting in his unconscious mind?

S: Yes, and also my husband is very mentally tired from my death.

Dr. N: Wouldn't red roses suit your purpose just as well?

S: (flatly) No. It was then I switched my energy to Sabine, the woman I knew who ran the store. She was at my funeral and was aware I loved white roses.

Dr. N: I don't think I know where this is going, Nancy. There were no white roses. Charles bought the red roses and then left for home. Wasn't this enough for you?

S: (laughing at me) You men! The white rose is *me*. The next morning Sabine personally drove to my house and delivered a big pot of white roses. She told my husband that she got them from another nursery and this is what I would have wanted. Then she left Charles standing bewildered in our driveway. He carried them over to the hole he had dug where my old rose bush had been and stopped. The roses were in his face. He smelled their fragrance—but what was more important, the wash of white was combined with the scent. (my subject pauses tearfully as she re-creates this moment)

Dr. N: (in a low voice) You are making all this very clear—please go on.

S: Charles was . . . feeling my presence at last . . . I now spread my energy around his torso to include the roses in a symmetrical envelopment. I wanted him to smell the white roses and my essence filtering through the energy field together.

Dr. N: Was this effective?

S: (softly) Finally, he knelt down next to the hole, pressing the roses to his face. Charles broke down and sobbed for a long time while I held him. When it was over he knew I was with him still.

While the spirits of husbands might use cars or sporting equipment, I find that wives often utilize garden settings to reach their mates. Another client told me about his wife applying the planting of an oak tree to make her connection. Before this widower saw me he wrote:

> Even if what happened to me was not from my wife, does
> it matter? The main thing is that in some way I am using
> the emotional energy generated by my feeling she was
> with me to tap into my inner resources, which previously
> were not available. I am no longer in an abyss without a
> glimmer of light.

In talking with people about such experiences, which some call mystical, it is important to consider the possibility of a spiritual source. If we can feed into a highly charged state of emotion during our grief, we can both heal and learn more about our inner selves.

Spirits may prefer to communicate with us in the form of ideas. Here is a quote from a letter I received from a former client about his departed wife, Gwen. I believe our session together assisted in his discovery of the best way to receive his wife's thoughts:

> I have learned we don't all have equal abilities as souls to communicate with each other. Sending and receiving messages is a skill that needs to be refined with practice. I finally recognized the imprint of Gwen's thoughts after getting nothing during my meditations. She was a literary person who used word thoughts rather than pictures to generate feeling in me. I had to learn to integrate word flashes from her into my own manner of speaking— which she knows—in order to decipher what she was telling me. I see more clearly now how I can touch Gwen with my mind.

Strangers as Messengers

Case 9

Derek was a man in his sixties who came to see me from Canada to evaluate his life and try and resolve his greatest sadness. When he was a young man, he lost his beautiful four-year-old daughter, Julia. Her death was sudden, unexpected and so devastating that he and his wife decided to have no more children.

I placed Derek in deep hypnosis and took him to a scene following his last life where he appeared in front of his council. We then discovered that one of his major current life lessons was learning to cope with tragedy. Derek had been deficient in this area during his past two lives by falling apart and making life more difficult for family survivors who depended upon him. He is doing much better in his current life. What was especially interesting for me about this case was a single incident that happened to Derek some twenty years after Julia's death.

Derek had recently lost his wife to cancer and was in mourning. One day, feeling very despondent, he walked to a nearby amusement park. After a while he sat down on a bench near a carousel. Listening to the music, Derek watched the children happily going around in circles on colorful wooden animals. He saw from a distance one little girl who looked like Julia and tears flooded his eyes. Just then a young woman of about twenty appeared and asked if she could sit down next to him. It was a warm day. She was dressed in white muslin, holding a cold drink in her hand. Derek nodded but said nothing while the woman enjoyed her drink and talked about growing up in England and coming to Canada because she was particularly attracted to Vancouver. She introduced herself as Heather and Derek noticed a glow of sunlight around her that gave the young woman a shining, angelic quality.

Time seemed to be suspended for Derek as the conversation turned to family and what Heather was going to do with her new life in Canada. Derek found himself talking to her as a father and the more they conversed, the more he felt he knew her. Finally, Heather stood up and placed her hand tenderly on Derek's shoulder. She smiled at him and said, "I know you are worried about me—please don't be. I'm all right and it's going to be a wonderful life. We will see each other again some day, I know."

Derek told me that as Heather walked away and gave him a final wave he saw his daughter and felt at peace. During our session, Derek recognized that the reincarnated soul of Julia had come to him and provided the assurance he had not really lost her. When we suffer the absence of people we love they may come to us in mysterious ways, often when our minds are detached in a shallow alpha state. Take these moments as messages from the other side and allow them to bring sustenance to you.

Angels or Other Heavenly Hosts

In recent years there has been a resurgence in the popularity of angels. The Roman Catholic Church defines angels as spiritual, intelligent, noncorporeal beings who are servants and messengers of God. The position of the Christian church is that these beings have never incarnated on Earth. We think of angels as white-robed figures with wings and a halo—theological images which have come down to us from the Middle Ages.

Many clients initially think they see angels when I regress them into the spirit world, especially those with strong religious convictions. This reaction is similar to the devotional responses of some people who have had near-death experiences. However, regardless of prior religious conditioning, my subjects soon realize the etheric beings they are visualizing in hypnosis represent their guides and soul companions who have come to meet them. These spiritual beings are surrounded by white light and may appear in robes.

In my work, guides are sometimes described as guardian angels, although our personal teachers are beings who have incarnated in physical form long before graduating to the level of guides. An intimate soulmate in discarnate form can also come to the gate to comfort us in times of need. I feel believing in angels emanates from an inner desire for personal protection on the part of many people. In making this observation, it is not my intention to set aside the faith of millions of religious people in angels. For many years I lacked faith in anything beyond my own existence. I know the importance of believing in something greater than yourself. Our faith is what sustains us in life and this applies to believing that there are superior beings who watch over us. My case presentations are intended to give weight to the concept of benevolent spirits in our lives.

Our spiritual teachers have different styles and techniques, just as teachers on Earth. Their immortal character has been matched to our own essence in a variety of ways. The next two abbreviated cases illustrate my contention that personal guides and soulmates, however they are represented, contact us from the other side if we require consolation.

Case 10

The following statements come from René, a forty-year-old widow who lost her husband, Harry, three months before our appointment. I waited until after our session before asking her the series of questions that follow. My intent was to have René contrast the conscious versus superconscious imagery she had of her guide, Niath.

> **Dr. N:** Before our session today, have you had any contact with the being you saw in hypnosis as Niath?

> **S:** Yes, since Harry's death Niath has come to me during my dark hours.

Dr. N: Did Niath appear to be the same to you before and after this hypnosis session?

S: No, I didn't see her quite the same way. I . . . thought she was an angel before and now I see Niath is my teacher.

Dr. N: Were her face and demeanor different to you while you were under hypnosis, compared to what you saw when awake?

S: (laughs) Today there were no wings or a halo, but bright light—that was the same—and her face and gentle manner were the same too. I also see that in our spirit group she can be . . . sharply instructive.

Dr. N: More of a teacher and less of a grief counselor, you mean?

S: Yes, perhaps that's it. Right after Harry's death she was so sweet and understanding when she came to me . . . (rushing on) that doesn't mean she isn't nice in the spirit world, just more . . . exacting.

Dr. N: Did you do anything to summon Niath right after Harry's death?

S: I was crying for help after the funeral. I found out that I needed to be alone and very still . . . to listen . . .

Dr. N: Does this mean you heard Niath rather than actually saw her?

S: No, in the beginning I saw her floating over my head in my bedroom. I had my arms wrapped around a pillow pretending it was Harry, but I had stopped crying. She became fuzzy after I first saw her and I realized then I had to listen carefully for her voice. In the days that followed I heard Niath more than I saw her . . . but I had to listen.

Dr. N: Does that mean concentrate?

S: Yes . . . well, no . . . more allowing my mind to go free from my body.

Dr. N: What happens when you don't listen properly but you want her messages?

S: Then she communicates with me through my feelings.

Dr. N: In what way?

S: Oh, I might be driving alone or out walking by myself, wondering about doing something—taking a certain action. She will make me feel good about it if I am supposed to do it—if it is right.

Dr. N: And what if the action you are considering would be wrong for you, then what?

S: Niath will make me feel uneasy about doing it. I will know in my gut it is a wrong move.

My next case excerpt involves a young man who died in a car crash in 1942 at age thirty-six. He gives us another perspective on the mythology of angels from a soul reaching back to Earth.

Case 11

Dr. N: Tell me what you did for your wife after the crash?

S: I stayed around for three days with Betty to lessen her heaviness. I positioned myself over her head so our energy fields crossed in such a way that I could soothe her by matching our vibrations.

Dr. N: Did you employ any other techniques?

S: Yes, I projected my likeness in front of her face.

Dr. N: Was this effective?

S: (playfully) Initially, she thought I was Jesus. The second day she was confused and the third day Betty was convinced I was an angel. My wife is very religious.

Dr. N: Are you bothered that she didn't recognize you because of her religious convictions?

S: Not at all. (then, after some hesitation) Oh . . . I suppose it would please me if Betty realized it was me but her feeling better is my main concern. Betty is convinced I am a heavenly deity—and that is okay because I do represent spiritual help for her.

Dr. N: Would she feel even better knowing it was you?

S: Look, Betty thinks I'm in heaven and can't help her. Her angel is able to do so because it's really me. So, I'm in disguise—what's the difference as long as my goal to help her is accomplished?

Dr. N: Well, since Betty has not connected you with your disguise, is there any other way you can communicate on a more personal level?

S: (smiles) Through my best friend, Ted. He consoles her and gives her advice with day-to-day details. Later I hover over the both of them sending . . . permissive messages. (subject then laughs)

Dr. N: What do you find humorous?

S: Ted is not married. He has been in love with Betty for a long time, but she doesn't realize it yet.

Dr. N: Is this all right with you?

S: (cheerfully, yet with nostalgia) Sure. I'm relieved he can do what I can't anymore for her . . . at least until she returns home to me.

Finally, there are those angel-like spirits who regularly come to Earth between lives simply to help people they don't know who are in distress. They may be healers in training, as was true with the client who said to me:

> My guide and I assisted a boy in India who was drowning and consumed by fear. His parents pulled him from the river and were trying to resuscitate him, but he was not responding well. I placed my hands on his head to quiet his fear, sent a spike of energy into his heart to bring warmth into his body and superimposed his essence with mine for a moment to help him cough up the water and start breathing again. We were able to help a total of twenty-four people on that trip to Earth.

Emotional Recovery of Souls and Survivors

The last remarks from case 11 about his wife, Betty, and those of case 3 who talked about her husband, Kevin, touch upon the issue of later relationships by the survivor. Falling in love again after the death of a spouse sometimes causes feelings of guilt and even betrayal. In both these cases we saw that the departing spouses only wanted their surviving mates to be happy and loved. However, just because spirits want this for us does not mean that we can easily compartmentalize our expressions of intimacy to past and present loves.

People who have had long, happy first marriages and then lose a spouse make excellent candidates for a successful second marriage. This is a tribute to the first relationship. Having other relationships neither lessens nor dishonors our first love, it only validates that love, providing a state of healthy acceptance has been reached in between. I know placing aside feelings of guilt is easier said than done. I have received letters from widows and widowers asking me if their departed spouses could actually be watching them in the bedroom with someone else.

In my summary of the spirit world, I indicated that souls lose most of their negative emotional baggage when they shed their bodies. Although it is true we may carry the imprint of some emotional trauma from a past life into the next one, this condition is in a state of abeyance until we return to a new body. Also, a great deal of negative energy is expelled during the early stages of our return to the spirit world, especially after deprogramming during orientation.

When a soul once again returns to a pure energy state in the spirit world, it no longer feels hate, anger, envy, jealousy and the like. It has come to Earth to experience these sorts of emotions and learn from them. But after departing from Earth, do souls feel any sadness for what they have left behind? Certainly, souls carry nostalgia for the good times in all their past physical lives. This is tempered by a state of blissful omniscience and such a heightened sense of well-being that souls feel more alive than when they were on Earth.

Nevertheless, I have found two sorts of negative emotions that exist within souls, both of which involve a form of sadness. One of them I would call karmic guilt for making very poor choices, especially when others were hurt by these actions. I will treat these aspects later under karma. The other form of sadness for souls is not melancholy, dejection, or a mournful unhappiness in the way life has gone on without them since their departure. Rather, sadness in souls comes from a longing to reunite with the Source of their existence. I believe all souls, regardless of their level of development, have this longing to seek perfection for the same reason. The motivating factor for those souls who come to Earth is growth. Thus, the trace of sadness I discern in souls is the absence of elements in their immortal character that they must find to make their energy complete. And so it is a soul's destiny to search for truth in their experiences in order to gain wisdom. It is important for the survivor to know that longing does not compromise a soul's feelings of empathy, sympathy and compassion for those who grieve for them.

Since the immortal character of the soul is no longer encumbered by individual temperament and the chemistry of its last body, it is at peace. Souls have much better things to do than interfere with people on Earth. In rare cases, certain souls are so disturbed by an act of injustice against them in life that they won't leave Earth's astral plane after death until they gain some sort of resolution. I will discuss more of this phenomenon under the subject of ghosts. The spiritual conflict with these souls does not include sadness over you finding happiness with someone else, unless, of course, you did something like murder your lover to be with another. The one great advantage the departed soul has over a survivor is knowing it is still alive and will be seeing everyone who is meaningful to them again. The integrity of souls involves an all-consuming desire that those they love have the free choice to finish their lives in any way they want. If you wish a soul to come to you it probably will, otherwise your privacy is respected. Besides, a part of your energy which you left behind in the spirit world is always there for them.

Since souls lose so many negative emotions upon reentering the spirit world, it follows that their positive affections also undergo alterations. For instance, souls feel great love but this love places no conditions upon others for reciprocity because it is given freely. Souls display a universal coherence with each other that is so absolute it is incomprehensible on Earth. This is one reason why souls appear to be both abstract and empathetic to us at the same time.

I have heard of some cultural traditions which advise that survivors must let the deceased go and not try to communicate with them because souls have more important work to do. Indeed, souls do not want you to become dependent upon communication with them to the detriment of independent decision-making. Yet many survivors require not only solace but also some sort of approval in the forming of a new relationship. I hope my next case will help dispel the idea that the departed are uninterested in your future. Your privacy is respected by the spirit of your love when you are content. Still, if a prospective course of action, particularly bonding with someone else, leaves you unsettled, they might try to make their opinions known. Because of the nature of soul duality they are quite capable of performing many tasks at once. This includes a soul's quiet time in solitude where they focus energy on people they have left behind. Souls do this to bring us greater peace even when we are not calling on them for help.

Case 12

George came to me in a state of some distress over feelings of guilt about a new love in his life. He had been a widower for two years after a long and happy marriage to Frances. George wondered if she was looking down on him with displeasure over his developing relationship with Dorothy. I was told Dorothy and her deceased husband, Frank, had been close friends of George and Frances. Nonetheless, George felt his increased attraction to Dorothy might be considered an act of betrayal. I begin this case at the point in our session when George sees Frances after a former life together.

> **Dr. N:** Now that you have entered the circle of your soulmates, who comes forward first?
>
> **S:** (cries out) Oh God, it's Frances—it's her. I've missed you so much, dear. She is so beautiful . . . we have been together . . . from the beginning.
>
> **Dr. N:** You see that you never really lost her in your current life, don't you, and that she will be waiting for you when it is your time to go?
>
> **S:** Yes . . . I always felt it . . . but now I know . . .

Note: George now breaks down and we are unable to continue for a while. During this time I want my subject to get used to hugging his wife again and talking to her through his superconscious mind. He strongly believes that his guide and my own conspired to bring him to this juncture. I explain that the information he will gain should help him move on in his life with Dorothy. The catalyst for this awareness is evident when we start to identify other members of George's soul group.

Dr. N: I want you now to identify the figures standing near Frances.

S: (brightens) Oh, really . . . I can't believe . . . but, of course . . . it makes sense now.

Dr. N: What makes sense?

S: It's Dorothy and . . . (becomes very emotional) . . . and Frank, they are standing together next to Frances, smiling at me . . . don't you see?

Dr. N: What should I see?

S: That they have brought us . . . closer together, Dorothy and me.

Dr. N: Explain why you think this is so?

S: (impatient with me) They are happy that we have found each other in . . . an intimate way. Dorothy has grieved a long time herself over Frank and the grief we both feel is being dispelled by having the company of each other.

Dr. N: And you see that all four of you are in the same soul group?

S: Yes . . . but I had no idea this was true . . .

Dr. N: How are Frances and Dorothy different as souls?

S: Frances is a very strong teaching soul while Dorothy is more artistic and creative . . . gentle. Dorothy is a peaceful spirit and able to adapt more easily to existing conditions than the rest of us.

Dr. N: Now that you have the approval of Frances and Frank, what will Dorothy gain from associating with you as your second wife in this life?

S: Comfort, understanding, love . . . I can provide her with more protection because I am goal oriented. I challenge things Dorothy takes for granted. She is very accepting. We have a good balance.

Dr. N: Is Dorothy your primary soulmate?

S: (emphatically) No, it's Frances. Dorothy usually matches with Frank in their lives, but we are all very close.

Dr. N: Have you and Dorothy worked together before in other lives?

S: Yes, but in different situations. She often takes the role of my sister, a niece, or close friend.

Dr. N: Why are you usually matched with Frances as a mate?

S: Frances and I have been with each other from the beginning. We are so close because we have struggled together, helping each other . . . she was always able to make me laugh at my serious nature—at my foolishness.

When I closed this segment of our session I felt that George had gained much insight. He was overjoyed at learning that it was no accident he and Dorothy were drawn together. All four souls knew their current timelines in advance.

I have had similar information come to me from clients who were not in the same soul group as their new love interest, but were connected as affiliated souls from nearby groups. I find most people know if the person they live with is not a significant soulmate. This does not mean they can't have good relationships with souls out of their group. I will quote the statement from a client who died before his wife in their previous life together:

> When I reach out to comfort my wife after my death, I do so as a friend and partner. We were not really in love. She was not an intimate soulmate for me, nor was I to her. I have a great deal of respect for her. We needed this relationship to work on those things which played to our individual strengths and weaknesses. So, I don't say, "I love you" into her mind because she would know it isn't true. She might then confuse my spirit with her soulmate. Our life contract is done and if she wishes, I want her to take another person into her heart.

Reuniting with Those We Love

It is fitting that I close this chapter on death with a case illustrating what it is like for soulmates who reunite on the other side. The case involves a widow who meets her husband at the gateway following a long separation.

Case 13

Dr. N: Who meets you right after death?

S: IT'S HIM! Eric . . . oh . . . at last . . . at last . . . my love . . .

Dr. N: (after calming my client) This man is your husband?

S: Yes, we are coming together right after I cross over—before I see our guide.

Dr. N: Tell me how everything unfolds, including the way feelings of endearment are transmitted between you and Eric.

S: We start with the eyes . . . from a little distance away . . . looking deep into each other . . . the knowing of everything flowing between our minds . . . of all that we have meant to each other . . . our energy gets sucked up into a magnetic pool of indescribable joy blending the two of us together.

Dr. N: At this moment have you both assumed the physical form you had in the last life?

S: (laughing) Yes, very rapidly we start with the first time we met— how we looked to each other—and move through the phases of body changes during our long marriage. It's not definitive because we don't settle on just one year of our life together. It's more . . . swirling energy patterns right now. We even pick up on other bodies we had together in previous lives, too.

Dr. N: Were you usually female in those lives?

S: Mostly, yes. Later, we will revert to a mixed gender pattern because there were good times in our past lives when he was female and I was male. (pause) But it is just fun right now to be the people we were in our last life.

Note: My client asks me to please not ask her any more questions for a few minutes. She and Eric embrace and when she speaks to me again it is to describe how their energy flowed together.

S: It is an ecstasy of coalescing.

Dr. N: This spiritual passion sounds almost erotic to me.

S: Of course, but it is so much more. I can't really describe it, but the rapture we feel for each other comes from all our contact together in hundreds of lives combined with memories of the blissful state we spend reunited between lives.

Dr. N: And how does the blending of your energy with your husband make you feel afterward?

S: (bursts out laughing) Like really wonderful sex, only better. (then more seriously) You must understand that I died as an eighty-three-year-old, sick woman. I was tired. It was a long life and I was a cold stove that needed warming up.

Dr. N: Cold stove?

S: Yes, I need energy rejuvenation. There is always a transfer of positive energy when we are met by our guides or by someone we love. Eric sparks up my tired energy. He lights a fire inside me to make me whole again.

Dr. N: When this meeting is over, what do the two of you do?

S: Our teacher comes to welcome me back and I am escorted through the mist to our center.

When a subject tells me that reentering the spirit world has the effect of being made whole again, this requires qualification. We receive an infusion of new energy from soulmates and guides who may also transfer part of the energy we left behind back into us as well. However, as I said when discussing spiritual longing, complete wholeness will not take place until our work is done. Despite this, being restored to what we were before the life began is like feeling whole once again. A subject put it this way: "Death is like waking up after a long sleep where you had just a muddled awareness. The release you feel is one that comes after crying, only here you are not crying."

I have tried to show death from the perspective of the soul in order to ease the pain of those left behind. As Plato said, "Once free of the body, the soul is able to see truth clearly because it is more pure than before and recalls the pure ideas which it knew before." Survivors must learn to function again without the physical presence of the person they loved by trusting the departed soul is still with them. Acceptance of loss comes one day at a time. Healing is a progression of mental steps that begins with having faith you are not truly alone.

In order to complete the life contract you made in advance with the departed, it is necessary to rejoin the rest of humanity as an active participant. You will see your love again soon enough. I am hopeful my years of research into the life we lead as souls may assist survivors in recognizing that death only exchanges one reality for another in the long continuum of existence.

~3

Earthly Spirits

Astral Planes

When my hypnosis subjects describe their ascent into the spirit world as "rising through misty layers of translucent light," I am reminded of the astral planes we read about in Eastern texts. I must confess that I am not at all attracted to the rigid stair-step quality of exactly seven planes of existence, from low to high, which come from Eastern spiritual philosophy. This is due to the fact that my clients see no evidence of all these planes. It is a human failing to label concepts as a means of codification. In my descriptions about the spirit world I am as guilty of this practice as everyone else. Perhaps it is best that we simply take those precepts which make spiritual sense to us and reject the rest, regardless of the age of certain ideas or who tells us they are true.

The reason for my objections to a rigid formula of specific planes of existence from Earth to a Godhead is that these states are unnecessary inhibitors. All my research with subjects in a higher state of consciousness indicates to me that upon death we go directly from one astral plane around Earth through the gateway into the spirit world. It does not matter if my subject is a young soul or a highly advanced older soul, right after death they all tell me their soul passes through a dense atmosphere of light around the astral plane of Earth. This light has patches of darkish gray but no impenetrable black zones. Many describe a tunnel effect. All souls from Earth then quickly move into the bright light of the spirit world. This is a single ethereal space without zones or barriers around it.

In the spirit world itself, all the so-called spaces or places available to the reincarnating soul are congruent. For instance, the Akashic Record traditions of Eastern thought don't appear to my subjects as being on some fourth causal plane separate from other functional areas. My subjects call these records Life Books, which are stored in symbolic libraries that are seen adjacent to other spiritual places.

I acknowledge there is much beyond the spiritual experience of the reincarnating soul and therefore out of my range of inquiry. Perhaps the whole idea of cosmic planes is basically an attempt to conceptualize stages of ethereal awareness as opposed to movement prevented by barriers. Historically, specific demarcations of planes that enclose the "underworld"—designed for certain unworthy souls—have been more prevalent in human thinking. I will discuss this further in chapter 6.

When my subjects tell of traveling interdimensionally, I suppose one could interpret this as soul movement through planes. The term "plane" is not used nearly as much as the words levels, edges, borders and divisions, except when a client refers to Earth. People in hypnosis report that within the astral plane surrounding Earth, alternate or coexistent realities are part of our physical world. Apparently, within these realities, non-material beings can be seen by some people in our physical reality. I have been told of multitudes of interdimensional spheres that are used by souls for training and recreation from the spirit world.

Spiritual boundaries can be as small as the "glasslike" divisions between cluster groups, or as large as the zones between universes. I am told all spatial zones have vibrational properties that allow for soul passage only when their energy waves are attuned to the proper frequency. The more developed souls explain that absolute time as we know it does not seem to exist in these areas. Does the physical world of Earth have similar characteristics that are unseen by most of us? I had a thoughtful client who wrote me the following after his session:

> Working with you has made me realize that our reality is like a movie projector showing us images on a three-dimensional screen of sky, mountains, and seas. If a second projector, with its own imprint of alternating light frequencies and space-time sequences, was synchronized with the first, both realities could exist simultaneously with material and non-material entities in the same zone.

If what people in a trance state tell me about this system has validity, etheric beings would be capable of existing in different realities within the same astral plane surrounding Earth—indeed on Earth itself. The vibrational energy forces around Earth are in constant flux. It seems to me that if these magnetic fields change density, they would produce cyclic variations over centuries of human time. Therefore, we may be more or less receptive to viewing spirits on Earth in any given century. Perhaps the ancients really could see more than we do in the modern world.

Nature Spirits

On a national TV show, a woman reported that she had seen elves in her vineyard. She said that in the beginning she only heard them and was a little concerned about her sanity. In time she was able to talk to them and a few became visible to her. She described them as being about two feet high with pointed ears and wearing baggy pants. Of course, many people in her area thought she was crazy when this news got out. The advice she received from these beings about what to use in her soil to increase the quantity and quality of grape production over that of the neighboring farms soon caused many of them to take her more seriously. When the story was released, this woman was invited to have her brainwaves tested. When her senses were stimulated it was found that portions of her brain were capable of a much higher energy output than normal.

I had a client who also claimed to have such abilities. She was an old soul and in a deep trance state said, "Fairy folk were here long before the rise of our civilizations and have never left. Most of us do not see them today, as in ancient times, because they are so old their density has become very light, while our Earth bodies still have heavy energy." I questioned her further and she added, "While a rock has a l-D (density), a tree would be a 2-D and our bodies are at the 3-D level. Thus, the beings of nature would be invisible with a transparency registering between 4-D and 6-D."

When I think of the woman who saw elves in her vineyard, I see a picture in my mind. If we could look at Earth with x-ray vision it might resemble a series of overlaid, clear plastic topographical sheets. These vibrational energy layers vary in density and denote alternate realities to me. Certain gifted people might be able to see within these layers, but most of us are unable to do so.

It is also my belief that much of our folklore comes from the memories souls have of their experiences on other physical and mental worlds. What they have to say about these experiences while under hypnosis conforms in some respects to the myths and legends of Earth. These soul associations include spirits in trees and plants as well as connections to the elements of air, water and fire. Folklore and soul memory will be explored further in later chapters.

Ghosts

Many researchers into the paranormal have written about ghosts. I do not consider myself proficient in this field, although I have had some exposure with souls as ghosts. At my lectures I am often asked how benevolent spirit guides can allow these beings to wander around lost, unhappy and alone. My contribution to the study of ghosts will be to review what I feel are some misconceptions and to explain this phenomenon from the perspective of the ghost rather than from those who see them on Earth.

When I began to devote my hypnotherapy practice exclusively to the study of life between lives, it took years before a client came to me who had been a ghost for an appreciable amount of time after a former life. I don't consider short-timers ghosts in the traditional sense. For instance, I had a client who died young in a schoolhouse fire while saving the children. This teacher stayed around town for some months afterward just checking on the kids and other people who were grieving at her untimely death. When I asked what prompted her to finally leave she said, "Oh, eventually I got bored." I have come to the conclusion that only a small fraction of souls have ever been ghosts, beyond the normal amount of time it takes for the new discarnate to adjust before leaving Earth. I don't believe we are being haunted by that many ghosts around the world.

The cases which follow will demonstrate that our guides do not compel or coerce us to move into the spirit world if our unfinished business is so overpowering that we do not want to leave Earth's astral plane. I find this is especially true if the soul has a permissive guide. Some guides have much more of a hands-off approach. Then, too, our guides typically don't make personal appearances next to us at the moment of death at ground zero.

For most souls, the pulling sensation right after death is gentle and only grows more deliberate as we leave Earth's astral plane. There is no question that higher beings are instantly aware of our death. Yet the wishes of the deceased are respected. Keep in mind that time means nothing in the spirit world. Discarnates don't have a linear clock in their heads so staying behind for days, months, or years doesn't have the same relevance as with incarnates. A ghost who has haunted an English castle for four hundred years and finally returns to the spirit world may feel in spirit time this amounted to forty days, or even forty hours.

Some people have the misconception that ghosts don't know they are dead or how to escape their situation. Yes, in a sense, they are trapped but this is a condition of mental obstruction rather than any material hindrance. Souls are not lost in some confined astral plane and they do know they have made a transition out of life on Earth. The ghost's confusion lies in the obsessive attachment they have to places, people and events where they can't let go. These actions of self-displacement are voluntary but special guides, called Redeemer Masters, constantly watch for signs that the known disturbed spirits are ready to exit. We have the right to self-determination, even with our death experience. Spiritual guides will honor poor decision-making.

From what I have been able to observe, ghosts are less mature spirits who have trouble freeing themselves from earthly contaminations. This is particularly true if their stay in limbo is for prolonged periods in Earth years. The reasons for staying behind are varied. Perhaps the life ended in an unexpected manner, which caused a deviation from a major path. These souls may feel their free will has been thwarted in some way. Quite often there was a terrible trauma connected to the ghost's death. Perhaps they want to try and protect a person they care about from danger.

In 1994, a young woman driving at night on a road not far from my house in the Sierra Nevada Mountains tumbled down a steep embankment and was killed. No one had seen the accident or noticed the wreck fifty feet down the hill where for five days her three-year-old son clung to life. This accident attracted national attention when it was reported that a passing motorist saw a ghostly apparition of a nude young woman lying on the highway directly above the wreckage. This was a dramatic way for this ghost to be noticed and it worked because her child was found just in time to save his life.

I find the underlying cause behind disturbed spirits to be a sudden change in their planned karmic direction that they perceive to be not only unexpected but unjust. The most common cases of ghosts appear to involve souls who were murdered or wronged by another person in life. My next case begins as a typical ghost story but then reveals how these matters are resolved constructively for the ghost.

The Abandoned Soul

Belinda came to see me because of an overwhelming sense of sadness she was unable to comprehend based upon her current life experience. During my intake interview I learned she was forty-seven and had never been married. She moved to California from the East Coast after a stormy breakup with a man called Stuart some twenty years before. Belinda cared for Stuart but she had broken off their engagement after making a decision to change her life and come west to pursue a new career. She asked Stuart to come with her but he did not want to leave his job and his family. Stuart pleaded with Belinda to marry him and stay in the area where they had both grown up but she refused. Belinda told me that Stuart was devastated by her leaving him but he wouldn't follow her. Eventually, Stuart married someone else.

Some years later, Belinda said she met Burt and they had an intensely passionate relationship for a while but eventually he left her for another woman. I wondered if this was the source of Belinda's unexplained sadness but she told me no, she had been hurt, but that it was a good thing she hadn't married Burt. Belinda now realized that besides his being an unfaithful lover, she and Burt were temperamentally unsuited. Belinda added that, for some reason, long before her relationships with men began she had these strange feelings of abandonment and loss.

Case 14

It is my custom to move subjects into their most immediate past life before we enter the spirit world. This hypnosis technique allows for a more natural mental passage following a death scene. I asked Belinda to pick a critical scene to open our discussion about her former life. She chose one of great mental anguish. She said she was a young woman by the name of Elizabeth living on a large farm near Bath, England, in the year 1897. Elizabeth was on her knees holding the coattails of her husband, Stanley, who was dragging her through the front doorway of their manor house. After five years of marriage, Stanley was leaving her.

Dr. N: What is Stanley saying to you at this moment?

S: (now begins to sob) He says, "I'm sorry about this but I need to get away from this farm and go out to see the rest of the world."

Dr. N: How do you respond, Elizabeth?

S: I am imploring—begging Stanley not to leave because I love him so much and that I will try harder to make him happy here. My arms are aching from holding his coat and being dragged down the hall to the front steps.

Dr. N: What does your husband say?

S: (still crying) Stanley says, "It's not you, really. I'm just sick of this place. I'll be back."

Dr. N: Do you think he means it?

S: Oh . . . I know a part of him loves me in some way but his need to escape this life and all he has known since he was a boy is too overpowering. (after this statement my subject's body begins to shake uncontrollably)

Dr. N: (after soothing her a bit) Tell me what is happening now, Elizabeth.

S: It's about over. I can't hold him any longer . . . my arms are not strong enough—they hurt. (subject rubs her arms) I fall down the rest of the steps in front of the servants—I don't care. Stanley gets on his horse and rides away while I watch helplessly.

Dr. N: Do you ever see him again?

S: No, I only know he went to Africa.

Dr. N: How do you maintain yourself, Elizabeth?

S: He left me the estate but I do not manage it well. I let most of the staff and workers go. In time we have almost no livestock and I am barely subsisting but I cannot leave the farm. I must wait for him should he finally decide to come back to me.

Dr. N: Elizabeth, I now want you to go to the last day your life. Give me the year and the circumstances leading up to this day.

S: It is 1919 (subject is fifty-two) and I am dying of influenza. I haven't put up much resistance in the last few weeks because I have just been existing. My loneliness and sorrow . . . the struggle to keep the farm going . . . my heart is broken.

I now take Elizabeth through her death scene and attempt to bring her into the light. It is no use because she remains grounded to the farm. I soon discover this rather young soul is about to become a ghost.

Dr. N: Why are you resisting moving up away from Earth's astral plane?

S: I won't go—I can't leave yet.

Dr. N: Why not?

S: I must wait longer at the farm for Stanley.

Dr. N: But you have waited for twenty-two years already and he has not returned.

S: Yes, I know. Still, I just can't bring myself to go.

Dr. N: What do you do now?

S: I hover as a spirit.

I talk to Elizabeth about her ghostly appearance and behavior around the farm. She does not zero in on Stanley's energy vibrations to locate him anywhere in the world, as an experienced soul would do. Further questioning indicates that Elizabeth has the idea that if she can scare away any potential buyers the estate might remain in the family. Indeed, the property does sit idle with no new occupants because everyone in the district knows it is haunted. Elizabeth tells me she flies around the manor house crying over her abandonment.

Dr. N: How long do you wait for Stanley in Earth years?

S: Uh, four years.

Dr. N: Does this seem like a long time for you? What do you do?

S: It is nothing—a few weeks. I cry . . . and moan over my sadness, I can't help it. I know this scares people, especially when I knock things over.

Dr. N: Why do you want to scare people who have done you no harm?

S: To express my displeasure at what was done to me.

Dr. N: Please explain to me how all this comes to an end.

S: I am . . . called.

Dr. N: Oh, you have asked for a release from this sad situation.

S: (long pause) Well . . . not actually . . . sort of . . . but he knows I am about ready. He comes and says to me, "Don't you think this is enough?"

Dr. N: Who says this to you, and what happens?

S: The Redeemer of Lost Souls calls to me and I move further away from Earth with him and we talk while waiting.

Dr. N: Just a minute—is this your spirit guide?

S: (smiles for the first time) No, we are waiting for my guide. This spirit is Doni. He rescues souls like me. That's his job.

Dr. N: What does Doni look like and what does he say to you?

S: (laughs) He looks like a little gnome, with a wrinkled face and a top hat which is all beat up—his whiskers shake when he talks to me. He tells me if I want to stay longer I can but wouldn't it be more fun to go home and see Stanley there. He is very comical and makes me laugh but he is so gentle and wise. He takes me by the hand and we move to a beautiful place to talk more.

Dr. N: Tell me about this place and what happens to you next.

S: Well, this is a place for grieving souls like me and it looks like a beautiful meadow with flowers. Doni tells me to be joyful and he infuses my energy with love and happiness and purifies my mind. He lets me play like a child again among the flowers and tells me to chase the butterflies while he rests in the sun.

Dr. N: It sounds wonderful. How long does all this go on?

S: (rather put off by my question) For as long as I want!

Dr. N: During this time, does Doni talk to you about Stanley and your behavior as a ghost?

S: (reacts with distaste) He absolutely does not do that! The Redeemer is not Tishin (subject's guide). Those questions will come later. This is my time to rest. Doni's old face is so full of kindness and love, he never scolds. He just encourages me to play. His job is to bring my soul back to health by helping me cleanse my mind.

After Elizabeth's energy is rejuvenated, Doni escorts her to Tishin and kisses her goodbye. Then the preliminary evaluations begin as with a normal orientation for someone returning to the spirit world. I was able to access this conference with Elizabeth-Belinda and it was instructive. In the beginning she stated that her life as an abandoned wife was wasted. Certainly, Elizabeth pined away much of her life in suffering without making adjustments or accepting change. Under Tishin's guidance she saw that this lesson was not wasted. Belinda today is a very independent and productive woman who has weathered many emotional storms.

By now, I am sure the reader has figured out that Stanley is Stuart today. When I relate this part of the story to people, some say to me, "Oh, good, she was able to turn the tables on that bastard with the same treatment to get revenge for what he did to her." This thinking shows how we misunderstand karmic lessons. The souls of Elizabeth and Stanley volunteered to assume their roles today as Belinda and Stuart. Stuart needed to feel the emotional pain of what he had wrought on Elizabeth. As Stanley, he had made a commitment of marriage in a culture and time when women were quite dependent upon their husbands. Because his action to leave her was swift and uncompromising, it was particularly brutal. This does not excuse Elizabeth, who took no responsibility for making changes in her life. Her suffering and nonacceptance of the situation was so extreme she ultimately became a ghost.

By assuming Stanley's role in her current life, the soul of Belinda had to learn what motivated Stanley's feelings of entrapment in an undesirable location. Belinda was not Stuart's wife when she left the East Coast so the commitment was not quite the same as Stuart had with her in their former life when he was Stanley. Yet in this life they were lovers again and Stuart felt forsaken by Belinda's desire to leave their town, friends and family to seek adventure and opportunity elsewhere. Because she had the courage to do this alone, Belinda's soul has now acquired the insight that Stanley did not leave her out of a malicious desire to inflict emotional pain. Stanley wanted freedom and so did Belinda.

Belinda has carried the mental imprint of this past life into her life today. From a karmic standpoint, Belinda has a dose of residual sorrow as Elizabeth which she was unable to comprehend until our session. Belinda told me she still thinks about Stuart and he probably cannot forget her since she was his first love. They are soulmates in the same group and I think it is likely the two of them will assume a new role together in their next life, balancing what they have learned in the last two lives.

For those of you who are curious why Belinda had to endure the brief unrequited love affair with Burt, this was a test. Burt is another member of the same soul group and he volunteered to trigger Belinda's soul memories of being Elizabeth to see if she had learned to stand up to the emotional pain of a broken heart. Burt's actions also served as a wake-up call for Belinda to realize in her current life how Stuart felt when she left him. The blade of karma cuts both ways.

Spiritual Duality

Some years ago a magazine article recounted the travels of an American woman who was driving through the English countryside and felt inexplicably drawn to a small side road away from her intended destination. Soon she came to a deserted old manor house (not Stanley's). The woman was told by the caretaker the house was haunted by a ghost who looked very much like her. Walking around the grounds she felt an eerie connection to something. Presumably she was there to help release herself. The two portions of her soul could have been drawn to each other in the same mysterious way that two people living parallel lives with one soul might be if there was a compelling purpose.

In chapter 1, I touched upon the duality of souls and how they are able to divide their energy to live more than one life at a time. A portion of the energy of most souls never leaves the spirit world during their incarnations. I'll discuss soul division further in the next chapter, but splitting soul energy is particularly relevant to the study of ghosts. In my last case, even though Elizabeth was in limbo for a while as a ghost, another part of her energy remained in the spirit world working on lessons and interacting with other souls. That other portion may also incarnate again and move on to a new life, which is what I believe happened with the woman who found the haunted house.

I disagree with some ghost authorities who state that ghostly forms only represent an earthly shell without a soul's core of consciousness. There are life cycles when souls choose to take less energy than they should into a human body. However, even if they become ghosts, such souls are far more than an empty shell of energy. One would think that the balance of a ghost's energy remaining in the spirit world ought to be more helpful to their disturbed alter ego still hanging around Earth. From what I hear, most immature souls who cross over are unable to perform this transfer and integration of energy by themselves. The following excerpt is a report I received from the soulmate of a ghost. This ghost is a young level I soul who was my subject's first husband.

Case 15

Dr. N: You have told me that your first husband, Bob, was a ghost after his last life. Please explain the circumstances here.

S: Bob became a ghost because he was killed early in our marriage in that life. He was so overcome with despair and concern for me he wouldn't leave.

Dr. N: I see. Can you tell me approximately how much of his total energy he carried with him into that life?

S: (nods her head in assent) Bob had only about a quarter of his energy and it was not enough for him in this mental crisis . . . he misjudged . . . (stops)

Dr. N: Do you think that if Bob had taken more of his energy to allow for this contingency he might not have become a ghost?

S: Oh, I can't answer that, but I think it would have made him stronger . . . more resistant to sorrow.

Dr. N: Then why did he take so little energy to Earth?

S: Well, because he wanted to be more engaged with his work in the spirit world.

Dr. N: I'm confused about why Bob's guide didn't just make him take more energy to Earth.

S: (shakes her head negatively) No, no! We are not pushed around that way. We are free to make our choices. And Bob didn't have to become a ghost, you know. Bob was advised to take more but he is stubborn and he was also considering another life at the same time. (a parallel life)

Dr. N: Let me make sure I understand. Bob underestimated his capacity to function more normally in a crisis with a body having only 25 percent of his energy capacity?

S: (sadly) I'm afraid so.

Dr. N: Even though in death that body was gone?

S: It didn't matter. The effects were still with him and he didn't have enough strength to combat the circumstances.

Dr. N: How long did Bob stay a ghost before the rest of his energy was restored to him in the spirit world?

S: Not long, about thirty years. He couldn't seem to help himself . . . lack of experience . . . part of his lesson . . . then our teacher was called by . . . you know . . . those beings who patrol Earth watching over the disturbed ones . . . to go get the rest of him to come home . . .

Dr. N: They have been called the Redeemers of Lost Souls by some people.

S: That's a good name for them, only Bob's soul wasn't lost exactly, only tormented.

Souls in Seclusion

My next case involves a more advanced subject who provided me with details about entities who are not ghosts but won't go home after death. As the case unfolds we will see that there are two motivating factors that drive these types of souls into seclusion.

Case 16

Dr. N: Are there people who die who are not ready to return to the spirit world?

S: Yes, some souls who are released from their physical bodies don't want to leave Earth.

Dr. N: I suppose they are all ghosts?

S: No, but they can be if that is their desire—most are not. They simply don't want to be in contact with anyone.

Dr. N: And their spiritual energy does not go home right after death?

S: That's right, except there is a part of their energy which never left the spirit world.

Dr. N: So I have heard. But let me ask if you consider these secluded souls as short-timers or do they stay in limbo for a long time in Earth years?

S: It varies. Some want to return as quickly as possible in a new body. These souls don't want to give up their physical form for any length of time. They are different from most of us who want to rest and go home to study. Many of this type have been real front-line warriors on Earth. They want to maintain a continuity with their physical life.

Dr. N: Well, it is my understanding that our guides won't permit us to be in some kind of holding pattern near Earth and go right into a new life. Don't these souls know they must go through the normal process of returning back to their groups, receiving counseling, studying their lessons and taking some part in the selection of a new body?

S: (laughs) You're right, but the guides don't force those in extreme distress to return home until they see the benefits of doing so.

Dr. N: Yes, but they won't give them a new body right away until after some sort of period of readjustment.

S: (shrugs) Yes, that's true.

Dr. N: Is it also true that other disturbed souls don't want to go back to Earth and won't go back where they belong in the spirit world either?

S: That's right—another type . . .

Dr. N: But if both soul types don't prowl around Earth as discarnates bothering people as ghosts, should I be calling them disturbed when all they want is to be left alone?

S: They are divergent. Their actions are the result of something unfinished . . . traumatic . . . overwhelming. They are unwilling to let go and this conduct is not usual. They won't talk to their teachers because of the extent of their unhappiness.

Dr. N: Why don't their guides just take charge and pull them up deeper into the spirit world despite their resistance?

S: If souls were forced to do what is right for them they would learn nothing from getting into a funk and shutting themselves up from everyone.

Dr. N: Okay, but I still wonder why the souls who want to come back right away, with no stopovers in the spirit world, can't just be given a new body immediately?

S: Can't you see that placing a disturbed soul into a new body would be totally unfair to a baby just starting life? These souls have a right to be in seclusion, but they will eventually make the decision to ask for assistance. They must come to the conclusion they can't progress alone. Being given a new body won't help them.

Dr. N: Where do the souls go who don't want to wander the Earth as ghosts but won't go home?

S: (ruefully) It's any space they want to create for themselves. They design their own reality with memories of a physical life. Some souls live in nice places like a garden setting. Others—those who have harmed people, for instance—design terrible spaces for themselves like a prison, a room with no windows. In these spaces they box themselves in so they can't experience much light or make contact with anyone. It is self-imposed punishment.

Dr. N: I have heard that disturbed souls—the ones associated with evil—are taken into seclusion in the spirit world.

S: That's correct, but at least they are ready to face the music and have their energy healed properly with love and care.

Dr. N: Can you give me some indication of how our guides deal with all types of souls in self-imposed exile?

S: They give them time to sweat it out. This is a challenge for teachers. They know these souls are concerned about their evaluations and the reactions from their soul groups. They are full of negative energy and not thinking clearly. It may take many reassurances by those who wish to help them before these souls agree to give up their self-imposed places of confinement.

Dr. N: I assume there are as many techniques of persuasion as there are guides?

S: Sure . . . depending upon the range of skill. Some teachers will not go near a disturbed student until that soul is so sick of being in seclusion they voluntarily call for help. This can take quite a while. (pause, then continues) Other teachers drop in often for chats.

Dr. N: Eventually, will all these disturbed souls release themselves?

S: (pause) Let's put it this way. Eventually, all will be released one way or another through different forms of encouragement . . . (laughs) or persuasion.

Those of you who are familiar with my work know that I have strong convictions about the influence soul memory has on human thought. The isolation and solitude of souls expressed in case 16 might well give one the impression of a Christian purgatory as a place of atonement. Could this religious concept have sprung from the fragmented soul memories of seclusion in the spirit world only to be subverted on Earth? There are similarities and great differences between my findings about soul seclusion and purgatory as defined by the church.

Christian doctrine has purgatory as a state of self-purification for those who must eliminate all traces of sin before proceeding on to heaven. I hear that some souls in seclusion undergo self-cleansing while others may require energy restoration. However, we don't come out of seclusion totally purified or there would be no need to reincarnate again. Also, soul confinement is not banishment. In recent years the less conservative elements of the Christian church do not stress hell as much as in the past. Nevertheless, the church still rejects universalism, the belief that everyone goes to heaven. To them, souls who die in a state of unrepentant mortal sin bypass purgatory and descend into hell where they suffer the punishments of "eternal fire." To be eternally damned, according to the church, is a separation from God as opposed to those who are blessed. The Christian churches simply do not accept the concept that *everything* is forgivable in the afterlife. In my experience, all souls are repentant because they hold themselves accountable for their choices.

From all I have learned, soul energy cannot be destroyed or made nonfunctional but it can be reshaped and purified of earthly contamination. Souls who demand to be left in solitude after death on Earth are not self-destructing, rather some feel isolation is necessary out of concern for contaminating other souls with negative energy. There are also souls who don't feel contaminated but they are not ready to be consoled by anyone.

The important thing to keep in mind is that souls have the ownership of their energy and most ask their guides to be taken to the centers of healing and rejuvenation in the spirit world. These are therapeutic areas away from their soul groups where there is solitude and time for personal reflection. However, this is a form of directed therapy. The disturbed souls case 16 talked about had not yet chosen to receive help. All my case histories indicate to me that after death we have the right to refuse assistance from our spiritual masters for as long as we wish.

I have been asked at lectures if the places of self-imposed exile are "lower planes" or "lower worlds." I can't help but feel these ideas come from fear-based dogma. Perhaps it's a question of semantics. I think a better translation of this state is a self-imposed space, a vacuum of subjective reality designed by the soul who wants to be alone. Separated space, away from the soul's spiritual center, is one of its own making. I don't see these souls as being lost in some realm divided from the spirit world where others reside. The disjunction is mental.

Souls of silence know they are immortal but they feel impotent. Consider what they do in solitude without help. They relive their acts over and over again, playing back all the karmic implications of what they have done to others and what has been done to them in their last life. They may have harmed others or been harmed by them. Quite often I hear they feel victimized by events over which they had little control. They are sad and mad at the same time. They have no interaction with their soul groups. These souls suffer from self-recrimination and restricted insight. I must admit these conditions fall within some of the definitions of purgatory.

Sartre said, "We have an imaginary self of the world with tendencies and desires and a real self." To this statement I would add that of William Blake, "Perception of our true self may threaten mergence with that self." In their space, the souls of solitude have given up their imaginary Self for a large dose of self-flagellation. Solitude and quiet self-analysis is an important and normal aspect of soul life within the spirit world. The difference here is that these disturbed souls are not yet ready to seek relief from their torment by asking for help, moving forward and making changes. It's a good thing that these souls make up only a small fraction of the population of souls crossing over each day.

Discarnates Who Visit Earth

There are entities who travel to Earth as tourists and have never incarnated on our planet. Some are quite advanced while others are maladapts. The character of these beings has been described to me as friendly, helpful and peaceful, or distant, aggravating and even contentious. For thousands of years I believe they have been considered in our folklore as beings with the capacity to create both fear and enchantment. Our mythology alludes to the differences between light beings who are airy and whimsical and darker beings who are heavy with ugly temperaments. Some of these pre-Christian legends have spilled over into current religious beliefs of a light or dark tableau of grace or violence in the afterlife.

Quite a number of my subjects have told me that between their lives on Earth they travel as discarnates to other worlds both in and out of our dimension. Some explain that they see other nonphysical entities on these trips. This is why it has been surprising to me that only occasionally do I receive small amounts of information from clients about encountering other light beings on Earth. My clients see them when they decide to visit Earth as discarnates themselves between lives. The reports are intriguing, as the next case illustrates.

Case 17

Dr. N: Since you have described to me how much you enjoy traveling to both physical and mental worlds between your lives, I am curious what you know about other beings you might see when you come to Earth?

S: They float through our reality here on Earth just as I do in other dimensions.

Dr. N: Do you know many souls who regularly incarnate on Earth that visit here like yourself?

S: No, as a matter of fact, it's not all that common, but I like to come. Many of my friends enjoy a change in scenery between lives and stay away from Earth. When I come here, sometimes I see strange beings I don't know.

Dr. N: What do they look like?

S: Odd, strange shapes, wispy or dense . . . not human-looking.

Dr. N: Let's talk about this. You have told me of the ability souls have in the spirit world to project a human form. What do you and your friends look like as spirits on Earth?

S: Oh . . . rather the same, but on a dense world such as Earth, we shift more on the physical side . . . to add flavor to what we once were here.

Dr. N: You mean you are in more of a corporeal state?

S: Um . . . yes . . . sort of. On worlds such as Earth we are more defined around the edges—the way we outline a human body in a transparent fashion as soft, diffused light. In the spirit world when we assume body features, say of a former life, we glow all over with full-strength energy.

Dr. N: Can a non-physical being, even in a diffused state, be visible to living inhabitants?

S: (chuckles) Oh, yes . . . but only certain people can see us as apparitions and then not always.

Dr. N: Why is that?

S: It has to do with their level of receptivity—of perception—at certain moments when we are in their area.

Dr. N: If you will, please put yourself in the position of a transparent light being on Earth and tell me what you do here. I want you to include any non-human spirits you see who have had no incarnation experiences on our planet.

S: (happily) As visitors, we soar through the mountains and valleys, the cities and small towns. For us, there is a vicarious picking up of the energy of Earth's struggles. It's always interesting to bump into different kinds of beings who are also on tour here. They know Earth's inhabitants are afraid of us and most of these beings would like to dispel the fear . . . yet . . . those of us from Earth know we can't afford to get entangled with people's lives in any major way.

Dr. N: Meaning that some beings from other worlds have no such reservations?

S: Yes.

Dr. N: I assume by "entangled" you mean interfering in someone's karmic path?

S: Well . . . yes.

Dr. N: But why not help people if you can?

S: (abruptly, and maybe with some guilt) Look, we are not guides assigned to Earth. We are only visitors, as are the others we see here occasionally. It's a vacation trip for all of us. If we come across a condition going bad we might take a moment to briefly . . . turn a head toward a better alternative path. We do get pleasure out of . . . nudging people . . . to act in their better interest rather than turning the wrong way.

Dr. N: If you happen to be in the right place at the right time?

S: Right, to give . . . a gentle push in a better direction at a crucial moment (raises voice)—no fixing of major trouble spots, you understand.

Dr. N: Then you would be considered as good spirits?

S: (laughs) As opposed to what?

Dr. N: (in an attempt to draw this subject out) To bad spirits who interfere with life forms for the pleasure of doing harm.

S: (abruptly) Who told you this? There are no evil spirits, only inept ones . . . and those who are careless . . . and indifferent . . .

Dr. N: How about sad spirits, or ones who are disoriented, or playful spirits—can't they cause harm?

S: Oh, yes, but it is not premeditated evil. (pause, and then adds) Not all of us are in the same category . . . soaring around Earth on a lark.

Dr. N: That's what I was getting at. I'm thinking of ghosts.

S: These are spirits grounded here by their own volition.

Dr. N: How about the spirits who are strangers to Earth?

S: (pause) There are other spirits who travel interdimensionally who we consider to be maladapts. They do not seem to have any sensitivity to Earth. They are not knowledgeable about human beings.

Dr. N: (coaxing) And can they cause problems for the living?

S: (edgy) Yes, sometimes . . . although it might be unintentional. They are not bad or evil, just clumsy, mischievous children. The younger light beings can get lost between and within dimensions. Their amusements distract them. We consider them as naughty youngsters. These pranksters think Earth is their playground where they can engage in devilish behavior with susceptible, gullible people and scare the hell out of them. They have a hilarious time before they are caught by one of the Rovers (tracker guides) sent to recapture these truants.

Dr. N: Is this a common occurrence?

S: Actually, I don't think so. They are like children who escape from the watchful eyes of parents once in a while.

Dr. N: So you don't see malevolent spirits directed here by some demonic force?

S: (promptly) Nooo—sometimes we might run into a dark, heavy entity who is disoriented by the Earth sphere. This place is dense but they come from places even more dense. Anyway, they want to cling to us because they don't know what they are doing. We call them the "heavies" because of their lack of mobility.

Dr. N: What about the spirits you spoke of who are just indifferent to people on Earth?

S: (deep sigh) Yeah, they can scare people. This is because some of them have a disruptive nature. They are not considerate.

Dr. N: Bulls in a china shop?

S: Yeah—no adaption to local customs . . .

Dr. N: And, in these cases with different types of spirits who might be aggravating to the people here, do you try to intervene in some way?

S: Yes, if we come across them acting like rogues we put a stop to it and try and push them away. This is very infrequent . . . most out-of-worlders are serious and respectful. (pause) I want to stress that we are not philanthropists. This is our recreation time and we want to be free of responsibility.

Dr. N: Okay then, why would an inept spirit of any sort come to Earth for whatever reason and be allowed to cause trouble, even inadvertently, for the people living here? Do their guides lack good parenting skills?

S: (unruffled) Well . . . too much monitoring makes for dull children. If they were on a tight leash how would they learn? They are not going to be allowed to destroy or do great harm.

Dr. N: One last question. Do you think that all the kinds of spirits we have been talking about exist in large numbers swarming all over Earth?

S: Not at all. Compared to Earth's population, only a tiny fraction. Judging by my own experience here, there are times when only a few are around and I may not see them at all. It is not a constant thing . . . it's more cyclic.

There is a mystery to that which is invisible to the living, when only our senses tell us something is there. I wonder if spiritual travelers don't engender memories within us of recognition of what we once were and will be again.

Demons or Devas

I think it is fitting that I close this chapter with a summary of some misconceptions we have about the existence of evil spirits, good spirits and spiritual influences on Earth. If I step rather heavily on any pet theories of the reader, please understand that my statements come from the reports of many hypnosis subjects in my practice. These subjects do not see the devil or demonic spirits floating around Earth. What they do feel when they are spirits is an abundance of negative human energy exuding the intense emotions of anger, hate and fear. These disruptive thought patterns are attracted to the consciousness of other negative thinkers who collect and disseminate even more disharmony. All this dark energy in the air works to the detriment of positive wisdom on Earth.

The ancients thought demons were flying beings who occupied the regions between heaven and Earth and were not particularly wicked. The early Christian church elevated demons to the status of "evil rulers of darkness." As fallen angels, they were able to disguise themselves as messengers of God rather than Satan in order to deceive humans. I think it is fair to say that within the more liberal religious communities today, demons represent our own inner misguided passions that can get us into trouble.

In all my years of working with souls, never once have I had a subject who was possessed by another spirit, unfriendly or otherwise. When I made this statement at one lecture, a man raised his hand and said, "That is all very well, O great guru, but until you have placed everyone in the world under hypnosis don't tell me about the absence of demonic forces!" Of course, this is a valid argument against my hypothesis that such things as soul possession, evil demons, the devil and hell don't exist. Nevertheless, I can come to no other conclusion when all of my subjects, even those who came to me with conscious beliefs in demonic forces, reject the existence of such beings when they see themselves as spirits.

Once in a while a client comes to me convinced they have been possessed by an alien entity or some sort of malevolent spirit. I have had other clients who believe an evil curse has been placed upon them from some past life behavior. As my hypnosis regression session moves into the superconscious mind of these people, typically we find one of three conditions:

1. Almost always the fear proves to be absolutely groundless.

2. Occasionally, a friendly spirit, often a dead relative, has been trying to reach them. My distraught client has misinterpreted the intent of this spirit who only wished to bring comfort and love. There has been miscommunication between the sender and receiver. Souls have little trouble with telepathy between themselves, but this does not mean all souls are adept communicators with incarnated people.

3. Very rarely, a disturbed, inept spirit has made contact because of some unresolved karmic issues they have on Earth. We saw this in case 14.

Researchers into the paranormal have come up with three more reasons which ought to be added to my own as to why certain people believe they have been possessed by a demon:

4. Emotional and physical abuse as a child, which create feelings that the adult abuser represents an evil power who has total control.

5. Multiple Personality Disorder.

6. Periodic increases in the actions of electromagnetic fields around Earth which are sufficient enough to disrupt brain activity in a disturbed individual.

The possibility that people can be possessed by a satanic being comes right out of medieval belief systems. It is fear based and the result of theological superstition that has ruined countless lives over the last thousand years. Much of this nonsense has dissipated in the last two hundred years, but it lingers with the fundamentalists. The exorcism of demons is still practiced by some religious groups. Frequently, I find that clients who come to me with concerns about possession have lives which seem to be out of their control and filled with a variety of personal obsessions and compulsions. People who hear voices commanding them to do bad things are likely to be schizophrenic—they are not possessed.

Our physical world may have unhappy or mischievous spirits floating round, but they do not lock in and inhabit the minds of people. The spirit world is much too ordered to allow for such muddled soul activity. Being possessed by another being would not only abrogate our life contract but destroy free will. These factors form the foundation of reincarnation and cannot be compromised. The idea that satanic entities exist as outside forces to confuse and subvert people is a myth perpetuated by those who seek to control the minds of others for their own ends. Evil exists internally, initiated within the confines of the deranged human mind. Life can be cruel but it is of our making here on this planet.

Assuming that we are born evil, or that some external force has occupied the mind of an evil person, makes malevolence easier for some people to accept. It is a way of rationalizing premeditated cruelty, preserving our humanity, and absolving ourselves of responsibility individually and collectively as a race. When we see cases of serial killers, or those of children who kill other children, we might label these people as either "born killers" or under outside demonic influences. This saves us the trouble of finding out why these murderers enjoy inflicting pain by acting out their own pain.

There are no soul monsters. People are not born evil. Rather they are corrupted by the society in which they live, where practicing evil satisfies the cravings of depraved personalities. This emanates from the human brain. Studies of the psychopath have shown that the excitement of inflicting pain on others without remorse satisfies an emptiness they feel within themselves. Practicing evil is a source of power, strength and control for inadequate people. Hate takes away the reality of a hateful life. The warped minds of these executioners tell them, "If life is not worth living for me, why not take it away from somebody else."

Evil is not genetic, although if a family has a history of violence and cruelty to their children, these acts are often passed on from one generation to the next as learned behavior. Violence and dysfunctional behavior from one adult member of a family is an internal emotional reaction that spills over to contaminate other younger members. This can lead to compulsive and destructive behavior from children of that family. How do these genetic and environmental disruptions to the body affect our soul?

What I have found in my practice is that a soul's energy force may, during troubled times, dissociate from the body. There are those who feel they don't even belong to their bodies. If conditions are severe enough, these souls are prone to thoughts of suicide—but usually not taking the life of another. I will have more to say about this condition in upcoming chapters. Part of this turmoil stems from conflicts between the soul's immortal character meshed to the temperament of a host brain with all its genetic baggage. There may also be influences of abnormal brain chemistry and hormonal imbalances affecting the central nervous system that might contaminate the soul.

Another element I find is that immature souls often have difficulties handling the poor mental circuitry of disturbed human beings. There is a counteraction of the soul self versus the human self. A push-me pull-you force is struggling to present a single ego to the world and not doing very well in the process. These are internal, not external forces at work. A disturbed mind does not need an exorcist but a competent mental health therapist.

Souls don't represent all that is pure and good about a body or they wouldn't be incarnating for personal development. Souls come to Earth to work on their own shortcomings. In terms of self-discovery, a soul may choose to act in conjunction with, or in opposition to, its own character in the selection of a human body. As an example, a soul combating tendencies toward selfishness and indulgence might not mix well with a human ego whose emotional temperament is disposed to engaging in hostile acts for self-gratification.

Quite often, troubled people have suffered painful environmental trauma such as physical and emotional abuse as children. They have either internalized themselves, creating a shell to hide behind their pain, or externalized by mentally moving outside their bodies on a regular basis. These defense mechanisms are a means of survival to preserve our sanity. When a client tells me that they love to "tune out" and practice astral projection because the out-of-body experience makes them feel more alive, I look for disturbances. Indeed, I may not find anything other than curiosity, but an obsession with being away from the body indicates a desire to escape from current reality.

It is perhaps for this reason I am troubled by the walk-in theory as another escape mechanism. I believe the whole idea of walk-ins to be a false concept. According to the proponents of this theory, tens of thousands of souls now on this planet came directly into their physical body without going through the normal process of birth and childhood. We are told that these possessing souls are enlightened beings who are permitted to take over the adult body of a soul who wants to check out early because life has become too difficult. Therefore, the walk-in soul is actually performing a humanitarian act, according to devotees of this theory. I call this possession by permission.

If this theory is true, then I must turn in my great-guru white robe and gold medallion. Not once, in all my years of working with subjects in regression, have I ever had a walk-in soul. Also, these people have never heard of any other soul in the spirit world associated with such practices. In fact, they deny the existence of this act because it would abrogate a soul's life contract. To give another soul permission to come in and take over your karmic life plan defeats the whole purpose of your coming to Earth in the first place! It is deluded reasoning to assume that the walk-in would wish to complete their own karmic cycle in a body originally selected and assigned to someone else. If I am a senior in a high school trigonometry class, would I leave my class and go down the hall to a freshman algebra class where a student is struggling with an exam and tell him I'll finish the exam for him so he can leave early? This is a lose-lose situation for both students—and what teacher would permit it?

The whole walk-in theory is like suicide, although it is supposed to combat suicide by allowing the walk-out soul to escape responsibility for straightening out their life. The walk-out soul relinquishes ownership of its host body so a more advanced spirit who does not want to go to all the trouble of being in a child's body can take over. This is one of the major flaws of possession by permission. From everything I have learned about body assignments, it takes years for a soul to fully meld its energy vibrations with that of a host brain. The process begins when the baby is in a fetal state. All the essential elements of who we really are come from the soul assigned to a specific body from the beginning. Consider first the three I's emanating from the soul: imagination, intuition and insight. Then add such components as conscience and creativity. Do you think the adult human mind is not going to recognize the loss of its partner Self to a new presence? Now, that would drive a host body insane as opposed to healing it. I tell people not to worry about losing their soul—it's with us for the duration because there are good reasons for having the particular body you occupy.

Souls take their responsibility very seriously, even to the extent of being inside nonfunctional bodies. They are not materially trapped. For instance, a soul may inhabit a comatose host body for many years and not abandon it until death. These souls are able to roam freely across the land visiting other souls who might be making brief trips away from their bodies during normal sleep states. This is especially true of souls in the bodies of babies. Souls are very respectful of their host body assignments, even if they are bored. They leave a small portion of their energy so they can return quickly if needed. Their wavelengths are like homing beacons who have "fingerprinted" their human partners.

When a soul's energy does leave the human body, this does not provide an opportunity for some demonic being to rapidly move in and occupy a vacant mind. This is another superstition. Aside from the nonexistence of such demonic beings in the first place, the mind is never completely vacant of a traveling soul's energy. A malevolent entity would be unable to squeeze in, even if it did exist.

Evidently, residents of the spirit world are quite aware of our enthrallment with dark and nefarious specters who pose a danger to the soul. I have a most unusual and defining case which brought this to my attention. The ironic engagement of demonology employed in case 18 by my subject's teacher toward his hapless student is outrageous and unconventional but effective. This case illustrates how the almost brutal use of humor can be graphically applied in the spirit world to define our shortcomings on Earth.

Case 18 concerns the death experience of an evangelical preacher of the 1920s. This man had spent a lifetime seeing the devil in every nook and cranny of his town in the deep South. During my review of this life with the client who carried these memories, I was told, "My parishioners were shaken to their bones with my fiery sermons of the hell awaiting all sinful transgressors." I will begin this case with a scene as it unfolded right after my subject reaches the gateway.

Case 18

Dr. N: You say that although things are not too clear, you are floating in bright light and someone is coming toward you?

S: Yes, I am kind of disoriented. I haven't gotten used to things around here yet.

Dr. N: That's fine, just take your time and let the figure float toward you as you float toward it.

S: (long pause, and then with a loud horrified exclamation) OH, GOD. NO!

Dr. N: (startled by this outcry) What's going on?

S: (subject's body begins to shake uncontrollably) OH . . . OH . . . LORD ALMIGHTY! IT'S THE DEVIL. I KNEW IT. I'VE GONE TO HELL!

Dr. N: (grasping subject by the shoulders) Now, take a deep breath and try to relax as we go through this together. (then, softly) You are not in hell . . .

S: (cuts in with a shrill tone of voice) OH, YEAH—THEN WHY DO I SEE THE DEVIL RIGHT IN FRONT OF ME?

Dr. N: (my subject's face is now covered in sweat and I use a tissue to wipe some of it away while continuing to reassure) Try to calm yourself, there is some misinterpretation here and we will find it soon.

S: (paying no attention to me, the subject now begins to moan while rocking back and forth) Ohooo . . . it's over for me . . . I'm in hell . . .

Dr. N: (I break in now more forcefully) Tell me exactly what you see.

S: (whispering at first and then loudly) A . . . being . . . demonic . . . reddish-green face . . . horns . . . wild-eyed . . . fangs . . . the facial skin is like charred wood . . . O SWEET JESUS, WHY ME OF ALL PEOPLE, WHO SPOKE SO MUCH IN YOUR NAME?

Dr. N: What else do you see?

S: (with loathing) WHAT ELSE IS THERE TO SEE? CAN'T YOU UNDERSTAND? I'M IN FRONT OF THE DEVIL!

Dr. N: (quickly) I meant the rest of the body. Look below the head and tell me what you see.

S: (with a violent shudder) Nothing . . . just a wispy ghostlike body.

Dr. N: Stay with me. Doesn't this seem unusual to you—that the devil would appear with no body? Move forward in time rapidly now and tell me what this figure does.

S: (my subject's body jerks up violently and then with a great sigh of relief he sags back into the chair) Oh . . . that bastard . . . I might have known . . . it's SCANLON. He is taking his mask off and smiling wickedly at me . . .

Dr. N: (now I can relax) Who is Scanlon?

S: My guide. This is his crude idea of a joke.

Dr. N: What does Scanlon really look like now?

S: Tall, aquiline features, gray hair . . . full of mischief-making, as usual. (laughs with bravado, but still not fully recovered) I should have known. He caught me unawares this time.

Dr. N: Does Scanlon make a habit of this sort of thing? Why frighten you just as you were coming into the spirit world a little disoriented?

S: (defensively) Listen, he is a great teacher. That's his way. He has got our whole group using masks but he knows I don't like them much.

Dr. N: Tell me why Scanlon used a devil's mask to scare you right after this life? Talk to him now.

Note: I am quiet for a few moments while my subject mentally connects with Scanlon.

S: (after a period of silence) I had it coming. Oh, I know it! I spent a lifetime preaching about the devil, scaring good people . . . telling them they were going to hell if they didn't pay attention to me. Scanlon gave me a dose of my own medicine.

Dr. N: And how do you feel now about his methods?

S: (chagrined) He made his point.

Dr. N: I want to ask you a blunt question. Did you really believe what you told your parishioners about seeing demonic forces everywhere, or were you motivated by something else?

S: (intensely) No, no—I believed what I was saying about evil being everywhere in every person. I was not a hypocrite.

Dr. N: Are you sure it wasn't false piety? You did not pretend to feel and be what you were not?

S: No! I believed it. My undoing was my method of preaching and the love of the power over others that this ability gave me. Yes, I admit that failing . . . I made life miserable for some of my flock . . . not seeing the essential goodness in people. I was always suspicious because of my obsession with evil and this corrupted me.

Dr. N: Do you feel part of what you became was the result of the body you chose in this life?

S: (in a flat voice) Yes, I lacked restraint. I chose a body with a feisty mind and allowed myself to be swept away. I was too confrontational as a preacher.

Dr. N: And do you know why your soul mind chose to enter into this partnership in the body of a preacher who constantly intimidated people?

S: Oh, I . . . shit . . . I let it happen because it felt good to be in control . . . I was afraid of . . . not being taken seriously enough.

Dr. N: You were worried about the loss of control?

S: (long pause) Yes, that . . . I would be . . . inadequate.

Dr. N: By his use of a devil's mask, do you think Scanlon demeans what you stood for in the church?

S: No, that's my teacher's way. I chose the body of a minister and he helped me with all this. I took a wrong turn—it was not the wrong path. My faith was not a bad thing but I became misguided and I misguided others. Scanlon wants me to see what it feels like to scare people rather than reason with them. He wanted me to feel the same fear that I gave to others.

Note: I now move my subject into a group setting to learn more about how Scanlon teaches his students through the use of masks.

Dr. N: Who is the first person who comes to you?

S: (hesitates and is wary) It's . . . an angel . . . soft glowing white . . . wings . . . (then, with recognition) OKAY, I'M ON TO ALL OF YOU. ENOUGH!

Dr. N: Who is this angel?

S: My dear friend, Diane. She has removed her angel's mask and is laughing and hugging me.

Dr. N: I'm a little confused. Souls can assume any shape or create any features they want. Why bother with masks?

S: The mask is similar to a figure of speech, a symbol one can hold in the hand to put on and pull off for effect. Diane is offsetting Scanlon's huge joke by being a loving angel for me while the others are laughing at what happened to me.

Dr. N: What kind of individual is Diane?

S: Very loving and full of humor. She likes practical jokes, as does most of my group. They all know I take things too seriously. I don't like the masks very much so they tease me.

Dr. N: During your lessons, are masks used as a means of teaching about right and wrong behavior?

S: Yes, they are a means of acknowledgment of good or poor thinking, misconceptions . . . they identify aspects of our character which are positive and those which are undesirable and we can role play with each other.

Dr. N: Did Scanlon originate the use of this sort of prop for your group lessons?

S: (laughs) Yes, and what he does makes an impression.

This was a strange case and I'll admit Scanlon had me going for a few minutes when I thought this client was taking me to a place no other had before. The treatment this subject received at the gateway by the use of a devil mask is an anomaly. Moreover, I have never encountered a guide whose behavior had such extravagance and provocation.

In the chapters ahead we will see how drama plays an important part in soul group activity. The use of masks by Scanlon's group as a symbolic gesture to embody a belief system is rather unique in my experience. Masks do have a long tradition in our cultural life, where personification of divine and demonic power has been used to mock spirits which are feared and honor those spirits that are venerated. The devil mask has a history of tribal exorcism toward a harmful spirit. Case 18 is one where mythic spiritual practices were taken from Earth by a soul group director to serve as a wake-up call for his students.

~4

Spiritual Energy Restoration

Soul Energy

We cannot define the soul in a physical way because to do so would establish limits on something that seems to have none. I see the soul as intelligent light energy. This energy appears to function as vibrational waves similar to electromagnetic force but without the limitations of charged particles of matter. Soul energy does not appear to be uniform. Like a fingerprint, each soul has a unique identity in its formation, composition and vibrational distribution. I am able to discern soul properties of development by color tones, yet none of this defines what the soul is as an entity.

From years of study on how the soul interacts within a variety of human minds over many incarnations, and what it subsequently does in the spirit world, I have come to know something of its yearnings for perfection. This does not tell me what the soul is either. To fully understand soul energy, we would need to know all the aspects of its creation and, indeed, the consciousness of its source. This is a perfection that I cannot know, despite all my efforts investigating the mysteries of life after death.

I am left then with examining the actions of this profound energy substance and how it reacts to people and events and what it is striving to do in both physical and mental environments. If the soul's existence begins and is molded by pure thought, it is sustained by that thought as an immortal being. The soul's individual character enables it to influence its physical environment to give greater harmony and balance to life. Souls are an expression of beauty, imagination and creativity. The ancient Egyptians said that to begin to understand the soul, one must listen to the heart. I think they were right.

Standard Treatment at the Gateway

When we cross over and are met by our guides, I find the techniques they use at initial contact fall into two general categories:

1. **Envelopment.** Here returning souls are completely cloaked by a large circular mass of their guide's powerful energy. As the soul and guide come together, the soul feels as though they both are encased in a bubble. This is the more common method, which my subjects describe as pure ecstasy.

2. **The Focus Effect.** This alternate procedure of initial contact is administered a little differently. As the guide approaches, energy is applied to certain points at the edges of the soul's etheric body from any direction of the guide's choosing. We might be taken by the hand or held by the tops of our shoulders from a side position. Healing begins from a specific point of the etheric body in the form of a brushing caress followed by deep penetration.

The choice of procedures depends on the preference of the guide and the condition of our soul energy at the time. In both instances there is an immediate infusion of potent, invigorating energy while we are projected forward. This is the introductory phase of the journey to our eventual spiritual destination. The more advanced souls, especially if they are undamaged, usually do not require assistance from a loving energy force.

A review of the techniques employed by case 1 on his wife, Alice, demonstrates elements of both the focus effect and envelopment on a living person by someone who is not yet a guide. Other cases in the last chapter indicate this is one way we begin our training in the use of healing energy before acquiring the status of a guide. During the exhilarating moments after initial contact, our guides might also expertly apply what I call energy *permeation*. This follow-up effect of energy transference has been described as being similar to the percolating of coffee. In case 8 a soul used an energy filtration process involving smell on her husband, Charles.

Healing emotional and physical injury, both in and out of the spirit world, emanates from a source of goodness. Positive energy flows to every part of the soul's being from the sender, whose own essence and wisdom is transmitted as well. My subjects are unable to explain the beauty and subtlety of this assimilation except to say it resembles the flowing of rejuvenating electricity.

Emergency Treatment at the Gateway

When souls arrive at the gateway to the spirit world with energy that is in a deteriorated state, some of our guides engage in emergency healing. This is both a physical and mental healing exercise that takes place before the soul moves any further into the spirit world. One of my clients died in an auto accident in his last life where his leg was severed. He told me what occurred at the gateway as a result of this experience:

> When I reached the gateway, my guide saw the gaps in my energy aura and proceeded at once to push the damaged energy back into place. He molded it as clay to fill, reshape and smooth out the rough edges and broken intervals to make me whole again.

The etheric, or soul body is an outline of our old physical body which souls take into the spirit world. Essentially, it is an imprint of a human form we have not shed yet, like the skin of a reptile. This is not a permanent condition, although we might naturally create it later as a colorful, luminescent shape of energy. We know damaged body imprints from a past life can influence the current physical form of some people unless properly deprogrammed, so why not the reverse? There are souls who shed their body form completely at the moment of death. However, many souls with physical and emotional scars from life carry the imprint of this damaged energy back home.

In terms of afflictions and soul healing, I learn a lot from the students as well as the teachers in the spirit world. My next case was a rather unusual one for me where a student guide was unable to handle damaged energy properly at the gate. My subject in this case had just come off a difficult life after being blown up in an artillery bombardment during a battle in World War I.

Case 19

Dr. N: As you pass into the bright light following your death in the mud and rain of this battlefield, what do you see?

S: A figure coming toward me dressed in a white robe.

Dr. N: Who is this figure?

S: I see Kate. She is a new teacher, recently assigned to our group.

Dr. N: Describe her appearance and what she is communicating to you as she comes closer.

S: She has a young, rather plain face with a large forehead. Kate radiates peace—I can feel it—but there is a concern too and . . . (laughs) she won't come close to me.

Dr. N: Why not?

S: My energy is in bad shape. She says to me, "Zed, you should be healing yourself!"

Dr. N: Why doesn't she help in this endeavor, Zed?

S: (laughs again loudly) Kate does not want to get near all my scrambled negative energy from the war . . . and the killing.

Dr. N: I have never heard of a guide shying away from such responsibility with disassembled energy, Zed. Is she afraid of contamination?

S: (still laughing) Something like that. You have to understand Kate is still rather new at this sort of work. She is not happy with herself—I can see that.

Dr. N: Describe what your energy looks like right now.

S: My energy is a mess. It is in chunks . . . black blocks . . . irregular . . . totally skewed out of alignment.

Dr. N: Is this because you didn't escape from your body fast enough at the moment of death?

S: For sure! My unit was taken by surprise. I normally cut loose (from the body) when I see death coming.

Note: This case and many others have taught me that souls often leave their bodies seconds before a violent death.

Dr. N: Well, can't Kate lend some assistance in rearranging your energy?

S: She tries . . . a little . . . I guess it's too much for her at the moment.

Dr. N: So, what do you do?

S: I begin to take her suggestion and try to help myself. I'm not doing too well, it's so scrambled. Then a powerful stream of energy hits me like water from a fire hose and it helps me begin to reshape myself and push out some of the negative crap from that battle.

Dr. N: I have heard of a place where energy is showered upon newly returned, damaged souls. Is that where you are now?

S: (laughing) I guess so—it's from my guide, Bella. I can see him now. He is a real pro at this kind of thing. He is standing behind Kate, helping her.

Dr. N: Then what happens to you?

S: Bella fades away and Kate comes close to me and puts her arms around me and we start to talk as she leads me away.

Dr. N: (deliberately provoking) Do you have any confidence in Kate after she treated you like some sort of leper?

S: (frowns at me severely) Oh, come on—that's a mite strong. It won't be long before she gets the hang of working with this kind of messed-up energy. I like her a lot. She has many gifts . . . right now, mechanics isn't one of them.

Recovery Areas for the Less Damaged Soul

Regardless of the specific energy treatment received by the soul at the gateway to the spirit world, most all returning souls will continue on to some sort of healing station before finally joining their groups. All but the most advanced souls crossing back into the spirit world are met by benevolent spirits who make contact with their positive energy and escort needy souls to quiet recovery areas. It is only the more highly developed souls, with energy patterns that are still strong after their incarnations, who return directly to their regular activities. The more advanced souls appear to get over hardship more quickly than others after a life. One man told me, "Most of the people I work with must stop and rest, but I don't need anything. I'm in too much of a hurry to get back and continue my program."

Most recovery areas for the returning soul involve some kind of orientation back to the spirit world. It may be intense or moderate in scope, depending upon the condition of the soul. This usually includes a preliminary debriefing of the life just completed. Much more in-depth counseling will take place later with guides in group conferences and with our Council of Elders. I have written about these orientation procedures in *Journey of Souls*. The surroundings of recovery areas are identifiable earthly settings created out of our memories and what spiritual guides feel will promote healing. Orientation environments are not the same after each of our lives. One woman had the following to say, after dying in a German concentration camp in 1944:

> There are subtle differences in physical layout depending upon the life one has just lived. Because I have just returned from a life filled with horror, cold and bleak-ness—everything is very bright to lighten my sorrow. There is even a comfortable fire next to me so I'll have the feeling of added warmth and cheerfulness.

Upon returning to the spirit world, often my subjects describe themselves as being in a garden setting, while others might say they are in a crystalline enclosure. The garden presents a scene of beauty and serenity, but what does crystal represent? It is not just in the orientation rooms that I hear about crystals. Crystal caves, for example, appear in the minds of some people who are spending time alone in reflection right after a life is over. Here is a typical statement about a crystal recovery center:

> My place of recovery is crystalline in composition because it helps me connect my thoughts. The crystal walls have multicolored stones which reflect prisms of light. The geometric angles of these crystals send out moving bands of light which crisscross around and bring clarity to my thoughts.

After talking to a number of clients out of trance, and with others who are knowledgeable about crystals, I came to realize that crystals represent thought enhancement through a balancing of energy. As a shamanic tool, the crystal is supposed to assist in tuning our vibrational pattern into a universal energy force while releasing negative energy. Bringing forth wisdom from an expanded consciousness through healing is the primary reason for being in a place of spiritual recovery.

The next example involves a garden setting. I had a client who had been working on humility for many lives. In earlier incarnations, usually as a man, this soul had been caught up with host bodies that had become haughty, arrogant and even ruthless during my subject's occupancy. In a complete turnaround, this person's last life had been one of acceptance that bordered on passivity. Since this life was so out of character for my client, there was a feeling of failure when this soul reached the recovery area. I was then given this account:

> I am in a beautiful circular garden with willow trees and a pond with ducks in it. There is such tranquillity here and this scene softens the feelings of discouragement I have over my last performance. My guide, Makil, brings me to a marble bench under an arbor draped with vines and flowers. I am so down over my wasted life because I over-compensated at every turn—going from one extreme to

another. Makil smiles and offers me refreshments. We drink nectar and eat fruit together and watch the ducks. While we do this the aura of my old physical body moves further away from me. I begin to feel as though I am taking in his powerful energy as oxygen after a near drowning.

Makil is a gracious host and he knows I need nourishment because I am judging myself in such a critical manner. I am always harder on myself than he is. We talk about my overcorrections of past mistakes and what I wanted to do that didn't get done—or was only partially completed. Makil offers encouragement that I still learned from this life, which will make the next one better. He explains the important thing was that I was not afraid to change. The whole garden atmosphere is so relaxing. I am already feeling better.

From cases such as this I have learned that our guides use the sense memory we had in our physical bodies to assist in our recovery. There are many ways to achieve this, such as the use of taste memory by Makil in the above case. I have also listened to descriptive scenes involving touch and smell. After receiving streams of bright white "liquid energy," there have been subjects who describe additional treatments involving the sensations of sound and multicolored lights:

After my cleansing shower, I move to an adjacent room to the place of rebalancing. While I float to the center of this enclosure, I see a vast array of spotlights overhead. I hear my name called: "Banyon, are you ready?" When I give my assent, sounds vibrate into me which resonate like tuning forks until the pitch is just right to make my energy bubble—like frothy soapsuds. It feels wonderful. Then the spotlights come on one at a time. In the beginning I am scanned by an intense beam of healing green light. It casts a circle around me as if I were on a stage. This light is designed to pick up my level of displaced energy—to see what I have lost or damaged—and make corrections. I think this is more effective because my energy is bubbling from the sound vibrations. Then I receive a wash of gold light for strength and blue for awareness. Finally, my own pinkish-white color is restored by one of the spotlights. It is soothing and loving and I'm sorry when this is over.

Regenerating Severely Damaged Souls

There are certain displaced souls who have become so contaminated by their host bodies that they require special handling. In life they became destructive to others and themselves. This spectrum of behavior would primarily include souls who have been associated with evil acts that caused harm to other people through deliberate malice. There are souls who slowly become more contaminated from a series of lifetimes, while others are totally overcome by one body alone. In either case these souls are taken to places of isolation where their energy undergoes a more radical treatment plan than with the typical returning soul.

Contamination of the soul can take many forms and involve different grades of severity during an incarnation. A difficult host body might cause the less experienced soul to return with damaged energy where a more advanced being would survive the same situation relatively intact. The average soul's energy will become shadowed when it has lived within a host body obsessed by constant fear and rage. The question is, by how much?

Our thoughts, feelings, moods and attitudes are mediated by body chemicals which are released through signals of perceived threats and danger from the brain. Fight or flight mechanisms come from our primitive brain, not from the soul. The soul has a great capacity to control our biological and emotional reactions to life but many souls are unable to regulate a dysfunctional brain. Souls display these scars when they leave a body that has deteriorated in this fashion.

I have my own theory of madness. The soul comes into the fetus and begins its fusion with the human mind by the time the baby is born. If this child matures into an adult with organic brain syndromes, psychosis, or major affective disorders, abnormal behavior is the result. The struggling soul does not fully assimilate. When this soul can no longer control the aberrant behavior of its body, the two personas begin to separate into a dissociated personality. There may be many physical, emotional and environmental factors that contribute to a person becoming a danger to themselves and others. Here the combined Self has been damaged.

One of the red flags for souls who are losing their capacity to regulate deviant human beings is when they have had a series of lives in bodies demonstrating a lack of intimacy and displaying tendencies toward violence. This has a domino effect with a soul asking for the same sort of body to overcome the last one. Because we have free will, our guides are indulgent. A soul is not excused from responsibility for a disturbed human mind it is unable to regulate because it is a part of that mind. The problem for slow learner souls is they may have had a series of prior life struggles before occupying a body that escalated wrongdoing to a new level of evil.

What happens to these disturbed souls when they return to the spirit world? I will begin with a quote from a client giving me an outsider's view of a place where severely damaged souls are taken. Some of my subjects call this area the City of Shadows:

> It is here where negative energy is erased. Since this is the place where so many souls are concentrated who have negative energy, it is dark to those of us outside. We can't go into this place where souls who have been associated with horror are undergoing alteration. And we would not want to go there anyway. It is a place of healing, but from a distance it has the appearance of a dark sea—while I am looking at it from a bright, sandy beach. All the light around this area is brighter in contrast because positive energy defines the greater goodness of bright light.
>
> When you look at the darkness carefully, you see it is not totally black but a mixture of deep green. We know this is an aspect of the combined forces of the healers working here. We also know that souls who are taken to this area are not exonerated. Eventually, in some way, they must redress the wrongs they perpetrated on others. This they must do to restore full positive energy to themselves.

Subjects who are familiar with damaged souls explain to me that not all of the more terrible memories of bad deeds are erased. It is known that if the soul did not retain some memory of an evil life it would not be accountable. This knowledge by the soul is relevant for future decisions. Nevertheless, the resurrection of the soul in the spirit world is merciful. The soul mind does not fully retain all the lurid details of harming others in former host bodies after treatment. If this were not true, the guilt and association with such lives would be so overpowering to the soul they might refuse to reincarnate again to redress these wrongs. These souls would lack the confidence to ever dig themselves out of pits of despair. I understand there are souls whose acts in host bodies were so heinous they are not permitted to return to Earth. Souls are strengthened by regeneration with the expectation they can keep future potentially malevolent bodies in check. Of course, once in our new body, the amnesiac blocks of certain past life mistakes prevent us from being so inhibited we would not progress.

There are differences in the regeneration process between moderately and severely damaged souls. After listening to a number of explanations about kinds of energy treatments, I have come to this conclusion: The more radical approach of energy cleansing is one of *remodeling* energy while the less drastic method is *reshaping*. This is an oversimplification because there is much I don't know about these esoteric techniques. The fine art of energy reconstruction is handled by nonreincarnating masters who are not in my office answering questions. I work with the trainees. Case 20 will provide some insight into the mechanics of energy reshaping while case 21 will address remodeling.

Case 20

My subject in this case is a practitioner of chiropractic and homeopathic medicine who currently specializes in repolarizing the out-of-balance energy patterns of patients. This client has been a healer for thousands of years on Earth and is called Selim in the spirit world.

> **Dr. N:** Selim, you have told me about your advanced healing group in the spirit world and how the five of you are in specific energy training. I would like to know more about your work. Would you begin by telling me what your advanced study group is called and what you do?
>
> **S:** We are in training to be regenerators. We work to reshape . . . to reorganize . . . displaced energy in the place of the holding ground.

Dr. N: Is this place a designated area for souls whose energy has been disrupted?

S: Yes, the ones in bad condition. Those who will not be returning to their groups right away. They will stay in the holding ground.

Dr. N: Do you make this determination at the gateway to the spirit world?

S: No, I do not. I have not yet reached that status. This decision is made by their guides, who will call upon the masters who are training me.

Dr. N: Then tell me, Selim, when do you enter the picture after a severely damaged soul crosses back to the spirit world?

S: I am called by my instructor when it is felt I can assist in this energy healing. Then I move to the holding ground.

Dr. N: Please explain to me why you use the term "holding ground" and what this place is like.

S: The damaged soul is held here until their regeneration is complete so they are healthy again. This sphere is designed . . . as a beehive structure . . . covered with cells. Each soul has its own place to reside during the healing.

Dr. N: This sounds very much like the descriptions I have heard about the incubation of new souls after their creation and before they are assigned to groups.

S: That's true . . . these are spaces where energy is nurtured.

Dr. N: So, are these beehive spaces all in the same place and used for the same purpose—both for regeneration and creation?

S: No, they are not. I work in the place of damaged souls. Newly created souls are not damaged. I can tell you nothing about those places.

Dr. N: That's fine, Selim, I appreciate learning about those areas where you do have knowledge and experience. Why do you think you were assigned this sort of work?

S: (with pride) Because of my long history in so many lives of working with wounded people. When I asked if I could specialize as a regenerator, my wish was granted and I was assigned to a training class.

Dr. N: And so when a severely wounded soul is returned to the holding ground, are you a soul who could be called to assist?

S: (shakes his head negatively) Not necessarily. I am only requested to go to the regeneration areas to work with energy that has been moderately damaged. I am a beginner. There is so much I don't know.

Dr. N: Well, I have a great deal of respect for what you do know, Selim. Before I ask you about your level of work, can you explain why a damaged soul would be sent to the holding ground?

S: They were overcome by their last body. Many are souls who have been repeatedly suppressed in previous lives as well. These are the ones who become stuck in life after life making no progress. Each body has contaminated them a little more. I work with these souls more than the ones who have had terrible energy damage, either from one life or many lives.

Dr. N: Do the souls whose energy has been gradually depleted ask for help, or are they forced to come to the holding ground?

S: (promptly) No one is forced. They cry for help because they have become totally ineffectual, repeating the same mistakes over and over again. Their teachers see they do not recover sufficiently between lives. They want regeneration.

Dr. N: Does the same cry for help come from souls who have been severely damaged?

S: (pause) Perhaps less so. It is possible that a life is so destructive it has damaged the . . . identity of the soul.

Dr. N: Such as being involved with cruel acts of violence?

S: That would be one reason, yes.

Dr. N: Selim, please give me as many details as you can about what happens when you are called to the holding ground to work on a case with severely depleted or altered energy.

S: Before meeting the new arrival one of the Restoration Masters outlines the meridians of energy we will be regenerating. We review what is known about the damaged soul.

Dr. N: This sounds like you are surgeons preparing for a procedure with x-rays before the operation.

S: (with delight) Yes, this gives me an idea of what to expect in three-dimensional imagery. I love the challenges involved with energy repair.

Dr. N: Okay, take me through this process.

S: From my perspective there are three steps. We begin by examining all particles of damaged energy. Then these dark areas of blockage are removed and what is left—the voids—are rewoven with an infusion of new purified light energy. It is overlaid and melded into the repaired energy for strengthening.

Dr. N: And does reweaving energy mean reshaping to you, as opposed to something even more radical?

S: Yes.

Dr. N: Are you personally involved with all phases of this operation?

S: No, I am being trained in the first step of assessment and can assist a little with the second step—where the modifications are not as complex.

Dr. N: Before you actually begin to work, what do you see when a soul's energy has been severely damaged?

S: Damaged energy looks like a cooked egg where the white light has solidified and hardened. We must soften this and fill the black voids.

Dr. N: Let's talk a moment about this blackened energy . . .

S: (interrupts) I should have added that the damaged energy can also create . . . lesions. These fissures are voids themselves, caused by radical physical or emotional damage.

Dr. N: What are the effects of disrupted energy on the incarnated soul?

S: (pause) Where the energy is mottled—not distributed evenly— this is due to long-term energy deterioration.

Dr. N: You talked about rearranging and repairing old energy with new purified energy for healing. How is this done?

S: By intense charge beams. It is delicate work because you must keep your own vibrational tuning . . . in matched sequences with that generated by the soul.

Dr. N: Oh, so this becomes personal. A master's own energy is used as a conduit?

S: Yes, but there are other sources of new purified energy that I don't use or know much about because of my lack of experience.

Dr. N: Selim, you have told me how warped energy is softened and allowed to flow back onto the right spaces, but introducing new purified energy concerns me. With all that reconfiguration aren't you changing the immortal identity of these souls?

S: No, we have . . . altered . . . to strengthen what is there . . . to bring the soul close to its original form. We don't want this to happen again. We don't want them back.

Dr. N: Is there some way you can test your repair work after it is completed?

S: Yes, we can place a field of simulated negative energy around the regenerated soul—as a liquid—to see if this can filter through the structure of our repairs. As I said, we don't want them back.

Dr. N: One last question, Selim. When you are finished, what happens to the regenerated soul?

S: It varies. All of them stay with us a while . . . there is healing with sound . . . vibrational music . . . light . . . color. And when these souls are released, much care is taken with their next incarnations and the selections of bodies. (sighs) If the soul has been in a body that damaged others in former lives . . . well . . . we have fortified these souls to go back and begin again.

My next case is an example of severe remodeling. Case 21 involves a particular class of soul I call the hybrid soul. In chapter 8, case 61 is another representative of this type of soul. I believe the hybrid souls are especially prone to self-destruction on Earth because they have incarnated on alien worlds before coming here fairly recently. There are hybrid souls who have great difficulty adapting to our planet. If I find this to be true, it is probable their first incarnation here was within the last few thousand years. The others have already adapted or left Earth for good. Less than a quarter of all my clients are able to recall memories of visiting other worlds between lives. This activity by itself does not make them hybrids. An even smaller percentage of my cases have memories of actually incarnating on alien worlds before they came to Earth. These are the hybrid souls.

The hybrid is usually an older soul who, for a number of reasons, has decided to complete their physical lives on our planet. Their old worlds may no longer be habitable or they may have lived on a gentle world where life was just too easy and they want a difficult challenge with a world like Earth that has not yet reached its potential. Regardless of the circumstances for a soul leaving a world, I have found these former incarnations typically involve life forms which were slightly above, about equal, or slightly below the intelligence capabilities of the human brain. This is by design. Hybrid souls who have formally incarnated on planets with civilizations possessing a much higher technology than Earth, such as those with space travel abilities, are smarter because they are an older race. Also, I have noticed that when I do have a hybrid soul as a client with former experience on a telepathic world, they tend to have greater psychic abilities than normal.

Sometimes a hybrid client will confuse their early incarnations on other physical worlds with being on Earth until we sort out that their first world only resembled a place on Earth. Visions of once living on the island nation of Atlantis is a good example. Without discounting the possibility that Atlantis once existed on Earth thousands of years ago, I believe the source of many earthly myths come from our soul memories of former existences on other worlds.

I think hybrid soul is an appropriate term for those souls among us of mixed incarnation origins. Such souls have developed from being in hosts that are genetically different than humans. I have seen gifted people in this life who started their development on another world. Nevertheless, there is a dark side to this experience, as a level V subject in training to be a Restoration Master will explain.

Case 21

Dr. N: Since you work with the severely damaged souls, can you give me a little more information about your duties?

S: I'm in a special section working with those souls who have become lost in a morass of evil.

Dr. N: (after learning this subject works only with those souls from Earth who have incarnated on other worlds before they came to Earth) In this section, are these the hybrid souls I have heard about?

S: Yes, in a restoration area where we deal with those who have become atrocity souls.

Dr. N: What a terrible name to call a soul!

S: I'm sorry you are bothered by this, but what else would you call a being associated with acts of evil that are so serious they are unsalvageable in their present state?

Dr. N: I know, but the human body had a lot to do with . . .

S: (cutting me off) We don't consider that to be an excuse.

Dr. N: Okay, then please continue with the nature of your work.

S: I am a second-stage restorer.

Dr. N: What does that mean?

S: When these souls lose their bodies, they are met by their guides and perhaps one close friend. That first stage does not last long and then the souls who have been involved with horrible acts are brought here to us.

Dr. N: Why doesn't the first stage last as long as with other souls?

S: We don't want them to begin to forget the impact of their deeds—the harm and pain they caused on Earth. The second stage separates them from the uncontaminated souls.

Dr. N: This sounds like you are running a leper colony.

S: (abruptly) I am not amused by that remark.

Dr. N: (after apologizing) You are not saying that all souls who commit evil acts are hybrid souls, as you define them?

S: Of course not, that's my section. But you should understand some real monsters on Earth are hybrids.

Dr. N: I thought the spirit world was a place of order with masters of superior knowledge. If these hybrid souls are contaminated abnormalities in human form—souls with the inability to adjust to the emotional makeup of the human body—why were they sent here? This indicates to me the spirit world is not infallible.

S: A vast majority are fine, and they make great contributions to human society. You would have us deny all souls the opportunity to come to Earth because some turn out badly?

Dr. N: No, of course not. Let's move on. What do you do with these souls?

S: Others, way above me, examine their contaminated energy in light of just how the world of their earlier experience impacted on their human body. They want to know if this was an isolated case, or if other souls from that planet have had problems on Earth. If that is true, other souls from that world might not be permitted to come to Earth again.

Dr. N: Please tell me more about your section.

S: My area is not devoted to souls who have committed one serious act of wrongdoing. We work with habitually cruel life styles. These souls are then given a choice. We will do our best to clean up their energy by rehabilitation and if we think they are salvageable, they are offered a choice to come back to Earth in roles where they will receive the same type of pain they caused, only multiplied.

Dr. N: Could a salvageable soul be one who committed terrible atrocities in life but showed great remorse?

S: Probably.

Dr. N: I thought karmic justice was not punitive?

S: It's not. The offer represents an opportunity for stabilization and redemption. It usually will take more than one life to endure an equal measure of the same kind of pain they caused to many people. That's why I said multiplied.

Dr. N: Even so, I suppose most souls take this option?

S: You are mistaken. Most are too fearful that they will fall again into the same patterns. They also lack the courage to be victims in a number of future lives.

Dr. N: If they won't come back to Earth, then what do you do?

S: These souls will then go the way of those souls we consider to be unsalvageable. We will then disseminate their energy.

Dr. N: Is this a form of remodeling energy—or what?

S: Ah . . . yes . . . we call it the breaking up of energy—that's what dissemination means. Certainly, it is remodeled. We break up their energy into particles.

Dr. N: I thought energy could not be destroyed. Aren't you destroying the identity of these contaminated souls?

S: The energy is not destroyed, it is changed and converted. We might mix one particle of the old energy with nine particles of new fresh energy provided for our use. The dilution will make that which is contaminated ineffectual, but a small part of the original identity remains intact.

Dr. N: So, the negative badness energy is mixed with overdoses of new goodness energy to render the contaminated soul harmless?

S: (laughs) Not necessarily goodness but rather freshness.

Dr. N: Why would any soul resist dissemination?

S: Even though those souls who accept these procedures for their own benefit recover and eventually lead productive lives on Earth and elsewhere . . . there are souls who will not stand for any loss of identity.

Dr. N: Then what happens to these souls who refuse your help?

S: Many will just go into limbo, to a place of solitude. I don't know what will eventually happen to them.

As I have said before, soul contamination does not only come from the physical body. Certainly, the energy damage described in the last two cases indicates that souls themselves are impure beings who also contribute to their own distress.

Before continuing, I want to make a statement about karmic choices here that is important for all of us to keep in mind. When we see people who are victims of great adversity in life, this does *not* necessarily mean they were perpetrators of evil or wrongdoing of any kind in a former life. A soul with no such past associations might choose to suffer through a particular aspect of emotional pain to learn greater compassion and empathy for others by volunteering in advance for a life of travail.

There are cases when a soul's energy damage is moderate, requiring special attention, but not to the degree where a Restoration Master is needed. The following quote is a report from a client about a gifted healing soul who works at a recovery station. I think of her as a combat nurse managing a field hospital and my client agrees:

> Oh, it's Numi—I'm so glad. I haven't seen her in about three or four lives, but her deprogramming and restoration energy techniques are just superlative. There are five others being attended to in this place whom I don't know. Numi comes over and clasps me to her. She gets inside me and blends my tired energy with her own. I feel the infusion of her stimulating vibrations and she performs a tiny bit of reshaping. It is as if I am receiving a gentle reaffirmation of that which created my own energy. Soon, I am ready to leave and Numi gives me a beautiful smile goodbye till next time.

Souls of Solitude

In the last chapter I explained how certain dysfunctional souls who have just experienced physical death leave their bodies and go into seclusion for a time. They are not ghosts but they don't accept death and they don't want to go home. The low percentage of souls in my practice within this category are at an impasse with themselves. Their major symptom is one of avoidance. Eventually, they are coaxed by empathetic guides to return to the heart of the spirit world. I called them the souls of silence. I also mentioned that it is considered a part of normal activity for healthy souls in the spirit world to engage in periods of quiet time away from others. Besides reflecting upon their goals, souls may use this interval to reach out and touch people they left behind on Earth.

However, there is another category of silent soul whom I see as a soul in solitude as opposed to a soul in seclusion. It may seem as if I am splitting hairs here, but there are major differences. Souls who wish solitude are healthy souls who have been through the recovery process and yet they still strongly feel the effects of negative energy contamination. Here is a case in point:

> After every life, I go to a place of sanctuary for quiet reflection. I review what I want to save and integrate from the last body and what should be discarded. Right now, I am saving courage and getting rid of my inability to sustain personal commitment. For me, this is a place of sorting. What I decide to keep becomes part of my character. The rest is thrown off.

Only a certain type of soul engages in this activity for a prolonged period. Often, they are more advanced souls who are more reflective if they are alone. This type of soul might be a natural leader who is drained of energy by defending other people. One such soul of this class is Achem, who is a soul devoted to causes for the betterment of others, often at his own expense.

Case 22

In this subject's past life he fought against the final subjugation of Morocco by the French military and was captured in 1934. As a resistance fighter, my client was taken from the Atlas Mountains into the Sahara Desert and tortured for information he did not give. After being staked to the ground, he was left to die a slow death in the hot sun.

Dr. N: Achem, please explain to me why you require such a long period of solitude after your life in Morocco?

S: I am a protector soul and my energy has still not recovered from the effects of this life.

Dr. N: What is a protector soul?

S: We try to protect those people whose innate goodness and intense desire to better the lives of large numbers of people on Earth must be preserved.

Dr. N: Who did you protect in Morocco?

S: The leader of the resistance movement against French colonization. He was more effective in helping our people fight for freedom because of my years of sacrifice.

Dr. N: This sounds demanding. Do you usually work with political and social movements in your lives?

S: Yes, and in war. We are warriors for good causes.

Dr. N: What attributes do protector souls have as a group?

S: We are noted for our enduring perseverance and calmness under fire while assisting others who are worthy.

Dr. N: If you challenge those who would seek to harm the people you want to protect, who decides if they are worthy? It seems to me this is a very subjective thing.

S: True, and this is why we spend time analyzing in advance where we can best be utilized to help people. Our work can be offensive or defensive in nature but we do not engage in any aggressive action lacking principle.

Dr. N: All right, let's talk about your energy drain after these endeavors. Why hasn't the shower of healing or some other restoration center returned you to normal?

S: (laughs) You call it a shower, I call this the car wash! It's an undulating tube which rubs you all over with positive energy, like the brushes of a car wash. I just took a few of my young students through it from the last life and they feel great.

Dr. N: So why didn't the car wash help you?

S: (more serious) It was not nearly enough, although the negative impurities are essentially gone. No, the core of my being has been affected by the cruelty of that life and the torture I endured.

Dr. N: What do you do?

S: I send the students away and go to the place of sanctuary where I can fully connect with myself.

Dr. N: Please tell me all you can about this place and what you do there.

S: It is a darkened enclosure—some call it a slumber chamber—where there are others resting but we do not really see each other. I sense there are about twenty of us now. We feel so washed out we have no desire to relate to anyone for a while. The Keepers attend to us.

Dr. N: Keepers? Who are they?

S: The Keepers of Neutrality are skilled at noninterference. Their talent lies in ministering to us with absolutely no intervention into our thoughts. They are the custodians of the slumber chambers.

Note: Apparently, the Keepers of Neutrality are a subspecialty within the ranks of Restoration Masters. They have other names but neutrality means they facilitate healing indirectly without any communication. My clients say these beings are devoted to absolute quietude for souls in their care.

Dr. N: What do these passive custodians look like?

S: (tersely) They are not passive. The picture I can give you is one of monks moving about a sanctuary. The Keepers have cloaks and a hood over their faces so they present no identity to us. Their thoughts are closed, but they are very watchful.

Dr. N: So they simply watch over you while you rest?

S: No, no—you still don't understand. They possess great skill in ministering to us. Their concern is the proper regulation and infusion of the energy which we have stored in the spirit world before going into a physical life.

Dr. N: I have heard a great deal about this attribute of the soul to divide itself. Why can't you just go to your own spiritual area and take the rest of your energy and meld with it? Or why not have a team of Restoration Masters regenerate your contaminated energy?

S: (takes a deep breath) I'll try to explain it. For us, all that is unnecessary. It is the *effects* of the impurities which we want healed by a slow, even return of our own purified, rested energy. The Keepers assist us in the restoring of our own energy.

Dr. N: Rather like getting a blood transfusion from your own blood bank?

S: Yes, exactly, now you are beginning to comprehend. We don't want it in a rush. We don't need major restoration either. We receive slow energy infusions of our own energy over a prolonged period for greater . . . elasticity. We want the strength we had before a rough life—and more—from having gone through the physical experience.

Dr. N: What's a prolonged period of time in Earth years for your recovery in this sanctuary?

S: Oh, that's hard to say . . . 25 to 50 years . . . we would always like it to be longer because the Keepers use their own vibrational frequencies to . . . massage our energy—which is fantastic. They are very private beings though, who don't want to be seen or spoken to, but they know we are grateful for their care. They also know when it is time for us to rejoin our friends and get back to work. (laughs) Then we are pushed out.

It was from cases such as these that I learned one of the best ways to repair damaged energy is to receive it back slowly. Many souls of solitude are quite advanced and don't require restoration in the normal recovery areas. These vigorous souls can be too overconfident. Achem admitted that he only took about 50 percent of his energy to Morocco and should have "charged up" more before departing into that life.

The next section will address planetary healers who work in physical environments. Since these souls are generally still incarnating, my sub-

jects do not consider them as masters. This would include the transformer souls mentioned in the next case. Planetary work is where our
exposure to many specialties begins and is a basic training ground for
developing souls.

Energy Healing on Earth

Healers of the Human Body

When I learned about souls who were specializing in restoring damaged energy in the spirit world, I was curious how these souls might
apply their unconscious spiritual knowledge when they were working
in physical form. Some place great emphasis on this aspect of their skill
development to help human beings. My next case is a woman who
works with many energy modalities, including reiki. However, until our
hypnosis session, she had little idea of the source of her spiritual power
to heal. Her spiritual name is Puruian and during our time together she
explained how and why energy adjustments are necessary for incarnates as well as discarnates.

Case 23

Dr. N: Puruian, I would like to know if your spiritual training in
soul restoration is used by you in your earthly assignments?

S: (subject evidenced some surprise as this information began to
unfold in her mind after my question) Why . . . yes . . . I didn't
realize how much until now . . . only those of us who want to
continue working in this way on Earth are called transformers.

Dr. N: What is the difference? How would you define a transformer?

S: (laughs in recognition) As transformers we do repair jobs on
Earth—we are the cleanup crew—transforming bodies to good
health. There are people on Earth who have gray spots of energy
which cause them to get stuck. You see it when they make the
same mistakes over and over in life. My job is to incarnate, find
them and try and remove these blocks so they make better decisions and gain confidence and self-value. We transform them to
be more productive people.

Dr. N: Puruian, I would like to clarify the differences in spiritual training, if any, between restoring souls in the spirit world and transforming energy on a physical world?

S: (long pause) Some parts of our training are the same but . . . transformers are sent to other worlds between lives to study—those of us who like working with physical forms.

Dr. N: Describe the last training you had as a transformer before you came back to Earth.

S: (struck by my question, there is a dreamy response) Oh . . . two light beings came from another dimension to work with the six of us. (Puruian's independent study group) They showed us how . . . to keep our vibrational energy into a tight, beamed focus—not scattered. I learned to pinpoint my energy to be more effective.

Dr. N: Were these beings from a physical world?

S: (in a soft tone) More like a gas sphere where their intelligence exists in . . . bubbles . . . but they were so good. We learned . . . oh . . . we learned . . .

Dr. N: (gently) I'm sure . . . Let's return to the practical use of what you learned now that you are more aware of the origins of your skills. Tell me how you apply this spiritual knowledge in your energy work today as a transformer soul on Earth?

S: (a look of wonder) It's . . . there now . . . in my mind . . . I see why it works . . . (stops) . . . the focused beam . . .

Dr. N: (pressing) The focused beam . . . ?

S: (earnestly) We use it as a laser—rather like a dentist would drill out a decayed tooth—to pinpoint and clean up gray energy. This is the fast way. It is harder for me to use a slow procedure which is longer lasting and even more effective.

Dr. N: Okay, Puruian, remember you are explaining to me how you use your spiritual training and earthly training in combination to heal energy. You have the memory right now of both aspects. Tell me about the slow method.

S: (takes a deep breath) I close my eyes and kind of go into a semi-trance when I cup my hands near my patient's head. I see now that what I have learned in the spirit world helps me more than what I learned in my classes down here. I guess that doesn't matter, really.

Dr. N: We receive power to help others from many sources. Please go on about your healing by the slow method with your patients on Earth.

S: Well, I work with geometric shapes, such as spirals of energy, forming them in my mind to match the configuration of the particular trouble spot. Then I lay these energy structures around the gray areas. This sets up the areas to be repaired with my slow healing vibrations, like placing a hot pad on a sore muscle. (pause) You see, these souls were damaged on the way in and this ... infirmity ... only grows worse as the body develops on Earth.

Dr. N: (surprised) Back up a minute. What do you mean, "damaged on the way in"? I thought your work on Earth mostly involved contaminated energy from life's trials?

S: That's only part of the problem. When souls enter the human body on Earth they come into dense matter. Their host bodies, after all, contain primitive animal energy which is thick. The soul has a natural sort of pure, refined energy which does not easily blend with some human hosts. It takes experience to get used to all this. The younger souls especially can be damaged. They get knocked off their tracks early on and are ... twisted.

Dr. N: And you might project different energy configurations with different people who are your patients.

S: Uh-huh, that is the job of the transformer. Their damaged energy lines are so ... squiggly ... they must be rearranged to remove the toxic energy. These muddled souls are so unbalanced that a lot of our work must be directed at all the cells of the body where negative energy is trapping the free flow of the positive. When this is performed properly the soul is more fully engaged with the human brain.

Dr. N: This sounds very worthwhile, indeed.

S: It is gratifying although I still have a lot to learn. (laughs) We call ourselves psychic sponges for refined energy.

It is not surprising that case 25 uses reiki in her work on Earth. Reiki is an ancient art of healing by the hands. After evaluating and working on damaged energy, practitioners of this art close gaps in the human energy field with body alignments to bring symmetry. There are theories that damaged energy, physical or mental, in the human body causes gaps in our auras through which a demonic negative force can enter. This is another of those fear-based myths that receives undeserved attention. I have been told by restoration specialists that this does not happen because there is no outside force of evil trying to take over your body. However, negative energy blockages in our energy field do cause a reduction in functional capacity.

I am also disturbed by scientific articles debunking energy work with the hands, such as therapeutic touch, because I have seen the power of this kind of healing with the sick. It is often freely given by certain nurses in hospital settings out of a genuine concern to nurture and heal. Our bodies are composed of an energy field of particles that appears solid but is fluid and acts as a vibrational conductor. One of my transformer souls had this to say about her therapeutic touch methods:

> The secret to healing is removing my conscious self so as to avoid inhibiting the free flow of energy between us. My objective is to merge with the energy flow of the patient to bring out the highest good in that body. This is done with love as well as technique.

If the receiving party is resistant and inhibits the free-flowing passageways of chi, or life force, through their own mental negativism, they are perfectly capable of blocking the detection of their energy field by a healer. As we begin a new millennium, more people are becoming aware of the healing properties of meditation and guided imagery to build energy within themselves. There are many ways to reach the center of our inner wisdom by tapping into a higher energy source. Massage, yoga, acupuncture and biomagnetic healing are some of the techniques available to help balance our chi.

Body energy and soul energy are adversely affected by vibrational resonances not in harmony with each other. Each person has their own fingerprint of natural rhythm. Body and soul must smoothly coexist for humans to be productive. If we take a holistic approach to body health, our creative self is better able to function with the human brain. Being in harmony with our outer and inner self positions us to more energetically engage in physical, spiritual and environmental interrelationships.

spirit world, I had no idea of the special s on our planet. I have learned the Earth ate and there are people capable of tuning he of the cases that opened my eyes was a rest Service in the Pacific Northwest. In , she explained:

> In the last few years I have felt a tingling, sparking sensation in my hands whenever I am around heavy vegetation. It is not painful, but there is an urgency for something to be released during my work in the forests. Lately, I have dreams about lightning going out of my hands and my wanting to pull it back into a bottle to save it. These dreams seem to fulfill a need inside me and upon awakening I feel happy. Am I going crazy?

I am drawn to people who think they are going crazy because of unexplained phenomena in their lives. I know what this feels like personally. Many of my old, traditional colleagues are convinced I have lost my marbles. Therefore, I was glad to take this woman as a client after she agreed to see a physician to make sure there was nothing causing neurological problems with her hands. I will pick up the dialogue of this case at the point where we are discussing her participation in an advanced independent studies group in the spirit world.

Case 24

Dr. N: Why did the five of you come together in this study group?

S: Because we work with energy the same way. It helps raise our consciousness—our abilities—when we are together.

Dr. N: Please explain this to me.

S: Well, our situation right now is that individually we cannot sustain an energy flow of sufficient quality to last very long and have the necessary effect.

Dr. N: So you accomplish what you wish to do collectively?

S: Yes, to some degree. That's why we enjoy working together so we can throw energy out in unison and bottle it up in concentrated reserves. Working alone our energy is not as potent, not as refined—it goes in all directions.

Dr. N: Is this why you are having these dreams and feeling these hand sensations right now in your life?

S: (reflects) Yes, I see that it is a message for me. I must alter my life to include more energy work.

Dr. N: You mean to store and use energy to heal people?

S: (quickly responds to my wrong assumption) No, my study group works with energy differently. We are healers of plants, trees and the land. That is why we pick lives as caretakers of the environment.

Dr. N: Did you choose your current vocation for a specific reason related to your skills?

S: Yes.

Dr. N: How about other members of your spirit world study group?

S: (with a big grin) Two of them work with me in the forest service.

Dr. N: I would think as planetary healers you and your friends have your work cut out for you with all the environmental destruction going on around Earth.

S: (sadly) It's terrible and we are so needed here.

Dr. N: Tell me, have you and the members of your study group been involved with using energy environmentally in many past lives on Earth?

S: Oh, yes . . . for a long time.

Dr. N: Give me an example.

S: In my last life I was an Algonquian Indian with the name of Singing Tree. My job was to insure our land would continue to supply us with food. I used to stand out in the forest for hours and hold out my hands. The tribe thought I was talking to the trees and the soil but actually I was exchanging energy with the land. It's an extension of mind and body with some help from our guides.

Dr. N: And how about today?

S: (pause) When you create and support beauty and growth from the land, you also give power to others who live here. From your hands you provide a means by which others are motivated with the beauty of what they see around them, as well as receiving sustenance from the environment.

Sometimes I receive letters years later from clients who want to say they finally reached their goals in life. A person with environmental healing talents might write me to announce they have become a landscape architect, opened a garden nursery, or joined a protest group to stop the logging of old redwood trees. I enjoy these aspects of career counseling in my work that begin with the question, "Why am I here?" When I became involved with delving into the mysteries of the spirit world, I thought people would mostly want to know about their spirit guides and soulmates. Instead, I found their primary interest was their purpose in life.

Before leaving the subject of our environment on Earth, and the manner in which people are able to tune into the energy vibrations of this planet, I should say a word about sacred sites. A number of researchers have reported on the fact that there are places in the world which give off intense pulses of magnetic energy. In the last chapter I spoke about vibrational energy layers which vary in density around the Earth. Some sacred sites on Earth are well-known to the public, such as the places of stone in Sedona, Arizona; Machu Picchu in Peru; and Ayers Rock in Australia, to name a few. People standing in these places feel a heightened awareness and physical well-being.

Planetary magnetic fields do affect our physical and spiritual consciousness, and I find a curious similarity here with descriptions about
the spirit world. My clients say the home ground of their cluster group
is "a space within a space" whose non-solid boundaries have a specific
vibrational concentration of energy generated by that particular group.
Perhaps certain human habitations on Earth, considered to be sacred
by the ancients, contain vortexes of energy concentrations caused by
what are called natural "ley lines." The places where these magnetic
gridlines converge are said to enhance unconscious thought and make
it easier to open our mental passages into spiritual realms. Knowledge
of vortex locations are very useful to planetary healers. In chapter 8,
under the section of soul explorers in other worlds, I will touch again
on planetary vibrational grid patterns which affect intelligent life away
from Earth.

Soul Division and Reunification

The capacity for souls to divide their energy essence influences many
aspects of soul life. Perhaps soul extension would be a more accurate
term than soul division. As I reported in the section under ghosts, all
souls who come to Earth leave a part of their energy behind in the spirit
world, even those living parallel lives in more than one body. The per-
centages of energy souls leave behind may vary but each particle of light
is an exact duplicate of every other Self and replicates the whole identity.
This phenomenon is analogous to the way light images are split and
duplicated in a hologram. Yet there are differences with a hologram. If
only a small percentage of a soul's energy is left behind in the spirit
world, that particle of Self is more dormant because it is less concentrated. However, because this energy remains in a pure, uncontaminated
state, it is still potent.

When I made the discovery of our energy reserve in the spirit world,
so much fell into place for me. The grandeur of this system of soul duality impacts many spiritual aspects of our life. For example, if someone
you loved died thirty years ahead of you and has since reincarnated, you
can still see them again upon your own return to the spirit world.

The ability of a soul to unite with itself is a natural process of energy regeneration after physical death. A client emphatically told me, "If we were to bring 100 percent of our energy into one body during an incarnation, we would blow the circuits of the brain." A full charge of all a soul's energy into one human body would totally subjugate the brain to the soul's power. Apparently, this could happen with even the less potent, undeveloped souls. I suppose this factor of soul occupation in a host body was evaluated in the early stages of human evolution by those spiritual grandmasters who chose Earth as a planetary school.

Moreover, having all the soul's energy capacity in one body would negate the whole process of growth for the soul on Earth because it would have no challenge coping with the brain. By strengthening a variety of parts of a soul's total energy in different incarnations, the whole is made stronger. Full awareness at 100 percent would have another adverse effect. If we did not divide our energy, we would experience a higher level of spiritual memory retention in each human body. Amnesia forces us to go into the testing area of the laboratory of Earth without the answers for the tasks we were sent here to accomplish. Amnesia also relieves us of the baggage for past failures so we may use new approaches with more confidence.

The ghost in case 15 indicated how it is possible for souls to miscalculate the percentage of energy concentration they bring into a life. One client called this "our light quotient." In a strange fashion, I find my level IV and V subjects shortchange themselves more than the less developed souls. This was demonstrated by the warrior soul in case 22. Typically, a highly advanced soul will bring no more than 25 percent of its total capacity to Earth where the average, less confident soul has 50–70 percent. The energy of a more evolved soul is refined, elastic and vigorous in smaller quantities. This is why the younger soul must bring more energy into their early incarnations. Thus, it is not the volume of energy which gives potency to the soul but the quality of vibrational power representing a soul's experience and wisdom.

How does this information help us understand the combined force of soul and human energy? Every soul has a specific energy field pattern which reflects an immortal blueprint of its character, regardless of the number of divided parts. When this spiritual ego is combined with a more structured personality of a physical brain, a higher density field is produced. The subtleties of this symbiosis are so intricate I have only scratched the surface. Both blueprints of energy react to each other in an infinite number of ways to become one to the outside world. This is why our physical well-being, senses and emotions are so tied to the spiritual mind. Thought is closely associated with how these energy patterns are shaped and melded together and each nourishes the other in our bodies.

I frequently use the analogy of a hologram to describe soul division. Holographic images are exact duplicates. This analogy is helpful but it does not tell the whole story. I have mentioned one variable in the process of soul division as involving the potency of energy concentration in each divided part. This element relates to the experience of the soul. Another variable is the density of material energy in each human body and the emotional makeup which drives that body. If the same soul joins two bodies at the same time and brings 40 percent of its energy into each body, there will be different manifestations of energy.

Think of taking a photograph of the same scene in the morning, at noon and in the evening. The changes in light refraction would create a different effect on the film. The energy of souls begins with a specific pattern but once on Earth these patterns are changed by local conditions. When we review our future life from the spirit world we are given advice about the energy requirements of the body we will occupy. The decision of how much energy we should take is ours. Many souls want to leave as much behind as possible because they love their home and the activities going on there.

Emotional and physical trauma drains our energy reserves. We can lose shards of positive energy to people whom we give it to voluntarily, or by others who drain it out of us with their negativity. It takes energy to erect and maintain defense mechanisms to protect ourselves. A subject once said to me, "When I share my light with those I think worthy of receiving it, I can recharge it faster because it was given freely."

One of the best ways we revitalize our energy is through sleep. Once again, we can further divide the energy we brought with us and roam freely while leaving a small percentage behind to alert the larger portion to return quickly if needed. As I mentioned earlier, this capacity is especially useful when the body is in a state of illness, unconsciousness, or in a coma. Since time is not a limiting factor for a freed soul, hours, days, or weeks away from the body are all rejuvenating. I might add that souls can also be recharged by loving spirits during a crisis. We interpret these energy boosts as profound revelations. A few hours' rest from the human body can do wonders for a soul as long as the remaining portion left behind is on cruise control and not coping with a complex dream analysis. That circumstance may cause us to wake up exhausted.

Since living parallel lives is another option for soul division, what are the motivations and effects from this decision? Many people feel it is common for souls to live parallel lives. I have found this not to be true at all. The souls who choose to split into two or more bodies within the same general time frame on Earth want to accelerate their learning. Thus, a soul might leave up to 10 percent of its energy behind and place the rest in two or three bodies. Because we have free will, our guides will allow for these experiments but they advise against it. On the whole, since the energy drain is enormous, most souls who try parallel lives do so only a time or two before giving it up. Souls don't wish to lead parallel lives unless they are extraordinarily ambitious. Also, souls don't split their energy to incarnate as twins. Dividing your energy to be in a family with the same genetics, parental influence, environment, nationality and so forth would be counterproductive. Such lack of diversity would provide little motivation for living a parallel life.

People are curious about the origins of two souls in the bodies of identical twins. I had two sisters in their late twenties as clients, born one minute apart. The souls of these women are intimately connected in the same spirit group, however they are not strictly primary soulmates. Each has met and lives with their own male soulmate with whom they are deeply in love. These two souls have lived for thousands of years as close friends, siblings, parents and children of one another but not as mates. They have never been twins before and the reason for their doing so currently was two-fold. They had unresolved trust issues in their past life relationship, but they said the major reason was "together, our combined energy field is doubled, which makes us more effective in reaching other minds."

People ask me if a soul did not bring enough energy into its body during the fetal state, can it retrieve more later in life? I find that once the energy formula of a given percentage is chosen in advance by a soul, it stays. To permanenty add more "fresh" energy from the spirit world during a life would likely disrupt the delicate balance initially established between the soul and a new human brain. Also, it seems improbable that an incarnated being could retrieve an ethereal substance from its discarnated self. However, with the help of their guides, some people have the ability to communicate—or temporarily tap into—their own energy reserve during a crisis.

The process of souls reuniting with the rest of their energy becomes most evident for me when I regress my subjects through a former death experience. Unless there are complications from the last life, most souls reacquire the balance of their energy at one of the three primary spiritual stations: near the gateway, during orientation, or after returning to their soul group. The advanced souls usually disembark only at the final stop on their journey home.

The Three Stations

Receiving our own energy at the gateway is not really a common occurrence. This is probably due to the initiation of recovery by a shower of healing near the gate. I do hear about it once in a while though, as with the soul in my next quote whose deceased husband brought a small remaining portion of her energy to the first stop. She explained the circumstances this way:

> My love could easily handle the little energy I saved. He brought this to me and spread it over me gently with his hands like a blanket as we were embracing. He knew how old and tired I was and he asked to come. Once contact is made, the rest of my energy comes into me as a magnet. I feel so expanded by it. The first thing I notice is that I can read his mind so much better telepathically and I sense so much more of what is around me.

When our guides conclude that it would be an advantage to have more of our energy at the second station during orientation, this decision has different ramifications. Basically, the decision rests on the belief that our debriefing from a difficult life will be more productive. Then, too, we might not be returning to our spirit group for some reason right after orientation. Here is an example of soul reunification at this stop:

> I am in a plain room which looks futuristic with smooth, milk-white walls. There is a table and two chairs—this furniture has no edges. My guide, Everand, is concerned over my lack of responsiveness. She is about to perform what we call "melting the physical form." She holds the rest of my energy in a beautiful, translucent vessel which radiates. Everand comes forward, pressing it into my hands. I feel the upsurge of my energy as an electrical charge. Then she moves close to me, stimulating my natural vibrational frequency to accept more easily what I left behind. As my core center is filled with my own essence, the outer shell of my physical body imprint is melted off. It is as if I were a dog shaking off water droplets from my fur after getting wet. The unwanted earthly particles are jarred loose—dissolved—and my energy now begins to sparkle again instead of being a dull light.

The usual way most souls reunite with the balance of their energy is after returning to a cluster group. A subject put it this way. "It is smoother for me to reunite with myself after I arrive at home base with my friends. Here the infusion of my rested energy can be assimilated at my own pace. When I am ready, I go get it myself."

Case 25

This case excerpt is from a discussion I had with a soul called Apalon, who discussed her reunification upon arriving home in a more flamboyant way than the soul in the quote above. Apalon is a level II soul who has just returned to the spirit world from a hard life in Ireland as a poor woman who died in 1910. Although physically strong and self-reliant, Apalon was married to a domineering, alcoholic husband and had to raise five children virtually alone. She suffered from a lack of personal freedom and self-expression. I see Apalon's welcoming home party as a reflection of a job well done after this difficult life.

Dr. N: Tell me, Apalon, after you have finished with the initial greetings from your spirit group, does the time soon arrive when you unify with your own energy reserve?

S: (grinning) My guide Canaris enjoys making a ceremony out of unification.

Dr. N: With the energy you left behind?

S: Yes, Canaris goes to an alcove in our enclosure where my energy is stored in a glass urn, waiting for me. It is under his care.

Dr. N: I gather your reserve energy has not been too active since your absence. What percentage of the total did you leave behind?

S: Only 15 percent—I needed a lot for my Irish life. This part was able to engage with my group and I could move around our area but I didn't participate in recreational diversions.

Dr. N: I understand, but is this weakened 15 percent a completely whole representation of your soul?

S: (vehemently) Absolutely—only a smaller version of me.

Dr. N: And was this 15 percent of you able to keep up with group lessons and greet people while the other 85 percent was on Earth?

S: Mmm . . . to an extent . . . yes. I continue to gain knowledge in both settings. (Earth and the spirit world)

Dr. N: (offhanded) I'm curious about something. If that 15 percent is still viable, why don't you just go get it yourself? What do you need Canaris for?

S: (offended) That would spoil his ceremony. Canaris is the keeper of my flame, so to speak, while I am gone. Besides, what you suggest would be an infringement on his prerogatives to assist me with melding with my energy. He wants to make a ceremony of it.

Dr. N: I'm sorry if I was too presumptuous, Apalon. Why don't you give me a visual picture of the ceremony.

S: (joyfully) Canaris goes to the alcove and, with the proud flourish of a nurturing father, brings it out while all my friends gather around and cheer about a job well done in Ireland.

Dr. N: Does this party include the soul who was your husband in the Irish life?

S: Yes, yes. He is in the front row cheering the loudest. He is not really the same person out of his Irish body.

Dr. N: All right, then what does Canaris do?

S: (laughs) He takes my energy in the greenish glass urn out of the alcove. It is glowing but he rubs it with his hands to make it shine brighter while enjoying our expressions of pleasure. Then he comes close and throws the cloud of light energy over me like a mantle of high office. He assists with my melding with his own powerful vibrations.

Dr. N: At this moment, what does having all your energy feel like?

S: (softly) Joining with oneself resembles two globs of mercury coming together on a glass plate. They flow into each other naturally and instantly become homogeneous. I feel a resurgence of power and identity. The warmth of the merger gives me a sense of serenity and peace as well. I feel . . . well . . . my immortality.

Dr. N: (rhetorically, to elicit a response) Isn't it a shame we don't take 100 percent of our energy to Earth?

S: (reacts immediately) Are you serious? No human mind could retain much of itself under those conditions, but I needed a lot for the Irish life.

Dr. N: What percentage do you have in your current body?

S: Oh . . . around 60 percent and it's plenty.

Dr. N: I have been told of physical planets where souls go that allow for all of our energy and the retention of full memory.

S: Sure, and many of these life forms allow for mental telepathy, too. Physical worlds like Earth—with the type of body we have—it's a stage of mental development. Right now, our evolutionary development sets up conditions which we must work through on our own. The limitations are good for us right now.

Dr. N: Apalon, explain to me what you understand about how much energy you should take to Earth before every life?

S: My energy level is monitored by Canaris and my council for each body depending upon the physical and mental characteristics of that body. Certain bodies require more spiritual energy than others and they know what conditions exist before we enter the life.

Dr. N: Well, you told me this Irish woman was physically strong and, I assume, she had a strong will as well for you to have survived intact. Nevertheless, you took a lot of your energy to Ireland.

S: Yes, she was stronger than I am today, but she needed my spiritual help and I needed her strength to assert what influence I could to survive with some identity in a life of deprivation. We were not always in harmony.

Dr. N: So when you are not in harmony with a body it takes more personal soul energy?

S: Oh, yes. And if your environment is harsh, that too must be taken into consideration. I feel very much in sync with my current body although I sometimes wish I had the stamina of the Irish body. There are many variables. That is the challenge. That's what is fun.

Note: Today, Apalon has incarnated as an independent businesswoman who travels all over the world for an international financial consulting firm. She has had numerous offers of marriage, all of which she has refused.

Occasionally, a client will tell me that after a former life they preferred to wait longer than normal before unifying with their energy. This is illustrated by the following quote:

> Sometimes I like to wait until after my council meeting because I don't want the fresh energy to dilute the memories and feelings I had in the life just lived. If I did infuse myself (by taking in reserve energy), that former life would be less real to me. I want my thoughts to be centered on answering questions about my work in that body with a clear, lucid memory of each event. I want to retain every emotional feeling I had of these events as they occurred so I can better describe why I took certain actions. My friends don't like to do this, but I can always recharge and rest later.

~5

Soul Group Systems

Soul Birthing

I think it is appropriate to begin an exploration of soul life with the creation of that life. Very few of my subjects have the memory capacity to go back to their origins as particles of energy. Some details of a soul's early life come to me from the rank beginners. These young souls have a shorter life history both in and out of the spirit world so they still have fresh memories. However, at best, my level I subjects have only fleeting memories about the genesis of Self. The following quotes from two beginner souls are illustrations:

> My soul was created out of a great irregular cloudy mass. I was expelled as a tiny particle of energy from this intense, pulsating bluish, yellow and white light. The pulsations send out hailstorms of soul matter. Some fall back and are reabsorbed but I continued outward and was being carried along in a stream with others like me. The next thing I knew, I was in a bright enclosed area with very loving beings taking care of me.

> I remember being in a nursery of some sort where we were like unhatched eggs in a beehive. When I acquired more awareness I learned I was in the nursery world of Uras. I don't know how I got there. I was like an egg in embryonic fluid waiting to be fertilized and I sensed there were many other cells of young lights who were coming awake with me. There was a group of mothers, beautiful and loving, who ... pierced our membrane sacs and opened us. There were swirling currents of intense, nurturing lights around us and I could hear music. My awareness began with curiosity. Soon I was taken from Uras and joined other children in a different setting.

The most revealing reports about soul nurseries come my way only infrequently from a very few highly advanced subjects. These are the specialists known as Incubator Mothers. The next case is a representative of this branch of service who is an exceptional level V called Seena.

Case 26

This individual is a specialist with children both in and out of the spirit world. Currently, she works through hospice with severely ill children. In her past life, she was a Polish woman who, although not Jewish, volunteered to enter a German internment camp in 1939. She did so ostensibly to wait on the officers and perform kitchen duties, which was a ruse. She wanted to be near the Jewish children entering the camp and to help them in any way possible. As a local resident of a nearby town, she could have left the camp at any time in the first year. Then it was too late and the soldiers would not allow her to leave. Eventually, she died in the camp. This advanced soul might have survived longer if she had brought more than 30 percent of her energy to sustain herself during the hardships of this assignment. Such is the confidence of a level V.

Dr. N: Seena, what has been your most significant experience between your lives?

S: (without hesitation) I go to the place of ... hatching—where souls are hatched. I am an Incubator Mother, a kind of midwife.

Dr. N: Are you telling me you work in a soul nursery?

S: (brightly) Yes, we help the new ones emerge. We facilitate early maturation . . . by being warm, gentle and caring. We welcome them.

Dr. N: Please explain the surroundings of the place to me.

S: It's . . . gaslike . . . a honeycomb of cells with swirling currents of energy above. There is intense light.

Dr. N: When you say "honeycomb," I wonder if you mean that the nursery has a beehive structure, or what?

S: Um, yes . . . although the nursery itself is a vast emporium without seeming to be limited by outside dimensions. The new souls have their own incubator cells where they stay until their growth is sufficient to be moved away from the emporium.

Dr. N: As an Incubator Mother, when do you first see the new souls?

S: We are in the delivery suite, which is a part of the nursery, at one end of the emporium. The newly arrived ones are conveyed as small masses of white energy encased in a gold sac. They move slowly in a majestic, orchestrated line of progression toward us.

Dr. N: From where?

S: At our end of the emporium under an archway the entire wall is filled with a molten mass of high-intensity energy and . . . vitality. It feels as if it's energized by an amazing love force rather than a discernible heat source. The mass pulsates and undulates in a beautiful flowing motion. Its color is like that on the inside of your eyelids if you were to look through closed eyes at the sun on a bright day.

Dr. N: And from out of this mass you see souls emerge?

S: From the mass a swelling begins, never exactly from the same site twice. The swelling increases and pushes outward, becoming a formless bulge. The separation is a wondrous moment. A new soul is born. It's totally alive with an energy and distinctness of its own.

Note: Another one of my level Vs made this statement about incubation. "I see an egg-shaped mass with energy flowing out and back in.

When it expands, new soul energy fragments are spawned. When the bulge contracts, I think it pulls back those souls which were not successfully spawned. For some reason these fragments could not make it on to the next step of individuality."

Dr. N: What do you see beyond the mass, Seena?

S: (long pause) I see this beatific glow of orange-yellow. There is a violet darkness beyond, but not cold darkness . . . it is eternity.

Dr. N: Can you tell me more about the line of progression of new souls moving toward you out of the mass?

S: Out of the fiery orange-yellow the progression is slow as each hatchling emerges from the energy mass. They are conveyed off to various points where mothering souls like myself are positioned.

Dr. N: How many mothers do you see?

S: I can see five nearby . . . who, like me . . . are in training.

Dr. N: What are the responsibilities of an Incubator Mother?

S: We hover around the hatchlings so we can . . . towel-dry them after opening their gold sacs. Their progression is slow because this allows us to embrace their tiny energy in a timeless, exquisite fashion.

Dr. N: What does "towel-drying" mean to you?

S: We dry the new soul's . . . wet energy, so to speak. I can't really explain all this well in human language. It's a form of hugging new white energy.

Dr. N: So, now you see basically white energy?

S: Yes, and as they come next to us—up close—I see more blue and violet glowing around them.

Dr. N: Why do you think this is so?

S: (pause, then softly) Oh . . . I see now . . . this is an umbilical . . . the genesis cord of energy which connects each one.

Dr. N: From what you are saying, I get a picture of a long pearl necklace. The souls are the pearls connected in a line. Is this at all accurate?

S: Yes, rather like a string of pearls on a silvery conveyer belt.

Dr. N: Okay, now tell me, when you embrace each new soul—dry them out—does this give them life?

S: (reacts quickly) Oh, no. Through us—not from us—comes a life force of all-knowing love and knowledge. What we pass on with our vibrations during the drying of new energy is . . . the essence of a beginning—a hopefulness of future accomplishment. The mothers call it . . . "the love hug." This involves instilling thoughts of what they are and what they can become. When we enfold a new soul in a love hug it infuses this being with our understanding and compassion.

Dr. N: Let me carry this vibrational hugging one step further. Does each new soul have an individual character at this point? Do you add or subtract from its given identity?

S: No, this is in place upon arrival, although the new soul does not yet know who they are. We bring nurturing. We are announcing to the hatchling that it is time to begin. By . . . sparking . . . its energy we bring to the soul an awareness of its existence. This is the time of the awakening.

Dr. N: Seena, please help me here. When I think of obstetric nurses in a hospital maternity ward holding and nurturing new human babies, they have no idea what kind of person a baby will turn out to be. Do you function in the same manner—not knowing about the immortal character of these new souls?

S: (laughs) We function as nursery caregivers but this is not a human maternity ward. At the moment we embrace the new ones we know something of their identity. Their individual patterns become more evident as we unite our energy with them to give them sustenance. This allows us to better utilize our vibrations to activate—to ignite—their awareness. All this is part of their beginning.

Dr. N: As a trainee, how did you acquire this knowledge of the proper employment of vibrations with new souls?

S: This is something new mothers have to learn. If it is not performed properly, the hatchling souls move on not feeling fully
ready. Then one of the Nursery Masters must step in later.

Dr. N: Can you take me a little further here, Seena? During your
love hug, when you first embrace these souls, do you and the
mothers discern an organized selection process behind the
assignment of a new soul's identity? For instance, could we have
ten courageous type souls come through followed by ten more
cautious souls?

S: That is so mechanistic! Each soul is unique in its totality of characteristics created by a perfection that I cannot begin to describe.
What I can tell you is that no two souls are alike—none—ever!

Note: I have heard from a few other subjects that one of the basic reasons each soul is different from the other is that after the Source "breaks
off" energy fragments to create a soul, what is left of the original mass
becomes infinitesimally altered so it is not exactly the same as before.
Thus, the Source is like a divine mother who would never create twin
children.

Dr. N: (pressing, wanting my subject to correct me) Do you think
this is a totally random selection? There is no order of characteristics with matched similarities of any kind? You know this to be
true?

S: (frustrated) How could I know this unless I was a Creator? There
are souls with similarities and those with none, all in the same
batch. The combinations are mixed. As a mother I can tweak
each major trait that I sense and this is why I can tell you no two
have exactly the same combinations of character.

Dr. N: Well . . . (subject breaks in to continue)

S: I have the sense that there is a powerful Presence on the other
side of the archway who is managing things. If there is a key to
the energy patterns—we do not need to know of this . . .

Note: These are the moments I wait for in my sessions, where I try to
push open the door to the ultimate Source. The door never opens more
than a crack.

Dr. N: Please tell me what you feel about this Presence, about the energy mass which is bringing these new souls to you. Surely, you and the other mothers must have thought about the origins of souls here even though you cannot see it?

S: (in a whisper) I feel the Creator is ... close by ... but may not actually be doing the work of ... production ...

Dr. N: (gently) Meaning the energy mass may not be the primary Creator?

S: (uncomfortable) I think there are others who assist—I don't know.

Dr. N: (taking another tack) Is it not true, Seena, that there are imperfections to the new souls? If they were created perfect, there would be no reason for them to be created at all by a perfect Creator?

S: (doubtfully) Everything here seems to be perfection.

Dr. N: (I temporarily move in another direction) Do you work only with souls coming to Earth?

S: Yes, but they could go to all kinds of places. Only a fraction come to Earth. There are many physical worlds similar to Earth. We call them pleasure worlds and suffering worlds.

Dr. N: And do you know when a soul is right for Earth based upon your incarnation experience?

S: Yes, I do. I know that the souls who come to worlds such as Earth need to be strong and resilient because of the pain they have to endure along with the joy.

Dr. N: That's my understanding, too. And when these souls become contaminated by the human body—particularly the young ones—this is because they are less than perfect. Might that be true?

S: Well, I suppose, yes.

Dr. N: (continuing) Which indicates to me that they must work to acquire more substance than they had originally in order to acquire full enlightenment. Would you accept that premise?

S: (long pause, then with a sigh) I think perfection is there . . . with the newly created. Maturity begins by the shattering of innocence with new souls, not because they are originally flawed. Overcoming obstacles makes them stronger but the acquired imperfections will never be totally erased until all souls are joined together—when incarnation ends.

Dr. N: Isn't this going to be difficult with new souls being created all the time to take the place of those ending their incarnations on Earth?

S: This too will end when all people . . . all races, nationalities unite as one. This is why we are sent to places such as Earth to work.

Dr. N: So, when the training ends, will the universe we live in die as well?

S: It may die before. It doesn't matter, there are others. Eternity never ends. It is the process which is meaningful because it allows us to . . . savor the experience and express ourselves . . . and to learn.

Before continuing with the evolution of a soul's progress, I should list what differences I have learned about their existence once they are created.

1. There are energy fragments which appear to return to the energy mass that created them before they even reach the nursery. I do not know the reason for their being aborted. Others, who do reach the nursery, are unable to handle learning "to be" on an individual basis during early maturation. Later, they are associated with collective functions and, from what I can determine, never leave the spirit world.

2. There are energy fragments who have individual soul essences that are not inclined, or have the necessary mental fabric, to incarnate in physical form on any world. They are often found on mental worlds, and they also appear to move easily between dimensions.

3. There are energy fragments with individual soul essences who incarnate only on physical worlds. These souls may well receive training in the spirit world with mental spheres between lives. I do not find them as interdimensional travelers.

4. There are energy fragments who are souls with the ability and inclination to incarnate and function as individuals in all types of physical and mental environments. This does not necessarily give them more or less enlightenment than other soul types. However, their wide range of practical experience positions them for many specialization opportunities and assignments of responsibility.

The grand scheme for the newborn soul starts slowly. Once they are released from the nursery, these souls do not enter into incarnations, nor are they even formed into soul groups right away. Here is one description of this transition period from the still-fresh memory of a young level I soul with only a couple of incarnations under his belt:

> Before I was assigned to my soul group and began coming to Earth, I remember being given the opportunity to experience a semi-physical world as a light form. It was more a mental world than physical because my surroundings were not completely solid and there was no biological life. I saw other young souls with me and we could move easily around the ground as luminous bulbs with a semblance of the human form. We were not doing—just being—and getting the feel of what it would be like to be solid. Although the setting was more astral than temporal, we were learning to communicate with each other as beings living in a community. We had no responsibilities. There was a Utopian atmosphere of tremendous love, security and protection everywhere. I have since learned that nothing is static and this—the beginning time— would be the easiest of our existence. Soon we would exist in a world where we would not be protected, in places where we would have memories of pain and loneliness— and pleasure too—and that these experiences are the teaching memories.

Spiritual Settings

While in trance, my subjects describe many visual images of the spirit world in earthly symbolisms. They may create structural images from their own planetary experiences or have these images created for them by guides seeking to raise their comfort level with familiar surroundings. After discussing this aspect of unconscious memory at lectures, I have had people say that, regardless of the consistency of these observations, they strain credibility. How could schoolrooms, libraries and temples exist in the spirit world?

I address these questions by explaining that past observational memory is metaphoric as a current perspective. Original scenes from all our lives never leave our memory as souls. In the spirit world, seeing a temple is not a literal record of stone blocks but rather a visualization of the meaning the temple has to that soul. Back on Earth, memories of past events in our soul life are reconstructions of circumstances and events based upon interpretations and conscious knowledge. All client memory retrieval is based upon observations of the soul mind processing information through a human mind. Regardless of the visual structures of spiritual settings, I always look to the functional aspects of what a subject is doing in them.

Once the new souls leave their protective cocoons they enter into community life. As they begin their incarnations, descriptions of the places and structures they see between lives take on the same flavor as that of older souls who go to Earth. Sometimes these descriptions are not so earthly. I hear reports of cathedral-like structures of glass, great halls of crystals, geometric buildings with many angles and smooth, domed enclosures without lines. Then, too, my subjects might say their surroundings have no structures, only fields of flowers and countryside scenes with forests and lakes. People in hypnosis display a sense of awe as they report floating toward their destinations in the spirit world. Many are so overcome they cannot adequately describe what they see.

I hear many accounts about the sheer movement of souls in transition going from place to place. The following account is from a level IV subject who uses geometric shapes to describe the properties of the various settings he sees:

I do a lot of traveling around in the spirit world. The geometric shapes I see represent certain functions to me.
Each structure has its own energy system. The pyramids
are for solitude, meditation and healing. The rectangular
shapes are for past life reviews and study. The spheroids
are used to examine future lives and the cylinder portals
are for traveling to other worlds to gain perspective.
Sometimes I pass great hubs of soul activity—like an air-
port—with people being paged telepathically. The hubs
are huge prismatic wheels with directional spoke-lines
which curve away from you. It's busy but well-organized.
(laughs) You can't rush in too fast or you might over-
shoot the particular line you want out of these great
hubs. These centers are ports of call with host souls
directing traffic and looking out for inquiries from travelers. Everything moves with a soft, comfortable floating
motion and there are beautiful harmonic tones upon
which souls can vibrationally lock onto, keeping them on
track to their destinations.

There is a statement from the Upanishads of India about our senses
being carried in memory after death. I believe this old philosophical
text is correct in the assumption that the senses, emotions and human
ego are a path to infinite experience, which provides a physical consciousness to the immortal Self. These sentiments were expressed by a
client of mine in a cogent way:

We can create anything we want in the spirit world to
remind us of places and things we enjoyed on Earth. Our
physical simulations are almost perfect—to many they
are perfect. But without a body . . . well . . . to me they
have the flavor of imitations. I love oranges. I can create
an orange here and even come close to reproducing its
pithy, sweet taste. Still, it is not quite the same as biting
into an orange on Earth. This is one reason why I relish
my physical reincarnations.

Despite this client's comments, I have had subjects tell me they see
the spirit world as true reality and Earth as an illusion created to teach
us. There may be no contradiction here. People from Earth have keen
taste buds. Oranges and human beings are therefore in harmony with
each other in one existence. There are degrees of reality. Simply
because our universe is a training ground does not make it unreal,

only impermanent. What may be a temporary illusion in the span of human surroundings does not take away from the fact that an orange on Earth eaten by an earthling *does* taste better than one created in the spirit world and eaten by a soul. By the same token, the reality of an interdimensional spirit world with its lack of absolutes allows the soul a magnitude of experience far beyond physical conceptions.

When my subjects describe seeing their spiritual centers, it is a wondrous image for them. All cultural stereotypes mixed with aspects of metaphoric symbolism recalled by the human mind are in play, to be sure, but these dramatic reenactments in a person's spiritual life are no less real. When the soul returns to Earth with the shroud of forgetfulness, it must adjust to a new brain without conscious memory. The new baby has no past experiences yet. The reverse is true right after death. For the spiritual hypnotherapist there are two forces operating in regression. On the one hand, we have the soul mind at work with its great storehouse of past life and spiritual life memories. On the other side, we also have the conscious memories of a current body engaged in descriptive imagery while the subject is in hypnosis. The conscious mind is not unconscious during hypnosis. If it were, the subject would be unable to speak to the facilitator coherently.

Memory

Before continuing with my analysis of what subjects in hypnosis see in the spirit world, I want to provide more information about divisions of memory recall and DNA. There are people who have the belief that all memories are carried by DNA. In this way they derive comfort from what they consider to be a scientific position against reincarnation. Certainly, everyone has a perfect right not to believe in reincarnation for a number of personal reasons, religious and otherwise. But to say that all past life memory is actually genetic in origin, carried in our DNA cells from remote ancestors, is an argument that, for me, fails in several ways.

Unconscious memories of past life trauma are capable of carrying a severely damaged physical imprint of that long-dead body into our new body, but this is not the result of DNA. These molecular codes are brand new and came with our current material body. Attitudes and beliefs from the soul mind do affect the biological mind. There are researchers who believe our eternal intelligence, involving energy imprints and memory patterns from past lives, may influence DNA. Indeed, there are countless other elements involving thought sequencing which we bring into our host body from hundreds of former lives. This also includes our experiences in the spirit world where we have no body.

A sound argument against past life DNA memory is the volume of research we have accumulated about past lives. The former bodies we had in prior lives are almost never genetically related to our current family. I could have been a member of the Smith family, along with others in my soul group, in one life and we might all choose to be part of the Jones family in the next life. However, we would not come back to the Smith family, as I will explain more fully in chapter 7. The average subject has led past lives as Caucasians, Orientals and Africans with no heredity connections. Moreover, how can our memories of being on other worlds in other species come from human DNA cells created only on Earth? The answer is simple. So-called genetic memory is actually soul memory emanating from the unconscious mind.

I divide memory into three categories:

1. **Conscious Memory.** This state of thought would apply to all memories retained by the brain in our biological body. It is manifested by a conscious ego Self that is perceptive and adaptive to our physical planet. Conscious memory is influenced by sensory experiences and all our biological, primitive instinctual drives as well as emotional experiences. It can be faulty because there are defensive mechanisms related to what it receives and evaluates through impressions from the five senses.

2. **Immortal Memory.** Memories in this category appear to come through the subconscious mind. Subconscious thought is greatly influenced by body functions not subject to conscious control, such as heart rate and glandular functions. However, it can also be the selective storeroom of conscious memory. Immortal memory carries the memories of our origins in this life and other physical lives. It is a repository of much of our psyche because the subconscious mind forms the bridge between the conscious and superconscious mind.

3. **Divine Memory.** These are the memories that emanate from our superconscious mind which houses the soul. If conscience, intuition and imagination are expressed through the subconscious mind, they are drawn from this higher source. Our eternal soul mind has evolved from superior conceptual thought energy beyond ourselves. Inspiration may seem to spring from immortal memory, but there is a higher intelligence outside our body-mind which forms a part of divine memory. The source of these divine thoughts is illusive. Sometimes we conceive of it as personal memory, when actually divine memory represents communication from beings in our immortal existence.

Community Centers

My next case illustrates the visual associations subjects in a superconscious state bring to descriptive memories of arriving back home. It involves an identification with classical Greece, which is not unusual. I have listened to visualizations so futuristic and surreal as to allow for few comparisons with Earth. People do say to me that words cannot adequately describe the images of what they see at this junction. Once I take a client past the gateway to spaces where they begin to make contact with other spirits they become exhilarated.

In case 27 a subject, whose spiritual name is Ariani, will associate a Greek temple with her experience after death from her most immediate past life. Perhaps this is not surprising since so many of my subjects had incarnations during the time when ancient Greece brought the light of a high civilization into a dark world. In art, philosophy and government they left a legacy and a challenge for those who followed. This society sought to unite the rational with the spiritual mind, which is remembered by those clients who were part of this Golden Age. Ariani had her final life in ancient Greece during the second century B.C., just before Rome began its occupation.

Case 27

Dr. N: When you approach your spiritual center, Ariani, what do you see there?

S: A beautiful Greek temple with bright white marble columns.

Dr. N: Are you creating this image of a temple yourself or is someone else placing it in your mind for you?

S: It's really there in front of me! Just as I remember it . . . but . . .
someone else could be helping me . . . my guide . . . I'm not sure.

Dr. N: Is this temple familiar to you?

S: (smiling) I know it so well. It represents the culmination of a
series of meaningful lives that I was not to know again for a long
time on Earth.

Dr. N: Why is that? What is it about this temple that means so
much to you?

S: It is a temple to Athena, goddess of wisdom. I was a priestess—
with three others. Our job was to tend the flame of knowledge.
The flame was on a flat, smooth rock in the center of the temple
with writing etched around it.

Dr. N: What does the writing mean?

S: (pause) Ah . . . essentially . . . to seek truth above all things. And
the way to seek truth is to look for harmony and beauty in that
which surrounds us in life.

Dr. N: (deliberately obtuse) Well, is that all you did—just making
sure the flame didn't go out?

S: (with some exasperation) No, this was a place of learning where a
woman could participate. The flame symbolized a sacred flame
in our hearts for knowing truth. We held the belief in the holi-
ness of a single god with lesser deities representing parts of that
central power.

Dr. N: Are you telling me that you and the other women had
monotheistic beliefs?

S: (smiling) Yes, and our sect went beyond the temple. We were seen
by the authorities as being pure in heart and not as an intellectual caste. Most of them did not realize what we were about.
They saw Athena in one light while we saw her in another. To us,
the flame meant that reason and feeling were not opposed to one

another. To us, the temple placed the mind above superstition. We also believed in equality between the sexes.

Dr. N: This kind of radical thinking could get you into a lot of trouble with a patriarchal establishment, I suppose?

S: It did, eventually. Their tolerance eroded and we had deceit and intrigue within our own ranks and then betrayal. Our motives were mistrusted. We were disbanded by a sexist state which was losing power and felt our sect was contributing to corruption within the state.

Dr. N: And after this series of lives in Greece, you wanted your temple with you in the spirit world?

S: That's one way of putting it. To my friends and me, this life and a few earlier ones in Greece represented the high point of reason, wisdom and spirituality. I had to wait a long time before openly being able to express these feelings again in a female body.

Once I took Ariani into her temple she saw a huge rectangular gallery without a ceiling, filled with approximately 1,000 souls. These souls were a large secondary group whom she saw bunched into smaller clusters, called primary groups, made up of souls numbering from three to twenty-five. Her own cluster was midway back on the right side (see figure 1, circle A). As she made her way back, Ariani was accompanied by her guide. She then described how this entrance appears to a returning soul. This scene is one I hear repeated over and over again involving large numbers of soul groups, regardless of the structural setting. In the superconscious minds of people, these gatherings could just as well be in an amphitheater, palace courtyard, or school auditorium as in a temple.

Dr. N: Ariani, give me a sense of what it feels like to make your way through this crowd of souls to your cluster.

S: (with excitement) It's uplifting and awesome at the same time. With my guide leading, we start to weave our way left and right between the clusters, some of whom are seated in a circle and others are standing, talking. In the early stages most people pay

Figure 1: The Great Hall Community Center

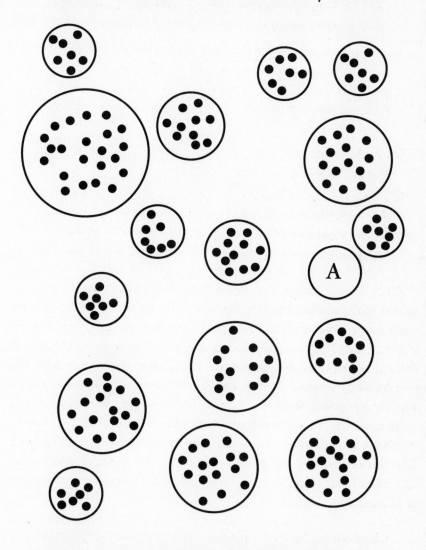

This diagram represents the first view by many people of large numbers of primary soul cluster groups which make up one big secondary group of some 1,000 souls. Primary group A is the subject's own cluster of souls.

> no attention to me because we are strangers. Souls who are
> nearby my path might nod their heads in polite acknowledgment
> of my arrival. Then, about midway through, people who see me
> become more animated. A man who was my lover two lives ago
> stands up and gives me a kiss and asks how I am doing. More
> people in other clusters begin now to smile and wave at me.
> Some whom I have known in lives only slightly give me a
> thumbs-up greeting. Then—as I get to a group next to my own
> cluster—I see my parents. They stop what they are doing and
> drift over the short space between our two clusters to embrace
> me and whisper encouragement. Finally, I reach my own group
> and everyone is welcoming me back.

About half of all my clients see large groups of souls upon their return. The other half report that after their arrival they see just their own cluster. The visual images of either large or small gatherings of souls can vary with the same soul after different lives. The primary group of souls, with whom we are most closely bonded, may also appear to these same subjects as people milling about in outdoor scenes of recreation, such as a countryside field of flowers.

Regardless of an exterior or interior setting, figures 2 and 3 illustrate what a majority of subjects see when they first make contact with their groups. In these instances, no other groups are observed in the area. In figure 2, the welcoming souls are rather bunched together, each soul coming forward in turn to the front position. Figure 3 shows the customary way a group forms a semicircle around the newly arrived soul. Most of my subjects experience this circular form of greeting. A descriptive representation of this practice will be found in chapter 7 with case 47.

Those subjects who report going directly into a classroom setting upon returning from a past life have a clear picture in their minds of hallways that connect a series of spaces for study. Unerringly, they seem to know in which space they belong. In these cases, cluster groups commonly stop their activities to welcome any new arrival. Figure 4 represents the usual design layout of a learning center where numerous groups of souls work. The consistency of reporting about the settings

Figure 2: Cluster Group Position 1

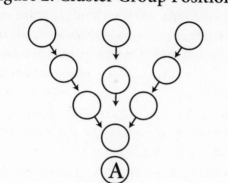

Figure 2 indicates the phalanx-diamond position of a primary cluster group greeting returning soul A with the group guide B behind. Here many souls are concealed behind one another before their turn to greet the incoming member.

Figure 3: Cluster Group Position 2

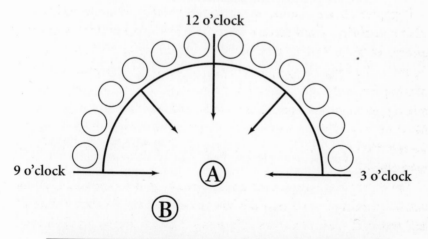

Figure 3 indicates the more common semicircle positioning of a soul group waiting to greet returning soul A with (or without) teacher-guide in position B. On the hands of this clock diagram, souls come forward, each in their own turn, from positions within a 180-degree arc. Typically, greeting souls do not come from behind A in the 6 o'clock position.

144 ~ Destiny of Souls

shown in figure 4 is astonishing. Only a very small percentage of my subjects say that their initial meeting with groups of souls involve just floating in air with nothing around. The absence of landscape scenes or physical structures does not last long, even in the minds of these people.

Classrooms

Any gathering of souls outside a classroom setting, including the large assembly halls, indicates it is a time of general socializing and recreation. This doesn't mean serious discussions are not taking place in these areas, only that soul activities are not directed as in study areas. Here is a typical description from a subject who is moving into a classroom setting (see figure 4):

> My guide takes me into a star-shaped structure and I know this is my place of learning. There is a round domed central chamber which is empty now. I see corridors going off in opposite directions and we move down one of these halls where the classrooms are located. They are offset in such a way that no two classrooms face each other. This is so we will not bother another room of souls. My room is the third cubicle on the left. I never see more than six rooms to a hallway. Each room has an average of eight to fifteen souls working at desks. I know this sounds ridiculous, but that's what I see. As I pass down the hall with my guide, I notice in some rooms souls are studying quietly by themselves while others are working in groups of two to five. A different room has the students watching an instructor lecturing at a blackboard. When I enter my room everyone stops what they were doing and gives me a big smile. Some wave and a few cheer as if they were expecting me. The ones nearest the doorway escort me to a seat and I get ready to participate in the lesson. The whole time I have been gone seems like a brief trip down to the corner grocery store to buy a carton of milk.

Most of my subjects visualize the structures of their spiritual classrooms as being single story, although there are exceptions, such as the next case, with an intermediate level soul called Rudalph.

Figure 4: Spiritual Learning Center

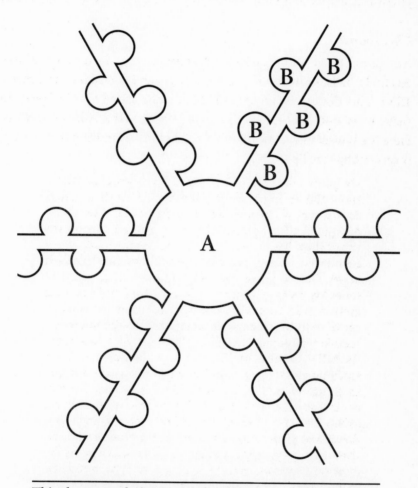

This classroom design is visualized by many souls as having a central rotunda A, with primary cluster group rooms B down adjacent corridors. Usually there are no more than six rooms per hallway. These round rooms are offset from each other. The number of reported corridors varies.

Case 28

Dr. N: After your last station stop, Rudalph, describe to me what you see as you approach your destination—the place where you belong in the spirit world.

S: As I come near my pod, there is a park-like atmosphere where the countryside is so quiet and peaceful. I see clusters of bubbles that are smooth and transparent with souls inside.

Dr. N: And do you recognize your own pod?

S: Oh . . . yes . . . although my . . . references . . . take some getting used to again. I'm doing fine. I could have done this myself but my guide Tahama (who appears as an American Indian) came to escort me on this trip because she knew I was tired after a long, hard life. (subject died at age eighty-three in 1937) She is so considerate.

Dr. N: All right, describe your pod for me.

S: I see my pod as a large bubble—which is a school building—divided into four floors. Inside the bubbles there are many bright, colorful points of soul energy.

Dr. N: And all this is transparent from the outside to you?

S: Semitransparent . . . milky.

Dr. N: Okay, now go inside and describe how you see these four floors and what they mean to you.

S: The four floors are transparent and look like glass. Each level is connected by a stairway with a compartment for study at one end. On each floor there are groups undergoing instruction. I enter on the first floor where a beginning level group of eighteen souls is listening to a visiting lecturer called Bion. I know her—she is very aware of the pitfalls of young people. She is strong but tender.

Dr. N: Do you know all the teachers in this school?

S: Oh, sure. I'm one of them—just starting, of course. Please don't think I'm bragging, I'm just a student teacher, but I'm very proud.

Dr. N: As well you should be, Rudalph. Tell me, does each floor have one primary cluster group?

S: (hesitates) Well, the first two do—there are twelve working on the second level. The upper floors have souls from other groups working on their individual specialties.

Dr. N: Rudalph, is this the same thing as an independent studies program?

S: That would be accurate.

Dr. N: All right, what happens next to you?

S: Tahama tells me where I need to be—reminding me that I belong on the third level but to take as much time as I want. Then she leaves me.

Dr. N: Why does she do that?

S: Oh, you know . . . our guides maintain a teacher-student relationship with us in this center. They try not to be real familiar with us . . . in a social way, because of their . . . professional status. I don't mean for this to sound as though they act like some pompous professors on Earth. This is different. The master teachers, such as my other guide, Relon, keep a little distance from the students when not engaged in teaching to give them space and allow for individual expression among themselves. They feel it is important for the student's growth not to be hovering around them all the time.

Dr. N: That's most interesting. Please continue, Rudalph.

S: Well, Tahama says she will see me later. To be honest, I'm not completely tuned into this place yet. It's just the way I am when I come back. It always takes me awhile to acclimatize, so I'm going to relax and enjoy the children on the ground floor.

Dr. N: Children? You call these first level souls children?

S: (laughing) Well, now I'm sounding a bit pompous myself. It's just how we describe the beginners, who can be rather childlike in their development. This group is really just starting. They acknowledge me, because I have been active with them. I know the ones who are repeating the same mistakes because of a lack of self-discipline. They are not making much effort to move up in development. I don't stay too long because I don't want them to be distracted from Bion's lesson.

Dr. N: What is the teacher's attitude about the slow ones?

S: Frankly, the teachers of the first level do get tired of certain students who almost refuse to progress, so they leave them alone a lot.

Dr. N: Are you saying the teachers stop pushing those students who are difficult?

S: You have to understand that teachers have infinite patience because time is meaningless. They are content to wait until the student is disgusted with treading water and offers to work harder.

Dr. N: I see. Please continue with your tour of this school.

S: I am looking up through the glass ceiling to the second level. That's where I'm headed next. These souls have a fleecy, gauze appearance from here. I don't really need a stairway but it represents a means of passage in my mind. As I climb to the second floor I see the adolescents. They are like super-active teenagers . . . full of restless energy . . . sponges absorbing a lot of information fast and trying to act on that knowledge. They are learning to get a grip on themselves but many don't know yet how to give back to others in effective ways.

Dr. N: As a teacher, would you say that these souls are self-absorbed?

S: (laughs) That's normal, along with a constant need for outer stimulation. (more seriously) I am not yet qualified to teach on this level. Enit is in charge here—a disciplinarian with a big heart. Right now they are on a break. I find them fun to be around because they all pump me for information about the manner in which I have learned to accomplish things on Earth. Soon it's time for me to go to the third level.

Dr. N: What would happen if one of these students followed you up into the third level?

S: (smiles) Once in a while a curious one will wander into more advanced areas. It's similar to a third grader walking down the hall into a sixth-grade class. The kid would be lost. They might be teased a little on Earth but someone would quietly take them back to their own classroom. It's the same here.

Dr. N: Well, I guess you are ready to take me up to the third level. May I have your impressions of this place?

S: (brightly) This is my area and we are like young adults. Many of us are training to be teachers. The mental challenges here are more constant. Now we are working on resourcefulness, not just reacting to situations. We are learning to protect and inform, to keep our eyes open, and to see the spirit of others through the light in their eyes on our earthly rotations.

Dr. N: Do you recognize people you know?

S: Oh, I see Elan. (husband in both past and current life, a primary soulmate) He appears to me as we were in our last life. Elan sparks up my tired energy with his love—like lighting a fire in a cold stove. I was a widow for a long time. (tearfully) We are sucked up into a pool of happiness together for a few moments.

Dr. N: (after a pause) Anyone else?

S: Everybody! There is Esent (mother in current life) and Blay (a best girlfriend in her current life). (subject is suddenly distracted) I want to go up briefly to the fourth level to see my daughter Anna. (also in current life)

Dr. N: Tell me what you can about the fourth level.

S: There are only three souls there and from below they appear as shapeless shadows of goldish and silver blue. There is such warmth and love with these souls growing into full adulthood. They are becoming very wise in helping souls really make use of their human bodies. I sense they feel more touched by a divine essence. They are in tune with their existence. When they come back from a physical life they don't need adjusting as I do.

Dr. N: Where are the older adults, such as the senior guides, the Elders and others like them?

S: They are not in this bubble, but we see them elsewhere.

The Library of Life Books

Many of my clients speak about being in research library settings soon after rejoining their soul groups. I have come to accept the idea that it is a standard learning imperative that we begin to study our past lives in depth right away. After I wrote about the place where our life records are stored in my first book, people asked if I was able to supply them with more details.

The people who describe earthly structures in their spiritual home also include the library, and descriptions of this setting are quite consistent. On Earth, a library represents a systematic collection of books arranged by subjects and names which provide information. The titles of spiritual Life Books have my client's names on them. This may seem odd, but if I were working with an intelligent aquatic being from Planet X who had never been to Earth and whose place of study was an ocean tide pool, I'm sure that is what this entity would report seeing in the spirit world.

I have reported on spiritual classrooms and smaller adjacent cubicles where primary groups interact, including even smaller isolated rooms where souls can be completely alone for quiet study. There is nothing small about the library. Everyone tells me the location of the Life Books is seen as a huge study hall, in a rectangular structure, with books lined along the walls and many souls studying at desks who do not seem to know each other. When my subjects describe a spiritual library they see the floor plan design in figure 5, an image that is very prevalent in their minds.

Once inside this space, librarian-guides are the Archivist Souls in charge of the books. They are quiet, almost monastic beings who assist both guides and students from many primary clusters in locating information. These spiritual libraries serve souls in different ways depending upon their level of attainment. Souls may be assisted either by their own guides, the Archivists, or both. Some of my clients go to the library

Figure 5: Life Books Library

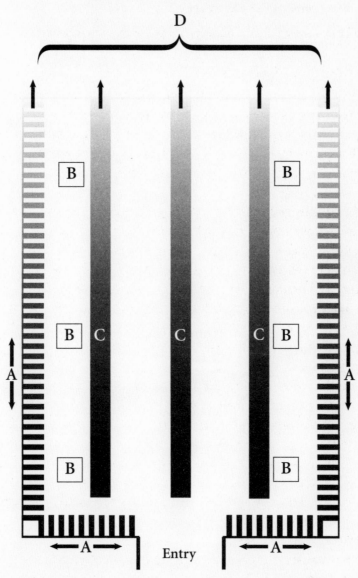

A: Bookshelves lining the walls of a large rectangular structure.

B: Pedestals for archivists and guides assisting souls in locating the proper Life Books.

C: Long study tables.

D: Walls of books and study tables stretching far into the distance, out of the soul's line of sight.

alone upon returning to the spirit world, while others have guides who routinely accompany them into this space. A guide might get his student started and then leave the room. Many elements come into play here, including the complexity of the research and the timeline to be reviewed by the student soul. When students are in these study halls they sometimes work in pairs but mostly they do their research alone after being assisted by the Archivists in finding the proper Life Books.

Eastern philosophy holds that every thought, word and deed from every lifetime in our past, along with every event in which we participated, is recorded in the Akashic Record. Possibilities of future events can also be seen with the help of scribes. The word "Akasha" essentially means the essence of all universal memory that is recording every energy vibration of existence, rather like an audio/visual magnetic tape. I have discussed the connections of divine, immortal and conscious memory. Our human conceptualization of spiritual libraries, timeless places where we study missed opportunities and our accountability for past actions, is an example of those memory connections. People of the East have conceived that the substance of all events past, present and future is preserved by containment within energy particles and then recovered in a sacred spiritual setting through vibrational alignments. I feel the whole concept of personal spiritual records for each of us did not originate in India or anywhere else on Earth. It began with our spiritual minds already having knowledge of these records between lives.

I find it unsettling that certain aspects of recovered memory about spiritual libraries can be subverted by human belief systems which are intended to frighten people. Within Eastern cultures there are those who have been led to believe the Life Books are analogous to spiritual diaries that can be used as evidence against the soul. Visions of spiritual libraries are interpreted as scenes where cases are prepared as depositions against errant souls based upon their karmic records. A further step in this misguided belief system brings us to the dreaded tribunal for sentencing after testimony about the soul's shortcomings in the last life. Certain psychics claim they have privileged access to events of the future through Akashic Records and that by working exclusively with them they can divert their followers from catastrophe.

Human extravagance has no bounds when it comes to instilling fear. A prime example is the fear of terrible punishment for those who commit suicide. It is true that being kept out of heaven has been a deterrent to suicide, but it is the wrong approach. I have noticed in recent years that even the Catholic church is not quite so adamant about suicide being a mortal sin subject to the extremes of spiritual punishment. There is now a Vatican-approved catechism which states that suicide is "against natural law" but adds, "by ways known to God alone, there is opportunity for salutary repentance." Salutary means conducive to some good purpose.

My next case represents a subject who killed herself in her last life. She describes her examination of this act in a library setting. Repentance in the spirit world often begins here. Since I will be reviewing her suicide, this is a suitable point to briefly digress from the library and address some of the questions I have been asked about suicide and subsequent retribution in the spirit world.

When I work with clients who have committed suicide in former lives, the first thing most exclaim right after the moment of death is, "Oh, my God, how could I have been so stupid!" These are physically healthy people, not those who are suffering from a debilitating physical illness. Suicide by a person, young or old, whose physical state has reduced the quality of their life to almost nothing is treated differently in the spirit world than those who had healthy bodies. While all suicide cases are treated with kindness and understanding, people who killed themselves with a healthy body do have a reckoning.

In my experience, souls feel no sense of failure or guilt when they have been involved with a mercy death. I shall give a realistic example of this sort of death with a brother and sister under the free will section in chapter 9. When there is unendurable physical suffering, we have the right to be released from the pain and indignity of being treated like helpless children connected to life-support systems. In the spirit world, I find that no stigma is attached to a soul leaving a terribly broken body who is released by its own hand or from that of a compassionate caregiver.

I have worked with quite a number of people who have attempted suicide in the years before they saw me and I feel my working with them has provided a helpful perspective. Some were still in emotional turmoil when I met them, while others had pulled away from thoughts of self-destruction. One thing I have learned is that people who tell me they don't belong on Earth need to be taken seriously. They may even be potential suicide cases. In my practice, these clients fall into one of three spiritual classifications:

1. Young, highly sensitive souls who began their incarnations on Earth but have spent little time here. Certain souls in this category have had great difficulty adjusting to the human body. They feel their very existence to be threatened because it is so cruel.

2. Both young and older souls who incarnated on another planet before coming to Earth. If these souls lived on worlds less harsh than Earth, they may be overcome by the primitive emotions and high density of the human body. These are the hybrid souls I discussed in the last chapter. Essentially, they feel they are in an alien body.

3. Souls below level III, who have been incarnating on Earth since their creation but are not merging well with their current body. These souls accepted a life contract with a host body whose physical ego mind is radically different from their immortal soul. They cannot seem to find themselves in this particular lifetime.

What happens to souls involved with suicide in healthy bodies? These souls tell me they feel somewhat diminished in the eyes of their guides and group peers because they broke their covenant in a former life. There is a loss of pride from a wasted opportunity. Life is a gift and a great deal of thought has gone into allocating certain bodies for our use. We are the custodians of this body and that carries a sacred trust. My clients call it a contract. Particularly when a young, healthy person commits suicide, our teachers consider this an act of gross immaturity and the abrogation of responsibility. Our spiritual masters have placed their trust in our courage to finish life with functional bodies in a normal fashion, no matter how difficult. They have infinite patience with us, but with repeated suicide offenders their forgiveness takes on another tone.

I worked with a young client who had tried to commit suicide a year before I saw him. During our hypnosis session we found evidence of a pattern of self-destruction in former lives. Facing his master teachers at a council meeting following his last life, this client was told by an Elder:

> Once again you are here early and we are disappointed. Have you not learned the same test grows more difficult with each new life you terminate? Your behavior is selfish for many reasons, not the least of which is the sorrow you caused to those left behind who loved you. How much longer will you continue to just throw away the perfectly good bodies we give you? Tell us when you are ready to stop engaging in self-pity and underestimating your capabilities.

I don't think I have ever heard of a council member come down any harder on one of my subjects over the issue of suicide. Months later, this client wrote me to say that whenever thoughts of committing suicide entered his head he pushed them aside because of a desire to avoid having to face this Elder again after killing himself. A little posthypnotic suggestion on my part made recovering this scene in his conscious mind especially easy and serves as a deterrent.

In suicide cases involving healthy bodies, one of two things generally happens to these souls. If they are not a repeat offender, the soul is frequently sent back to a new life rather quickly, at their own request, to make up for lost time. This could be within five years of their death on Earth. The average soul is convinced it is important to get right back on the diving board after having taken a belly flop in a prior life. After all, we have natural survival instincts as human beings and most spirits tenaciously fight to stay alive.

For those who display a pattern of bailing out when things get rough there are places of repentance for a good purpose. These places do not contain a pantheon of horrors in some dark, lower spirit region reserved for sinners. Rather than being punished in some sort of bleak purgatory, these souls may volunteer to go to a beautiful planetary world with water, trees and mountains but no other life. They have no contact with other souls in these places of seclusion except for sporadic visits by a guide to assist them in their reflections and self-evaluation.

Places of isolation come in many varieties and I must admit they seem terribly boring. Maybe that's the whole idea. While you are sitting out the next few games on the bench, your teammates continue with challenges in their new lives. Apparently this medicine seems to work because these souls come back to their groups feeling refreshed but knowing they have missed out on a lot of action and opportunities for personal development with their friends. Nonetheless, there are souls who will never adjust to Earth. I hear some are reassigned to other worlds for their future incarnations.

My next two cases represent the exposure of souls to spiritual libraries and the impact seeing their records has on them. In both cases there is evidence of the use of altered reality, with some differences. The woman in case 29, a suicide case, will be shown a series of alternate choices she could have made in her past life, presented in four coexisting time sequences. The first timeline was the actual life itself. She will be more of an observer than a participant in these scenes. With case 30, however, we will see the employment of a single scene with an altered reality where the soul will dramatically enter a scene from his past life to actually experience a different outcome. Both cases are designed to show the many paths in life involving choices.

Our guides decide on the most effective means for self-discovery in the library. The design and scope of these investigations then comes under the jurisdiction of the Archivists.

Case 29

Amy had recently returned to the spirit world from a small farming village in England where she killed herself in 1860, at age sixteen. This soul would wait another hundred years before coming back due to her self-doubts about handling adversity. Amy drowned herself in a local pond because she was two months pregnant and unmarried. Her lover, Thomas, had been killed the week before in a fall off a thatched roof he was repairing. I learned the two were deeply in love and intended to marry. Amy told me during her past life review that she thought when Thomas was killed her life was over. Amy said she did not want to bring disgrace upon her family from the gossip of local villagers. Tearfully, this client said, "I knew they would call me a whore, and if I ran off to London that is exactly what a poor girl with child would become."

In suicide cases, the soul's guide might offer seclusion, aggressive energy regeneration, a quick return, or some combination of these things. When Amy crossed over after killing herself, her guide, Likiko, and the soul of Thomas were there to comfort her for a while. Soon she was alone with Likiko in a beautiful garden setting. Amy sensed the disappointment in Likiko's manner and she expected to be scolded for her lack of courage. Angrily, she asked her guide why the life didn't go as planned in the beginning. She had not seen the possibility of suicide before her incarnation. Amy thought she was supposed to marry Thomas, have children and live happily in her village to old age. Someone, she felt, had pulled the rug out from under her. Likiko explained that Thomas' death was one of the alternatives in this life cycle and that she had the freedom to make better choices than killing herself.

Amy learned that for Thomas, his choice to go up on a high, steep and dangerously slippery roof was a probable one—more probable because his soul mind had already considered this "accident" as a test for her. Later, I was to learn Thomas came very close to not accepting the roof job because of "internal forces pulling him the other way." Apparently, everyone in this soul group saw that Amy's capacity for survival was greater than she gave herself credit for, although she had shown tenuous behavior in her earlier lives.

Once on the other side, Amy thought the whole exercise was cruel and unnecessary. Likiko reminded Amy that she had a history of self-flagellation and that if she was ever going to help others with their survival, she must get past this failing in herself. When Amy responded that she had little choice but to kill herself, given the circumstances of Victorian England, she found herself in the following library scene.

Dr. N: Where are you now?

S: (somewhat disoriented) I'm in a place of study . . . it looks Gothic . . . stone walls . . . long marble tables . . .

Dr. N: Why do you think you are in this sort of building?

S: (pause) In one of my lives I lived as a monk in Europe (in the twelfth century). I loved the old church cloister as a place for quiet study. But I know where I am now. It is the library of great books . . . the records.

Dr. N: Many people call them Life Books. Is this the same thing?

S: Yes, we all use them . . . (pause, subject is distracted) There is a worrisome-looking old man in a white robe coming toward me . . . fluttering around me.

Dr. N: What's he doing, Amy?

S: Well, he's carrying a set of scrolls, rolls of charts. He is muttering and shaking his head at me.

Dr. N: Do you have any idea why?

S: He is the librarian. He says to me, "You are here early."

Dr. N: What do you think he means?

S: (pause) That . . . I did not have compelling reasons for arriving back here early.

Dr. N: Compelling reasons . . . ?

S: (breaking in) Oh . . . being in terrible pain—not able to function in life.

Dr. N: I see. Tell me what this librarian does next.

S: There is a huge open space where I see many souls at long desks with books everywhere but I'm not going to that room now. The old man takes me to one of the small private rooms off to the side where we can talk without disturbing the others.

Dr. N: How do you feel about this?

S: (shakes head in resignation) I guess I need special treatment right now. The room is very plain with a single table and chair. The old man brings in a large book and it is set up in front of me like a TV viewing screen.

Dr. N: What are you supposed to do?

S: (abruptly) Pay attention to him! He sets his scroll in front of me first and opens it. Then he points to a series of lines representing my life.

Dr. N: Please go slowly here and explain what these lines mean to you, Amy.

S: They are life lines—my lines. The thick, widely spaced lines represent the prominent experiences in our life and the age they will most likely occur. The thinner ones bisect the main lines and represent a variety of other . . . circumstances.

Dr. N: I have heard these less prominent lines are possibilities of action as opposed to the probabilities. Is that what you are saying?

S: (pause) That's right.

Dr. N: What else can you tell me about the thick versus thin lines?

S: Well, the thick line is like the trunk of a tree and the smaller ones are the branches. I know the thick one was my main path. The old man is pointing at that line and scolding me a bit about taking a dead-end branch.

Dr. N: You know, Amy, despite this Archivist fussing about these lines, they do represent a series of your choices. From a karmic standpoint all of us have taken a wrong fork in the road from time to time.

S: (heatedly) Yes, but this is serious. I did not just make a small mistake in his eyes. I know he cares about what I do. (there is a pause and then loudly) I WANT TO HIT HIM OVER THE HEAD WITH HIS DAMN SCROLL. I TELL HIM, "YOU GO TRY MY LIFE FOR A WHILE!"

Note: At this point Amy tells me that the old man's face softens and he leaves the room for a few minutes. She thinks he is giving her time to collect herself but then he brings back another book. This book is opened to a page where Amy can see the Archivist as a young man being torn apart by lions in an ancient Roman arena for his religious convictions. He then puts this book aside and opens Amy's book. I ask her what she sees next.

S: It comes alive in three-dimensional color. He shows me the first page with a universe of millions of galaxies. Then the Milky Way . . . and our solar system . . . so I will remember where I came from—as if I could forget. Then, more pages are turned.

Dr. N: I like this perspective, Amy. Then, what do you see?

S: Ahh . . . crystal prisms . . . dark and light depending upon what thoughts are sent. Now, I remember I have done this before. More lines . . . and pictures . . . which I can move forward and backward in time with my mind. But the old man is helping me anyway.

Note: I have been told these lines form vibrational sequences representing timeline alignments.

Dr. N: How would you interpret the meaning of the lines?

S: They form the patterns for the life pictures in the order you wish to look at—that you need to look at.

Dr. N: I don't want to get ahead of you, Amy. Just tell me what the old man does with you now.

S: Okay. He flips to a page and I see myself onscreen in the village I just left. It isn't really a picture—it's so real—it's alive. I'm there.

Dr. N: Are you actually in the scene or are you simply observing the scene?

S: We can do both, but right now I am supposed to just watch the scenes.

Dr. N: That's fine, Amy. Let's go through the scene as the old man is presenting it to you. Explain what is going on.

S: Oh . . . we are going to look at . . . other choices. After seeing what I actually did at the pond where I took my life—the next scene has me back at the pond on the bank. (pause) This time I don't wade in and drown myself. I walk back to the village. (laughs for the first time) I'm still pregnant.

Dr. N: (laughing with her) Okay, turn the page. Now what?

S: I'm with my mother, Iris. I tell her I am carrying Thomas' baby. She is not as shocked as I thought she would be. She is angry, though. I get a lecture. Then . . . she is crying with me and holding me. (subject now breaks down while tearfully continuing to talk) I tell her I am a good girl, but I was in love.

Dr. N: Does Iris tell your father?

S: That is one alternative on the screen.

Dr. N: Follow that alternative path for me.

S: (pause) We all move to another village and everyone there is told I am a widow. Years later, I will marry an older man. These are very hard times. My father lost a lot when we moved and we were even poorer than before. But we stay together as a family and life eventually becomes good. (crying again) My little girl was beautiful.

Dr. N: Is that the only alternative course of action you study right now?

S: (with resignation) Oh, no. Now, I look at another choice. I come back from the pond and admit I am pregnant. My parents scream at me and then fight with each other about who is to blame. I am told they do not want to give up our small farm they worked so hard for and leave the village because I am disgraced. They give me a little money to get to London so I can try to find work as a serving girl.

Dr. N: And how does this work out?

S: (bitterly) Just what I expected. London would not have been good. I wind up in the streets sleeping with other men. (shudders) I die kind of young and the baby is a foundling who eventually dies too. Horrible . . .

Dr. N: Well, at least you tried to survive in that alternative life. Are any other choices shown to you?

S: I'm growing tired. The old man shows me one last choice. There are others, I think, but he will stop here because I ask him to. In this scene my parents still believe I should go away from them but we wait until a traveling peddler comes to our village. He agrees to take me in his cart after my father pays him something. We do not go to London but rather to other villages in the district. I finally find work with a family. I tell them my husband was killed. The peddler gave me a brass ring to wear and backs up my story. I'm not sure they believe me. It doesn't matter. I settle in the town. I never marry but my child grows up healthy.

Dr. N: After you are finished turning these pages with the old man and have contemplated some of the alternatives to suicide, what are your conclusions?

S: (sadly) It was a waste to kill myself. I know it now. I think I knew it all along. Right after I died I said to myself, "God, that was a stupid thing to do, now I'm going to have to do it all over again!" When I went before my council they asked if I would like to be retested soon. I said, "Let me think about it awhile."

After this session my client discussed some of the choices she has had to make in her current life involving courage. As a teenager she became pregnant and dealt with this difficulty through the help of a school counselor and finally her mother, who was Iris in her life as Amy. They encouraged her to stand up for herself regardless of the opinions of others. In our session together my subject learned her soul has a tendency to prejudge serious events in her life in a negative manner. In many past lives there was always a nagging thought that whatever decision she made in a crisis would be the wrong one.

Although Amy was reluctant to return to Earth again, today she is a woman of much greater confidence. She spent the hundred years between lives reflecting on her suicide and decisions made in the centuries before this life. Amy is a musical soul and she said at one point:

> Because I wasted the body assigned to me, I am doing a kind of penance. During recreation I can't go to the music room, which I love to do, because I need to be alone in the library. I use the screens to review my past actions involving choices where I have hurt myself and those around me.

When a client uses the word "screen" to describe how they view events, the setting is relevant. Small conference rooms and the library appear to have tables with a variety of TV-size books. These so-called books have three-dimensional illuminated viewing screens. One client echoed the thoughts of most subjects when she said, "These records give the illusion of books with pages, but they are sheets of energy which vibrate and form live picture-patterns of events."

The size of these screens depends upon usage within a given setting. For instance, in the life selection rooms we use just before our next incarnation, the screens are much larger than seen in spiritual libraries and classrooms. Souls are given the option of entering these life-sized screens. The huge, shimmering screens usually encircle the soul and they have been called the Ring of Destiny. I will discuss the Ring further in chapter 9.

Despite the impressive size of the screens in future-life selection rooms, souls spend far more time looking at scenes in the library. The function of the smaller library screens is for monitoring past and current time on Earth on a continuing basis. All screens, large or small, have been described to me as sheets of film which look like waterfalls that can be entered while part of our energy stays in the room.

All cosmic viewing screens are multidimensional, with coordinates to record spacetime avenues of occurrence. These are often referred to as timelines and they can be manipulated by thought scanning. There may be other directors of this process not seen by the soul. Quite often a subject will employ mechanical contrivances in their scanning descriptions such as panels, levers, and dials. Apparently, these are all illusions created for souls who incarnate on Earth.

Regardless of screen size, the length, width and depth in each frame allows the soul to become part of a procession of cause and effect sequences. Can souls enter the smaller screens associated with books in the same way as with the larger screens found in the Ring? While there are no restrictions for time travel study, most of my subjects appear to use the smaller screens more for observing past events in which they once participated. Souls take a portion of their energy, leaving the rest at the console, and enter the screens in one of two ways:

1. As observers moving as unseen ghosts through scenes on Earth with no influence on events. I see this as working with virtual reality.

2. As participants where they will assume roles in the action of the scene, even to the extent of altering reality from the original by re-creations.

Once reviewed, everything returns to what it was since the constant reality of a past event on a physical world remains the same from the perspective of the soul who took part in the original event.

As the dialogue progresses in my next case, it will be obvious that an unseen entity is re-creating a past life scene, but with alterations. These adjustments are intended to elicit empathy and teach the soul in case 30. This case is an example of what some of my clients mean when they talk about entering worlds of altered time and causality through screens found in books, desk consoles and viewing theaters. Although these spacetime training exercises do not change the course of the original historical event on Earth, there may be other forces at work here.

I concede the possibility that my subject's memories could demonstrate that they are moving through parallel universes which might nearly duplicate our own spacetime. Yet in spiritual classrooms and libraries they do not see past events on Earth as being outside the reality of our universe. I do have the feeling that what a soul from Earth is able to see and explain to me is regulated by the resonances of their personal guides. When they reach the life selection room, with larger, theater-type screens to look solely at the future, their perspective about a constant reality changes more to a fluctuating reality.

Events on any screen can be moved forward or backward. They can be placed into fast or slow motion or suspended for study. All possibilities of occurrences involving the viewer are then available for study, as if they were using a movie projector. One can sense from case 30 that a past event on our physical world has not been indelibly changed for this individual even though his soul is existing in the eternal *now* time of the spirit world. Some would call these projections "no time" for souls, because the past can be blended with future possibilities in the next life from an always-present spirit time.

Case 30

This case involves a soul called Unthur, who has just completed a life of aggressive behavior toward other people. His mentors decided to begin Unthur's life review in the library with a scene from his childhood in a play yard.

Dr. N: When you return to the spirit world, Unthur, is there some highlight of your past life review that you particularly remember and would like to tell me about?

S: After I have time to visit with my group for a while my guide, Fotanious, escorts me to the library for some private study while my past life is still very fresh.

Dr. N: Is this the only time you will come here?

S: Oh, no. We often come here by ourselves to study. It is also a way to prepare for the next life too. I will study vocations and avocations for the new life in light of my objectives, to see if they fit.

Dr. N: All right, let's move into the library. Please describe everything you see in the order that you see it.

S: The room is in a large, rectangular building. Everything is a glowing, transparent white. The walls are lined with big thick books.

Dr. N: Has Fotanious brought you here?

S: Just in the beginning. Now I am with a woman with pure white hair who has met me. Her face is very reassuring. The first thing I notice when I enter are the long rows of tables that stretch off so far into the distance I can't see where they end. I see many people sitting at the long tables looking at the books in front of them. The people studying are not too close to one another.

Dr. N: Why is that?

S: Oh . . . not facing each other is a matter of courtesy and respect for privacy.

Dr. N: Please go on.

S: My librarian looks so scholarly . . . we call these people the Scholastics. (to others they are Archivists) She moves to a nearby wall section and pulls down a book. I know these are my records. (in a faraway voice) They contain stories which have been told and those that are untold.

Dr. N: (with some levity) Do you have your library card?

S: (laughs) No cards are required—just mental attunement.

Dr. N: Do you have more than one Life Book assigned to you?

S: Yes, and this is the one I will use today. The books are stacked in order on the shelves. I know where mine are and they glow when I look at them from a distance.

Dr. N: Could you go into the stacks yourself?

S: Mmm . . . no . . . but I think the older ones do.

Dr. N: So at this moment the librarian has brought you the book you are supposed to study?

S: Yes, there are large pedestals positioned near the tables. The Scholastic opens the page where I am to begin.

Note: We are now at the stage when each case takes on a unique quality of personal engagement with the Life Book screens. The conscious mind may or may not be able to translate into human language what the superconscious mind fully sees in the library.

Dr. N: Then she is getting you started at the pedestal before you take this book to a table by yourself?

S: Yes . . . I am looking at a page with . . . writing . . . gold lettering . . .

Dr. N: Can you read this writing for me?

S: No . . . I can't translate it now . . . but it identifies that it is my book.

Dr. N: Can't you make out even one word? Look closely.

S: (pause) I . . . see the Greek pi symbol (Π).

Dr. N: Is this symbolic of a letter in the Greek alphabet or does it have a mathematical significance for you?

S: I think it has to do with ratios, how one thing relates to another to me. The writing is a language of motion and emotion. You feel the writing as . . . musical vibrations. These symbols represent the causes and effects of a set of proportional relationships between similar and dissimilar circumstances in my lives. There is more, but I can't . . . (stops)

Dr. N: Thank you for that. Now, tell me—what you are going to do with this book?

S: Before I carry it down to an empty space at one of the tables, we are going to do an exercise together. The writing symbols tell us where to turn the pages . . . but I can't tell you how . . . I don't know how to explain it.

Dr. N: Don't worry about that. You are doing a fine job with explanations. Just tell me how the librarian helps you.

S: (takes a deep breath) We turn to a page which shows me as a child playing in my schoolyard. (subject now begins to shake) This . . . isn't going to be fun . . . I'm directed to the time when I was a mean, rotten kid . . . I am supposed to experience this again . . . something they want me to see . . . a part of my energy . . . crawls into the page itself . . .

Dr. N: (encouraging) All right, let the scene unfold and tell me all you can.

S: (squirming in his chair) After I . . . crawl into the book . . . I am totally engaged with the scene in every respect as if it was being replayed all over again. I'm . . . in grade school. I am a tough kid who picks on the smaller, less aggressive boys . . . punching them and throwing rocks at everybody when the schoolyard monitors aren't looking. And then . . . OH, NO!

Dr. N: What's happening?

S: (alarmed) Oh . . . for God's sake! Now, I am the smallest kid in the yard and I'm being punched BY ME! This is incredible. After a while I am me again, being pelted by rocks from everyone else. OW, THIS REALLY HURTS!

Dr. N: (after quieting the subject down and moving him totally back into the library) Were you in the same time frame as you were as a child or in a form of altered reality?

S: (pause) In the same time, with altered reality. None of this happened in my early life, but it should have. So the time has been played back to me in a different way. We can relive an event to see if we can get it better. I felt the pain I inflicted upon others by my bullying.

Dr. N: Unthur, what have you learned from all this?

S: (long pause) That I was an angry kid driven by fear of my dad. Those are the scenes I am going to do next. I am working on compassion and learning to control my rebellious nature as a soul.

Dr. N: What is the significance of your Life Book and being in this whole library atmosphere?

S: By studying my book I am able to recognize mistakes and experience alternatives. Being in this quiet study area—watching all the other souls at the tables doing the same thing—well, it gives me a feeling of camaraderie with them and all we are going through together.

Later in our session we discovered that Unthur needed self-discipline and to be more considerate of people. This had been a pattern of conduct over many lives. When I asked if it was possible to study future lives in the library I received this answer. "Yes, we can scan a variety of possibilities here on the timelines, but future events are very indeterminate and this is not the space where I would make any decisions about what is to come."

When I hear statements such as this I do think of parallel universes where all possibilities and probabilities can be examined. In this scenario, the same event could occur from a slight to radically altered range on the same timeline in multiple spaces and you would exist in many universes simultaneously. Yet, the Source of all spacetime might well employ alternate realities without parallel universes. In later chapters, I will cite reports of multiple universes around us which are not duplicates of our universe. In the spirit world, souls watching the orchestrated screens seem to move from past to present to future and back simultaneously in the same space.

When souls are in the library, I'm told certain event sequences of the future may look shadowy on some lines and almost disappear. On the other hand, in the classrooms with larger screens, and especially in the place of life selection, which has huge panel screens, the timelines are bolder. This allows for easier scanning and entry by the soul for future life study. Newer souls must acquire these skills by learning to blend their light waves with the lines on the screens. By concentrating their essence in this way, images come into focus that pertain to them. The timelines on the screens move back and forth, crossing one another as resonating waves of probability and possibility from the *now* time of the spirit world where past and future are joined and all is knowable.

Cases 29 and 30, as with all my cases, raise the question of what true reality is. Are classrooms and the library with viewing screens of past and future time *real*? Everything I know about our life after death is based upon the observations of people. The observer communicates to me in trance from their soul mind through the brain. It is the observer who defines the properties of matter and ethereal substance both on Earth and in the spirit world.

Consider the last case. Unthur told me he cannot change his past by a second-time-around visitation. Yet after death he returned to the playground of his childhood as an active participant. Once again he was a boy playing with other children with all the sights, sounds, smells and feelings connected to that event. Some of my clients say these are simulated events, but are they? Unthur became part of the scene where he bullied children and then was attacked by them. He could feel the hurt and squirmed in my office chair from pain he had not received in the timeline of this boyhood. Who is to say an altered reality does not simultaneously exist for all events, where both origins and outcomes are interchangeable? The observer soul may work with many realities at a time in the spirit world while studying. All are placed in the soul's path to teach.

We question whether our universe is all an illusion. If eternal thoughts of the soul are represented by intelligent light energy that is timeless and formless, it is not restricted by matter in our universe. Thus, if a cosmic consciousness controls what the observer mind sees on Earth, the whole concept of cause and effect within given time intervals is a manipulated illusion designed to train us. Even if we believe that everything we think is real is an illusion, life is anything but meaningless. We know if we hold a rock in our hand it is as real to us as an observer-participant in a physical world. We must also keep in mind that a divine intelligence placed us in this environment to learn and grow for a greater good. None of us are here by accident and neither are those events which affect us in our own reality at this moment in time.

Colors of Spirits

The Mixture of Colors in Soul Groups

When people in trance mentally leave the spaces of energy rejuvenation, orientation and the library to engage actively with other souls, their contrasting colors become more evident. One aspect of understanding the dynamics of cluster groups is the identification of each soul by color. In *Journey of Souls*, I described my findings about the energy colors of souls. What I want to do in this section is to try to correct some misconceptions people have regarding color recognition. During the course of my explanations, it might be helpful for readers who have my first book to compare figure 3 in *Journey of Souls* with figure 6 in this section.

In figure 6, I have charted the full spectrum range of core colors that identify the level of soul development as seen by subjects in deep hypnosis. More importantly, I have attempted to indicate the subtle overlaps and mixes of energy colors within these levels. The basic core colors of white, yellow and blue generated by souls are the major markers of their growing development. As their light waves take on deeper hues from light to dark during advancement, they become less scattered and have greater focus in their vibrational motion. The transition is slow and there is much spilling over of color tints as souls develop. Because of this it is restrictive to lay down hard definitive rules about color transmission.

Referring to figure 6, box 1, we see the pure white tones reflected in beginner souls. It is a mark of innocence and yet this color can be seen throughout the spectrum for all souls. The universal color of white will be explained further in the next case. White is often associated with the halo effect. Guides, for instance, may suddenly charge up their normally intense, steady light and surround themselves with a brilliant white halo. Souls returning to the spirit world often tell me that when they notice any soul coming toward them from a distance, they see white light.

Souls whose core level of development are in boxes 1, 5, 9, and 11 are usually seen with no overlapping of other color tints in the center of their energy mass. I don't see many clients exclusively displaying the colors shown in box 7. This may indicate we need more healers on

Figure 6: Color Spectrum of Spiritual Auras

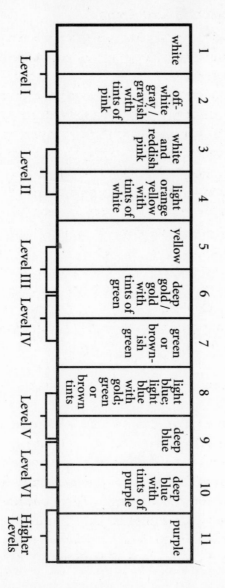

This classification chart indicates how a soul's primary core colors deepen from beginners in box 1 to ascended masters in box 11. Halo color overlaps of different hues may surround the primary core colors of a soul. There is also an overlapping of color aura between soul levels I to VI.

Earth. I have never had a subject whose energy is totally in the violet-purple range in box 11. The color ranges beyond level V are ascended masters who do not appear to be incarnating, so the little I know about them comes only from my subject's observations.

There are individual variables within each soul cluster group in terms of their basic core color because they are not all developing at the same rate. However, a soul's energy color may also be affected by another factor, which initially confused me. Besides the primary core colors indicating the stage of overall development, certain souls carry secondary colors. These have been called halo colors because they usually appear to the observer to be outside the core center of a soul's energy mass.

Halo colors are undiluted by tints or shades of other colors, as can be the case with central core colors. The only exception here would be if the halo and core color were exactly the same. Reports from my subjects in distinguishing colors are made easier because this overlaying effect is not often seen. The halo colors represent attitudes, beliefs, and even unattained aspirations of the soul. Because they are learned in each life, the halo tints may fluctuate more quickly between lives than the core colors, which display a slower development of character. During a hypnosis session, these secondary halo colors are like flashing self-portraits the moment the observer sees them. Case 31, a highly advanced level V, will describe this effect. This individual was among a group of clients who helped me decipher the color coding of halos.

Case 31

Dr. N: If I were standing in front of you in the spirit world holding up a full-length mirror, what colors would we see?

S: You would see a light blue center with goldish white at the edges of my energy—my halo.

Dr. N: And when you look at your master teacher, what does his energy look like?

S: Clandour has . . . a dark blue center . . . working outward to a pale violet . . . crowned with an edge halo of white.

Dr. N: What do "core energy" and "halo energy" mean to you?

S: Clandour radiates the solid state of his learning experience at the center of his energy while the violet trim is his advancing wisdom from that knowledge. The white transmits that wisdom.

Dr. N: Eventually, what do you think Clandour's core center will be and how will it appear?

S: The deep violet of divine spirituality radiating from all positions in his energy mass.

Dr. N: Can you define the difference between core and halo color variations in soul energy?

S: The central core represents accomplishment.

Dr. N: Such as the light blue in your own energy—this would be your present learning attainment?

S: Yes.

Dr. N: And the edges—the halos—your own goldish white, what can you say about that?

S: (pause) Ah . . . my attributes . . . well, I have always tried to watch out for other people in my lives—this is who I am—but it is also what I wish to become . . . rather, I should say, I want to strive to grow stronger in this aspect.

Dr. N: You are not a beginner soul and yet you display some white in your energy. I'm curious about this bright white halo ring around so many souls with other colors to their energy.

S: The vibrancy of white energy indicates we are able to meld our vibrations easily with all others (souls) for clear communication.

Dr. N: I suppose this is why teacher-guides often display bright white halos, but how does this white differ from the solid white light of a young soul?

S: White represents the energy color base for all souls. It is the shading of white with other color mixtures which identify each soul. White is very receptive energy. The newer ones are receiving vibrations in great quantities while teachers are sending information in large amounts to be absorbed as uncluttered truths.

Dr. N: And the beginner soul has had so little experience you don't visualize any other colors except white?

S: That's correct, they are undeveloped.

Although there is much I don't know about the entire matrix of soul energy color, I have learned that changes in color cores become much less evident after level IV. Over many years of research, I have kept a record of what people have told me about these secondary halo colors. The major colors each have their own range of attributes. Over 90 percent of my subjects agree on the qualities these colors represent in a soul. I have condensed what I have learned into three of the most commonly reported character traits for each color without regard to shade variations. Black is either tainted, damaged, or defiled negative soul energy which is generally seen in the soul restoration centers.

White: Purity, Clarity, Restlessness.

Silver: Ethereal, Trust, Flexibility.

Red: Passion, Intensity, Sensitivity.

Orange: Exuberant, Impulsive, Openness.

Yellow: Protective, Strength, Courage.

Green: Healing, Nurturing, Compassion.

Brown: Grounded, Tolerant, Industrious.

Blue: Knowledge, Forgiveness, Revelation.

Purple: Wisdom, Truth, Divinity.

In the next chapter there will be other spiritual references to the significance of colors. This pertains to the colored garments council members wear as perceived by the souls who come before them. In addition, I will show how the designs of certain emblems worn by these Elders, some of which are gemstones, convey certain meanings through color.

Figure 7 is a representation of a level II soul group displaying both core and halo colors. I have deliberately avoided charting a case where the same core color of development also appears as a halo color. To avoid confusion, figure 7 shows no white, yellow, or solid blue halos. There are twelve members of this primary soul group, including my subject, a level II male. The diagram indicates relationships of family members in their current incarnation. A more typical primary soul group would not all incarnate in one family.

Under hypnosis, this subject (3B) is looking at the eleven souls in his primary group who are members of his current family in this life plus a best friend. His sister has a core color that is almost solid yellow because she is moving into level III. If she also had a strong protective side to her of yellow, instead of the blue (knowledge) that she actually has, it would have been harder for my subject to report that fact based on color alone because her halo and core color would have been nearly the same.

Besides his sister, other aspects of figure 7 indicate that the subject's grandparents and son are slightly more advanced than other members, while his father and aunt are slightly less so. The grandfather and mother of this family are healers. Note that almost half the group have no secondary halo colors. It is not at all unusual for me to encounter groups with none. My subject's bright red halo over an energy core mass of white and reddish pink confirmed his fiery, intense nature. His son in this life has similar behavioral traits. His wife is more contemplative, with an open, trustful nature. His daughter is nonjudgmental and very spiritual. When I asked this subject to give me his thoughts about the red in his energy, here is what he had to say:

> Because of my intense nature I have a problem with anger in my lives. I often choose bodies which are highstrung emotionally because they match my character. I don't like passive bodies. My guide doesn't mind these choices because she says I will learn to control myself by relaxing the brain of these bodies. This sort of control is hard because of my own impulsive reactions and passion in difficult situations. It has taken many centuries of past lives, but I am getting better at self-discipline. In the past I have too easily entered into aggression and now this is slowly changing. I also have the help of my soulmate (current wife).

Figure 7: Energy Colors Displayed by a Soul Group

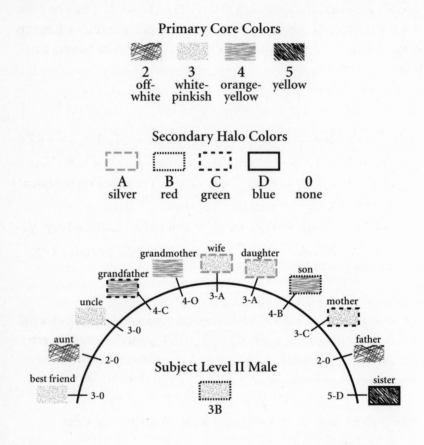

This chart indicates the currently incarnated relatives and one friend of subject 3B. The boxes for each relative are keyed to figure 6 for both core and halo colors. Numbered boxes 2, 3, 4, and 5 are primary core colors. Lettered boxes A, B, C, and D are secondary halo colors displayed by group members.

It sometimes happens that I will encounter souls who are anomalies in the way their development progresses. This becomes evident to me when clients describe souls in their groups with core colors that seem out of place. A prime example is the white lights of younger souls. The following case involves a group of level III to IV souls. I had just finished reviewing all the yellow-blue members of this group when this subject disclosed there was a soul who was mostly white standing next to her.

Case 32

Dr. N: What is a white light doing in your group of advanced souls?

S: Lavani is in training with us because of her gifts. It was decided that although she is young, without much experience, she should not be held back.

Dr. N: Isn't Lavani rather lost in your group? How can she keep up?

S: She is being tested right now and, to be honest, Lavani is a little overwhelmed.

Dr. N: Why was she assigned to your group?

S: Our group is rather unusual because we have a high tolerance for working with inexperienced souls. Most groups of our type are so busy they would probably ignore her. I'm not saying they would be unkind, but after all she is still a child and looks to us like a child with her small, wispy energy patterns.

Dr. N: I suppose most advanced groups would not want this responsibility?

S: Quite right. Developing groups are very absorbed with their own work. To a child, they can appear almost disdainful.

Dr. N: Then explain to me why Lavani's guide permitted her to come over here with your people.

S: Lavani has great talent. We are a group of quick learners and our lives have been immensely difficult and fast paced. (my subject has only spent 1,600 years on Earth) Despite our rapid advancement we have a reputation for being very modest, some say overly so. We are studying to be teachers of children and Lavani is good for us, too.

Dr. N: I am very puzzled by this. Has Lavani been cut off from association with her own group at this early stage of her existence?

S: Oh my, no! Where did you get that idea? She is with her own group most of the time (laughs) and they do not know about her adventures with us. It is better that way.

Dr. N: Why?

S: Oh, they might tease her and ask too many questions. She is very attached to them and we want Lavani to have a normal association with her own friends even though we know she will be moving out of her group early because of her gifts. They are not yet motivated by the same desire.

Dr. N: Well, if souls are telepathic and know everything about each other, I don't see how Lavani could hide all this from her friends.

S: It is true the whites are not able to set up blocks as we do about certain private things. Lavani has been taught to do this, I told you she had potential. (pause, and then adds) Of course, everyone respects the private thoughts of others.

It is not uncommon to find that when souls such as case 32 do incarnate, the younger souls they are working with ask to be their children in life. Lavani is the child of this subject today. The reverse may also be true where it is the child who is the advanced soul living with a parent having the younger soul.

There are instances when I hear about a soul whose color is described as being in retrograde. Most of us in our existence have slipped backward after some lives, but when our color regresses to any great extent it is due to a condition that is both serious and prolonged. Here is a statement from one client which carries a poignant message for all of us:

> It's a shame about Klaris. His green used to be so brilliant. He was a great healer who became corrupted by power. For Klaris things were almost too easy—he was so

talented. His downhill slide happened over a number of lives involving many abuses. He loved the veneration and adulation so much, his vanity became a disguise from himself. Klaris began losing his gifts and we noticed his color fading and growing more muted. Finally, Klaris became so ineffective he was sent down for retraining. We all expect he will eventually come back.

Colors of Visitors in Groups

Once in a while I hear that a color presentation from one or two souls in a group appears to be out of place with everybody else. I have learned this may signify temporary visits by a highly specialized guest or a soul from a nearby group. Once in a while, I hear about a visitation by an interdimensional traveler whose experience far exceeds that of the group. I have a condensed quote from an interesting report about such visitors:

> When we look at advanced beings who come to visit our group through other dimensions that are not familiar to us, it is like they have passed through a screen, which we call the Lens of Light, to reach us. They come once in a while at the invitation of our guide, Joshua, because they are friends of his. We see these souls as having the silver of flowing water as they pass in front of us. To us the silver stream is . . . a cloak of passage . . . the purity of a translucent interdimensional intelligence. They are elastic beings with the ability to pass through many physical and mental spheres and function well. They come to help push away the darkness of our ignorance, but these beautiful beings never stay long.

I should add that these colorful characters who briefly appear in soul groups have a profound effect. In the case above, when I asked my client to give a specific example of an insight gained from the teachings by these silvery beings I was told, "They widen our vision to see more probabilities in making choices by becoming astute at reading people. This skill develops critical thinking and allows for informed decisions based upon larger truths."

Human versus Soul Color Auras

There is another misconception about color I have encountered since *Journey of Souls* was published. Many people seek to find comparisons between my color classifications with souls and that of human auras. I believe these assumptions can lead to the wrong conclusions. Color and energy vibrations are closely linked in souls and are reflective of the nonmaterial environment of the spirit world. Thus, in a physical environment the frequency of the same soul energy is altered. The human body changes the color of these energy patterns further.

When healers identify color auras around human beings, these colors are largely reflections of physical manifestations. Besides thoughts from a human brain, which are influenced by our emotional makeup, central nervous system and chemical balances, all the vital organs of the body are involved in human auras. Even muscles and skin play a part in creating the physical energy around us. Certainly, there are correlations between the soul mind and our bodies, but physical and mental health are the prime determinants in human auras.

I should state that I do not see human auras. All my information about them comes from specialists in this field and from my subjects. I am told that as we go through life our temporary body fluctuates rapidly and this affects the external color arrangements of our energy. It takes many centuries for soul colors to change. Eastern philosophy holds, and I agree, that we have a spirit body which exists in conjunction with the physical and that this etheric body has its own energy outline. True healing must take into account both the physical and subtle body. When we meditate or practice yoga we work to unblock our emotional and spiritual energy through various parts of the body.

On occasion, when I am talking to a subject in trance about the distribution of light energy from other souls in their group, I will be told about stronger energy patterns emanating from particular areas of what seems to be a human shape. Just as we may bring imprints from a former life into our current life, we can also take body imprints into the spirit world as silhouetted energy reminders of our physical incarnations. For a while, during my questioning in the next case, I wondered if this subject was letting her conscious memory about chakras seep into her unconscious explanations. Chakras are supposed to be vortex power sources that emanate from within us outward at seven major points on the human body. This subject felt that chakras were a spiritual expression of individuality through physical manifestations.

Case 33

Dr. N: You have said that Roy is one of the members of your family in this life who is in your soul group. When you look at Roy's focal point of energy, what do you see?

S: I see a concentration of pinkish-yellow coming from the middle of his body form—the place where the solar plexus would be.

Dr. N: What body form? Why is Roy presenting a physical body to your group?

S: We show the features of the bodies we have occupied that pleased us in life.

Dr. N: Well, what does an energy concentration from the stomach area mean to you?

S: Roy's strongest point of personal power in his lives is his gut, regardless of his body. He has nerves of steel. (laughs) He has other appetites in this area, too.

Dr. N: If Roy's metabolic energy rate shows that attribute, can you pinpoint a distribution of extra light energy coming from certain places of the body in other members of your group?

S: Yes, Larry has his greatest development from his head. He has been a creative thinker in many lives.

Dr. N: Anyone else?

S: Yes, Natalie. Her power essence is developing faster from the heart area because of her compassion.

Dr. N: How about yourself?

S: Mine comes from the throat, because of my communication skills through speech in some lives and singing in my current life.

Dr. N: Do these energy points have anything to do with the projection of human color auras?

S: As far as color, not generally. As far as strengths in energy concentration, yes.

Spiritual Meditation Using Color

The healing properties of multicolored lights for energy rebalancing in a recovery area were quoted in the last chapter from a soul called Banyon. People who have read my work about the spirit world have asked if this sort of information about color can be useful for physical healing. Spiritual meditation as a means of getting in touch with our inner self is of great benefit in healing the body. There are many good self-help books on the market which explain the various forms of meditation. Since color transmission is the expression of a soul's energy and that of our guides, perhaps I ought to cite one example of meditation using color.

The six-step meditative exercise I have chosen comes from a mixture of my own suggested visualizations and those of a courageous fifty-four-year-old woman I worked with whose weight dropped to sixty-nine pounds during her fight with ovarian cancer. She is now in remission after chemotherapy and the speed of her recovery baffled doctors.

A number of my clients generate a sense of spiritual empowerment by the use of meditation with colors. Those who have severe physical health problems tell me the best results come from meditating once a day for thirty minutes or twice a day for fifteen to twenty minutes. Please know I do not offer these steps of meditation as a cure for physical ailments. The power of each person's mind and their ability to concentrate is different, just as is the nature of their illness. Nevertheless, I do feel one's immune system can be boosted by connecting with our higher Self.

1. Begin by calming your mind. Forgive people for all the real and imagined wrongs that have hurt you. Spend five minutes cleansing, where you visualize all negative thought energy—including fears about your illness—as a black color. Think of a vacuum cleaner moving from the top of your head to the bottom of your feet, sucking up and pushing out of your body all the darkness from the pain and hurt of your disease.

2. Now, create a light blue halo above your head that represents your spirit guide, whom you call upon for help while sending out loving thoughts. Then spend another five minutes concentrating on your breathing while counting the breaths. Measure your breaths carefully while thinking comfort in and tightness out. You want to harmonize your breathing with the rhythm of the body.

3. At this point, start to think of your own higher consciousness as an expanding white-gold balloon to help protect your body. Say in your mind: "I want that part of me which is immortal to defend the mortal." Now begin your deepest concentration. You will pull the purity of white light from the balloon and send it as a power beam into your body organs. Since your white blood cells represent the strength of your immune system, visualize them as bubbles and move them around your body. Think of the white bubbles as attacking the black cancer cells and dissolving them with the power of light over darkness.

4. If you are receiving chemotherapy, support this treatment by sending out a lavender color as you would see from an infrared heat lamp to all parts of your body. This is the divine color of wisdom and spiritual power.

5. Now, send out the color green for healing these damaged cells from the effects of the cancer. You might blend this color with the blue of your spiritual guide intermittently during the most difficult periods. Pick your own shade and think of the green as a flowing liquid mending your insides.

6. Your last step is to once again create the blue halo of light around your head to sustain mental strength and courage over a weakened body. Expand it around the external parts of your body as a shield. Feel the healing power of this light of love both inside and outside. Think of yourself in a state of suspension and close by repeating a mantra such as "Heal, Heal, Heal."

Meditation as a daily discipline is hard work which pays big dividends. There is no right way to meditate. Each person must find a program which links their intellectual and emotional systems in a framework that suits their needs. Deep meditation brings us into a divine consciousness and a temporary release of the soul from personality. With this liberation one is able to transcend into a different nondimensional reality where everything in the focused mind is unified into a single whole.

The woman with ovarian cancer was able to help her doctors by bringing total mental concentration to bear on healing her body. When the mind is in a pure, centered state we can find who we really are—that essence we may have lost somewhere along the road of life. Daily meditation is also beneficial as a means of connecting with the presence of loving spirits.

Forms of Energy Color

Besides the effects of color, another external means of investigating souls in groups is to compare their shapes. These energy forms would include symmetry versus irregularity of shape, brightness or dimness of light configurations and the qualities of motion, all of which provide spiritual signatures of the group members. When observing other souls, many people in a trance state are aware of a soul's vibrational resonance. After I review the nuances of color tone with a client, together we will study the pulsation and vibrational rates of motion of their soul companions.

In discussing the energy form of any soul, my first question is, "How much energy was left behind in the spirit world before the current incarnation?" This question has much to do with the activity or passivity of the soul and relates to brightness and dimness of energy. Despite the amounts of energy, however, all manner of energy generation is identified by character, capacity and mood of the soul. These are variables that can change after a series of lives.

During my prehypnosis intake interview with a new client, I inquire about the cast of characters in their current life. I make notes about all their relatives, friends and past loves as well. This is because I will have a front-row seat in the play that is about to unfold from their minds and I want a theater program. My client will be the leading actor in this drama, with others in supporting roles.

In the case excerpt which follows, it can be seen how quickly information is gained through questions involving both color and form about a supporting cast member within a client's soul group. During my intake interview with Leslie, my client, I learned of her sister-in-law, named Rowena, who was a real thorn in her side. Leslie, whose spiritual name is Susius, described herself as someone who seeks security in her lives and tends to be around peaceful people. In her current life this subject remarked, "Rowena seems to enjoy confronting me and challenging all my convictions." What follows is the opening scene of Leslie's mental picture of her spirit group.

Case 34

S: (very upset) Oh, I don't believe it! Rowena is here—or rather it's Shath—that's Rowena.

Dr. N: What's wrong with seeing the soul of Rowena in your spirit group?

S: (frowning, with a tightening of the mouth) Well, Shath is one of the . . . disruptive ones . . .

Dr. N: Disruptive in what way?

S: Oh . . . compared to those of us who have smooth, unruffled energy vibrations.

Dr. N: Susius, as you observe your sister-in-law, how is she different in terms of color and shape?

S: (still verifying the recognition of Rowena) There she is, all right! Her orange energy is pulsating rapidly—the usual sharp, jagged edges—that's Shath. Sparks—that's what we call her.

Dr. N: Does the form she presents to you indicate she is as antagonistic to you here in this spiritual setting as in your current life?

S: (Leslie is now adjusting to Rowena's presence and her voice softens) No . . . actually she draws us out . . . she is good for our group . . . I can see that.

Dr. N: I want to consider how her projections are different from your own energy in color and form. What can you tell me about yourself in the spirit world?

S: Mine is soft white with rose variations . . . I am called Bells by my friends because they see my energy as fluid droplets of steady rainwater which give off an echo . . . of faint tinkling bells. Shath has a sharp clarity to her energy and I see tints of gold. Her energy is bright and very overpowering.

Dr. N: And what does all this mean to you and your group?

S: We just can't be complacent around Sparks. She is so restless—a swirl of constant motion—there are always questions from her and challenges about our performance. She enjoys taking parts in our lives which shake our complacency.

Dr. N: Do you think she is less abrasive in the spirit world than in her current body as Rowena?

S: (laughs) You bet. She chose a high-strung body with a short fuse, which amplifies everything. This time (current life) she came as my husband's sister. Shath can be so annoying but now that I see who she really is, I know her motives come from love and wanting the best we have to give. (laughs again) We help her to slow down, too, because she has a tendency to jump into fires without looking.

Dr. N: Is there anyone in your inner circle of friends whose energy is similar to Shath—to Rowena?

S: (grins) Yes, that would be my best friend Megan's husband, Roger. His name here is Siere.

Dr. N: How does his energy appear to you?

S: He sends out geometric, angular patterns that zigzag back and forth. They are sharp waves—like his tongue—and from a distance his energy reverberates like crashing cymbals in an orchestra. Siere is a daring, intrepid soul.

Dr. N: Based on what you have been telling me about energy shapes, could Shath and Siere—Rowena and Roger—have a compatible match-up in life?

S: (bursts out laughing) You must be joking! They would kill each other. No, Rowena's husband is Sen—my brother Bill—a peaceful soul.

Dr. N: Please describe his energy.

S: He has a grounded energy which is greenish-brown. You know Vines is around when you hear a gentle swishing.

Dr. N: Vines? I don't understand what that means.

S: In our group when you get a nickname, it sticks. Sen has vibrational waves which look like a vine . . . with the patterns forming braided strands—you know—as with long hair.

Dr. N: Does this energy pattern identify Sen—your brother Bill—in some way?

S: Sure. Complex but constant—very dependable. It reflects his ability to weave a variety of elements together in lovely harmony. Vines and Sparks blend beautifully because Rowena never lets Bill get too complacent and he gives her an anchor in life.

Dr. N: Before I go on, I have noticed that the spirit names you have given for your soul group all start with the letter S. Does that mean anything? I'm not sure I am even spelling them correctly.

S: Don't worry about that—it is the sound which gives off the intonations of their energy motion. That reflects who my friends really are.

Dr. N: Sound? So besides the color and form of your group's energy, their waves have sound linked to each of them as we might hear on Earth?

S: Well . . . sort of . . . with us, it's energy resonance we identify with Earth, although you could not hear these vibrations with a human ear.

Dr. N: Could we go back to your best friend, Megan? You mentioned her, but I don't know her vibrational pattern color.

S: (with a warm smile) Her wispy, pale yellow energy is like flickering sunlight on a field of grain . . . smooth, even and delicate.

Dr. N: And her character as a soul?

S: Absolute, unconditional compassion and love.

Before going further with the issue of sound and the similarity of some spiritual names, I should explain the karmic link between my client, Leslie, and her best friend in this life, Megan. To me it is an emotionally compelling story. During my intake with case 34, Leslie explained to me that she was a professional singer and that occasionally her throat and larynx were especially tender. I regarded this as simply an occupational hazard and thought no more about it until we reached the death scene in her past life. It was then necessary to deprogram a former body imprint directly related to Leslie's throat.

In their past life, Megan was Leslie's younger sister. As a young girl, Megan had been forced by her father to marry a wealthy, brutal, older man called Hogar, who beat and sexually abused her. After a short while, Leslie helped Megan escape from Hogar in order to run away with a young man who loved her (Roger). An enraged Hogar found Leslie that night and dragged her to a secluded place where he raped and beat her for hours to learn the whereabouts of her sister.

Leslie told Hogar nothing until he began to strangle her for information. She then bought her sister more time to get away safely by giving Hogar the wrong directions. Hogar strangled Leslie to death and rushed away, but he never found Megan again. Later in our session Leslie had this to say. "Singing in this life is an expression of love because my voice was silenced over love in the last life."

Sounds and Spiritual Names

We have seen how color, form, movement and sound are individual markers of souls in their groups. These four elements appear to be interrelated, although light energy, vibrational shapes and their wave movement, as well as the resonance of sound, are not uniform among soul group members. However, there are resemblances with these elements between certain souls, and sound can be the one most obvious to the spiritual regressionist.

There is a language to sound in the spirit world that goes beyond the systemization of spoken language. I am told laughing, humming, chanting and singing exist, as do the sounds of wind and rain, but they are indescribable. Some subjects pronounce the names of souls within their group as if they were balancing musical chords in order to harmonize them with each other. Case 34 is an example of how the pronunciation of spiritual names within an inner circle of friends has an affinity of sound with the letter S. In case 28, two spiritual teachers were called Bion and Relon. There seems to be rhythmic interplay between certain soul energies in a cluster group manifested in this way.

Some hypnosis subjects have difficulty in producing spiritual names. These subjects say the names of souls in their minds consist of a vibrational resonance which is impossible to translate. It gets more complicated. One client stated, "In my experience, our real soul names are something similar to emotions, but they are not the emotions of humans so I can't reproduce our names by any sound." There is also vocal symbolism connected to names, which may have hidden meanings that a client is unable to decipher in human form.

Nevertheless, for many clients who are struggling to remember a spiritual name, the use of phonics and a cadence of sound may serve them well. A subject might use vowel sounds to characterize members of their cluster group. I had a client who named three souls in his group as Qi, Lo and Su. It is not at all uncommon for me to have cases, such as the last one, where group names emphasize one letter of the alphabet. For some reason, many spiritual guides have an A ending to their names.

I do have subjects in trance who find it easier to spell spiritual names for me rather than try to pronounce them. Yet these same clients will state that the spelling doesn't mean as much to them as the sound. My probes of spiritual names can also elicit shortened versions of the actual name. One client said, "In my spirit group, the nickname for our guide is Ned." Not satisfied with this, I persisted and eventually had this guide's full name down on paper. The result was Needaazzbaarriann. I got the message. During the rest of this session we stayed with Ned.

Privacy is also a factor when I have a client who feels that giving me the name of the spirit guide would somehow compromise that relationship. I must respect their concerns and be patient. As the session progresses this uneasiness might wear off. For instance, a client told me her guide was called Mary. Then she added, "Mary is letting me call her by that name in front of you." I accepted this and we continued on for a while when, abruptly, the guide's name became Mazukia. There are moments in a regression when it is not appropriate to push too hard for information.

Finally, I should report that our own soul names can change a little as we evolve. I had one highly advanced subject tell me her name as a young soul was Vina, which had now changed to Kavina. I asked why, and Kavina replied that she was now a disciple of a senior guide called Karafina. When I inquired as to the significance of the similar phrasing of these names in the spirit world, I was told it was none of my concern. There are clients who have no reticence in closing down questions in a hurry if they feel I have stepped over the line of privacy.

Soul Study Groups

In my first book, I devoted whole chapters to examining beginner, intermediate and advanced groups of souls and their guides. I also gave case examples of group energy training where souls learn to create and shape physical matter such as rocks, soil, plants and lower life forms. It is not my intention to repeat myself on these topics except when, by doing so, I can further the reader's knowledge of other aspects of life in soul collectives.

In this section I am going to examine the relationships between learners within soul study groups as opposed to the structural aspects of schoolhouses and classrooms reviewed earlier in this chapter. Spiritual learning centers are not necessarily visualized by my clients as having a classroom or library atmosphere. Quite often these centers are described as simply "the space of our home." Even so, the pictures of spiritual learning environments can change rapidly in the minds of clients discussing their instruction periods.

When my research into our life between lives was published, some people were critical of my analogies of human schoolhouses and classrooms as spiritual models for the instruction of souls. One Colorado couple wrote me to say, "We find your references to schools in the afterlife to be distasteful, and this is probably due to your own bias as a former educator." Others have told me that for them, schools were a long series of bad experiences with bureaucracy, authoritarianism and personal humiliation at the hands of other students. They did not want to see anything resembling human classrooms on the other side.

I know there are readers who have had bitter memories of the time they spent in school. Sadly, schools on Earth, as with other institutions, contain shortcomings wrought by human beings. Teachers and students can be guilty of arrogance, petty tyranny and indifference to the sensitivities of others. Wherever learning takes place, there is scrutiny. Nevertheless, many of us remember having caring teachers who gave us essential information while we formed lifelong friendships with fellow students as well.

The functional aspects of acquiring spiritual knowledge are translated by the human mind into learning centers and I am sure our guides have a hand in creating visualizations of earthly edifices for souls who come to our planet. People in hypnosis talk about the similarities of form and structure to Earth in some respects but there are great differences in other aspects of their reports. My clients tell me about the overwhelming kindness, benevolence and infinite patience of everyone in ethereal study areas. Even the analysis of each soul's performance by fellow students is conducted with total love, respect and a mutual commitment to make things better in the next incarnation.

Soul groups appreciate individualism. It is expected that you will stand out and make contributions. There are forceful souls and quiet souls but no one dominates, just as no one is obtrusive. Individualism is appreciated because each soul is unique, with strengths and weaknesses that complement others in the group. We are assigned to certain soul groups for our differences as well as similarities. These differences in character are honored because souls who share their lives bring a rich personal wisdom to every lifetime experience.

Souls love to tease and use humor in their groups but always they show respect for one another, even with those who have been in bodies that have hurt them in life. More than forgiveness, souls exercise tolerance. They know that most negative personality traits connected to the ego of the body of the person who brought them sadness and heartache were buried when that body died. At the top of the discarded list of negative emotions are anger and fear. Souls volunteer both to teach and learn certain lessons and karmic plans may not always work out in the way they were intended, given the variables of earthly environments.

I remember after one of my lectures, a psychiatrist raised his hand and said, "Your discussion about soul groups reminds me of tribalism." I responded that soul groups do appear to be tribal in their intense loyalty and mutual support for each other in a spiritual community. However, soul groups are not tribal in their relationships toward other groups. Earth societies have a nasty habit of mistrusting one another at best and demonstrating bitterness and cruelty at worst. Societies in the spirit world are inclined to be rigorous, moderate, or compliant in their interpersonal relationships but I see no evidence of discrimination or alienation either within or between soul groups. Unlike human beings, all spiritual beings are bonded together. At the same time, souls strictly observe the sanctity of other groups.

When I was a part-time evening college teacher, I found that some of my students, including the adults in my classes, would confuse facts with their own value patterns. While struggling with conceptual problems, there were times when they argued from a false premise and even contradicted themselves. This, after all, is the nature of students. Eventually, they learned to extrapolate and synthesize ideas more effectively. From this background, my introduction to instruction in the spirit world gave me perspective.

During the early years of my hypnosis research, I was astounded by the total lack of self-deception in spiritual classrooms. I saw that teacher-guides seemed to be present everywhere, although not always in a manifested form. Our teachers come and go in spiritual study sessions but never interfere with self-discovery. Although souls themselves are not yet omniscient, by having infinite knowledge of all things, they have no doubts about karmic lessons and the part they played in past life events. An axiom of the spirit world is that souls are always hardest on themselves in terms of performance.

Within soul study groups there is a wondrous clarity of rational thought. Self-delusion does not exist but I must say that the motivation to work hard in every life is not uniform among all souls. I have had clients tell me, "I'm going to skate for a while." This can mean slowing down their rate of incarnations, picking easy incarnations, or both. Although the soul's teachers and council may not be happy with this decision, it is respected. Even within the spirit world, some students choose not to give their best at all times. I believe they are a distinct minority of earthbound souls.

To the Greeks the word "persona" was synonymous with "mask." This is an appropriate term for the way in which the soul utilizes a host body for any life. When we reincarnate into a new body, the soul's character is united with the temperament of its host to form one persona. The body is the outward manifestation of the soul but it is not the total embodiment of our soul Self. Souls who come to Earth think of themselves as becoming masked actors on a world stage. In Shakespeare's *Macbeth*, the king prepares for death by telling us, "Life's but a walking shadow, a poor player that struts and frets his hour upon the stage and then is heard no more." In some ways this famous line describes how souls feel about their lives on Earth, the difference being that once the play has begun most of us don't know we are in a play until it's over, due to a variety of amnesiac blocks.

Thus the analogy of a play, like that of a schoolroom, befits what my clients see in a deep hypnotic trance state. I have had clients tell me that when they return to their soul groups after a particularly hard life there is clapping and shouts of "Bravo!" from their friends. The applause is for a job well done at the end of the last act of the play of life. One subject said, "In my group the major cast members of our last play in life will go off in a corner to study the individual scenes we played after it has ended and before rehearsals begin for the next play to come." I often hear my subjects laugh about being offered a certain part in the next play—which is their current life—and the debates that took place before final casting decisions were made as to who would play what part in the future.

Our guides become stage directors who go over past life scenes with us, frame by frame, of both good and bad times. Errors in judgment are presented in small bites. All possible outcomes are studied and compared by designing new scripts for these scenes with different sets of choices that could have been made in each circumstance. Behavioral patterns are minutely dissected with each player, followed by a review of all the roles in the script. Souls might then decide to switch roles with each other and replay key scenes all over again to test the results with a different actor from their group or by someone recruited from a

nearby group. I encourage my subjects to tell me about these role sub-
stitutions. Souls gain perspective from being witnesses to their own
past performance through other actors.

Re-creations of past life alternatives present a psychodrama I find
useful as a therapeutic tool in a soul's current life. These stage analogies
by soul groups do not trivialize what they go through on Earth as simple impersonations. They offer the soul an objective means of comprehension and foster a desire to improve. The system is ingenious. Souls
never seem to get bored in these educational exercises which invite creativity, originality and a desire to triumph over adversity by acquiring
wisdom from human relationships. Always, they want to do better next
time. Whatever the format, spaces of learning provide a fascinating
chessboard for souls when they go over all the possible moves for the
best solutions after the game is over. Indeed, some of my subjects call
the whole process of reincarnation "the Game."

The outcome of one's performance in the play may range from very
satisfactory to acceptable to unsatisfactory. I realize some readers might
conclude this sounds suspiciously like educational grading on Earth,
but this is not an idea of my origination. I'm told that in soul groups,
the evaluation of performance by our peers is not threatening; rather, it
encourages motivation. Most souls appear to me to be driven by a
desire to review the last game of life they have played in order to better
preview the next one. Like champion athletes, they want to try and
improve with each performance. Ultimately, they know at a certain
level of development and proficiency this aspect of the game will end
with the closing of the play and their physical incarnations. This is the
goal of souls who come to Earth.

As I stated at the beginning of this section, instruction in learning
centers is not limited to reviewing past lives. Besides all the other activities, energy manipulation is a major part of training. The acquiring of
these skills takes many forms in classroom work. I have said before that
humor is a hallmark of the spirit world. The student in the next case
gives us a sense of the whimsical when she explains how one of her creation classes got a little out of hand:

Case 35

Dr. N: You have explained about how your group has gathered into an enclosure resembling a school classroom but I'm not sure what is going on here.

S: We have gathered for practice in creation training with our energy. My guide, Trinity, is standing at a chalkboard working on a drawing for us to study.

Dr. N: And what are you doing now?

S: Sitting at my desk with the others—watching Trinity.

Dr. N: Give me a picture of this. Are you lined up in a row with the others at a long desk, or what?

S: No, we have our individual desks—they have tops which open up.

Dr. N: Where are you sitting in relation to your friends?

S: I am off to the left. Ca-ell, the mischievous one (my subject's brother in her current life), is next to me. Jac (subject's current husband) is just in back of me.

Dr. N: What is the mood in this room right now?

S: Laid back—very relaxed—because this assignment is so easy it's almost boring, watching Trinity drawing.

Dr. N: Oh, really? What is Trinity drawing?

S: He is drawing . . . ah, how to make a mouse quickly . . . from different energy parts.

Dr. N: Are you going to break up into groups to combine your energy with others for this assignment?

S: (with a wave of her hand) Oh, no. We are way past that. We will be tested individually.

Dr. N: Please explain the test.

S: We are to rapidly visualize a mouse in our minds . . . as to the necessary energy parts to create a whole mouse. There is an order of progression with how energy should be arranged in any creation.

Dr. N: So the test is the proper steps in creating a mouse?

S: Mmm . . . yes . . . but . . . actually, this is a test of speed. The secret of efficiency in creation training is rapid conceptualization—knowing which part of the animal to start with first. Then you tackle the amount of energy to be applied.

Dr. N: This sounds difficult?

S: (with a big grin) It's easy. Trinity should have picked a more complex creature . . .

Dr. N: (doggedly) Well, it seems to me that Trinity knows what he is doing. I don't see . . . (cuts me off with gales of laughter and I ask what is going on)

S: Ca-ell has just winked at me and opened his desktop and I see a white mouse scurrying out.

Dr. N: Meaning he is getting ahead of the assignment?

S: Yes, and showing off.

Dr. N: Is Trinity aware of all this?

S: (still laughing) Of course, he misses nothing. He just stops and says, "All right, let's all do this quickly if you are so ready to begin."

Dr. N: Then what happens?

S: There are mice running all over the room. (giggles) I put larger than normal ears on mine just for fun to liven things up even more.

I will close this section with a more serious case example of group energy usage. It represents a type of lesson I have not reported on before. Case 36 involves an inner circle of three companions who wish to help a fourth member who has just incarnated on Earth. Unlike the higher level of soul capability in the previous case, these souls are part of a learning group that has recently entered level II.

Case 36

Dr. N: As your mind visualizes all the meaningful activities going on in your study group, please take me to a significant exercise and explain what you are doing.

S: (long pause) Oh . . . you want that . . . well, my two friends and I are doing our best to help Kliday with positive energy after he entered the body of a baby. We want this to work because soon we are all going to follow him into life.

Dr. N: Let's go slowly here. What exactly are the three of you doing at this moment?

S: (takes a deep breath) We are sitting together in a circle—our teacher is in back of us directing things. We are sending a united beam of energy down into the mind of Kliday's child. He has just arrived and well . . . uh . . . I don't want to violate confidences, but he is not having an easy time.

Dr. N: I see . . . well, perhaps talking about it might clarify things. Don't you think it would be all right to discuss what you are doing a little further?

S: I . . . I guess so . . . I don't see the harm . . .

Dr. N: (gently) Tell me what month after conception did Kliday join the baby?

S: In the fourth month. (pauses and then adds) But we started to help Kliday in his sixth month. It is such hard work to continue to the ninth month.

Dr. N: I can understand that—the necessary concentration and all. (pause) Tell me why Kliday needs help from the three of you.

S: We are trying to send him encouraging energy shaped in such a way to assist Kliday in making a better adjustment to the temperament of this child. When you join with a baby it should be like placing your hand into a glove which is the exact size for you and the child. Kliday's glove is not fitting well this time.

Dr. N: Does this knowledge come as a surprise to you and your teacher?

S: Ah . . . not really. You see, Kliday is a quiet soul—peaceful—and this baby has a restless, aggressive mind and . . . the mesh is difficult for Kliday, even though he knew what to expect.

Dr. N: Are you saying he wanted a certain kind of challenge before this baby was chosen?

S: Yes, he knew he needed to learn to cope with this sort of body because he has had trouble before with not being able to control aggression.

Dr. N: Is this child going to be a hostile person? Perhaps one with few inhibitions . . . emotional conflicts and so forth?

S: (laughs) You got it—that's my older brother.

Dr. N: In your current life, you mean?

S: Yes.

Dr. N: What roles will the other two souls you are working with at the moment assume in Kliday's life, besides yourself?

S: Zinene is his wife and Monts, his best friend.

Dr. N: Sounds like a good support team. Can you explain a bit more why Kliday needs this sort of type A personality in a body?

S: Well, Kliday is very thoughtful. He ponders a lot and is tentative. He doesn't jump into situations. It was felt this body would help him expand his capabilities and assist the child, too.

Dr. N: Was Kliday's last life a problem?

S: (shrugs) Problems, problems . . . the same sort of body . . . he was caught up in obsessions and addictions . . . little control. He abused Zinene too.

Dr. N: Then why—?

S: (breaking in) We really studied that last life . . . reviewing everything over and over . . . Kliday wanted another chance in the same kind of body. He asked Zinene if she would be his wife again and she agreed. (subject begins laughing)

Dr. N: What amuses you?

S: Only this time I'm going along as his younger brother to help keep him in line with a very strong body.

Dr. N: Let's finish with your current energy beam exercise. Explain how you and your two companions use your energy in helping Kliday.

S: (long pause) The alignments of Kliday's energy and that of the baby are scattered.

Dr. N: The baby has scattered emotional energy and Kliday is having trouble melding with that?

S: Yes.

Dr. N: Does this involve the patterns of electrical impulses from the brain, or what?

S: (pause) Yes, the thought processes . . . from nerve endings (stops and then continues) we are trying to help Kliday in tracking this.

Dr. N: Is the baby resisting Kliday as an intruder?

S: Ah, no . . . I don't think so . . . (laughs) but Kliday thinks he got another primitive brain in some respects.

Dr. N: Where in the baby's body is your combined energy beam going?

S: We are being directed to work up from the base of the skull, starting at the back of the neck.

Dr. N: (I bring client into the past tense) Were you successful in this exercise?

S: I think we did help Kliday, especially in the beginning. (laughs again) But my brother is still a headstrong person in this life.

Additional illustrations of soul group interaction will be cited in later chapters. In chapter 9, under the section describing the body-soul partnership, I will go into more detail about the physiological aspects of our struggle with the primitive side of the human mind mentioned in the last case. The next chapter is devoted to the higher spiritual assistance we receive as an adjunct to soul study groups. The psychological ramifications of future life choices actually start with our first orientation upon returning to the spirit world. Ideas involving past performance and future expectations are brought into sharper focus with a soul's first council meeting.

∼6

The Council of Elders

Human Fear of Judgment and Punishment

Not long after souls return to their spirit groups they are called before a gathering of wise beings. A step or two above our guides, these ascended masters are the most advanced identifiable entities my still-incarnating clients see in the spirit world. They give them different names such as the Old Ones, the Sacred Masters, the Venerables, and pragmatic titles like the Examiners or the Committee. The two most common names I hear to describe these highly evolved masters are council and Elders, so I use these designations to describe this body.

Because the Council of Elders does represent authority in the spirit world, there are people at my lectures who immediately become suspicious when I talk about robed beings who wish to question souls about their past life performance. One man in Toronto couldn't contain himself and loudly proclaimed to everyone in the audience, "Ah ha, I knew it! A courtroom, judges, punishment!" Where does this fear and cynicism about the afterlife come from in the minds of so many people?

Religious institutions, civil courts and military tribunals give us codes of morality and justice which impact the conduct of millions. There is crime and punishment and cultural traditions of harsh judgment for human transgressions that have been with us since our tribal days. The positive effects of a code of behavior and ethics connected to all religions down through history have been enormous. It has been argued that fear of divine retribution is what keeps the masses at bay with better conduct than they would otherwise have. Nevertheless, I feel there is a downside to any religious doctrine that creates personal anguish over facing a harsh final authority and maleficent spirits after death.

Organized religions have only been with us within the last five thousand years. Anthropologists tell us that in the millennia before, primal people were naturists who believed all animate and inanimate things had good and bad spirits. In this respect, the old tribal practices were not so different from the idolatry of historical religions. Many gods of old were wrathful and unforgiving while others were benevolent and helpful. Human beings have always been uneasy about forces beyond their control, particularly with divinities who might rule their lives after death.

Since fears about survival have always been a part of our lives, it follows that human beings would find death to be the ultimate danger. Throughout our long history the brutality of life meant that judgment, punishment and suffering would likely continue in some way after death. Many cultures around the world have fostered these beliefs for their own purposes. People were led to believe that all souls, good and bad, would pass through a dark underworld of danger and trial right after death.

In the West, purgatory has long been pictured as a lonely way station for souls trapped between heaven and hell. In recent decades the non-evangelical churches have a more liberal definition of purgatory as a state of isolation for the purification of sins and imperfections before the soul can enter heaven. With Eastern philosophy, especially among the canons of Hinduism and the Mahayama Buddhist sects, there has been a long tradition of spiritual prisons of lower, defiled planes of existence, which is also being liberalized. This concept is another reason why I am against the use of concentric circle imagery of multiple astral planes as a map for describing soul travel after death. Historically, they were designed to show multi-purgatorial cells in an underworld of judges, courts and demons.

Seekers of truth who turn to the ancient metaphysical traditions of the East find a confusing mix of superstitions, just as with Western theology. While reincarnation has long been embraced by the East, there has been the retention of the doctrine of transmigration. In my travels through India, I found transmigration to be an intimidating concept which has been used to control behavior. Under this credo, a wide variety of sins are met with the very real possibility of the soul being transmigrated back to a lower subhuman form of life in its next cycle of existence. In my research, I have found no evidence to support transmigration of souls. My subjects indicate the soul energy of different forms of life on Earth do not appear to intermingle their energy in the spirit world. For me, the intimidation and fear transmigration engenders is a coercion of karmic justice. I have found the souls of humans on other worlds in prior incarnations to be in host bodies slightly more or less intelligent than our own species. I have never had a client assigned to another world where they were not the most dominant intelligence on that particular planet. This is by design.

Rather than stages of punishment, we go through stages of self-enlightenment. Yet large segments of human society are unable to shake off the nagging feeling, built over thousands of years of cultural conditioning, that judgment and punishment must exist in some form in the afterlife as it does on Earth. Maybe it won't be a hell with torture by the forces of darkness, but it's something unpleasant. It is my hope that what I have to say in this chapter will bring comfort to people inclined to be fearful about the possibility of punishment after death. On the other hand, there will be those who feel accountability to a Council of Elders may not be all that comfortable either. The Epicureanists of this world—those devoted solely to uninhibited pleasure in life while paying little attention to the plight of others—might also not be happy with this chapter. Neither will the Iconoclasts, who are opposed to authority of any kind, moral or otherwise.

The spirit world is a place of order and the Council of Elders exemplifies justice. They are not the ultimate source of divine authority, but they appear to represent the last station of beings responsible for souls still incarnating on Earth. These wise beings have great compassion for human weakness and they demonstrate infinite patience with our faults. We will be given many second chances in future lives. They won't be lives of easy karmic choices, otherwise we would learn nothing by coming to Earth. However, the risks of life and sanity on this planet are not designed to cause us any further pain after death.

The Setting for Soul Evaluation

My subjects state they appear before their council right after an incarnation and many report they will visit them a second time just before rebirth. Of the two assemblages, the first seems to have the most impact on the soul. During this meeting, the major choices we made in the life just lived are reviewed with us. Behavior and accountability for our actions at important forks in our karmic path are evaluated carefully. At the first conference we are acutely aware of our mistakes, especially if we have hurt others. If there is to be a second visit as the time draws close for reincarnation, it is more relaxed with discussions centering around potential life choices, opportunities and expectations for the future.

Our guides notify us when it is time to go before the council and usually they will escort us to the chambers of these ascended masters. To the average client, guides don't appear to play a large role at these hearings. However, when a more advanced soul tells me they go to this meeting alone, it is not unusual for them to see their guide sitting on the council while they are there. When our guides do appear with us in front of the council, they are rather quiet. This is because behind-the-scene discussions about our last life have already taken place between guides and council members.

As our primary teacher and advocate, guides may want to interject a thought for our clarification, or interpret some concept for us if they think we are confused at any point during the proceedings. It is my feeling that guides do far more at these hearings than many of my clients realize.

The descriptions about the form and procedure of council meetings are very consistent among all hypnosis subjects. When I begin this part of a client's session, my usual approach is to ask them what happens when the time arrives to go before a group of wise beings. Here is an example of a typical response:

> The time of my expectation has arrived. I am to see the Holy Ones. My guide, Linil, comes and escorts me from my cluster group down a long corridor past other classrooms. We move into another area with a larger hallway that is lined with marble columns. The walls are textured with what looks to be frosted glass panels of many colors. I hear soft choir music and string instruments. The light is a subdued, golden tone. Everything is so relaxing, even sensual, but I am a little apprehensive. We come to an atrium filled with beautiful plants and a bubbling fountain of water. This is the waiting area. After a few moments, Linil takes me into a round room with a high domed ceiling. There are rays of light shining down. The Holy Ones are seated at a long crescent-shaped table. I move to the center of the room in front of the table while Linil stands behind me to my left.

When I first heard about the council meetings, I wondered why it was necessary for them to be seen in any sort of authoritarian setting. Why not a simple countryside scene, if they are so full of benevolence? While the younger souls told me that this setting "was right and proper for their examinations," the older souls explained that there was a major reason for a domed enclosure. With this design, a higher Presence effectively focuses its light energy on the entire proceedings from above. I will discuss the powerful impact of this Presence later in this chapter.

A great majority of my subjects visualize a dome design for the chamber of the Council of Elders, as shown in figure 8. They see the chamber structure as a manifestation of a holy place on Earth. This "celestial shell of compassion," as one client called his council chamber, is symbolic of temples, mosques, synagogues and churches. Figure 8 shows the central table (D), which is usually long in front and may curve around at the edges to accommodate larger numbers of Elders. Some clients report that they see this table on a slightly raised dais just

Figure 8: The Council Chamber

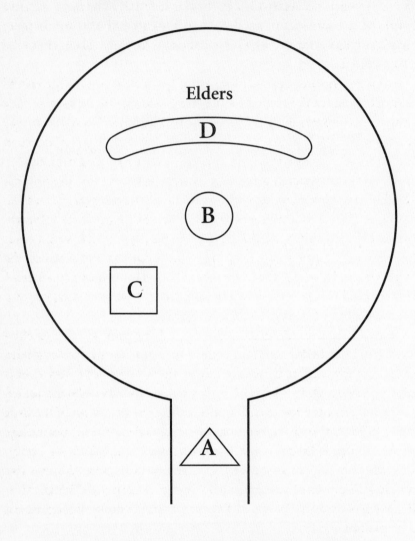

A typical structural design where Elders meet souls. This spacious room appears to most people as a large rotunda with a dome ceiling. Souls enter the chamber at the end of hallway (A), or from an alcove. The soul is positioned in the center (B), with their guide in back, usually on the left (C). The Elders generally sit at a long crescent-shaped table (D), in front of the soul. The table may appear to be rectangular.

above eye level. I have learned these nuances in setting relate to what the soul feels is necessary for a particular meeting to be most effective for them. If a soul sees its council in more of an authority mode, there might be reasons for this which I will then probe with a client about the life just lived.

Subjects who are regressed to the spirit world do not readily volunteer details about the scope of a specific inquiry from the Elders. They must feel comfortable that the hypnosis facilitator knows their way around a council chamber. On an unconscious level, this confidence in the spiritual regressionist seems to give them mental permission to speak about their sacred memories. This is the reason why my research into human memory of the spirit world took so many years. It was like fitting the pieces of a jigsaw puzzle together. Small pieces of information about the spirit world led to larger implications which would never have occurred to me to ask about in a whole context. For instance, the reason behind a raised dais in the council chamber was one small detail that expanded into a larger meaning. Another was the position of a client's guide, particularly at the first hearing.

As can be seen in figure 8, the position of the guide (C) in this illustration is on the left. For a long time I did not understand why guides were usually positioned behind and to the left of most of my clients being questioned. If the soul has two guides, occasionally the junior guide will enter the room and stand on the right side. Most of the time we have just our senior guide in attendance and only a low percentage of my subjects tell me this guide stands on the right. Whenever I asked why this was so, I received rather vague answers such as, "Oh, it is less restrictive" or "It is customary for our communication" or "We all stand in certain places out of respect." For a long time I simply stopped asking this question.

Then came the day when I was working with a very perceptive advanced subject who told me about the importance of distinguishing all council communication. I revived my question about guide position and received this answer.

Case 37

Dr. N: Why is your guide standing behind you on the left?

S: (laughs) Don't you know? With most human bodies the right side of the head is not as predominant as the left.

Dr. N: What does that have to do with his position?

S: The left side-right side thing . . . not in sync.

Dr. N: Are you talking about an imbalance between the left and right brain hemispheres in humans?

S: Yes, my problem—and that of many others recently returned from Earth—is a slight weakness of energy reception on our left side. It doesn't last too long.

Dr. N: And, as you stand in front of the council, you are still feeling the effects of your human body? You still have that physical imprint with you?

S: Yeah, that's what I am telling you. We don't shake off these effects by the time of our first council meeting. It seems like only a few hours since my death. It takes a while for us to get rid of the density of the physical body . . . the constrictions of it . . . before we are completely free. This is one reason why I don't need Jerome (guide) so much at the second meeting.

Dr. N: Because . . . ?

S: By then, we are sending and receiving telepathic communication more efficiently.

Dr. N: Please explain to me what Jerome actually does to help you by standing on your left side.

S: In most humans the left side is more rigid than the right. Jerome assists in the energy reception coming into my right side from the council by blocking thoughts which might escape out the left.

Dr. N: Are you saying your energy aura is like a sieve?

S: (laughs) Sometimes it seems like it—on the left. By serving as a blocking agent for thoughts which might escape he serves as a backboard, bouncing thought waves back into me for better retention. This assists in my comprehension.

Dr. N: Do you think he adds his own thoughts to this process?

S: Sure he does. He wants it all to penetrate and stay with me.

Subsequent questioning with other clients confirmed the backboard effect case 37 told me about. At the beginning of their incarnations, while souls are learning to utilize unique and complex circuit patterns, they find that most human brains are not balanced between the right and left hemispheres. I am told that no two host bodies are the same in the way our brain hemispheres are linked to process critical judgment, creativity and language communication. This is a primary reason why the wiser souls join the fetus of a new body early rather than late in a mother's term.

Past life regression therapists work with the physical body imprints of former lives that may be disabling to their client's current body. Typically, these people come to us after traditional medicine has not given them relief. For example, a physical problem may be referred discomfort from a violent past life death. Part of our job is to deprogram these carryovers whenever they become debilitating to the client.

In chapter 4, we saw how body imprints also affect souls who cross back into the spirit world with physical energy damage. I must say that before case 37 I never imagined a human body imprint could affect communication at council meetings. I was aware that during the course of these hearings, council members might communicate with each other in a rapid pitch of high and low vibrations. The average soul misses most of this sort of intercommunication between Elders. The scrambling effect here is apparently intentional. I think it is safe to conclude that any conversation at council meetings requiring interpretation is usually handled by our guides.

I have a rather unorthodox but effective procedure for a spiritual regressionist to use that relates to communication and the council. When I am working with a subject in front of their council, I frequently tell them to ask the Elders and attending guide if they know *my* spirit guide. The client usually answers in the affirmative, saying something to the effect that all masters know each other in the spirit world. I will then follow up with a question about why the client thinks these masters, their guide, and my guide conspired to bring them to my office on this particular day. The answers can be very revealing since my clients feel synchronicity is at work. Within this process of hypnosis methodology, more often than not a subject will remark, "You know, I see your guide suspended over your left shoulder helping you and laughing at your efforts to acquire more information about the spirit world than you need to know."

Souls who come before their respective councils have been debriefed during orientation sessions with their guides. However, it is in front of the council where souls feel most vulnerable about their past performance. The object of council meetings is not to demean the souls who come before them or to punish them for their shortcomings. The purpose of the Elders is to question the soul in order to help them achieve their goals in the next lifetime. Every soul has an awareness of the inquiry format for their life review, although they know that no two council visits will be the same. At the meetings for the younger souls, I have noticed both guides and council members are especially indulgent and solicitous. During my early research on council meetings, I learned that directed questioning by these spiritual masters toward my subjects was both firm and benevolent at the same time.

I'll admit that when I initially heard about these hearings there were doubts in my mind. I felt that if a soul was summoned to appear before a body of higher beings, there were going be certain punitive aspects to a karmic review. This was due to my own cultural conditioning. Finally, I came to the realization that going before a council has many facets. The Elders are like loving but firm parents, managing directors, encouraging teachers and behavioral counselors all rolled into one. What souls feel for their council is reverence. Actually, souls themselves are their own severest critics. I find evaluations by our soul group companions to be far more acerbic than any council Elder, although our peers do lace their criticism with humor.

During the time when souls are moving toward the space where their council is waiting, there are mixed reactions. I have had subjects say they are looking forward to seeing the Elders to get a higher perspective on their progress. Others are apprehensive, but this soon passes once the proceedings begin. The Elders have a way of making the souls who come before them feel welcome almost at once. One of the most obvious differences between a courtroom on Earth and a spiritual gathering of grandmasters is the fact that every one in the chamber is telepathic. Thus, all in attendance know the whole truth about every aspect of our conduct and the choices we made in the last life. Deception is impossible. There is no need for rules of evidence, defense attorneys or juries. So that they can properly plan for our future, the Elders want to make sure that we totally understand the consequences of our actions, particularly toward others.

The Elders ask us how we feel about major episodes in our life and our courses of action. Desirable actions and those that were counterproductive are discussed openly with us without acrimony or finger pointing. Regardless of the number of times we continue to make the same mistakes, our council has enormous patience with us. We have much less patience with ourselves. I believe if the councils of all the souls from Earth I have worked with were not so indulgent, the average soul would simply give up and not come back. Souls have this right of refusal to return to Earth.

The Elders probe for answers of how we think our host body served or hindered development. The council is already considering our next potential body and future environment. They wish to know how we feel about another incarnation. Many subjects have the sense that their council has not yet made up their minds about future lives for us. Nothing about this meeting appears to be rubber-stamped.

Our intent in life is of utmost importance at council meetings. The Elders know all about us before we appear, but during the deliberations how our soul mind interfaced with a human brain is carefully analyzed. They know our past record with other host bodies. This includes the control, or lack of it, we exercised over the baser natures and negative emotions of bodies on Earth. Compulsions, illusions and attachments are never offered as excuses by souls for their conduct. I am not saying souls don't complain about their difficulties in front of councils. However, rationalizations about life's trials are not substituted for brutal honesty.

The council is looking to see if the inner immortal character of our soul maintained its integrity in terms of values, ideals and action during incarnation. They want to know if we were submerged by our host body, or did we shine through? Did our soul effectively merge as a partner to the human brain as one harmonious outward human personality? Council members question souls about the use of power. Was our influence positive, or corrupted by the need to dominate others? Were we led by the convictions of others, demonstrating no personal power, or did we make original contributions? The council is not so concerned about how many times we fell down in our progress through life, but whether we had the courage to pick ourselves up and finish strong.

Appearance and Composition of the Council

The word Elder is considered appropriate by many clients because the advanced beings who sit on their councils are visualized as elderly men. They are frequently depicted as having bald heads, or white hair and perhaps beards. In questioning people about the gender of these beings, I have come to some conclusions. The high predominance of older males seen on the councils is a cultural stereotype. Wisdom is associated with age and men are seen more often than women because of our long history of male dominance in positions of authority.

There are two factors that create these stereotypical images: One, what is projected to you from the council is intended to impact your own experiences and conceptions as a soul from Earth. Two, memory recall in regression involves an overlaying process. While subjects relive their experiences in front of the council in a pure soul state, they are also communicating to me from their current body with all the cultural influences which exist in life today.

We are under the same influences as discarnates when we project a set of facial features from a past life to members of our spirit group. This reflects both our character and mood at the moment, as well as creating a form of instant recognition to souls who might not have seen us in a while. I am certain that regression therapists who perform my sort of work in future years will find as many women as men on these councils. Bear in mind that when I review a council meeting, it is usually between former lives in past centuries. I always take timelines into consideration when evaluating the reality of a spirit world scene in the mind of a client.

Having made this statement about gender bias, I must add that most of my advanced clients, along with large numbers of intermediate souls, see their councils as androgynous. An Elder may appear as sexless or be of mixed gender, flashing both male and female images to the soul. Nevertheless, since almost all my clients either cannot or will not give me the names of their council members, they tend to call them he rather than she, despite a genderless appearance. Spirit guides, on the other hand, are represented equally as male and female between clients.

Returning to figure 8, the reader will notice that the position of the council table (A) is toward the back of the rotunda. The soul (B) stands directly in the center of the room. Most of my clients say, "We stand out of respect." I'm not sure they have a choice. I have had more advanced souls actually sit at one end of the table with their council, but this is quite uncommon and considered presumptuous by the average soul. When I am told that there is no table and the Elders wish my client to join them informally, I know I am working with a highly developed soul who is approaching guide status.

The very young soul, who has been to Earth less than five times, sees their council differently than all my other subjects, as the following quote illustrates:

> There are four of us who play a lot. We do silly things when our teacher, Minari, is not around. My friends and I hold hands when it is time to be taken to see two important people. We go to a place which has bright colors everywhere. There is a man and woman sitting in two high-backed chairs with big smiles on their faces. They have just finished with a small group of kids who wave at us on their way out. This couple are in their early thirties, I would guess. They could be our parents. They are loving and kind and beckon us forward. They just ask a few questions on how we are getting along and what we would like to do in our next life. We are told to pay close attention to everything Minari tells us. It's like Christmas in a department store with two Santas.

The fact that more than one soul would appear before a council meeting is a dead giveaway that my subject is still considered a "child soul." I learned that this individual had only been to Earth once before his current life. In my experience, somewhere between the second and fifth life this sort of council scene is altered. One client who had just made such a transition exclaimed:

> Oh, how things have changed! This meeting is more for-
> mal than last time. I am a little anxious. There is a long
> table and I am being asked by three older people to
> describe my progress to them. It's similar to having just
> finished an exam and now it's time to find out how you
> scored.

The typical client sees between three to seven members on their council. An advanced soul might have from seven to twelve Elders. This is not a hard and fast rule by any means. However, as souls develop and become more complex they appear to require more specialists on their panels. I do find that less-developed souls are frequently unable to dif-ferentiate between individual council members, except for their chair-person and perhaps one other Elder at the table. These two Elders seem to be most engaged with the case while those Elders who are not directly questioning the soul are rather hazy in the background.

It strikes me that there is some sort of protocol connected with council seating arrangements. The members arrange themselves in a row with the less-active participants located at the ends of the table. Almost always, there is a chairperson seated at the center, directly in front of the soul. This Elder is the primary questioner and may also be referred to as a director or moderator. The number of council members who attend these meetings can change each time we see them, depend-ing upon the circumstances of the life just lived and the one to come. Our chairperson, and perhaps one or two other Elders, are normally present over great spans of time between many lives. Another curious aspect of this procedure to me is that members of the same soul group usually go before different councils. I suppose this is due to the differ-ent character aspects of each soul and their state of development. My clients are unable to explain why this is so.

When I am told by a client that a member of their council has just reappeared on the panel after an absence involving a number of lives, or if a new member has appeared, I take notice. A male client told me:

> After my last life I saw a new female member on my council. She was not unkind, but gently critical of my continued insensitivity to women in my past lives. She is here to help me develop a plan to overcome my tendency to shut women out of my life. This is hindering my development.

Apparently, specialists come into our panels at certain times to lend their expertise if we continue to fall into the same ruts. While facing three Elders a subject remarked:

> Only the director in the center speaks to me. The Elder on my left emanates warm, benevolent energy toward me while the one on the right sends me serenity. It is as if I needed tranquillity at this moment because we are talking about my coping with angry emotions in life.

Another client of mine explained what had been happening at her recent council meetings in this way:

> After many of my recent lives, my council has changed from three members to four, then back to three, then four. I noticed this fourth member appears to be a bright silver color while the others have deep hues of violet. I call him my counselor for confidence. Invariably, when I see him sitting on my panel I know I am going to get a lecture on my lack of confidence. He tells me I'm a reticent soul, afraid to push myself with others even when I know I'm right. I tell him how fearful I am on Earth and he gently explains that when I extend myself I become greatly loved and appreciated. I am afraid of confrontation and lives of adversity. He says, "We never give you more than you can handle; keep extending yourself, you have much to offer."

This subject chose to be a woman of small stature and ordinary features in her current life, rather than accepting a tempting offer of another body choice as a dazzling beauty. She told me there was the expectation that this silver counselor of confidence would be happy with this added challenge, along with her also accepting a life with parents who belittled and devalued her while she was growing up. I asked this client what single statement from the silver council member was most sustaining to her over the last few centuries. She replied, "That which you gain from each difficult life, you gain for all eternity."

Where a personal guide will review how we prioritized our objectives and analyze each step after a life, our Elders ask more overview-type questions. The council just doesn't inquire into our most immediate past life. Lines of questioning follow across the sum of all our lives and cover the larger picture of our progress toward self-fulfillment. The Elders wish to explore if we are developing to our potential. I have come to believe that the committee is carefully balanced by certain Elders whose character and background have some sort of common ground with the souls who come before them. Sometimes I see a personal affinity between an Elder and one of my clients. Individual Elders seem to identify with a soul's character, strengths and weaknesses, interests and purposes.

Despite what I have just said, I must add that the vast majority of people in hypnosis do not feel really close to the Elders on their councils. They have reverence and veneration for them but not the deep affection they display toward their spiritual guides. This is why the following case is so exceptional.

Case 38

Dr. N: Do you see any new faces on your council since the last time you went before them?

S: (with a sudden gasp, then a deep sigh of pleasure) AT LAST! Rendar has come back. Oh, am I glad to see him again.

Dr. N: Who is Rendar?

Note: Subject is shaking and does not respond.

Dr. N: Now, take another deep breath and relax for me so together we can discover what is going on. Where is Rendar sitting?

S: To the left of center at the table. (still musing) It's been so long . . .

Dr. N: How many Earth years have passed since you last saw Rendar?

S: (tearfully, after a long pause) Some . . . 3,000 years . . .

Dr. N: This must represent a multitude of lives for you—why has Rendar been away so long?

S: (still tearful, but regaining composure) You don't understand the significance of his coming back on my council. Rendar is very old and wise . . . he is so . . . peaceful . . . he was with me before my Earth cycles (past lives) had numbered so many. Rendar told me I was showing great promise and developing rapidly— I was receiving assignments of importance—and then . . . (subject stops, choking up again)

Dr. N: (softly) You are doing fine. Please go on and tell me what happened to you.

S: (after another long pause) I . . . fell from grace. I fell into the traps that so many of us do here. I grew too confident with my power. Assuming positions of authority over others was fun. It didn't matter what kind of body I had. I became self-indulgent and self-ish in life after life. Rendar warned me about slowing down my progress and I made promises to him I did not keep. So many lives . . . wasted . . . I squandered away opportunities . . . and corrupted my knowledge and power.

Dr. N: Well, obviously you have turned things around recently or Rendar would not be here?

S: I have been working so hard to improve in the last 500 years. To care about others—to engage in service to others—to feel compassion—and now my reward. Rendar is BACK! (subject begins to shake violently and cannot talk)

Dr. N: (after a break where I do my best to compose this client) What does Rendar first say to you at the moment you see him after his long absence?

S: He gives me a warm smile and says, "It's good to be working with you again."

Dr. N: Just like that? That's it?

S: Nothing else is necessary. I feel the power of his great mind and know that once again he has confidence in my future.

Dr. N: What do you say to him?

S: I vow not to slip back again.

Rendar's color was reported as a phosphorescent violet robe. The garment worn by both guides and council members is almost always a robe, sometimes described as a tunic. Spirits don't need clothes any more than they require buildings as places to live in the spirit world. As with so many other images people have of their spiritual life, this too is metaphoric. As pure energy, Elders have deep shades of purple but the colors of their robes may be different. The symbolism of wearing robes confers dignity, honor and a sense of history in the minds of people who report on them. People associate robes with the fields of law, academics and theology in human society.

There are many clues a therapist can gain from questioning hypnosis subjects about the colors of the robes worn by each Elder on their council. These robes appear for the edification of souls from Earth. When I began to gather information about the variety of robe colors, I assumed that these differences conferred some sort of status or rank to an Elder in the minds of people. During my early investigations into this aspect of the spirit world, I asked questions based upon my faulty assumptions about authority. I found the garments worn by these beings, their seating positions at the table, and the degree of participation by each council member was not hierarchical.

White and purple are the most common robe colors seen by my clients. Since they are at opposite ends of the color spectrum this may seem incongruous. However, as case 31 explained, white is receptive energy to beginners while it is also a color of transference or intervention by advanced senders of thought. The white energy of younger souls denotes a process of continual self-cleansing and renewal. For the more advanced, it signifies purity and clarity. The reason white robes are seen so frequently on council members—and with guides at the gateway to the spirit world—is that here white represents the transmission of knowledge and wisdom. White energy robes, or white as a halo aura on an enlightened being, signifies harmonizing and aligning thought with universal energy.

Purple is the color of wisdom and deep understanding. Council members with purple and violet robes reflect their ability to govern the affairs of the souls who come before them with benevolence and love born out of vast experience. These energy colors reflected on an Elder's robe have an idealistic quality of perfection bestowed upon the wearer by my clients. Black robes are never seen, but once in a while an apprehensive subject will call the Elders "judges" when they initially enter the council chamber. Once inside, though, no soul visualizes this meeting space as a courtroom.

Hoods, four-square hats and skull caps, all having an antiquarian flavor, may be seen on the Elders. Hoods are usually thrown back from the head, which is less ominous to the viewer. These visualizations remind me of religious orders, such as the Dominicans, who wear hoods with white robes.

These earthly influences of robes and tunics made out of cloth go back a long way in our history. The garments and other accoutrements reported by my subjects on Elders are trappings which engender respect and reverence to wise beings who, like oracles, interpret events in a soul's existence. The next case is a level I soul who has just entered the council chamber after his last life ended in 1937.

Case 39

Dr. N: How many Elders do you have on your council?

S: I prefer to call them the Wise Ones. There are six sitting at the table.

Dr. N: Explain to me what each Wise One is wearing and give me your impressions of what you see.

S: (pause) Well, the one in the center is wearing a purple robe and the others are white mixed with purple . . . ah . . . except the one on the far right . . . she is mostly white with a touch of yellow. She is more animated toward me than the others.

Dr. N: What do all these colors mean to you?

S: It kind of depends upon the life I have just lived. The Wise One in white on the right wants me to see things more clearly. The yellow-robed person . . . has something to do with my giving and receiving support . . . but I don't know what that has to do with me right now. I remember someone else was in her place two lives ago who wore a crimson robe. That was when I returned home (to the spirit world) after being physically crippled.

Dr. N: What did you think of when you saw her red robe two lives ago?

S: It's physical—a body-oriented color. The crimson One dealt with karmic influences involving that body. I was really worn down and angry after that life. There was a Wise One wearing green then, too, which I don't see now.

Dr. N: Why green?

S: They are skilled at healing . . . mental and physical.

Dr. N: And do you usually see all these colors in the robes worn by the Wise Ones?

S: As a matter of fact, no. Mostly, I see them all wearing about the same purple color tones. This time I'm supposed to be getting some special messages.

Dr. N: Let's talk about the purple-robed being in the middle. Do you think this is someone important?

S: (laughs at me) Hey, they are all important!

Dr. N: Okay, someone more significant to you than the others.

S: Yeah, he's the leader. He sort of directs things.

Dr. N: Why is that, do you think?

S: Because the others seem to defer to him. He conducts things. Mostly, the others seem to speak through him.

Dr. N: Do you know his name?

S: (laughs) No way! We don't circulate in the same social circle around here.

Dr. N: How does the meeting open for you?

S: The director says to me, "Welcome, we are glad to have you with us again."

Dr. N: What do you say?

S: "Thank you"—but I'm thinking, "I hope this goes all right."

Dr. N: What kind of thoughts do you pick up then from the chairman who seems to be running things?

S: He doesn't want me to feel the Wise Ones are so superior that I can't talk to them. This meeting is for me. Then he says, "How do you feel about your progress since we saw you last? Did you learn anything new we can talk about?" (pause) This is the way these meetings open. They want to hear what I have to say.

Dr. N: Do you feel more relaxed now?

S: Yeah.

Dr. N: Give me an idea of how things proceed from here?

S: (pause) We start with what I did right. I had a successful company which employed many people in my past life. I'm turning this over in my mind. I want to make a good impression by telling them about my charity contributions—you know, my good acts. (pause) Then things drift into the way I ran my company . . . my inability to avoid conflicts—disagreements and anger with my employees. (subject grows agitated) It's so frustrating . . . and I'm working on this . . . but then . . . (stops)

Dr. N: Please go on. Does your guide assist you in any way with this?

S: My guide Joaquin speaks from behind me. He sums up the main parts of my life and my objectives to contribute to society by employing people during the Depression.

Dr. N: Sounds good to me. Are you happy with the manner in which Joaquin is presenting you to the Wise Ones?

S: Well, yes. He states what I wanted to do and then what actually happened. His tone is even. Joaquin does not defend or praise me—he simply relates my participation in the events during a bad time in America.

Dr. N: Do you think of Joaquin as your defense attorney?

S: (abruptly) No, that's not the way things are here.

Dr. N: Is Joaquin objective in his summation of your life?

S: Yeah, but we've hardly started. I'm forming my thoughts about how well I provided for my family but this kind of gets mixed up with my professional life . . . I can't get how I treated my employees out of my mind. This really bothers me. Joaquin is quiet now—he doesn't want to interfere with my thoughts.

Dr. N: Then let's stay focused with the thoughts between you and your council of Wise Ones. Please continue.

S: I'm trying to anticipate their questions. I know I enjoyed accumulating material possessions in my life. They want me to tell them why and I say that it made me feel valuable as a person, but I stepped on people. Then they bring up similar actions on my part from former lives . . . and if I feel I am doing better.

Dr. N: Do you think their thought probes about your past are jeopardizing the summary of your current life in some way?

S: No, there is no harsh edge to their questions. I'm okay with this but now my mind is racing and I think of my charity work again as something I should stress . . . then . . . (stops)

Dr. N: (encouraging) You are doing just fine with this, tell me what happens next.

S: The Wise One in the center . . . his powerful mind envelops me.

Dr. N: What does he communicate to you exactly?

S: (slowly) This is what I hear in my mind: "Emmanual, we are not here to judge you, punish you, or to override your thoughts. We want you to look at yourself through our eyes, if you can. That means to forgive yourself. This is the most challenging aspect of your time with us because it is our desire that you accept yourself for who you are with the same unconditional love we have for you. We are here to support you in your work on Earth. Toward that end, we would remind you of the bus stop incident."

Dr. N: The bus stop incident—what does that mean?

S: (pause) I was confused myself when he said it. I look back at Joaquin for assistance.

Dr. N: Explain what happens then, Emmanual.

S: The Wise One in the center . . . his thoughts come to me once more: "You do not remember this incident? The woman who you helped one day while she was sitting at the bus stop?" I said, "No, I don't." Then, they wait for my memories to kick in and someone sends a picture into my mind. I'm beginning to see . . . there was a woman once . . . I was walking toward my office with my briefcase. I was in a hurry. Then I heard this woman crying softly to my left. She was sitting at a bus stop next to the sidewalk. It was during the Depression, people were desperate. I stopped. Then on an impulse, I sat down next to her and put my arm around her, trying to comfort her. This was a very unnatural thing for me to do. (pause) My God, is this what they are interested in? I was with this woman for only a few minutes before the bus came. I never saw her again.

Dr. N: How do you feel now about the Wise One bringing up this incident during your hearing?

S: It's so crazy! An entire lifetime of giving money to charity and they are interested in this! I gave this woman no money, we only talked . . .

As my client and I evaluated this meeting I reminded him why I thought the smiling female council member on the far right wore a robe of yellow. This might be to acknowledge his spontaneous act of support to a stranger at the bus stop. Less developed souls standing in front of their councils often have entanglements of memory as they purge themselves. While they are self-absorbed, they may miss what is important. Emmanual felt sorry for the woman at the bus stop. Although he was in a hurry to get to his office, he sat down next to her. His brief, compassionate gesture did not last long. Yet in those moments, I learned that Emmanual reached her pain, looked into her eyes, and told her she was going to make it through her troubles because he was confident she could be strong. She stopped crying and when her bus came she stood up and told him she would be all right. Then he hurried off and forgot this brief act of kindness for the rest of his life.

The bus stop incident in this case appears to be a small thing when stacked up against a lifetime of other acts. It was not a simple act to the council. As we move through life, there are many gestures between people that are uplifting. They may be so momentary that we are not conscious of them at the time. In the spirit world nothing is insignificant. No act goes unrecorded.

There are no hard and fast rules about the meaning behind every color the Elders might choose to show the souls who come before them. For instance, the red robe worn by the council member in the last case related to the need of Emmanual to sustain the passion for life within a broken host body in a former life. In the next section I will explain the meaning behind other symbols worn by council members. A red robe, or red stone on a medallion or ring displayed by an Elder, can have several meanings depending on the setting. Red is the color of passion and intensity and Emmanual saw a crimson robe after one of his lives with physical disabilities. However, in another case an Elder could display a ruby medallion to denote the need for a soul to have a greater passion for truth than was shown in a former life. The subtle variations of color translation at council meetings are unique to every soul's own perceptions. As one of my subjects said:

> The wearing apparel of my council shows their mastery over a certain discipline. The colors they display in different forms also relate to the topic under discussion. These represent gifts of awareness to me as I face my council. No Elder is greater than the other because each is an aspect of ultimate perfection.

Signs and Symbols

From the dawn of human history our race has sought hidden spiritual meanings through interpretations of what we see around us. I remember how I felt climbing into the cave sanctuaries of Paleolithic humans along the Dordogne Valley in France. Inside these caves, one is taken back to the Stone Age by the symbolic art along the walls. They are among the earliest representations we have of human spiritual consciousness. For thousands of years primal cultures around the world used rock pictures and diagrammed pictographs to represent ideas relating to magic, fertility, sustenance, courage and death.

Indeed, down through the long centuries since that time, we have sought personal revelation through signs from the supernatural. The earliest signs were taken from the animal kingdom, from stones and the elements. We use symbols of all sorts as embodiments of power and instruments of insight and self-development. Ancient cultural attachments to mystic symbolism were often associated with a desire for transfiguration of our higher Self over the primitive side of human nature. The rites and symbols of secret mystical societies, such as the Gnostics and Kabbalists, may well represent soul memory on Earth and human memory in the spirit world.

Perhaps I should not have been surprised to have found emblems with meaningful signs in the spirit world. As with all physical objects visualized by subjects in hypnosis, the emblems they see worn by some Elders are grounded in past life experience. Conversely, why shouldn't we carry messages from the council to Earth within our soul mind as well? Anthropologists who have studied clay tablets, seal stones, scarabs and amulets from our past believe that their influence to both wearer and observer went beyond physical life into the realm of disembodied souls. This custom continues today with engraved pendants, rings and charms. Many people who wear these symbolic talismans believe they protect but are also reminders of personal power and opportunity. The following cases may shed some light on the origins of our feelings about prophetic signs.

About half my subjects see medallions hanging around the necks of one or more Elders on their council. The other half see no objects at all. Frankly, I have found no correlation between these two groups of clients in any way, including their level of development. When a medallion is seen by people, some 85 percent of them visualize a circular design. The others may see squares, rectangles, triangles, and starlike designs, some of which are seen in three dimensions. All these medallion shapes, in association with the designs on them, are significant and represent a continuity of spirit, both morally and spiritually, to the evolving soul.

The medallions typically hang from a chain or sometimes just a cord. Usually the metallic disk is gold but they can also be silver or bronze. Most clients are focused on only one medallion on the council, which is almost always worn by the chief questioner. This Elder is generally positioned directly in front of the soul.

Case 40

Dr. N: How many members of your council are sitting in front of you?

S: Five.

Dr. N: How are they dressed?

S: They all have white robes.

Dr. N: I want you to look carefully—do you see any of these wise beings wearing anything on their robes? If you don't see anything, fine, don't worry about it, I'm just curious.

S: (pause) Well, the one in the center has something around his neck.

Dr. N: Please describe what you see.

S: I don't know. It's on a chain.

Dr. N: What is on a chain?

S: Something round, a metal disk.

Dr. N: (I always ask this question) Is it close to the size of a grapefruit, orange, or walnut?

S: (the usual response) An orange.

Dr. N: What color is this ornament?

S: Gold.

Dr. N: What do you think this gold medallion means?

S: (the normal response) Oh, probably some sort of badge of office, or maybe his particular area of expertise.

Dr. N: Really. Do you think it is necessary for council members to wear emblems to signify to each other what their position is, or any particular talent they may have?

S: (confused) Well . . . I don't know . . . I mean, how could I know?

Dr. N: Let's not give up on this so easily. We might learn something together.

S: (No answer)

Dr. N: Describe what you see on the gold medallion.

S: (the usual response) I can't see it very well.

Dr. N: I want you to move closer so you can see the emblem more clearly.

S: (reluctant) I'm not sure I should.

Dr. N: Let's look at this logically. If you were not supposed to see the emblem, your chairperson would not allow you to see it. Think about this. Does it make sense that these highly developed beings would openly display adornments on their robes which you are not supposed to see? And why would they need to display them for each other?

S: I suppose you're right. (still reluctant) I guess it would be okay for me to move a little closer.

Dr. N: Just so you know, talking to me about this is not a violation of confidentiality. Look at the expression on the face of the Elder wearing the emblem. He knows what you are thinking. Tell me what you see?

S: A kindly expression . . . helpful to me.

Dr. N: Then I am sure he would not want you to miss anything pertaining to this meeting. Move forward and tell me what you see on the metal disk.

S: (now more confident) I can't make out the writing around the side, it looks like filigreed lace, but on the raised part of the disk in the center I see a big cat with its mouth open.

Dr. N: Give me more details about the cat. Is it a house cat?

S: (more forcefully) No, it's a profile of a mountain lion with a fierce face and large teeth.

Dr. N: Anything else?

S: (with recognition) Oh, there is a hand holding a dagger under the lion's neck. (long pause) Ah . . . yes . . .

Dr. N: You know now what this is all about, don't you?

S: (quietly) Yes, I think I do. It is from my Indian life.

Dr. N: We haven't talked about that life. Tell me when and where this life took place and how the big cat fits in.

This client, whose spirit name is Wan, proceeded to explain that in 1740 she was a young Indian woman in North America. She was out in the forest one day digging roots with her two children. The men of her village were off hunting. Suddenly, she saw a big cat jump out of a tree and move toward the children. Wan dropped her basket and ran directly at the cat. She said, "There was only time to pull out my stone knife—then he was on top of me. Just before the lion killed me I was able to thrust up deep into his neck. Later the men found me and the lion dead, but the children were safe." When I asked Wan why she was being shown this emblem of the cat, she said, "To signify I displayed courage here and I must use it more in other lives."

I always verify the design of medallion carvings with a posthypnotic suggestion at the end of my sessions. I have my clients draw me a picture of what they saw. Wan's visual picture of this event is shown in figure 9A.

The depiction of Wan's hand killing a mountain lion on the medallion was intended to send a strong message of capability and courage. My client came to me because she was fearful of dying at age thirty-nine because her brother had died two years before in his thirty-ninth year while driving recklessly. She just had her thirty-ninth birthday and we found there was a tenuous quality about her existence.

In the course of our session my subject learned that in the life following her Indian life, she and her two children had been abandoned by her trapper husband in a Wyoming cabin during a harsh winter in the nineteenth century. This husband, who was her brother today, was restless and wanted his freedom from family responsibilities. Thus, this case involved a karmic transference of roles by an unsettled soul in Wan's spirit group who went from an errant past life husband in the nineteenth century to a rather wild brother in the twentieth.

As the trapper's abandoned wife, Wan told me she did not fight hard enough to save herself and the children by putting on snowshoes, a backpack, and trying to get out to civilization while she still had food. She was afraid, and rationalized that her husband would return before she and the children starved. The council showed Wan the cat medallion not only as a counterpoint to the lack of resolve in the Wyoming life but also for her fearfulness today. I'm glad Wan saw the contemporary message of this symbol of courage in our session because the soul of her brother had volunteered for the probable short life to test my client again and deal with his own karma of abandoning people.

I know it seems odd that these ethereal beings on the council would be seen by souls as having a body of light energy in human shape wearing robes with ornaments. When I initially detected the medallions I did wonder if they were chains of office. I learned that these pendants and their designs had nothing to do with an Elder's status on the council but everything to do with offering a message of inspiration to the souls who come before them. As with so many aspects of the spirit world, these symbols did not reveal themselves easily to me.

In the early stages of my inquiries into medallions, my questions would elicit enigmatic responses to the effect that an emblem's meaning was unfathomable, or that the Elder was sitting too far away to make it out. For too long I accepted these explanations. Then I changed tactics. As can be seen from the last case, I now tell subjects that it does not make sense that Elders would wear an insignia for personal recognition with each other. Since these wise beings already know everything about

Figure 9 (A-D): Medallion Designs Worn by Council Members

A

B

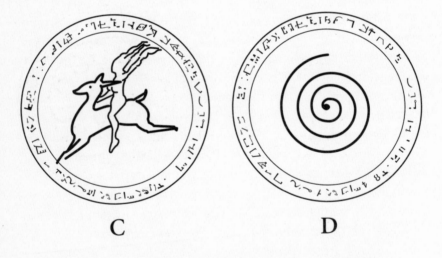

C

D

These designs are not drawn to scale. Souls see them in different sizes and colors but they are almost always round and hang from an Elder's neck. All emblems are illustrated with the usual double-circle edge etched with indecipherable linguistic markings.

Figure 9 (E-H) continued

E

F

G

H

each other, these medallions have to be for the benefit of the soul they are interviewing. They might be changed over time after a karmic lesson is learned; however, some scenes appear not to change at all.

Once a person in hypnosis realizes the emblems are not symbols of a secret society belonging only to their particular council, they open up. This allows the client to make the mental distinction between an observer caught up in an event over which they have no control to that of an active participant. Responses improve by giving the client permission to recognize what essentially already belongs to them as a soul. The therapy I am able to utilize in their current life from this aspect of interlife council meetings is worth the effort. The passages from the next case are unusual because the subject knows the names of three council members, all of whom have medallions. The chairman's emblem design is figure 9B.

Case 41

Dr. N: As you look more closely at the emblem worn by your chairperson, please describe it to me.

S: Drit wears the head of an eagle. It is turned sideways on the gold disk in bold relief. Its beak is wide open. I can see the bird's tongue.

Dr. N: Okay, what does all this mean to you?

S: Drit is giving me a message to fly high and scream into the silence.

Dr. N: Can you tell me more?

S: Drit says I must engage with my silence in life. I can't live in my own world all the time. Unless I break out and rise above life's circumstances, I will not progress.

Dr. N: And how do you respond to Drit's message?

S: I just don't accept this—I tell Drit that there was enough noise by others in my past life. I didn't need to add to it.

Dr. N: What does Drit answer?

S: He says I could have made the world louder—but better—by being more vocal in what I knew to be the truth.

Dr. N: Do you agree with his assessment?

S: (pause) I suppose . . . I probably could have participated more . . . to engage others . . . and fought for my convictions.

Dr. N: Do you always see the eagle design after your lives?

S: No, only when I fall into my old patterns of silence. Sometimes his disk is blank.

Dr. N: Are you having trouble with this same issue in your current life?

S: Yes, that's why I came to you and why Drit has now reminded me of this lesson.

Dr. N: Does anyone else on your council wear an emblem?

S: Yes, that would be Tron. He sits to the right of Drit.

Dr. N: Please describe the design on Tron's medallion for me.

S: He wears an emblem engraved with a cluster of golden grapes.

Dr. N: Are you saying the grapes are gold, rather than appearing in their natural colors?

S: (shrugs) Yes, they are gold because the disk is that color. The emblems are always metallic.

Dr. N: Why is that?

S: I'm really not sure. For me, they represent objects that are precious and long-lasting.

Dr. N: What does the symbol of a cluster of grapes mean to you?

S: (pause) Tron wears the sign of . . . the fruit of life . . . which can be eaten . . . ah, absorbed . . . that is, to grow with knowledge.

Dr. N: Why a bunch of grapes rather than, say, an apple?

S: The cluster of grapes represents—not a single fruit—but multiples of the same fruit . . . to absorb different aspects of the same whole.

Dr. N: Would you care to expand on this message by Tron?

S: That by absorbing this symbol—each grape—into myself I will grow and flourish from every experience.

Dr. N: Do any other members of your council wear emblems?

S: (pause) Shai, she wears the emblem of the key as a reminder to open the door of knowledge and by doing so accept the fact that the answers to my problems lie within my abilities to solve them.

With case 41, it was the eagle design which had the greatest prominence. Birds on medallions are not unusual. One man told me that his chairperson had an emblem of bird feathers with a thistle in the center to remind him of a number of lives in the Highlands of Scotland. He stated, "In those lives as a clansman I soared up mountain crags, fighting British oppression for the freedom of my people."

A female client saw a swan emblem on an Elder, which denoted growth through change. She said, "I am being reminded that at birth this beautiful creature is awkward and can't fly. This represents my own metamorphosis from an ugly duckling into someone imposing—a productive person in my last series of lives." Occasionally, a fish is seen on a medallion. A client told me that for him, this symbol represented a creature who could swim against a current and still be in harmony with its environment.

For some reason, human figures are rarely seen on council emblems. When I do hear of them I find their symbolic meanings to be intriguing. To illustrate the use of a human figure on a medallion, I refer the reader to figure 9C. This represents the case of a thirty-year-old woman called Noreen who came to me because she did not want to live anymore. Her husband had committed suicide some months before and she wanted to follow him. During the session we found out this soulmate had lost his life in a logging accident at age twenty-six in their previous life together.

Couples in life each have their own karmic paths which may involve different issues from each other. However, these issues are frequently intertwined when souls from the same cluster group agree to work together, especially in a marriage. Noreen did not do well as a young widow in her last life, particularly in her refusal to open her heart to anyone else. For the remainder of that life, Noreen was inconsolable and died in bitterness from self-inflicted emotional wounds.

Facing her council at the end of this past life, she was told by the chairperson, "You didn't let your spirit grow, did you?" Apparently, the same lesson has been presented to Noreen in her current life to see how she will handle it. I want to stress that this was not why her husband committed suicide. I have had cases where a spouse will intentionally choose a body that has a high probability of dying young from a variety of natural causes to allow the surviving spouse to again work through grief in a more healthy fashion. Suicide is not one of these options. Suicide by a physically healthy young person is not a prearranged karmic option for anyone. From my experience, I believe the odds are that if Noreen's husband had not committed suicide he probably would have died young from some sort of accident.

At the time of our meeting, my client believed it was not possible to go on without the man she loved. Her extreme despondency also carried feelings of guilt that somehow she might have been responsible, although her husband's suicide note carried just the opposite message. I feel that taking this client back to her last council meeting and viewing once again the medallion she saw is making a difference in her life today.

Case 42

Dr. N: I want you to tell me exactly what design you see on the chairman's medallion.

S: The first thing I see is an animal . . . a deer. No, I think it is a gazelle. It is jumping in mid-flight.

Dr. N: Good, and do you see anything else you can talk about?

S: (pause) There is a human on its back. This really stands out boldly in the center.

Dr. N: I see. Is it similar to a bas-relief carving?

S: Yes, the gazelle and human figure are turned sideways to me. You know, like I'm watching them from an angle as they race across a plain. The human is faceless, but has long hair and the delicate body of a woman. The one leg I can see is bent . . . she is riding. One arm is raised, holding up a torch.

Dr. N: (a shift to present time, and then a command) All right, what I want you to do is rediscover the meaning of what you are seeing. It is no accident that we are here today discussing this emblem together. It represents something you need to remember. You are a young widow for the second time in two successive lives. Ask for assistance from your guide if necessary.

S: (after a long pause, she responds tearfully) I know the meaning. The human is me and I am riding east into the sunrise. The direction signifies the dawn of a new day. This animal would normally never trust a human to be near it, much less ride on its back. The gazelle trusts me and I must trust myself to go where the animal takes me because we must travel swiftly.

Dr. N: And why must you travel swiftly?

S: (after some prompting from me and few false starts) Because in life there is danger. Parts of this danger lie within us, our weakness—the way we sabotage—and this prevents us from reaching a destination. It is easy to get bogged down.

Dr. N: Are you saying the gazelle represents a liberating force?

S: Yes, I must have the courage and strength to continue on with my life with a greater sense of purpose. The gazelle also represents freedom to conquer fear and have faith in myself.

Dr. N: What about the torch you are carrying on the emblem?

S: (softly) Always . . . the light of knowledge. Our search for wisdom. This flame is never extinguished or made ineffective by shadows.

Dr. N: Do you see anything else on the pendant?

S: (still in a state of reverie) Oh, it is not important to me, I think. I am unable to read the Greek letters within the circle around the edge.

Unfortunately, I must report that none of my subjects who see medallions can decipher the strange symbols between the two outer rings near the edge. The secret writing remains a mystery in my research and I have reluctantly come to the conclusion this is one feature of the emblems that my clients and I are not supposed to know about. I should also add that much of what souls see and hear at their council meetings cannot be re-created in my office. Over the years of my work, I have come to expect that people in hypnosis cannot adequately explain all that happens in their spiritual lives because of human limitations in communication and translations which must be processed through the human brain. My subjects do not know why they cannot decipher the "squiggles" on medallions. They refer to them as hieroglyphics, cuneiform writing, runes and even mathematical symbols. The script does not seem to be translatable. It could be pictorial or ideogrammic. Perhaps it is an unspoken spiritual language.

I suspect the same types of symbols appear on the Life Books in spiritual libraries, such as the Greek pi symbol on the front of the book described by case 30. While the Life Books are very personal and undoubtedly used as a chronicle of the soul's past by their guides and councils, the writing around the edges of an Elder's medallion may have nothing to do with the soul. I have come to the conclusion that if my subjects were supposed to know about this writing while in a trance state, their spiritual guides would assist them. Regardless of whether the symbolic marks they see represent sounds, ideas or words of some sort, there may be a good reason why people cannot translate them, which has nothing to do with the client. One had this to say, "I think I'm not supposed to understand their meaning because this is a message to my Elder from a higher Source. Maybe this is his lesson wheel that he must decipher for his own goals."

I divide what is seen on council emblems into two general categories. The first involves living or natural objects. These symbols could also include minerals, such as gemstones. The second category is the geometric designs, such as circles and straight line drawings. Gemstones may appear on both types of medallions. Council medallions are symbolic of pain and purpose, triumphs and shortcomings of the souls who go before them. The colors of the gemstones presented to the soul relate to both the Elder presenting them and also to the soul observer. The general design of a medallion involves soul attributes, accomplishments and goals. Like the oracles of old, the Elders may show a sign as a warning of impending trouble if what we strive for in life is set aside.

The case examples that follow are of clients who saw geometric designs and gemstones on their council emblems. The deciphering of line drawings in geometric designs is not quite as readily discernible as with objects of nature, which include gemstones. There are cultures, such as in Japan, where personal emblems involving line drawings have heraldic overtones. In the Orient, these family symbols worn on clothing could be of natural objects or geometric designs to identify members of a specific clan. As opposed to Japanese clan traditions, members of a soul group would not likely see exactly the same emblem displayed by their respective councils.

I find the meaning behind swirl designs on geometric emblems to be particularly intriguing. There is a universal aspect to some of them, such as with the next design listed under figure 9D. I have personally seen minor variations of this swirl design on rocks in such diverse locations as Europe, North Africa, Australia and in the deserts of North America. Many archeologists call it the life source design. When I asked the subject who saw the design in figure 9D about its meaning at a council meeting, I was told, "The council woman who wears the swirl design is reminding me that—starting from within the core of the spirit world—we spiral outward in development and will someday return to the Source of our origins." When a swirl, or concentric circle design appears on a medallion, the meaning usually relates to a soul's existence within the continuum of life. This sign projects a connotation of spiritual protection, as well.

In figure 9E the lines are crooked. Here is what the client who saw this design on an Elder had to say:

> There are four rippled lines which come from the outer edges of the insignia from different directions. They converge within the circle of unity, indented in the center of the disk. The crooked lines represent different pathways toward our goal. They are not straight paths because we

are imperfect souls. The lines make the insignia look fractured just as most every life seems to be disjointed at times. We may take many turns in our travels, but eventually we will all arrive at the same place in the center.

I have also been told about celestial signs with star, moon and sun symbols. After a long while of keeping records of all medallion signs, I realized that a crescent moon design was seen more often than other celestial designations. Figures 9F and 9G (which I will present in case 44) represent different variations of the crescent moon design in the minds of two clients:

> The sun gives us golden rays of life-giving light while the partial moon is a symbol of growth for me. This silver light represents the forces of my potential. As it grows, so does my higher Self.

> I am an interdimensional traveler between lives. The upside-down moon represents the covering and containment of the spirit world, which has jurisdiction over the Earth, our universe, and the dimensions around it. The lines at the top of the emblem are pivotal points of my soul travel, which epitomize grounding me to my work. At the bottom of this emblem is the atom-star, the purifier light and connector of universes.

Generally, when a client speaks of seeing a crescent moon on a medallion it represents the increasing power of the soul on Earth. My subjects say this is a waxing moon, which is growing, as opposed to a waning moon. The sign is often reported to be silver on a gold disk. Straight lines which are looped, angled, horizontal or vertical have countless meanings. For instance, figure 9G has five straight, angled lines at the top of the medallion. One subject who saw such lines all the way around a disk with no other markings said, "The great-star design of these long lines converging down to the center of the disk means I am supported on all sides by the Elders on my council." I find it impossible to classify the large variety of signs and symbols I hear about because each is so individual to the soul.

I will offer one more medallion design as figure 9H. This last design combines a geometric pattern with a gemstone. This emblem was reported by a woman, whose spiritual name is Unz, who lives in constant pain from fibromyalgia, a disease which inhibits muscle function.

Case 43

Dr. N: Explain to me what you see on the robe of your chairman?

S: Kars wears a gold medallion for my observation. For as long as I can remember it has had intertwined circlets all around the face of the disk.

Dr. N: Tell me, Unz, what does this design mean to you?

S: The circlets are a reminder to me that each life we live fits together with all our other lives in a continuum toward fulfilling our primary purpose.

Dr. N: Do you see anything else on the disk worn by Kars?

S: (joyfully) Yes, yes—I have graduated to the emerald stone, which is in the center.

Dr. N: And what does this stone mean to you?

S: (with great satisfaction) It is the stone of the healer.

Dr. N: Does this have anything to do with your having fibromyalgia in your current life?

S: Absolutely. I specifically asked for a body in this life which would be subjected to incurable pain.

Dr. N: (with surprise in my voice) Can you expand upon why you did this?

S: I chose this path long ago. I found that whenever I was suffering myself with a malady that generated pain, it helped my healing art. When one is in constant pain, even of low-grade intensity, it presents an opportunity—especially for a healer.

Dr. N: To do what?

S: To experiment with the vibrational levels of pain with the body. You can learn the fine art of adjustments in energy to relieve sections of pain. By working with my own energy in this way I learned to assist others more skillfully.

Dr. N: What else can you tell me about this experience?

S: Being in constant pain keeps one grounded, anchored to the human experience. For pain relief one must be completely focused. It helps to have confidence that there is a higher purpose in learning to work through pain. I pay a lot of attention to other human beings who suffer from physical infirmities in life. I am able to help those who are receptive to the use of mind control for relief.

Dr. N: It seems to me you feel quite proud of having earned the emerald stone as presented by Kars.

S: The stone represents the lineage of the wearer as a healer. It is an embodiment of my personal character and that of Kars, who has been assigned to monitor the progress of my trials through the ages. It represents my attainment.

Dr. N: Is it fair for me to assume that you are being shown this stone by a master healer who has the expectation that you will carry on this work to become a teacher specialist yourself?

S: Yes, and Kars' confidence in me is empowering.

Case 43 is what I would call an accelerated soul. Unz has only been incarnating on Earth for some five thousand years, a very short time considering her advancement. This is because she never skates in any of her lives. She accepts no healthy bodies, which really astonished me. In her life today, Unz is a Science of Mind minister who incorporates an eclectic mix of spiritual disciplines. Through her ministry, she assists many people with health problems through the use of guided imagery and meditation.

Another aspect of case 43 that I found interesting was that Unz only began to see the green stone on this medallion in the last four or five lives. Before that there was an amber stone in the center of the disk. Unz told me this was the color of nurturing and protection for the weak and sick, which came before the green stone. She called this gemstone "my growing-up stone," and added, "The green emerald displays my current placement." This indicates to me Unz is a level IV soul. Further questioning revealed something else. Unz said in her early lives on Earth the circlets (loops) had no stone at all in the middle of the emblem.

I remember a level V who told me, "There are five jewels on my overseer's emblem, a diamond, ruby, amber, emerald and sapphire, which symbolize my achievements over different levels of development." Thus, it is not the gemstone itself as a mineral of value that has significance on a spiritual medallion but rather the color of attainment the jewel represents. Gemstone metaphors reported by people in trance offer useful parallels with earthly traditions. The ancients of the Middle East, India and China thought that certain colors represented in gems and semiprecious stones possessed a kind of living personality of their own. For example, the Sumerians believed the wearer of a blue lapis stone had their personal spirit god with them "who must be listened to." Most of my clients see their spirit guides as dark blue light. The ancients also felt that amethyst-purple conferred transcendental knowledge and wisdom. This gem color represents level VI souls and above.

Of those hypnosis subjects who do see medallions worn by their council members, some see only gemstones. They may not be shown on a disk. I have had cases where the stones—or glowing balls of colored energy—appear on necklaces, rings, or are simply held in an Elder's hand and exhibited to the souls who come before them. Essentially, the displaying of certain colors of light energy represents different aspects of our physical and spiritual life. Certain colors emanating from an Elder as a halo, robe, or medallion can also indicate an Elder's specialty area, which might directly relate to what the soul in front of them hopes eventually to achieve.

The hypnosis facilitator must be cautious about their own preconceptions about color meanings. Color interpretations on images presented to the hypnosis client visualizing council meetings won't have quite the same meaning for everyone. Nevertheless, I think it is fair to say that to people in a trance state, signs and symbols presented to them through soul memory relate to the effects of forces over which they wish to exert some control in their current lives. My subjects associate all the medallions I have talked about on their councils with perception and wisdom. Their meanings are intensely personal things, and are displayed with the intention to instruct and motivate souls from Earth to an awareness of Self. The impact of viewing these signs and symbols under hypnosis is so compelling with some clients that after their sessions they have ordered duplicates on personal jewelry to remind them of their karmic path.

The Presence

"When you take people into the spirit world, do they see God?" This is a question I am frequently asked about at lectures and there is no short answer. I can say my subjects do feel the Source of their origins all about them in the spirit world. The more advanced explain that all souls will eventually coalesce back into conjunction with the Source of purple light. However, is there someplace in the spirit world where a being superior to the Elders is evident to the still-incarnating soul? The answer is yes, at council meetings.

During the time we are meeting with the Council of Elders there is the overwhelming feeling of an even higher force which is simply called "the Presence." Many subjects state, "This is as close to God as we get." My more advanced clients, who are nearing the end of their regular incarnations, indicate that they don't think the Presence is God, exactly. To them it is a deified entity, or entities, with capabilities immensely superior to those on the council. Everyone agrees that the Presence is there to assist the work of the council.

Typically, people who come to me do not like to use the word God in describing a higher Presence, which they feel more than see in the spirit world. They prefer to use such words as Source, or Oversoul, because the word God has been too personalized on Earth. As many souls approach the more advanced stages of development, the Presence may become pluralized in their minds as a part of the many divine forces in the spirit world with infinite knowledge. They feel this higher force does influence council meetings but might not be the ultimate Creator. My subjects see the greatest evidence of the Presence at council meetings. Even so, the Presence is equated with a larger omnipotent and omnipresent energy force in the spirit world.

After reviewing hundreds of case notes describing the Presence, I decided to offer a few of them in a series of quotes. In their sessions, each subject speaks of the Presence in just a few sentences. I hope the list of quotes I have selected will capture the flavor of what the average soul feels about this aspect of their council meetings:

> I do not actually see the Presence, but feel it as the ultimate energy. It is there for the council, but mostly for me. The Elders don't serve as intermediaries between myself and this Source of power. I feel a direct connection with the divine purple light.

> When I am in the council chamber the Presence oversees the Elders with its pulsating violet light. Sometimes it turns to a bright silver to calm and purify my mind.

> The Presence is above and in back of the council. Only with difficulty can I look up at this power. I feel its sanctity so strongly that I don't think I should try to look at it directly during the council meeting. If I did, I could not stay focused on the Elders.

> The council seems to acknowledge the Presence without being too deferential to it in such a way as to slow down the proceedings. I think it intended that my council and I pay attention to each other. Still, I have the impression that the magnitude of all this combined intelligent energy is designed just for me at this moment. My guide, the Elders, and the Presence are keepers of the wisdom behind my experiences.

> The Presence represents a purity of energy which assists the council on my behalf. I believe that the council needs the help of the Presence because it has been so long since they themselves incarnated in biological form. The pure wisdom of this energy allows both the council and myself to see more clearly where we all should be going.

> The brilliance and drawing power of the Presence is a calling . . . an eagerness . . . directed at everyone in the chamber for all of us to join it someday. It is like a parent waiting for us to grow up and unite with it in adult understanding.

> When you stand in the council chamber and feel the
> Presence it is like a penetrating resonance in your mind.
> Even my master guide encounters the sense of bliss that I
> do. I know this is why she really enjoys coming to council
> meetings with me. It is a fountainhead of love and under-
> standing. When my time with the council is over and I
> leave the Presence . . . there is such a yearning to go back
> and be close to it once more.

People have asked me if I have ever had anyone who could shed
some light on what it is like to be a council member and be closer to the
Presence. I have had very few subjects with such experience who are in
transition from level V. However, one individual stands out in my
mind.

Chinera was one of the most advanced clients I have ever had. No
one has taken me closer to the Presence than this soul. Chinera trained
in another dimension before coming to Earth several thousand years
ago. Today, this client is an acupuncturist who practices a variety of
healing arts. The medallion worn by Chinera's council chairman is
shown in figure 9G. Further details about the interdimensional travel
capabilities of souls will be examined with the Explorer Soul specialists
in chapter 8.

Case 44

Dr. N: When your work as a personal guide is completed, do you
expect to be assigned to the Council of Elders?

S: No, this won't happen yet. I must become a master teacher working with younger teachers . . . helping them get in touch with
their students on many levels.

Dr. N: How do you know this?

S: Because I am still in training here (incarnating), learning more
about Earth's biological life forms.

Dr. N: Chinera, it is my belief we are together today to help each
other understand certain things. Let's begin this part of our discussion by my asking you about your relationship with the
Elders on your council. Begin by telling me how many you see.

S: I have twelve members on my council right now. After my last life, the four in the center of the table were the ones who questioned me about becoming more centered on Earth. I still have some blocks which need adjustment. The four on the right-hand side are from my original dimension. They are here to assist in the better utilization of the energy I brought with me into Earth's universe.

Dr. N: What about the last four members of your council?

S: The four on the left-hand side of the table act as stabilizers of universal light and sound between all the dimensions around the Earth universe. They act as a pivotal point to ground me in a physical world.

Dr. N: Can you give me some idea of what blockages are hindering your progress on Earth?

S: Primarily, the council wants me to enlarge my influence with more people. I have been resistant to extending myself. I complain to them that it would dilute my power. They disagree with my arguments about spreading myself too thin.

Dr. N: I know the feeling. Do you accept this evaluation?

S: (long pause) I know they are right but I still feel sometimes I am an alien on Earth.

Dr. N: Tell me, Chinera, have you ever appeared with members of your council to discuss certain students you work with?

S: Yes, I have briefly.

Dr. N: Then perhaps you can help me understand the progression of soul advancement. Where would you classify yourself?

S: I'm working on being a master teacher.

Dr. N: Would the next elevation above this level of a guide be a position on the council?

S: Not necessarily. There are many other choices for specializations. One might not be suited to be on a council.

Dr. N: Let's say you were suited and were given a seat on the council and were effective there. Where could you go next as a soul?

S: (hesitates in responding) To the place of the Oneness.

Dr. N: Is this represented by the Presence at council meetings?

S: (vaguely) Into that essence, yes.

Dr. N: Describe the Oneness—is it an oversoul?

S: I believe it is many who are One . . . it is the creation center as I know it . . . it is where the creators of new souls shape light energy for certain functions.

Dr. N: Chinera, please describe this process further for me.

S: I . . . can't tell you too much . . . it is where the energy of new souls is sparked off the oversoul. Where we help the young ones grow, to find their unique identity.

Dr. N: Is the Oneness what we call God?

S: It is a divineness.

Dr. N: Since you have said this divinity could be composed of many who are One, are they the ultimate deity of all universes and all dimensions connecting these universes, including our spirit world?

S: (long pause) I don't think so.

Dr. N: Where do you think the essence of the Presence comes from?

S: (faintly) Everywhere . . . (stops)

Dr. N: How do you know of these things?

S: I have a mentor on the council . . . we talk a lot . . . my friends and I have flashes of thought . . . and we ask questions about the ultimate reality.

Dr. N: When you talk to your mentor and your friends of a force that might be above even the Presence, what have you heard and felt?

S: It may be the same force of which the Presence is a part, I don't know . . . it is . . . massive, but soft . . . powerful . . . yet gentle. There is a breath . . . a whisper . . . of sound . . . so pure . . .

Dr. N: (placing the palm of my hand on the subject's forehead) Stay with these thought fragments, Chinera. Float with them as far as they will take you toward the sound. (speaking in a whisper myself) Is this sound created by some sort of light energy?

S: No, the sound creates all . . . including light and energy.

Dr. N: Move closer as if you were floating without effort—closer toward the origin of the sound. (a command) NOW, WHAT DO YOU SEE AND HEAR?

S: I'm at the edge . . . I can't . . .

Dr. N: (loudly) KEEP GOING CHINERA!

S: (quietly, with great difficulty) I . . . with my friends . . . when we have unified our minds to the sound we see pictures in our minds . . . they are . . . geometric designs . . . aligned in patterns . . . (stops)

Dr. N: (now softly coaxing) A little further . . . just beyond . . . what is there?

S: I . . . feel . . . the sound holds this structure . . . and . . . makes it move . . . shifting and undulating . . . creating everything. It is a reverberating deep bell . . . then a high-pitched pure humming . . . like an echo of . . . (stops)

Dr. N: Reach in, Chinera, one last effort. An echo of what?

S: (a deep sigh) A mother . . . full of love . . . singing to her child.

I pushed Chinera hard for information because I knew, in my lifetime, I probably would never have another client to quite match her. This individual, and other highly advanced subjects, have indicated that the Council of Elders exists within a reality of deeper meaning beyond the conception of souls still coming to Earth.

The Chain of Divine Influence

To many of my clients, the Presence seems not to be a "Who" but that which "Is." For others, the Presence is an entity who functions as an equalizer, harmonizing the greater awareness of Elders to the lesser awareness of the souls who come before them. This effect causes the council chamber to breathe with synchronized energy. A handful of my level Vs have actually had the chance to briefly participate as members of a council as part of their guide training. When I asked one of them what this experience was like, I received the following response:

> When I sat on a panel it was like being inside the soul in front of you. What you feel is much more than empathy toward someone who has just come back from a life. You are really in their shoes. The Presence gives you the power to feel everything the soul feels at the moment. The prism of light from the Presence touches every council member in this way.

Does the same Presence move from council to council, is there more than one entity, or is "It" simply God, which is everywhere? These questions, of course, I cannot answer. Despite the overlapping of jurisdiction between soul groups, how many councils must exist who are responsible for all the souls just from Earth? This too is impossible for me to gauge, but the numbers must be immense. If it is true that other worlds in our universe have souls needing councils and other universes that the spiritual masters must manage, their task is beyond conception.

Unlike the highly advanced souls, such as case 44, most of my clients are unable to recognize that the Elders could be fallible beings themselves. Other than fleeting moments with a more powerful and loving Presence, the Council of Elders is the highest authority people directly encounter in their spiritual visions. As a result of what they see in a trance state, my subjects do have the sense of a vertical tier effect of soul attainment in the spirit world. This perception of the cosmos is not a new belief system in human civilization.

Indian, Egyptian, Persian and Chinese texts of the past speak of "the agencies of God" who were personified as metaphysical entities, some of whom were even anthropomorphic. Early Greco-Hebrew religious philosophy also identified with a stair-stepped concept of spiritual masters, each one more divine than the last. Many cultures believed that while God is the Source of all creation and is totally good, the management of our universe was delegated through a combination of lesser beings who were mediators of reason and the purveyors of divine thought between a perfect being and a finite world. They were considered to be emanations of the Creator, but beings who were less than perfect. Perhaps this helped explain the imperfections of our world with God still being the First Cause.

The pantheistic view is that all manifestations in the universe *are* God. Over a long span of time the spiritual philosophy of some cultures evolved into a conception that the divine forces which govern our lives were essentially words of wisdom, analogous to the reasoning powers of human beings. In other societies, these forces were thought of as Presences capable of influencing our world. The Christian church found the whole idea of intermediaries emanating from a supreme Source to be unacceptable. The position of Christianity is that a perfect being would not delegate a less than perfect being—who could make mistakes—to run our universe.

The Old Testament God spoke through prophets. In the New Testament, the word of God comes through Jesus who, Christians believe, is the image of God. Still, the prophets of all the major religions are reflections of God to their followers. I feel the acceptance of prophets in many religions around the world has its roots in our soul memory of sacred intermediaries—such as guides and Elders—between ourselves and the creator Source. In our long history on this planet there have been many cultures with mythological figures having cosmological functions as mediators between the unknowable God and a hostile world. I don't feel we should relegate myths, as a means of explaining the world, to primitive thought. What we rationally know today still does not answer the mystery of creation any more than in the past.

In terms of the First Cause, I have found both old and new spiritual concepts can be reconciled in one significant way. Souls are able to create living things out of an energy source provided for them. Thus, souls are able to make something out of something in a variety of settings.

In religious theology, divine creation is making something out of nothing. There are those who believe that the Godhead does not create physical matter but only the conditions which allow highly advanced beings to do so.

Is Earth a laboratory created by higher forms of energy for the lower to advance through many stages of development? If so, these higher beings are our Source but not *the* Source. In *Journey of Souls,* I wrote about the possibility of a creator lacking full perfection and having the need to grow stronger by expressing its essence. However, it could have the need to do this even if it was perfect. The philosophy of a divine stair-stepping authority validates the belief of many people that Earth and our physical universe is far too chaotic to have been formed by ultimate perfection. In my view, this whole idea takes nothing away from a perfect Source somewhere who set everything in motion for all souls eventually to become perfect. Our transformation from total ignorance to perfected knowledge involves a continual process of enlightenment by having faith that we can be better than we are.

Processing Council Meetings

There comes that time during a hypnosis session when the subject tells me their council meeting is over and they are ready to leave the chamber and return to their soul group. It is a moment of intense reflection and together, we will evaluate the information received. Above all else, appearing in front of our spiritual council involves matters of accountability for the life just lived and I want to use the relevant portions of this evaluation in my client's current life.

Within the texture of any soul evaluation by one's council there runs the thread of divine forgiveness. The Elders provide a forum of both inquiry and compassion and display their desire to bolster the confidence of the soul for their future endeavors. One departing soul had this to say:

> When the Elders are finished with me I feel they told me much more about what I did right than where I went wrong. The council knows I have had critical meetings with my guide about my performance. They don't

patronize me, but I think part of their job is to raise my expectations. The council says they foresee great things from me. The last thing the Elders said was to stop looking to others for self-validation. When I leave them, I feel they have absorbed all my self-doubt and cleansed me.

People ask me if souls feel remorse both during and after the council meeting if they were involved in acts of cruel wrongdoing. Of course they do, but often I must remind those who ask this question that accountability for wrongdoing frequently comes with the selection of the next body for the payment of karmic debts. Souls are directly involved with this selection process through their council because this is what *they* want for themselves. Although karma is associated with justice, its essence is not punitive but one of bringing balance to the sum of our deeds in all past lives.

There is another follow-up question I am asked about regarding the conclusion of these council meetings. "Is it all sweetness and light for those souls who have not been involved with cruel acts, or do some souls come away unhappy with the general temper of the meeting?" I answer these queries by explaining that I have had a few clients who left the council chamber a little unsettled. These are souls who feel they could have presented themselves a little better to a particular Elder. There are other uncommon cases, especially with young, rebellious souls, where I have had the impression they are fighting what they call "an act of contrition" by standing in front of the Elders. The following quote is an example:

> I get a little upset with the All-Knowing Ones. They lull you into complacency because they want you to spill your guts out to them. Sure, I made a lot of mistakes but it's their fault in sending me to Earth in a body that got me into trouble. When I complain about Earth they don't level with me completely. They are stingy with information. I tell them that life makes you take risks, and my director talks to me about moderation! I said to him, "That's all very well for you to say sitting here safe and comfortable while I'm fighting to survive down in a war zone."

These immature souls do not realize that to be on a council, an Elder has survived many war zones. By contrast, the next quote comes from an old, advanced soul nearing the completion of her incarnations on Earth:

> As my session with the council comes to an end, the Elders stand and close around me in a circle. Once in position, they raise their arms—outstretched like a giant bird—enfolding me with wings of unification. This is their accolade for a job well done.

I don't believe I have ever had a client come away from visualizing themselves attending a council meeting without some sense of awe, penitence and the need for atonement. They carry these sentiments back to their soul groups. For this reason, I was unprepared to learn about the Law of Silence.

I will cite a case excerpt involving privacy of the mind which extends not only to soul groups but also to my own questioning of clients about council meetings. There are aspects of council meetings that are out of the scope of current reality for my subjects. For a variety of personal and spiritual reasons, people are unable to recall all the details of these meetings. Some parts of this blockage can be deliberate on the part of the client. In case 45, the subject evidently knows what he wishes not to tell me. With other subjects, they don't know why they can't remember.

Case 45

Dr. N: I now want to move forward to the most significant part of your discussion with the Elder sitting to the right of the chairperson on your council.

S: (uneasy) I'm not comfortable with this.

Dr. N: Why?

S: I don't want to break the Law of Silence.

Dr. N: You mean with me?

S: With anyone, including members of my group.

Dr. N: Don't group members exchange information on everything?

S: Not on everything, especially with very private and personal communication from the council. The Law of Silence is a way of testing us to see if we can hold the truths of that which is sacred.

Dr. N: Could you be more specific here?

S: (laughing at me) Then I would be telling you!

Dr. N: I don't want to violate anything you consider too sacred to discuss but, after all, you came to see me for a reason.

S: Yes, and I have gained much. It is just that I don't wish to share with you all that I am now seeing in my mind.

Dr. N: I respect that. However, I find it curious that you don't wish to share this with your soul companions.

S: Most of them have a different council than I do, but there is another reason. If we share all our knowledge, it can create havoc if that person is not ready for certain things. The profound may be improperly used and thus by violating the Law of Silence we generate interference with another soul.

Dr. N: I understand, but does this law also have to apply to our conversation about your growth and personal aspirations?

S: (smiling) You just don't give up, do you?

Dr. N: If I was easily dissuaded from asking questions about life in the spirit world, I would know very little and would be less effective in helping people.

S: (sighs) I won't talk to you about certain sacred things which pertain to me.

The larger implications of what this case had to say about mental privacy between souls in groups has been corroborated by others. It seems very odd to me that souls would not want to compare notes with their friends about all that happened to them in council meetings. Perhaps this is one reason why members of the same soul group are rarely given the same council. Here is another example of privacy:

> I don't discuss my panel with anyone other than two of my friends. Even the three of us are careful about dis-

cussing what transpired at our meetings. We talk in a general way, like, "I know I need to do this or that because an Elder said so-and-so about me."

Considering that our life between lives is in a telepathic world, early in my research I wondered how souls could keep any thoughts hidden from each other. I found that young souls have great difficulty in masking thoughts from the more experienced souls, especially their guides. By level III, mental telepathy becomes an art form, and this includes blockage for privacy. Without the emotional restrictions of the human body, such as shame, guilt and envy, there is no motivation for subterfuge. In a telepathic world, the paramount consideration between souls is their respect for personal privacy. Souls live in communities with intense group socialization where they work on their own lessons and those of others. They open their minds to each other to such an extent it seems impossible to conceal intent. This fosters complete openness on karmic matters which affect those souls who will be connecting on Earth.

How are telepathic souls able to engage in selective mind screening and blockage? This is a process I know little about but I have discovered a few details. From what I can gather, every soul has a distinctive mental vibrational pattern, like a fingerprint. The pattern is similar to a tightly woven basket with interlocking energy strands surrounding an individual core of character. The strands are motion pictures of thought where transference is voluntary to the soul. These involve ideas, concepts, meanings, symbols and personal distinctions particular to that soul. With experience, the soul has the ability to mask any picture frame at any moment. Thus, while nothing is hidden in a general way, no strand opens to the core to release a fine distinction of thought unless a soul wishes another to enter.

Having said all this, I find it is usual for guides and Elders to probe below a particular mental threshold of the less-advanced souls. This is for the benefit of these souls. I know this sounds ominous. It would be, if all this was taking place on Earth. Our teachers also engage in selective mind screening toward souls who wish to mind-probe them. This is because guides don't wish to burden the younger souls with concepts they are not yet ready for, particularly those involving the future.

Everyone respects the sanctity and wisdom of their council. The information is considered privileged and very personal. Upon returning to their individual groups from these meetings, souls don't want their peers to be tempted to second-guess certain meanings derived from the Elders. One client told me, "It would be like cheating on an oral exam to tell my friends. They would be unable to resist their own interpretations of the meeting in order to help me." On the other side of the council table, the Elders encourage silence because they know that if privacy is honored this insures greater openness with the souls who come before them. Undue interference by group peers later, however well-intentioned, might skew the Elders' messages. The one exception I see to the Laws of Silence involves more advanced souls, training in specialized groups. They appear to enjoy sharing what they consider to be "guild information" from their council meetings.

Since the spirit world has a timeless environment, I use council meetings as a therapeutic springboard for rapid karmic reviews spanning centuries. Placing everything in the chamber on hold, I take my subject back to key junctions of their past lives involving critical choices. I direct the hypnosis subject to pick moments in their past lives that are relevant to the topic under discussion by the Elders. Many of our attitudes and ego hang-ups come from other lifetimes and seeing this in a different context gives the client a new perspective in current time. Frequently, I feel the assistance of both my guide and the client's guide.

Through this form of therapeutic intervention, my client and I look for clues to current behavior patterns. This will open the door to healthy reframing. Reincarnation therapy is more than cognitive understanding. People need to see that the twists and turns in their lives all have meaning and purpose. I may also move clients forward to the life selection room to discuss why the Elders offered them their current bodies. If the soul is not yet supposed to know about aspects of the future in this life, it will be blocked. When I am finished I take the Elders out of suspended animation and the council meeting continues without missing a beat.

I never forget I am only a temporary intermediary in the dynamics between my client, their guides and council Elders. I know they are helping me because otherwise my subject would not be able to visualize the council meeting in trance. With the use of deep hypnosis I have the advantage as a spiritual regressionist of utilizing both the soul mind and current human ego. The superconscious mind operates within an eternal framework which the subconscious is able to process into current reality.

The importance of an awareness of our real inner Self cannot be overemphasized for a productive life. I am not suggesting that the one three-hour spiritual regression session I offer is a quick fix for disturbed people. Nevertheless, a renewed conscious awareness of our true nature, knowing about our past lives, and our immortal life in the spirit world can provide a solid foundation for more conventional therapy later in a client's local area. On the other hand, a single spiritual regression for the mentally healthy client can do wonders for the recognition of their inner wholeness and purpose.

$\backsim$7

Community Dynamics

Soulmates

Between the first and second council meetings is a period of renewal for the soul. As ethereal beings, our growth actually began in the mental realm of the spirit world with other souls before any of us incarnated. So while our internal being is uniquely individual, a vital part of spiritual life between incarnations is devoted to empathetic relationships with other souls. Thus, our development as souls becomes a collective one. Part of the expression of this collectivity is the association we have with these souls in a material reality, such as Earth. During reincarnation, the closeness souls feel for each other in a mental setting is severely tested by karmic challenges in our host bodies. This interruption of a blissful mental existence is one means by which spiritual masters expand our consciousness.

I have listened to many intriguing past life love stories of soulmates who come across time and space to meet each other in life once again. Here are a few examples:

Where love was tormented; in a Stone Age culture by a lustful clan chief who took my client's mate on a regular basis and then gave her back.

Where love was deprived; from a woman who was a slave in ancient Rome serving meals to the gladiators, one of whom she loved. This captured fighter told my client he would love her forever the night before he was killed in the arena.

Where love was cruel; to a stable hand flogged to death in a castle dungeon during the Middle Ages by a nobleman who caught his daughter and my client in their secret meeting place.

Where love was heroic; when a Polynesian bridegroom drowned after saving his mate of a few hours—my client—after their canoe was struck by a sudden storm three centuries ago.

Where love was deadly; when my client, a German husband in eighteenth-century Europe, stabbed his wife in a fit of jealous rage over her alleged affair. Falsely accused by local gossips, she died proclaiming her innocence, saying she loved only him.

Where love was unforgiving; by a returning Civil War veteran whose lonely wife, my client, had married his brother a year after the veteran was officially declared dead.

All the couples listed above are happily married to each other today. Their past trials in each life prepared them for the next and strengthened their bond as soulmates. Past life age regression produces interesting information about coupling, but placing these clients between their lives provides them with far more perspective on these relationships.

There are many tests wrapped in the package of love. Mixed into those lives where we have had a long and happy life with a soulmate are those lives where we have destroyed the relationship or been devastated by the actions of our soulmate toward us. In the difficult lives with soulmates something stood in the way of an acceptance of love. Being with soulmates can bring joy and pain, but we learn from both. Always, there are karmic reasons behind the serious events involving relationships in our lives.

I had a client, called Valerie, who lived the life of a beautiful woman in China two centuries ago. In that life she rejected her primary soulmate, the man she most cared about, because he argued with her and refused to feed her vanity while others did so. "Besides," Valerie told me in trance, "he was so ungainly and rough-looking I was embarrassed to be seen with him because of what others might think. Out of pride, spite and feelings that I was being taken for granted, I married a handsome man who catered to my whims. I lost the happiness that could have been mine."

In her next life, in nineteenth-century America, Valerie was the daughter of a Cherokee Indian chief who ordered her to marry the son of another chief as part of a treaty arrangement. This man repulsed her physically and made her life miserable after she assented to her father's wishes. The warrior she loved in her own tribe was the rejected soulmate in her China life. Upon returning to the spirit world after her death as an Indian woman, Valerie told me:

> My love and I could have run away together. Aside from the great danger of this act, something inside told me I had to endure what my father had set in motion. I see now that it was a test. We have the capacity to severely hurt the person who loves us and also ourselves in the bargain. My life as a Cherokee woman was a reminder of my pride and vanity as a Chinese woman.

Being with the "wrong" person for a period in your life does not mean that time was wasted. The relationship was probably intended in advance. In fact, you might see this soul again in the spirit world in a different light. This was true of the man my subject was forced to marry in her Indian life. His soul belonged to a neighboring group to Valerie's own. The soul of both men Valerie loved in her past two lives is again united with her in the twentieth century as her husband. I should add that Linda, who is Valerie's best girlfriend today and a member of her own soul group, was the eventual mate of the warrior she loved in the Cherokee Indian life. After our session, Valerie grinned while telling me, "Now I know why I have always been a little uneasy seeing Linda around my husband."

Before I go further, it would be a good idea to consider some ramifications involved in the magical experience of meeting a soulmate. When I first sit down with a client and we establish a rapport, I will ask about prior and current relationships that have had significance in their life. In this way I acquire a feel for the cast of characters who exist in the play of their current life. Since I am going to be sitting in the front row as this play unfolds during hypnosis, I want a theater program.

Once in a deep trance state, many soul connections will become clear. People in my client's cast may be lovers, devoted friends and relatives, mentors or associates. Our relationships with people take many forms in life and usually involve souls from other groups as well as our own. Usually, clients have a strong desire to identify these soul connections in their current life, although most already have a good idea who they are.

In a broad sense, love is endearment, which can take many forms in life. There is always a mental connection of one sort or another with a soulmate, regardless of the role they play. We connect with people on many levels for a multitude of karmic lessons in every life. When friendship catches fire it turns to love, but without abiding friendship deep love cannot thrive. This is quite different from infatuation, which exists on a superficial level where we have those nagging doubts about whether the connection has any real meaning. Without trust, intimacy suffers and love cannot grow. Love is the acceptance of all the imperfections of our partners. True love makes you better than you would be without that person in your life.

People often equate love with happiness. Yet happiness is a state of mind that must develop within you and not be dependent upon someone else. The most healthy kind of love is one where you already feel good about yourself and so extending your love to someone else is totally unselfish. Love takes hard work and continual maintenance. I have had numerous divorced subjects who learn that their first loves were primary soulmates. Things might have worked out if they both had tried harder.

On the other hand, there may be reasons why we might not meet our primary soulmate until later in life. Soulmates will from time to time separate for a life or two and not appear at all. "My soulmate and I were becoming too dependent upon each other, we needed to grow a while on our own" is a statement I often hear when soulmates are apart. Every era on Earth is different as to the sort of attachment and experience we will have with a soulmate. However, each life with them builds upon former lives.

We learn valuable lessons from broken relationships. The important thing is to move on in life. Some clients may tell me before their session that true love seems to elude them. After the session they usually understand the reasons behind this situation. If the right love for you does not come along, liberate yourself with the understanding that you may be here to learn other lessons. We mistakenly assume people who choose to live alone are lonely when actually they have rich lives that are calm, reflective and productive. Connecting with someone for whom you have no feelings just for the sake of not being alone is more lonely than being by yourself. As the song says, "Falling in love with love is falling for make-believe." This kind of love is a fantasy because it's driven by an addiction to have love at any price. If your soulmate is supposed to appear they will come into your life, often when you least expect it.

Over many years of exposure to souls in the spirit world I have developed a means of classifying soulmates. I find the position of souls within one of three categories bears upon their relationship to us in the drama of life. Our guides and beings who come from spiritual areas far from our own are not included in these three divisions.

Primary Soulmates

A primary, or principal soulmate is frequently in our life as a closely bonded partner. This partnership may be our spouse, brother or sister, a best friend, or occasionally a parent. No other soul is more important to us than a primary soulmate and when my subjects describe lives with these souls as their mates most will say their existence is enriched beyond measure. One of the greatest motivations for souls to incarnate is the opportunity for expression in physical form. This is certainly an attraction for primary soulmates. They may change genders from life to life together if they are more advanced souls. The average soul usually chooses one gender over another about 75 percent of the time.

A primary soulmate should not be confused with the use of the term primary cluster group where many souls interact with each other as companions. People use the term "true soulmate" to define their primary soulmate, which is fine as long as this does not imply that all other soul companions are something less than true. The disagreements people in my field have about such terms are often more symbolic than literal, but I take issue with another concept related to primary soulmates that bothers me.

I have been questioned on road tours about how my descriptions about primary soulmates and statements of soul duality relate to the theory of twin souls. My answer is, they don't. I have discussed how we are able to divide our soul energy to live parallel lives, although most souls don't wish to accelerate learning in this way. Also, I have stated this capacity to divide allows us to leave part of our energy behind in the spirit world as an exact duplicate while we incarnate. Almost all souls engage in this practice, which represents soul duality. My findings of primary soulmate relationships and the capacity for souls to divide have no correlation with the twin soul or twin flame theory. My truths are mine alone but to be blunt, I have never found a single piece of evidence in my research to support the concept of twin souls.

As I understand the theory of twin souls, you and your twin were created at the same moment out of one energy egg and then separated, not to be reunited with your twin—your true soulmate—until the end of your respective karmic incarnations. I remember clients, such as case 26, who said no two souls are alike at the moment of conception. Each energy particle is unique in its own right and created as a single entity. What is so illogical to me about the twin soul theory is why would we have a primary soulmate with whom we could not work out our karmic lessons with before reaching a perfected state? Primary, or true, soulmates exist to help one another achieve goals; they are not twins of ourselves.

Companion Soulmates

Our primary soulmate is our eternal partner but we have other souls in our primary cluster group who can be called soulmates. Essentially, they are our soul companions. These souls have differences in character and a variety of talents which complement each other, as my case histories illustrate. Within this cluster group there is usually an inner circle of souls who are especially close to us, and they play important support roles in our lives and we do the same thing for them. This number varies but the average client has from three to five souls in their inner circle.

Although the companion souls in a cluster group started together, they do have different rates of development. This has as much to do with drive and motivation as talent. Each soul does possess certain strengths that their companions can draw upon during group incarnations. As the group gets smaller, many go off into different specializations but they do not lose contact with each other.

Affiliated Souls

This classification of souls pertains to members of secondary groups outside our own primary cluster but located in the same general spiritual vicinity. As I mentioned in chapter 5 under figure 1, secondary groups around our own primary group can total up to 1,000 souls or more. Many of these groups work in classrooms near us. There are certain affiliated souls in other groups who are selected to work with us whom we come to know over many lives, while others may only cross our path briefly. Quite often our parents come from one of these nearby cluster groups.

In terms of social interaction in the spirit world, as well as contact during their physical incarnations, souls of one cluster group may have little or no association with many of the souls in a secondary group. In the larger context all souls in a secondary group are affiliated in one way or another but they are not considered soulmates by my clients. Although they are not really companion souls, they do form a large pool of people available for casting calls by our directors in the life to come. A soul affiliate might have a specific characteristic that is exactly what is needed to bring a karmic lesson into your life. They are very likely to incarnate as people who carry strong positive or negative energy into their association with you. These decisions depend upon advance agreements between all parties and their respective teachers as to the benefits and disadvantages of certain character roles.

The role can be very brief. The reader may recall the bus stop incident related by the subject in case 39. The assistance given to the woman in that case was more likely spontaneous, and I feel this subject was a non-affiliated soul. I will cite an example of a brief positive contact reported to me by a subject who met a clearly defined affiliated soul:

> I was walking alone on a beach, totally devastated after being fired from my job. A man appeared and we struck up a conversation. I did not know him and was never to see him again in that life. But that afternoon he came up to me with ease and we talked. I felt myself unloading my problems on this stranger. He calmed me down and gave me greater perspective of my job situation. After about an hour he was gone. Now I see he was an acquaintance in the spirit world from another group. It was no accident we bumped into each other that day. He was sent to me.

However, it is with soulmates that we have our most profound contacts. While considering this book, I was asked by people to be sure and give them one detailed case of a love story between primary soulmates. Being a romantic myself, this request was irresistible.

Case 46

There was an urgency to Maureen's voice when she called me for an appointment. This was in the days before I had long waiting lists of over a year. Maureen lived close to my office in California and wondered if she might see me with a male friend who was on his way from New York to meet her for the first time. I asked her about this friend she had never met and the following story unfolded.

Three months before, on a computer website, a group of some twenty-five people interested in life after death formed what is known in computer parlance as a "chat room." Conversations are initiated on-line in this way for people with similar interests. All this had to be explained to me because I have little knowledge of computers. Maureen said that she and a man named Dale found they were so closely attuned in their discussions about the topic of soulmates they felt connected in a strange way. She added that it was uncanny how Dale mirrored her thoughts. They decided to set up their own private chat room for further computer conversations.

Maureen and Dale learned that they were born only a few months apart fifty years ago in an area around San Francisco. They talked about their unsuccessful marriages and a mutual feeling of unexplained sadness about seeking something neither had ever found that would open their hearts. Their conversations mostly centered around life after death and Dale mentioned reading my work. Soon, the two decided to meet each other in California and see me for a combined regression session at the same time.

I agreed to an appointment date that turned out to be the day after they first met. They arrived at my office starry-eyed and I remarked that they were already in a trance state and didn't need me. The moment they saw each other there was instant recognition. Maureen said, "The way we smiled at each other—the expression in our eyes—the sound of our laughter together—the connecting vibrations as we shook hands—created a euphoria that was so strong we were oblivious to everything going on around us."

I will relate this case from the standpoint of Maureen, since she was my initial contact. During intake, I learned that there had been times in her life when she had a feeling of déjà vu when she heard music from the 1920s or saw dancers do the Charleston wearing flapper dresses from that era. Maureen also told me that since childhood she had been bothered by a recurring nightmare of sudden death.

It is my custom to take subjects into the spirit world after death from their last life so they will not miss the natural wonders of normal spirit world entry. The advantages of this hypnosis technique are many, including learning if any disrupting body imprints from the last life have been carried forward into the client's current physical body. To speed up this process by taking subjects directly into the spirit world, say from their mother's womb, causes them to arrive disoriented. It would be like taking someone into the back of a house and asking them to describe the front. This accelerated procedure for spirit world entry would also cause them to circumvent a variety of orientation stations. These stops might be vital if the death preceding this entry was sudden and traumatic. By not skipping over death scenes, the client is actually better protected from painful physical memories.

Upon my direction to move to the most significant scene in her past life, Maureen took me to the events leading up to her death. This is often a signal of trouble ahead and past life facilitators must be prepared to deal with death scenes that can be horrific. What follows is a condensed version of Maureen's story.

Dr. N: Are you a man or woman?

S: A girl, really.

Dr. N: What is your name?

S: Samantha. Sam for short.

Dr. N: Where are you and what are you doing at this moment?

S: I'm at my bedroom dressing table getting ready to go to a party.

Dr. N: What is the party all about?

S: (pause, and then light laughter) It's . . . for me, today is my eighteenth birthday and my parents are giving me a coming-out party.

Dr. N: Well, happy birthday, Sam. What is the date today?

S: (after a brief hesitation) July 26, 1923.

Dr. N: Since you are at your dressing table, I would like you to look in your mirror and describe to me what you see.

S: I'm blond, with my hair up high tonight. I'm wearing a white silk gown. It's my first real grown-up party dress. I'm going to put on my new white high-heeled shoes.

Dr. N: You sound smashing.

S: (with a knowing smile) Rick better think so.

Dr. N: Who is Rick?

S: (now distracted and flushed) Rick is . . . my guy . . . my date for tonight. I've got to finish my makeup, he will be here soon.

Dr. N: Listen, Sam, I'm sure you can talk to me while finishing your makeup because I don't want to slow you down. Tell me, are you serious about Rick?

S: (flushes again) Uh-huh . . . but I don't want to appear too eager. I'm playing hard to get. Rick thinks he's the cat's meow, but I know he wants me.

Dr. N: I can see this is an important party. I suppose that he will be honking soon for you to run out to his car?

S: (annoyed) Absolutely not! Oh, he'd like that, all right, but he will ring the doorbell in a proper fashion and the maid will let him in and make him wait downstairs.

Dr. N: So the party is some distance from your house?

S: Not too far—it's in a posh mansion in downtown San Francisco.

Dr. N: Okay, Sam, now move forward in time to the party downtown and explain to me what is going on.

S: (bubbling) I'm having a wonderful time! Rick looks gorgeous, of course. My parents and their friends are telling me how grown-up I look. There is music, dancing . . . a lot of my friends are congratulating me . . . and (my subject's face grows dark for a fleeting moment) there is a lot of drinking my parents don't know about.

Dr. N: Does this trouble you?

S: (fighting off a new set of feelings by quickly running one hand through her hair and returning to the moment) Oh . . . drinking is always a part of these affairs—it makes us gay and carefree. I'm drinking too . . . Rick and some of his friends snuck in the liquor.

Dr. N: Move forward now to the next significant event this evening and explain what is taking place.

S: (subject's face softens and her voice is more halting) Rick and I are dancing . . . he is pressed so close to me . . . we . . . are on fire . . . he whispers in my ear that we must get away from the party to be alone for a while.

Dr. N: And how does this make you feel, Samantha?

S: Excited . . . but something seems to be holding me back . . . I overcome it . . . I'm willful. I assume it's a feeling of my parents' disapproval . . . yet, I sense it's something more. I shake it off in favor of the excitement of the moment.

Dr. N: Stay with this emotion. What happens next?

S: We leave by a side entrance to avoid being seen and go to Rick's car. It's a beautiful new red roadster convertible. It's a marvelous night and the top is down.

Dr. N: Then what do you and Rick do, Sam?

S: We get in the car. Rick takes the pins out of my hair so it will blow free. He gives me a deep kiss. Rick wants to show off . . . we roar out of a long driveway into the street.

Dr. N: Can you describe the location of the road and the direction you take?

S: (now growing very nervous) We are going south down the Pacific Coast Road out of San Francisco.

Dr. N: What is the ride like for you, Sam?

S: (for one final fleeting moment the subject is free of her premonitions) I feel so alive. It's a warm night and the wind in my hair blows the strands all over my face. Rick has one arm around me. He squeezes me and says I am the most beautiful girl in the world. We both know we're in love.

Dr. N: (I notice my subject's hands now start to shake and her body grows more rigid; I take her hand because I suspect what is coming) Now, Samantha, I want you to understand that as you continue to talk to me I will be with you every step of the way so I can move you quickly through anything that may happen. You know this, don't you?

S: (faintly) Yes . . .

Dr. N: Move to the time when things begin to change on this drive with Rick and describe the action.

S: (subject's entire body now starts to shake) Rick has been drinking too much and the road is getting more curvy. The turns are sharper and Rick only has one hand on the wheel. We are near a hilly section . . . close to the ocean . . . there is a cliff . . . the car is all over the road. (now shouting) RICK, SLOW DOWN!

Dr. N: Does he?

S: (crying now) OH, GOD, NO. HE WON'T! HE IS LAUGHING AND LOOKING AT ME AND NOT THE ROAD.

Dr. N: Quickly now, Sam—keep going.

S: (with a sob) We miss the next curve—the car is in space—we are crashing into the ocean . . . I'm dying . . . the water . . . so cold . . . can't breathe . . . Oh, Rick . . . Rick . . .

We stop while I begin rapid desensitization of this traumatic memory while at the same time bringing Samantha's soul out of her physical body. I remind her she has been through physical death many times before and she will be all right. Samantha explains that she is reluctant to go because her young life was only starting. She didn't want to leave Rick but the pulling sensation away from the ocean was "too insistent."

When I began my research on the soul, I assumed that when two people such as Samantha and Rick died together they would also enter the spirit world together. I have found this not to be true in death scenes, with one exception. Small children who are killed with those who love them rise with that person. I will elaborate on this further in chapter 9 under souls of the young. Even primary soulmates killed at the same moment will normally rise up by separate routes on their own vibrational lines. I felt that this loss of companionship was a little sad until it was made clear to me that souls are met by their guides and friends from the spirit world at the appropriate time and place. Each soul requires their own rate of ascension, which includes orientation stops and energy rejuvenation, even if they are returning to the same soul group. This was true for Rick and Samantha.

Dr. N: Do you see Rick anywhere?

S: No, I'm trying to resist the pulling which wants me to turn around and face upwards. I want to continue to face the ocean . . . I want to help Rick.

Dr. N: Does the force eventually turn you around in the proper direction away from the Pacific Ocean?

S: (subject is now quiet and resigned, but mournful as well) Yes, I am now far above the Earth.

Dr. N: (this is a question I usually ask people) Do you want to say goodbye to your parents before going further?

S: Oh ... no ... not right now ... later I will ... now I just want to go.

Dr. N: I understand. Tell me, what do you see next, Samantha?

S: The eye of a tunnel ... opening and closing ... coordinating its movement with my movement. I pass through and feel much lighter. It's so bright now. Someone in a robe is coming toward me.

In Dale's session, we learned he was Rick and his memories corroborated those of Maureen. While Samantha apparently lived a few seconds after the crash and rose out of the ocean, Rick's soul bailed out while the car was still in the air. When I related this story to a Dallas audience a lady loudly scolded, "Isn't that just like a man!" I told her that when the mind knows there is no chance of surviving imminent devastation to the body, souls may leave a moment before actual death. In this way the soul emerges with their energy more intact.

After the sessions with Dale and Maureen were completed, I met with these primary soulmates for a review of what we had learned. Maureen explained that whenever she drove down Highway 1, south of San Francisco, she would inexplicably get very nervous and apprehensive at a certain section on the coast road. Now she knew why. I hoped my deprogramming of her death scene in 1923 would also clear up the recurring nightmares of sudden death. A month later Maureen wrote and confirmed this nightmare was finally gone.

The wonders of synchronicity became evident in this case when Dale told me that one of the reasons he left the area where he was born was because he felt uncomfortable driving around San Francisco. You would think that the time we spend in the spirit world between lives should eliminate all residual effects of our past life experiences. In most cases it does but, as I have said, some people do carry physical and emotional body imprints from one life to the next. This is especially true if that imprint bears upon a particular karmic lesson in the life to come.

Why were these primary soulmates separated in their current lives for fifty years? To understand this we must start with the dynamics of their cluster group. Dale and Maureen come from a level I soul group. In varying degrees, these twelve souls are intense fighters and risk takers. Their guide regularly takes them to nearby groups just so they can see how other groups function with more peace and harmony. Dale and Maureen told me these visitations were interesting but they found peaceful souls "sort of boring." Certainly, there are members of their group who are less restless, but Rick/Dale isn't one of them. In his current life he was an Army Ranger who served three tours in Vietnam. "I didn't expect to come back," he told me, "and that would have been okay." Because he likes living on the edge of danger, he left the service after the war because being a peacetime soldier was too dull.

After the car crash in 1923 the group's senior guide picked up Rick, who spent considerably more time in debriefing and orientation than did Samantha. When he did return to the group, Rick was very chagrined. In a tender scene of energy caressing, Rick told his primary soulmate how sorry he was for cutting off her young life. It was not clear from the session just how much they both knew about the possibility of the crash in advance. They have been lovers in numerous past lives, many involving turmoil. Although Dale and Maureen incarnated at the same time in this life and in the same place as their life in the 1920s, they were not destined to meet while young. The same sensory experience and emotional energy from this geographical location simply were part of the conditions for meeting much later in their current lives.

These soulmates both knew going into their current life that conditions would not be right for their meeting until many years had passed. Dale especially needed to feel the frustration of years of longing for the right woman to come along. He is not a careless, irresponsible man today. Samantha/Maureen also required the maturity she did not yet possess in her relationship with Rick in the 1920s. Neither Dale nor Maureen take life for granted at this stage of their conjunction. They have both been through considerable heartache without each other. My work with this couple ended with both essentially making the same declaration. Maureen said, "We are completing our healing by a clear respect for the sanctity of life and importance of forgiveness. Now that we both know the meaning of loss, we are going to treasure the time we have left together in this life."

Before closing this section on soulmates, I should add that many soulmates have a preparation class just before their next incarnation. A feature of this dress rehearsal with our guides is a final review of important issues in the life to come. One aspect of this prep class might also include two soulmates going off alone and sending visual images to each other of what they will look like in their new human bodies and under what circumstances they are going to meet.

In *Journey of Souls* I wrote a chapter citing examples of this sort of preparation for embarkation. Soulmates don't always get together just before departure. Then too, depending upon the karma involved, sometimes one soul knows more than the other about their future meeting and what that person will look like. Here is a short example of a soulmate discussing meeting his future wife:

> I was permitted to see my wife in the screening room for the next life. She was an attractive aerobics instructor who I would meet in a gym. I studied her body and facial features carefully because I didn't want to mess up our meeting, as I had done in my prior life. The scent of her body bathed in sweat was embedded in my mind . . . her gestures . . . her smile . . . and most of all her eyes. The moment I saw her in this life it was like two magnets pulling together.

Linkages Between Spiritual and Human Families

As a rule, members of the same soul group do not return in their next incarnations as members of the same genetic human family. This means, contrary to American Indian tradition, a grandfather's soul would typically not return to the body of his grandson. I have emphasized the opposition souls have for genetic reincarnation in chapter 4 under soul division and again in chapter 5 with DNA. It is limiting and even redundant for souls who wish to learn fresh lessons to return to bodies having the same heredity, ethnicity, cultural environment, and perhaps the same geographic setting as they had in a former life. By incarnating in different families around the globe in each life, souls are able to take advantage of the great variety of human body choices. This variety is what gives depth to our incarnations on Earth.

In unusual cases, our guides may be indulgent with souls who have strong feelings about unfinished karmic business within a particular family and wish to return to the same family. These souls may be given another crack at addressing a serious wrong done to them, or to correct harm they have caused another in the family. They could return as children of a new generation, but within the same lifetime of those people who were involved with the karmic events requiring their attention. I want to stress these occurrences of genetic reincarnation for karmic purposes are rare. It is far more likely the soul would return to another family with peripheral associations to the family of their former life to redress a serious wrong. Nevertheless, this too would be a very unconventional decision, especially in cases of personal injury to the soul, because it smacks of revenge.

Although souls typically do not incarnate in the same hereditary family they had in past lives, members of the same soul group most definitely choose new families where they can be together. Members of soul groups tend to be associated in each life by blood ties and geographic proximity. What sort of roles do they choose? I'm sure readers of this book could sit down and draw up a chart showing significant members of their family, friends, lovers and even acquaintances to see who might be the most likely candidates for their own soul family.

In chapter 5, figure 7, I charted the color auras of a soul family in their current life. Figure 10 is a diagram showing how a group of souls incarnated into human families in order to stay connected to one another over the past three centuries. My central subject in this diagram is Ruth. Please note that from one century to the next, the family heredity is completely different despite the genealogical overtones of my chart. Figure 10 is an abbreviated version of Ruth's spiritual friends in human bodies. There are six souls listed from her own cluster group and two from an affiliated group to be found in each century.

Ruth appears in the center of the diagram and each of the connecting lines from the center outward represents the same soul assuming different family roles relating to Ruth from the twentieth century back to the eighteenth century. We can see that Ruth's primary soulmate in this life

Figure 10: Spiritual and Human Genealogy

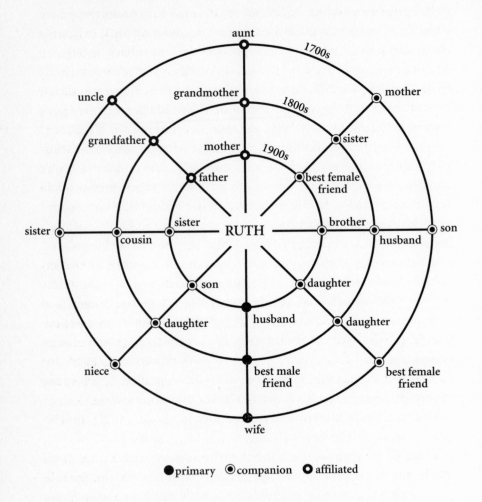

This webbed diagram illustrates primary, companion and affiliated soulmates who have incarnated into bodies related to the lives of the subject, Ruth, over the past three centuries. Each generational line outward from the center represents the same soul in different bodies.

is her husband. In Ruth's last life, this soul was her best friend, and in the life before, her wife when she was a male in the eighteenth century. Ruth's primary soulmate has a halo color tinted with protective yellow while Ruth's own halo is a mixture of white and blue tints, indicating clarity and love of learning. These primary soulmates have mated on a fairly regular basis for some 7,000 years since their first life together.

Besides the companion souls in Ruth's soul group, I have also shown two affiliated souls from a nearby group. These souls are my subject's current father and mother. The roles they played in the nineteenth century were her grandmother and grandfather respectively. In the eighteenth century, these same two souls were Ruth's aunt and uncle. Ruth's chart represents one typical client. Every soul group has its own subtle variations of human family preferences. I had a client the same week I saw Ruth who is extremely close to her mother. The mother's soul was a member of that client's soul group and was her sister in the life before.

Grandparents often have a great influence in our early lives as non-judgmental confidants. I often find that a favorite grandparent in this life was a sibling or best friend in a former life. The social dynamics of intimate human contact are so powerful that in most of my cases the roles souls play in our lives and we in theirs directly bear on a group's karmic lessons. When we are hurt by someone close to us in life, or caused them hurt resulting in alienation and separation, it is because they volunteered to teach us lessons of some sort while learning lessons themselves. These lessons better prepare both parties for future relationships, as case 47 will show.

I should also point out that peripheral roles in our lives by hundreds of affiliated souls in nearby groups may go on for generations. Because of space, I did not list all these souls on Ruth's past life chart in figure 10. An example of one important affiliated soul not included here is a soul called Zenda, who was Ruth's favorite teacher in the sixth grade. We found that in the last century, Zenda was a supportive next-door neighbor. In the eighteenth century Zenda was the owner of a business that employed this subject. The web design of figure 10 is appropriate when we consider all the interrelationships of people whose own lives are woven into our own.

The psychological profiles of primary, companion and affiliated souls in a client's current and past lives is very instructive when detailed in a genealogical-type chart. In each of the three past centuries we found another leading actor in Ruth's lives who was from an affiliated soul group. There was not space for her in figure 10 either. This soul, known as Ortier, assumed roles involving jealous, unemotional and manipulative people. She was sent to test Ruth's trusting nature so she would learn to recover more quickly from the hurt and deal with it in a healthy manner. While this same individual would also demonstrate good qualities in human temperament, the negatives were very constant. In Ruth's current life, Ortier is her mother-in-law. In the life before, this soul played the role of a close friend who betrayed her. There is evidence the karmic cycles with Ortier assuming roles as a protagonist will end soon for Ruth.

Ruth is a warm, passionate and tender person. Her primary soulmate has aspects of these qualities but is also tenacious, brutally frank and decisive. Many other souls in figure 10 are rather reserved and quiet. They also have character similarities of perfectionism and stubbornness.

One soul in the group is sloppy, easygoing and more complacent than the rest. He is my client's brother, Andy, in her current life. This soul volunteered to be Ruth's husband in the last century as a change of pace for her. During that life, Ruth's primary soulmate chose the role of a male friend. They were so drawn to each other they had an affair that almost destroyed Ruth's marriage with Andy. She finally realized in this past life that Andy, an uncustomary mate to be sure, was a person who opened her mind in a relaxed way to a more optimistic existence where she would learn to appreciate each day and see more humor in life to complement her naturally warm nature. Although not a great love match, Ruth found tolerance and playfulness with Andy as her husband in the nineteenth century. Meanwhile, her primary soulmate was coping with a new challenge of being married to someone else whose character was much more confrontative than Ruth's.

I don't wish to leave the impression that not being married to your primary soulmate is a formula for discontent. As a matter of fact, I have had clients who have deliberately alternated mates in a series of lives with three or four souls from their inner circle to meet certain challenges. Although the souls of Ruth and Andy tried this for the first time in the nineteenth century, the results were mostly positive.

Reuniting with Souls Who Have Hurt Us

Now that we have an idea of the roles different soulmates can play in our lives, I want to discuss a specific aspect of these associations that is of interest to people. I am often asked what it is like to see someone in our soul group right after a life where they have hurt us in some way. The philosopher Heidegger said, "No one else can love for you or feel your pain." This statement may be true on Earth, but not in the spirit world. Souls are capable of getting into the minds of their friends and feeling just what they feel. They do this for reasons of empathy, a desire for understanding and to evaluate the disruptive behavior of each other in the last life.

In case 47, I have chosen a man who had a rough start in his last life with an abusive, tyrannical father who was never satisfied with anything he did. For simplification, I will use the Earth names of these players with my subject being Ray and his father as Carl. Ray was a troubled boy who grew up lacking self-worth and his entire adult life was spent trying to conquer these negative feelings. Ray hid his sensitivity from others by building protective walls around himself. What happened when father and son met again in the spirit world is the substance of this case.

We are going to sit in on what Ray called "a motivational critiquing session" with Carl. The opening scene begins innocently enough with the usual greetings extended to an arriving soul by members of a cluster group. It might be helpful to refer back to figure 3 on page 143 where I have diagrammed the soul group as they would appear on the upper half of a clock. I employ my "clock technique" with incoming souls to help me determine soul position as my hypnosis subjects identify members of their cluster group.

Case 47

Dr. N: As you draw closer to these souls, how are they arranged in front of you?

S: Mmm . . . sort of a half circle with me coming into the middle.

Dr. N: I want you to imagine that their positions conform to the face of a clock. You are in the center, where the hands of the clock are located. The person directly in front of you would be at 12 o'clock. The one on your left is at 9 o'clock and the one on your right at 3 o'clock. Do you understand?

S: Yes, but my guide Ix-Ax is behind me right now.

Dr. N: That's usual at this first reunion, Ray. We will consider him to be between 7 and 5 o'clock. Now tell me, from what direction on the face of our clock does the first person come forward to greet you?

S: To my far left—at 9 o'clock.

Note: The first person to come forward and greet us after a life is always a soul of significance.

Dr. N: That's fine. Does this soul appear as a male or female to you, or is the soul genderless?

S: (tenderly) It's my wife, Marian.

Dr. N: And what does she do right now?

S: Cups my face in her hands . . . she gives me a soft, gentle kiss and then hugs my head.

Each spirit has their own style of greeting for the incoming soul. After Marian, Ray's grandmother wraps her energy completely around him lovingly, as a cloak. Then, his daughter Ann comes forward. Part of her energy is still on Earth because her current incarnation is not yet complete. Despite this reduction in energy mass, Ann clasps Ray in an exuberant rocking motion while laughing at his unsettled demeanor.

As we progressed around the clock, I noticed that my subject grew more uneasy. I suspected an important member of the group was not yet in Ray's line of sight. As we neared the end of the circle of souls, the mood began to change when Ray encountered what I call "the hunker-ing-down syndrome," which is caused by one soul hiding behind another. Sometimes the act is playful, rather like hide-and-seek, but not in this case.

Dr. N: Is that everybody?

S: (twisting uncomfortably in my office chair) No ... I see a shadow behind my Aunt Bess.

Dr. N: (after calming and reassurance) Ray, tell me exactly what happens next.

S: I see a flash of light now. (with recognition) Oh ... it's my father ... Carl. He is hiding behind the rest. He wants to be last. He is avoiding me. He is embarrassed at the lightness of the moment—all the hugging, laughing and excitement going on. My father doesn't feel like participating in this right now with me. (darkly) Neither do I.

Note: A little further on in the session I make the transition back to the soul who was Carl.

Dr. N: I want you to move forward to the time when you talk to Carl. Try to give me the details of just how your conversation with him unfolds.

S: We soon get to this ... the critiquing of what took place and why ... talking about our attitudes and judgments. Marian and Ann are there, and Carl is still chagrined. He starts by saying, "I was too severe with you as your father. I know what we planned got out of hand. That life—it just got away from me ..."

Dr. N: What does this admission mean to you, Ray?

S: (with a sense of revelation) Carl's soul is not like the alcoholic, abusive man who was my father ... oh, I see some similarities ... but his innate goodness was shut down. He was not able to control the obsessions of this body.

Dr. N: Forgive me, Ray, but aren't you making excuses for his per-formance? I mean, Carl had lessons to learn too, didn't he?

S: Okay, he volunteered to join with a body prone to emotional outbursts. Besides the plan of making things deliberately hard for me, he wanted to see if he could better moderate a body prone to violence. Carl's previous life was one of excesses. He admits this last life we had together did not work out well. Carl did not do the right thing by me or himself.

Dr. N: (pressing) You still don't think Carl is excusing what he did to you as your father because of his body type?

S: No, you can't get away with that here. Carl is explaining that he failed me in many ways this time around, but he learned from the life and he asks me if I did too. (pause)

Dr. N: Please continue with this, Ray.

S: (a deep sigh) I can see all his anger is gone and this is strange to me now because I haven't yet gotten used to his real self . . . but it won't take long.

Dr. N: As you consider all this, Ray, what negative inclinations does the soul of Carl have which carry into his incarnations?

S: He knows it is the desire to control events and people around him. His past life as my father fed into those tendencies. Both of us have trouble in life with confrontation. This is why we work so well with Ann and Marian. They seem to diffuse life's frustrations so much easier than we do.

Dr. N: Let's return to the circumstances which led to your need to be under the control of a stern father who was supposed to make things deliberately hard. Even if Carl had not gone overboard in his assignment, I don't understand why you volunteered to be his son.

S: (laughs) For that you would have to know our guide, Ix-Ax. He uses humor rather than being overly preachy. He doesn't push us hard as an authority figure because Carl and I react badly to a firm hand. Ix-Ax nudges us while letting us believe all the ideas we get come from our own perceptions. (pauses) Ix-Ax allows me to think I am getting away with something and then he tweaks my conscience. He is a coach, not a director.

Dr. N: Well, I'm glad to get that information about Ix-Ax, but how does all this relate to you and Carl and this past life of a damaged relationship between you?

S: (patiently) In my life before the last one with Carl I was an orphan and got into some bad habits. I lost my real identity in that body. It was a wake-up call.

Dr. N: In what way?

S: I had no directional support as a kid. My mother had died. Being alone as a kid can make or break you. The trouble was . . . as I grew stronger and more self-reliant, I had little concern for others. I created a life of taking and giving back little. I felt people owed me.

Dr. N: Look, Ray, do you have to go to such extremes? How about having a loving father in the life you planned with Carl to compensate for the one before as an orphan?

S: (shrugs) Too easy. After my life as an orphan, Ix-Ax asked me, "I suppose now you are ready for a life of being pampered by indulgent parents?" I said to him, "Say, that doesn't sound bad at all." Then he added, "Shall we also arrange for you to be an only child of wealthy parents?" We had some fun with this scenario for a while with Carl entering into the discussion with a few quips about wanting plenty of money as my rich father in order to play the horses. He loves horses.

Dr. N: So how did you and Carl finally come around to making the decision to have a stressful life together?

S: Ix-Ax knows us so well. I am too far along for a soft-soap approach to life. In the end we asked him for assignments together in a difficult environment.

Dr. N: Didn't things go from bad to worse for you as far as loneliness and alienation in your last two lives? I'm wondering if you and Carl learned anything from having such a poor relationship as father and son.

S: (pause, while rubbing his hands together in thought) Yes and no. It's true I let my alienation in both these past lives serve as an excuse for a lack of real progress but at least I had a father in my last life who didn't leave. I did better with Carl's abuse than total abandonment in my life before Carl, when I was an orphan.

Dr. N: That's not much of an endorsement. Was the soul of Carl your father in your life as an orphan?

S: No.

Dr. N: What was your primary lesson in the last two lives?

S: To keep my identity, no matter what the adversity. This will make me a stronger soul.

Dr. N: I'm sure it will, Ray. But I should think you might consider slowing down now and then and take easier lives as a change of pace. Would it be so bad to catch your breath and build a stronger foundation for identity retention in future bodies?

S: (clearly upset with this suggestion) No! I told you I can do this and Ix-Ax knows it, too. My strength is perseverance in fighting adversity. My life with Carl as my father was a recovery test from the previous life as an orphan and it was not a failure for me. (forcefully) I learned plenty for the next life and I tell Carl this to make him feel better.

Dr. N: How do the two of you bring all this to some sort of resolution in the spirit world?

S: (in a softer, more contemplative tone) When we are alone we agree to exchange the energy of our thoughts and all the memories of that life together.

Dr. N: Is this the full mind exchange I have heard about?

S: Yes, every particle of my identity as Carl's son in that life is transferred to Carl while he projects all his memories as my father to me. It's very subjective—and that's good. In my group we call this passing the cup of sorrows.

Dr. N: And is each perspective totally honest?

S: There can be no deception here.

Dr. N: Does this exchange last long?

S: No, the transfer is brief but complete. Then we know all the trials and burdens, pain and anger—the drives—from the other's perspective because it is like actually being inside their old body. We become the other person.

Dr. N: Does this mind exchange bring forgiveness?

S: It is so much more than that. It is an indescribable melding of two minds. We can both experience the circumstances which led the other to make certain choices. I feel Carl's lack of fulfillment and he feels mine. Once the exchange is made, it cuts so deep forgiveness toward another isn't necessary. You forgive yourself and then we heal each other. Understanding is absolute. We will try again in a different life until we get it right.

After some initial awkwardness in the spirit world following their last lives together, Ray and Carl were relaxed and happy once again in their soul group. This does not mean that Carl's conduct was quickly exonerated in the spirit world. During his life review and evaluation, before he saw Ray, Carl was keenly aware of the excessive pain and hurt he had wrought upon Ray. There are two forces at work here. The first is the potential subversion of the soul's full character by the biophysical attributes of a host body, along with the effects of specific environmental influences. The second factor is the role they were each assigned to play out in the stream of karmic causation.

Each life is a piece of fabric which makes up the whole tapestry of our existence. If a family member or friend is harsh and uncompromising, or perhaps weak and emotionally distant toward us in life, we are only seeing an external portion of the entire true character of that soul. Role assignments in life all have purpose. If you grew up with a particularly difficult parent, as Ray did with Carl, ask yourself this question: What did I learn at the hands of this person that has given me wisdom I would not possess if he or she had never been in my life?

Ray has had his difficulties in his current life with chemical dependency and obsessive behavior. Yet, at age 45, he is drawing on his inner resources and turning things around. From what Ray has told me, getting in touch with his true soul identity in our session together has been very helpful. The soul of Carl is now my client's older brother, who was not easy on Ray when they were growing up. Many of the same relationship patterns are being played out today as in the past. Even so, these two souls have been far more engaged with each other as brothers than they were as father and son.

By not burying unpleasant memories in this life, Ray's soul lives in a mentally healthier body. This time around the soul of Ann, a principal player, is Ray's mother rather than a daughter. She provides a different generational dimension to his current life. Gershen Kaufman has written that "shame is a kind of soul murder." One of Ray's issues is the handling of shame. Shame brings a numbness to our minds because it ushers in feelings of nonacceptance, of being no good and having no validity. It may be so overpowering as to preclude any soul progress in a human mind that has shut down. However, Ray is an unusually determined soul who, as we have seen, won't give up these hard lives for an occasional rest. He grows stronger by building on each hard life.

Case 47 illustrates that there are souls who continually ask for body types that challenge their weakness of soul character. Both Ray and Carl are souls who easily fall into addictive habits with certain types of body chemistry. Why do they continue to ask for these bodies? They do it for practice. Any obsessive mood-altering behavior is a fix and Ray is determined to conquer this before moving on. I know this soul is making progress. After two failed marriages, Ray told me he has met the woman of his dreams, but he had to be clean of drugs and alcohol to appreciate her. We learned his wife-to-be is the soul of Marian.

A final word about the hunkering-down syndrome, where a returning soul might not initially see a group member clearly. When this happens to someone sitting in my office it may be that the soul who is hiding from a client's conscious awareness is going to have a profound future impact. I recall a young widow who came to see me while still grieving over the recent loss of her husband. We had reviewed all the members of her soul group, including the soul of her departed husband. He embraced her in an emotional scene where he told her to stay strong and everything would turn out all right. Then she said, "Ah, there is one more. A dark figure, bending down behind the others. Oh—it's the soul of my future husband. I'm sure of this—but we haven't met yet in this life. I'm not supposed to know who he is right now because it would spoil the spontaneity of our meeting."

Interaction Between Soul Groups

I have said that almost all the younger soul groups remain in their own study areas. Particularly with the level I and IIs, their designated spaces are sacrosanct with self-imposed boundaries between classrooms. The underlying basis for these conventions is that all souls have respect for the privacy of the work going on in other study areas. Spiritual classrooms are not like earthly models where we need excuse slips for absences. Souls are free to avoid study engagements with their own classmates at any time. If a soul wants solitude, or to be involved in some private work which they feel is beneficial to them away from their companions, they are free to do so as long as this activity does not interfere with the work of another group.

I find that souls are not forced to study and some take long periods of rest. Even so, most souls I talk to feel left out if they are not with their classmates in some ongoing project. It is the excitement of mastering certain skills that drives them. Thus, most souls don't wish to get involved in the middle of projects by other groups. I find that no two groups in a vicinity are at exactly the same level in all departments of study. So regardless of your developmental level, it is not all that easy to visit another classroom and gain something from a lesson in progress.

Visits between soul group members are selective and designed for specific reasons. Since such visitations are by invitations emanating from teacher-guides, they are the exception rather than the rule in the spirit world. There are groups who consort with sojourners while others don't appear to see souls from other groups at all, except when they are away from their study areas. When souls arrive near the end of their level II training, they begin to push very hard. It is during this time when my subjects most frequently talk about the opportunity of visiting other cluster groups. The client in my next case had the following to say about one of his visits.

Case 48

Dr. N: Why did you want to visit this nearby soul group?

S: I come from a less serious group than many. I like to visit with this cluster because they are slightly ahead of my own. It helps my game of life to be around better players. Most of them are about ready to move up into independent study and they are very determined. I tell them a few jokes about my group to loosen them up and they give me practical ideas.

Dr. N: Do you visit with them often?

S: No, we know how busy everyone is and I respect that. I don't like to interrupt them too much.

Dr. N: Tell me about your last visit and what took place.

S: (pause) They were in the middle of a heated discussion. One of their members, called Orick, was going over a dream sequence he had from an incarnation that recently ended. Orick thought they might like to know about this incident.

Dr. N: An incident involving a dream by Orick when he was last in human form on Earth?

S: That's right. Someone out of incarnation in his group had sent Orick information while he was asleep that his human mind misinterpreted.

Dr. N: Well, was that the fault of the sender—this discarnate—or Orick?

S: You must understand the group I am visiting are pros at this sort of thing. They don't like mistakes. They are a very serious bunch.

Dr. N: Please go on. What did you learn from the retelling of this incident by Orick about his dream?

S: The morning after his dream on Earth, Orick said he went into deep meditation to try and sort out the message he had received during the night. I guess it was too muddled in his human mind to make much sense. Orick was lightly chiding his friend—the one who sent the message—that he ought to perfect his message-sending through dreams.

Dr. N: What did the sender of the dream say to Orick?

S: He said in an offhanded way, "No, you just translated the information I sent you in an imperfect fashion and then you acted wrongly on your own misinformation."

Dr. N: And what did the group you were visiting conclude from this discussion between Orick and his friend?

S: I think everyone decided that even though two souls are very close the imperfect aspects of the receiving human brain can screw up any transmission. The safe thing for a soul in the spirit world to do is transmit more than once and not rely on one medium, such as the dream state. Also, to keep the messages short and very clear.

Dr. N: So, this was a productive visit for you? You learned something?

S: I always do. Mostly I keep quiet and listen with this particular group. The discussion about transmitting spiritual messages was useful to me and I took what I learned from this visit back to my group for study.

Those groups who are uncomfortable with ordinary visitors may welcome an advanced specialist or high-profile soul unique to their experience. I presented an example of this sort of visitation under colors of visitors in groups in chapter 5. Yet even the clannish groups seem to enjoy socializing out of their study areas. I have already reviewed the community areas where large numbers of primary groups meet to engage in conversation with each other. To many souls this practice is considered recreation.

Because many souls do become restless at times with their formal work, instructor souls often arrange for gatherings at the community centers to hear guest speakers. The visiting speakers at these functions give souls a break from their regular teachers, which allows for different perspectives with topics of general interest to the soul groups. These messages could center around how to appreciate others, the benefits of kind acts, loyalty and integrity, and how to be generous with the gifts

each of us possesses. I know the expressions of all these moral sentiments doesn't sound much like recreation, but the speakers spice things
up with personal anecdotes and many allegories where they draw parallels to their earthly experiences. There are also other subtle conversations here between masters of their craft and members of an audience
of souls that my subjects are unable to translate for me. I have a quote
which gives the flavor of such a gathering:

> Our training is helped by the roving guest speakers. They
> are different in approach and character from my own
> guide, and that's helpful. There is one woman called Sha-
> lakin whom I adore. She comes to our center once in a
> while and I never miss her. Her particular skill is the abil-
> ity to take any problem and quickly boil it down to the
> heart of the matter. She can take a complex idea and get
> through to me so quickly I somehow know I am going to
> respond much more effectively the next time it confronts
> me in life. She tells us to listen to people we don't partic-
> ularly like on Earth because we can learn something from
> everyone.

Recreational Activities in the Spirit World

Leisure Time

This section is dedicated to all those who are afraid that life between
lives involves only work and no play. The term R & R, rest and recreation, is quite appropriate in the spirit world and I have listened to the
statements from hundreds of clients about what they do outside of
their training areas. After physical death our spirit continues to carry all
the fond memories of earthly life. The poignancy of tasting food and
drink, touching human bodies, the smell, sights and sounds of walking
the deserts, climbing mountains and swimming in the seas of Earth
remain with the soul. An eternal mind can reminisce about the motor
movements and sensory pleasures of a human vessel and all the feelings
it generated. Thus, it is natural souls would want to maintain these
planetary memories by re-creating their former bodies in the spirit
world. After all, it was here (in the spirit world) where the conceptual
design and eventual energy models for physical organisms began.

In this section, I will also discuss soul travel to Earth between lives as a part of R & R. Chapter 8 will deal with souls who travel to worlds other than Earth. These soul trips could be construed as "working vacations" for exploration and study, or they could be devoted exclusively to leisure time. The allocation of study versus leisure time on physical and mental worlds away from the soul's home is flexible, depending upon the primary purpose of the trip and the mood of the soul. Since I am devoting this section to soul recreation, my case examples involving trips to Earth and other activities in the spirit world will be confined to soul entertainment.

Recess Breaks

My subjects differentiate between the shorter breaks from soul study and those involving more recreation time. This is an example from a male client relating a typical intermission from class work:

> There are ten people in my group and we separate from each other during the short breaks. I like to wander about, away from our enclosure. I might go down the hall and out into an open area where people from many other groups are milling around and talking. What I like about these casual rest periods is the spontaneity. We can easily meet someone who we might like to be paired up with in some way in a future life. It isn't that we talk shop at these breaks as much as the exposure of just meeting and getting to know other sorts of souls. Of course, there is always the fun of bumping into someone from a past life who we haven't seen in a while and comparing notes.

Another subject had this to say about lesson breaks with members of her group who are inclined to choose female bodies:

> We go to a space surrounded by a lush garden of flowers. It has a beautiful pool with vibrating, restorative, liquid energy. It is shallow so we can wade rather than actually swim. We float around as water nymphs and tell each other funny stories about our lives.

In those groups where souls are not yet fully androgynous I do hear about gender-oriented recreational activities. This does not surprise me. As I have said before, the younger souls are inclined toward one gender when they incarnate on Earth. One subject said to me, "During our picnics at the breaks, my women friends and I flirt with some of the male-oriented souls from other groups close by us. We threaten to become their wives in the next life if they don't behave."

Quiet Solitude as R & R

Because the work activities of soul groups is demanding, there are souls who prefer settings of solitude during their off time. We all know people who prefer to be alone rather than socialize. Many of us become so distracted by the hectic roles we play in life, it is difficult to learn who we really are. Under case 22 in chapter 4, I referred to souls of solitude, who require a lengthy period of adjustment alone after particularly hard lives. These souls are not usually the monastically-oriented beings who require steady doses of solitude throughout their existence. Certainly, most souls rejuvenate well with some solitude. Yet I have encountered certain souls who seem to require regular periods of seclusion mixed with group class time. I consider many souls of this type to be ascetics. I feel the appeal of periods of quiet time represents a form of mental contemplation similar to that experienced from abbeys to ashrams on Earth where we focus on spiritual principles. A client made the following symbolic statement:

> I am called the Wreathweaver by my group. I like to be by myself so I can see myself. Within my quiet time, I construct circular bands of energy—weaving them together as a tapestry of my lives and that of my six closest friends. I display the diversity of our life experiences by weaving different materials—attributes of energy— which represent the trappings of people and events. To execute this properly I must have total concentration.

My subjects say that the desire for time alone in the spirit world comes from an intense need to dwell within the sacred confines of pure thought to try and touch the Source from which they sprang. Many say they have profound moments of success but it is intense work. I have found that some of these ascetic souls have trouble participating in group activities and will shun recreation periods because they prefer contemplation. Despite their detachment during training, down the line these souls are capable of making great contributions in their specialty areas.

Going to Earth for R & R

There are souls who come to Earth as invisible beings between lives so they can re-experience former physical environments. The only problem with this is they must return to chronological time, which means these souls are caught up with change since they were last here. In chapter 3, the soul in case 17 described returning to Earth on a vacation trip and running into other discarnates, some of whom were disruptive. This factor, plus not wanting to dilute old, original memories, can dissuade souls from coming back to Earth between lives. There are souls who find this sort of nostalgic trip to be unrewarding and even frustrating out of a physical body. This situation does not apply to those souls who come back to comfort and aid loved ones and are not motivated by a desire for recreation.

From what I have observed, it is change that seems to have the biggest impact on the vacationing soul. Many won't return to Earth for recreation between lives because of the day-to-day modernization of the communities they once occupied. In dimensions away from ground zero on Earth, images of places and the people who once lived here are frozen in a timeless vacuum that never vanishes from existence. The patterns of energy particles representing moments in human history can be retrieved at will by souls who are out of absolute physical time.

Nonetheless, there are souls who still want to come back for planetary visits, despite the negatives. My next case is one of those souls who enjoys roaming around his old haunts on Earth. Out of a multitude of possible case selections, I chose the next case for personal reasons. The area described is where I grew up. Case 49 and I participated in the same activity, which even overlapped in time during the last few years of his life, ending in 1948. As I consider this case, I wonder if I will be imitating this soul's spiritual recreation myself in the twenty-first century?

Case 49

Dr. N: What do you find most enjoyable as a recreational activity between lives?

S: I like to come to Earth.

Dr. N: Where do you go?

S: I loved the beaches of southern California in my last life. So I return to sit on the sand in the sun, walk the beach among the sea gulls, and be in the surf. My passion are the waves—the feeling of movement and the crashing foam.

Dr. N: How can you fully experience all this at the beach without a physical body?

S: I take just enough energy with me for the experience but not enough to be seen.

Dr. N: I have been told that on many recreation jaunts a soul might take 100 percent of their energy. What do you do?

S: We don't do this on Earth because it would not be fair to scare people. I bring no more than 5 percent, usually a bit less.

Dr. N: Are you capable of riding waves?

S: (laughing) Absolutely, why do you think I come? I also soar with the birds and play with dolphins.

Dr. N: If you were a spirit sitting on the beach enjoying the sun and I walked past you, what would I see?

S: Nothing, I am transparent.

Dr. N: Would that mean if I were strolling along the beach would I just walk through you in your space without sensing your presence?

S: Well . . . a few people might sense something but they would probably dismiss this as a figment of their imagination.

Dr. N: Could you go to other physical worlds to experience what you have described?

S: Yes, but I loved this area and I have been here in more than one life. That is why I return. For me the sea is part of my soul. I could go to other water worlds, or create all this in the spirit world, but for me this would not be quite the same thing.

Dr. N: Where are your other favorite spots to play based upon your former lives on Earth?

S: Around the Mediterranean and Aegean Seas.

Creation of Earthly Settlements

The Apaches believe that "wisdom sits in places." Since it is possible to create any reality in the spirit world, it is not unusual that some souls wish to spend their off periods in the houses where they lived on Earth. Frequently, these souls prefer to suspend the timeline where they lived in a former life and not expose themselves to huge increases in population and alterations of their old neighborhoods. This is like freezing moments in past time, which souls who wish to spend their recreation time in the spirit world can do.

These souls may want to mentally construct an exact duplication of familiar settings around where they used to live, such as the surrounding countryside, parks and streets, and any structures which remind them of their old hometowns. They only have to conjure up these places from memory and use directed energy beams for the images to appear. To fully implement these projects created out of pure energy, the assistance of others may be required. Once in place, they will disintegrate only when the soul loses interest.

The bodies souls had during the time when they lived in certain locations are also re-created by them whenever they are in residence. Souls may wish to add their old pets to these scenes, which I will explain more about in the section on animals. I must say that many of the souls who appreciate this sort of recreation are fun-loving and humorous. They might ask their past life friends to come and socialize with them at re-created geographic locations of mutual interest. Soulmates have priority here, as the next quote clearly indicates:

> My wife Erika and I loved the small house we built in the Bavarian Alps. We wanted it again after death and so we built it with the help of our energy teacher. He thought it was good practice for us. The model was in my mind and he saw it perfectly before we began the energy transmissions. Additional touches of the exterior came from our friends Hans and Elfie, who lived near our house in Germany and are with us now. The interior furnishings Erika and I did without help. I created my old library and my wife set up her kitchen just as it was. It is wonderful to be alone again with her in this way.

People are curious if souls can have intimate physical relations with their re-created bodies. If good sex originates in the mind, then the pure soul has all the benefits without the physical inhibitors. No self-pretense is possible in the spirit world. From what I can gather, there is a loss of full tactile sensation by not being within a dense physical body having a nervous system. At any rate, in the spiritual re-creation of a human body, the lack of full sensory sensation is more than made up for by the erotic power of two minds that are completely joined.

Love is a desire for full unification with the object of that love. Spirits have the capability between lives of expressing love even more intimately than on Earth. Even so, some souls are still motivated by establishing the scenes of former lives where their love blossomed. Re-creating these scenes is meaningful to partners. After all, a major incentive for many souls to reincarnate is the pleasures of physical expression in biological form.

Animal Souls

I remember delivering a speech in downtown New York City and during the question and answer period a woman in the front row issued me the following challenge: "Do you believe cats have souls?" I responded with, "Are you a cat owner?" While the woman hesitated for a moment, a friend sitting next to her smiled and held up four fingers. Of all the animal lovers in the world who are interested in this question, I have to be most careful of those owning cats. I told the woman in Manhattan that since I have never hypnotized a cat, I can't personally attest to cats having souls. This did not make her happy until I added that some of my clients declare they do see animals in the spirit world between their lives.

The world's religions have long debated whether animals possess souls. Eastern religions, such as Judaism, say animal's souls are equal to those of humans. In Judaism there are different levels of the soul, with the lowest being animals and the highest humans. Muslims hold that animals do have spirits, but those souls are not immortal because animals cannot rationally choose between heaven and hell. The Christian religions reserve the eternal soul only for righteous human beings.

Pet owners who interact with their animals project much of their own spiritual energy toward these creatures, which is reciprocated in different ways depending upon the type of animal and its personality. Do these traits represent a soul? We know that animals think, but we are not sure of the degree of that thought. Dogs are protective, cats are resourceful and dolphins have complex speech patterns. Does any sort of rational thought, or the lack of it, establish a criteria for animals having souls?

Anyone who has pets will tell you that animals have individual personalities, feelings and even a sense of the needs of their owners. We know animals provide comfort during our bereavement and physical illnesses. Pets have the capacity to lift our spirits and foster healing while providing us with love and companionship without reservations. For those people who think that animals are mere sentient beings who only have instinctual sensations, I would say that if animals have thought perceptions then they have individualized energy at some level.

My subjects report that every animal has its own particular classification of intelligent energy and human souls don't move up and down the ladder from one form to another. These energy particles range from complex life forms, as in the case of chimps, to the simple structures. Despite the repudiation of transmigration by my subjects, perhaps all organic and inorganic matter projects vibrational energy on Earth and probably relates to one another in a purposeful way.

I have been told by clients who have had connections with a variety of animals in the spirit world that all of them do indeed have some sort of soul energy. They are not like human souls and also differ from one another. After death, the energy from these animals reportedly "exists in different spheres from that of the human soul." To the person in trance, *spheres* are spaces, each having their own specific patterns and functions. I have had a number of informative reports about animal souls in the spirit world. My next case is a good example from a subject whose name is Kimoye.

Case 50

Dr. N: Kimoye, what do you like to do for recreation?

S: Frankly, I am a rather quiet, unsocial soul and I enjoy doing two things. I garden and play with animals during the time I am away from my group.

Dr. N: Do you actually grow things in the spirit world?

S: Creating living things from energy is one of our important exercises here.

Dr. N: Tell me about playing with the animals.

S: I have a dog and cat as well as a horse. These are my pets from the last life.

Dr. N: Do they just appear when you want them?

S: No, I must call for them as they don't normally live in our spaces here. I can't go to their place. An Animal Caretaker brings them to me. We call them trackers.

Dr. N: Meaning the tracker has to find your pet and not one created out of energy, as you might do with a plant in your garden?

S: Absolutely.

Dr. N: Do animals have souls, Kimoye?

S: Yes, of course they do, but in many varieties.

Dr. N: What is the difference between animal and human souls?

S: The souls of all living things have different . . . properties. Animal souls have smaller particles of energy . . . less volume and are not as complex and multifaceted as the human soul.

Dr. N: What other differences do you know about between the souls of humans and that of animals?

S: The main difference, other than size and capacity, is that animal souls are not ego-driven. They are not overwhelmed by identity issues as we are. They also accept and blend with their environment rather than fighting to control it like human beings. (stops and then adds) We can learn from them.

Dr. N: You said that animal souls had their own domain in the spirit world. How then are you able to associate with them even with the help of a Caretaker Soul?

S: (perplexed with me) They have sensory energy on Earth like us . . . we share their physical existence . . . so why not the mental . . . ?

Dr. N: Well, Kimoye, you did say they have a different arrangement of properties than our intelligent energy.

S: So do my plants, but I am not denied their company if I wish it.

Dr. N: You mentioned that you play with your dog. Can plant energy become dog energy?

S: No, because each form of life does have its own assortment of energy—this energy does not cross the line into another physical form on the same planet.

Dr. N: Does this mean a cat won't transmigrate into a higher form of life and a human being will not become a lower form, say in the body of a cat, in a future life?

S: Yes, that's right. Energy is created and assigned to certain physical and mental forms.

Dr. N: Why is that, do you think?

S: (laughs at me) I don't know about the grand design here, except that mixing soul types is not expedient.

Dr. N: Tell me, Kimoye, do you see the animal souls of your pets in groups such as that of your own soul group?

S: Like I said, I don't go to their places. They have no need to call for us to come to them. I can't tell you about these areas except to say the Animal Caretaker told me there is a general division of land, air and water groups.

Dr. N: Are any connected with each other in the spirit world?

S: It is our understanding that whales, dolphins and seals are together—crows and hawks—horses and zebras—that sort of thing. Animals have their own connections with community bonding by general species that we are not supposed to under-stand—at least I don't.

Dr. N: Well . . . ?

S: (breaks in) I guess if we needed to know we would be told.

Dr. N: Okay, now let's go back to your original statement about playing with your pets during recreation time. Could you have a wild animal such as a wolf?

S: Only if the wolf was domesticated.

Dr. N: Can you explain this to me, Kimoye?

S: (subject frowns in concentration) The associations with animals need to be productive in certain settings for us to be motivated to work with certain life forms. My dog on Earth can be with me within my spiritual property where I built my house and garden because it is natural for him to be here. He belongs with me because we were bonded playmates. Our mutual love and respect for each other on Earth is being renewed because it is good. There is beauty in this for both of us—this must be why it is permitted.

Dr. N: Could you differentiate between the soul of a domesticated animal on Earth and one that was wild?

S: I think so. As I said, animal souls are much less complicated than human souls. The domesticated ones are able to extend love and affection to humans, which we need. The wild animal souls are not as focused in this area and don't understand us very much at all. Most cannot be constrained—and shouldn't be, just because we share the same environment.

Dr. N: Do you think there is more need for freedom with the wild animal?

S: Maybe, but the souls of all living things—especially us— require freedom of expression. With the domesticated animal soul, they are more willing to give up some freedom to bond with humans in exchange for love, affection and protection. There is a symmetry in having pets.

Dr. N: Kimoye, you make this sound as if domesticated animals are on Earth to serve humans.

S: It is a mutual benefit exchange, like I told you. Those of us who love animals on Earth believe we can communicate with our pets in small ways. When we return to the spirit world and see our pets again—each of us in a pure soul state—this becomes more evident.

Dr. N: Does everyone in the spirit world feel as you do about animal souls?

S: Many do not have my love for animals. I have friends here who have no wish to interact with animal energy, even some who connected with animals on Earth. They have other activities during their recreation time. (stops and then adds) This is their loss.

Animal Caretaker Souls appear to be specialists in the spirit world. It is not a popular specialty among my clients but their work is much appreciated by pet lovers. These caretakers are not considered to be zookeepers. I once asked a subject who was knowledgeable of the skills this specialty required about my old basset hound, Socrates, a much-loved family pet for fifteen years. My question was that if my soul mind could create a house and a physical body for myself between lives, could I conjure up my dog? I was told the following:

> You could do this if you were advanced enough in the creation of energy. But even if you had this ability, your dog would not be quite as real as a professional could do for you. An Animal Caretaker Soul has the skill to track and find the spark of soul energy which did not die with Socrates and reconstruct your dog exactly as you knew him on Earth. Your pet will know you and be able to play with you whenever you wish and then he will go.

Apparently, Animal Caretaker specialists associated with Earth are souls who are skilled at finding and reconstructing the essence of certain lower forms of life. I think of them as creator souls who seem to have the desire and ability to maintain these forms of life for us in the spirit world because of their own love for the creatures of our planet.

There can be past life karmic aspects to our associations with animals on Earth and this could be another reason why we have Animal Caretaker Souls. I have a client who is an intense animal rights activist today and has been devoted to the alleviation of animal suffering in all her past lives since a life in Austria in the early sixteenth century. As a young Austrian boy in that life, my client's family was engaged in the slaughtering of cows and pigs for market, which traumatized him. Today this client calls all animals "my children." During her life, and between lives, she spends her free time with them. She also melds with their energy in a place called the Space of Transformation, used to increase her perception of their consciousness. Kimoye essentially told me the same thing when she said in her session, "I enter this chamber, which has a field of programmed animal energy that allows me to feel what they feel. This gives me insight about animals on Earth." For both these clients this activity represents learning as much as recreation.

The Space of Transformation

During their long apprenticeship of training, souls are able to study and practice many arts. One of these areas of instruction, which I wrote about in *Journey of Souls,* is a sphere of soul transformation. Many souls, both young and old, can learn much from entering this enclosure between lives. The young are introduced to certain arts here that might interest them, while the older souls can hone their existing skills further. When I describe this space to people, I use an analogy of the holodeck on a spacecraft in the *Star Trek* television series. While there are similarities in the concept, the Space of Transformation goes much further than being a room of simulations.

The Space of Transformation is not limited to permitting souls to get inside the energy of animals. Here the soul can become any animate or inanimate object familiar to them. In order to capture the essence of all living and even nonliving things on Earth, souls are able to meld with multiple substances. This would include fire, gas and liquids. They may also become totally amorphous in order to meld with a feeling or emotion to become one with that state.

I have listed the Space of Transformation under recreation because the average soul begins to use this space for the sheer enjoyment of energy shape shifting. However, many souls I have worked with prefer to engage in these exercises in actual physical settings on other worlds. This will be covered in the next chapter. As I mentioned, all these activities have the potential to go far beyond recreation for most souls. The next short case is an illustration of how the Space of Transformation tempers and strengthens the soul mind in a process of mental annealing.

Case 51

Dr. N: Why have you come to the Space of Transformation?

S: There are periods when I am away from my soul group and I wish to experience what this room has to offer. I enter the energy screens here to absorb my energy into the strata of compassion. I am drawn to this energy stream . . . it is part of my soul.

Dr. N: Please explain this stream of energy to me.

S: They are specific belts of purified energy. I blend with the one of compassion.

Dr. N: Who creates this particular belt for you in this space?

S: I don't know. I enter and mentally concentrate on what I want and it is provided for me. As I practice, the more potent this energy gets, and the more benefit I receive.

Dr. N: I don't see why it is necessary for you to come to this place to experience compassion when you can get that from going to Earth.

S: Yes, but you must understand that when I go to Earth and devote my energy to the healing of others, my energy loses much of its integrity by the end of my life. This is because I am inexperienced as a full-fledged healer.

Dr. N: Well, if you are here for that sort of rejuvenation, why don't you give me a more precise example of what you do in the Space of Transformation.

S: (takes a deep breath) I can identify pain, but in order to diffuse it in the human body I assimilate it. This eventually makes me ineffective. I become a sponge rather than a mirror of light. Here I can practice my art.

Dr. N: By doing what?

S: I learn to manipulate my energy rather than absorb pain. The energy belt of compassion is like a liquid pool where I can swim and become part of the emotion in an experience which is so subjective I cannot describe it to you. It assists me in working on calmness within a sea of adversity. It is wondrous . . . it is . . . alive.

Listening to stories about the Space of Transformation gives me the impression the experience is euphoric. Whether these psychic pools of concentrated energy, which appear to transform souls for a time, are real or simulated from my frame of reference is moot. This is because while my clients see the spirit world as ultimate reality, they call this space one of altered reality. There is one constant criterion that helps me differentiate these concepts in my mind. Working models of reality which are temporary and will eventually die are illusory. The eternal world of the soul that analyzes and evaluates this process appears to my subjects as a permanent state of consciousness. The Space of Transformation is a creation for spiritual development.

Dancing, Music and Games

There are still people in the world living in remote settings who engage in spiritual dancing and singing that is important to their cultural life. Many years ago, I was privileged to watch and participate one night in the singing and dancing of a tribe of Lahu natives. These were Burmese hill people living deep in the mountains along the Burma-Thai border. I was with a small group of Westerners who were the first outsiders to be taken to see this particular isolated tribe. The trek was difficult, taking us through jungles and across mountain ranges. The experience was mystical.

When my subjects describe the way they express their inner being in the spirit world through dance movements combined with music, I think of the Lahu people. The Lahu are animists, who believe that all natural phenomena have souls and manifest a personal spiritual force. Many societies had these beliefs in ancient times, long before the rise of major religions. My clients explain that when groups of souls engage in this form of recreation there are elements of ritualism and a celebration of a sacred Source. As with both ancient and modern cultures on Earth, souls find this form of expression to be a means of heightening intensity. These movements evoke soul memories of their origins on Earth, other worlds and the spirit world itself.

Dancing and singing in unison brings a feeling of oneness with all thought. When my subjects describe the effects of this form of soul recreation, it is as if they feel suspended in the memory of spiritual bliss. They talk about how the sounds and rhythms of harps, lyres and chimes are an expression of their nature as a soul. The accounts of some clients remind me of my visit to the Lahu tribe when they speak of drums, flutes and dancing in a circle around a fire. One of these subjects had this to say:

> We engage in the ring dance, moving in graceful, free-flowing harmony around firelight accompanied by the humming of lilting melodies. Our energy whirls in circular, changing cadences as a shift in wind of moods. For us this is an offering of the intense relationships we have for each other born from a thousand lifetimes together. We come to participate in dance and song as an affirmation of our bonds and to resonate a collective wisdom.

Another subject reported the following about dance movements in the spirit world. Initially, the object was apparently speed, then the dance changed to something else:

> We start moving in a circle and then the pace accelerates faster and faster. We gather all this force, pushing it in front of us, until we look like a whirlwind with no space between. Now, the dance is gone—replaced by a cascading turbulence, which is a joining of our souls. As we slow down, the effects of unraveling energy are useful in observing our separation. At the end of this dance we have experienced the intricate differences between our vibrational energy patterns.

Some souls have described the scene above as "the tumbleweed game." This indicates to me there is only a fine line between spiritual dancing and games, all of which have their individual interpretations. Here is another example:

> When we dance we change our normal pear-shaped, elongated energy to that of a curved crescent which looks like a first-quarter moon. We move toward each other from two or four directions, depending upon the number of participants. By shifting our shapes from concave to convex—back and forth—to match the soul opposite us, we can blend—spoon fashion—and separate with great speed. We stretch out and intertwine our energy while swaying in and out like a mating dance.

Soul dancing may also become a form of acrobatics as indicated by the next statement from a client:

> My group especially enjoys acrobatics. We do not perform gymnastics in human form, as some of the others do. We retain our oval, or elongated shapes of pure energy. We set up an energy field resembling a kind of trampoline to be used for tumbling in relays. It includes a dance form which is too hard to describe, but it's all done with a great deal of laughter and fun. This movement during recreation draws us closer together.

I have noticed that these activities may be combined with comedy skits. Souls who engage in these forms of entertainment love to poke fun at each other. Yet I don't hear much about souls acting in full-scale plays as pure recreation. This is because the more serious aspect of role-playing, although not lacking in humor, is so often employed during past life reviews. This is enough theater for most souls.

Other recreational activities, such as art and composition, are pursued quietly and individually. The practice of music and sculpture may be pursued alone or collectively. Sculpting energy to design structural objects and the creation of small life forms is not really considered recreational. They represent an integral part of task-oriented classroom instruction although, as we have seen, these activities can be overlapped with leisure time. Music is in a special category all its own as far as almost universal soul appeal. Unlike Earth, where so many of us are unable to learn to play a musical instrument or sing, as souls we seem to be able to engage in these activities effortlessly. Melodic sounds are often heard throughout the spirit world by my subjects in spaces that are not recreational. Within the context of R & R, music is enjoyed by souls directly or interwoven into subtle frameworks for drama, dancing and even games.

From my research, I have come to believe that more than any other medium, music uplifts the soul with ranges of notes far beyond what we know on Earth. There seems to be no limit to the sounds used in the creation of music in the spirit world. People in deep hypnosis explain that musical thought is the language of souls. The composition and transmission of harmonic resonance appears to relate to the formation and presentation of spiritual language. Far beyond musical communication, I'm told spiritual harmonics are the building blocks of energy creation and soul unification.

Many souls enjoy singing in the spirit world but it took me years to find a soul who is a Musical Director. My next case is a subject who has had a multitude of past lives where he was connected to music in one form or another. In his last life he was an Italian opera singer in the 1930s.

Case 52

Dr. N: What is your major recreational activity in the spirit world?

S: To create music.

Dr. N: You mean with musical instruments?

S: Oh, there is always that—you can pull any instrument out of thin air and play it. But, for me, there is nothing more satisfying than creating a choir. The voice is the most beautiful of musical instruments.

Dr. N: Look, you don't have the vocal chords of an opera star any longer, so . . . ?

S: (laughs at me) Has it been that long since you were a spirit? No human body is needed. In fact, the sounds we create are lighter and of much greater range than those on Earth.

Dr. N: Can everyone sing the high and low notes?

S: (with enthusiasm) Of course they can. We all have the ability to be sopranos and baritones at the same time. My people can hit high and low notes and everyone is always on pitch—they just need a director.

Dr. N: Could you describe what you do?

S: (quietly, without boastfulness) I am a Musical Director of souls. A singing conductor—it is my passion—my skill—my pleasure to give to others.

Dr. N: Are you better at this than other souls because of your musical talent in your past life as an opera singer?

S: Oh, I suppose that one follows the other, but not everyone is as focused on music as I am. Some souls in musical groups may not be paying attention to the entire score. (smiles) Because of the musical range possessed by souls, they need a director to keep all these virtuosos on track. After all, this is recreation for them. They want to have fun as well as produce beautiful music.

Dr. N: So, you enjoy working with choirs rather than an orchestra?

S: Yes, but we mix it up to make the singing come together. When spirits apply themselves to instruments and voice sounds, it's wonderful. It's not stray notes. The harmonic meshing of musical energy reverberates throughout the spirit world with indescribable sounds.

Dr. N: Then all this is vastly different from working with a choir on Earth?

S: There are similarities, but here you have so much talent because every soul has the capability for perfection of musical sound. There is high motivation. Souls love this form of recreation, especially if they wanted to be able to sing on Earth but sounded like frogs.

Dr. N: Do you bring souls from groups other than your own to be in this heavenly choir?

S: Yes, but lots of groups like to sing opposite each other and see who can be the most innovative.

Dr. N: If you were to look into the deeper motivations for souls, can you help me understand why music is so important for them in the spirit world?

S: It takes you to new mental levels . . . moving your energy . . . communicating in unison with large numbers of other souls.

Dr. N: How large a choral group do you direct?

S: I am partial to small groups of around twenty, although there are hundreds of souls from many groups who are available for me to direct.

Dr. N: Large groups must be a great challenge for you?

S: (taking a deep breath) Their range is staggering . . . vibrations pouring out in many directions . . . everyone hitting incredibly high and low notes without warning while I am struggling with their cues . . . and yet it's all pure rapture.

I will finish this section on recreation with a list of the most popular games souls play in the spirit world. One of my reasons for presenting the lighter side of soul socialization is to exemplify the differences between group study time and that of recreation. I have previously discussed the clannishness and rather insular attitudes of some soul groups. I do not wish my readers to assume this is a representation of the "outsider-insider" mentality that we so often see in cultural groups on Earth. There is no jealousy, mistrust or prejudice between spirit groups. While the younger souls are conditioned to be centered on their own training groups, this does not mean these souls see themselves as being all that different from other groups. Xenophobia does not exist in the spirit world. The information I have about how spirits from many groups play games together is one way I have of demonstrating the nature of soul behavior.

Nevertheless, at my lectures, I do feel the necessity of being cautious in offering too many details about spiritual games. There are people who believe matters of life after death are far too serious for such frivolities. A few have even commented that my speaking about recreation detracts from the rest of what I have to say about soul life. Despite these criticisms, I consider it more important that the public is aware the afterlife is not so dreadfully serious that souls cannot have fun.

The spiritual games I have encountered are never strictly enforced by monitors nor directed by team captains. In fact, the "rules" are loosely interpreted. There are elements of playful competition but without the emotional aggression one sees in sports on Earth. Spiritual games are not played with the objective that somebody wins while others lose. Games are vigorous and carefree at the same time. Our guides encourage game participation as a means of practicing energy movement, dexterity and group thought transmission. On the other hand, I have had subjects whose groups do not participate in games in the spirit world. Their separateness is always respected. This is especially true with the more advanced souls who are so engaged in other forms of energy training that game playing would be a detraction.

There is a remarkable consistency to game descriptions by subjects in hypnosis. While we can take the memory of a game with us to the spirit world, it is my belief that certain games with origins in the afterlife are brought to Earth and modified from unconscious memory for use in a physical body. The reader can be the judge of the most likely game origins from the following quotes. I will start my list of a few popular games with what appears to be a form of tag:

> We chase around, trying to catch each other by flowing fast in straight lines and then maintaining that speed when turning sharply. The more maneuverable spirits are able to double back, stop and start again quickly without getting caught.

Simple interpretations of tag and other games may be combined with music and dancing. In these versions, especially with the young, souls will chase each other into areas that have been defined as personal playgrounds:

> I love the meadows with trees to climb and tall grass where we can roll around chasing after each other and playing leapfrog. We can also shape shift into objects to make our games more interesting.

There is a game I hear quite a bit about which reminds me of a kind of dodgeball, where large numbers of souls line up opposite each other and throw bolts of energy. One can also recognize elements of keep-away and volleyball in the descriptions of this game called bolt-banging, which requires quick position adjustments and dexterity:

In our game of bolt-banging, we line up in two long lines opposite each other. We create balls of energy and throw them high over an imaginary line or fire them in straight or low trajectories at the opposing players. We must stay in a confined area to exchange bolts without slowing our momentum. At first it's easy to get out of the way while making your own bolts at the same time. Then the tempo increases and our play area looks like a hailstorm. When our bolts are flying around, they can be dodged, or caught and thrown back. The object is not to be inadvertently hit by a bolt. A player who is zapped is not out—he just tries harder to be more agile. We feel the complexities of each soul carried in the bolts which hit us.

Another high-velocity game is something akin to red rover, or perhaps bumper cars, where souls line up opposite each other in a square. Instead of sending one player over at a time to try and break through a chain of arms, as in red rover, these souls rush at each other en masse. One subject said, "This is a game of collision, where we bounce off one another in a chain reaction of whirling energy." The object seems to be the creation of a high volume of concentrated energy. Another client who plays this game told me:

The energy flow from all of us is pooled so that each player receives a heightened awareness from all the other souls. It's an exhilarating game. There is a magnification of all our energy which is unified. Eventually, when the energy charge lessens, we all settle down and engage in a kind of folk dance.

There are many subtle games that my subjects have difficulty in describing to me. One I have heard about from a number of people, however, has the name of gemball. The game is a little like marbles and lawn bowling combined with the symbolism of gemstones, which I reviewed in chapter 6. From case 53, it can be seen how displaying colored energy objects, as embodiments of personal character, need not be limited to our appearances at the Council of Elders.

Case 53

Dr. N: Do all groups have some interest in playing games?

S: Not at all. My group is fun-loving and we don't like to be tied down in classrooms too much. Some of the others find us a bit wild and undisciplined. There are four souls in our group who are not so playful so we cherry pick from other groups to make up our teams.

Dr. N: Is it true that souls can bring all the games they enjoyed on Earth to the spirit world?

S: (hesitates) Well, yes . . . but you don't see them all . . .

Dr. N: Why not? Give me some examples of games you don't see.

S: I don't see golf because it is too self-centered, you are mostly playing against yourself. Tennis is a little better but I don't see that either because only two people play and that is limiting.

Dr. N: Does this mean football is popular in the spirit world?

S: Mmm . . . not really. We don't play games with stars like quarterbacks and team captains. Football is too uneven a game, with wide variations in positions. Soccer would be better. It's hard to explain. We enjoy group games with lots of souls where everyone has an equal position and is engaged in the same way . . . in their movements.

Dr. N: I enjoy swimming, so I suppose you wouldn't see that either?

S: (laughing) Then you'd be wrong. If you didn't want to go to Earth for this as a spirit you could create a semblance of water here—or a golf course—whatever you require to bring back happy memories. But if you want other souls to participate with you in games of sport, then that's more of a collective matter.

Dr. N: So, you see a difference between individual and group recreational activity?

S: Yes, I do.

Dr. N: All right, then tell me about a game which is not like the sports games we have been talking about, one perhaps which is not so robust and carefree even though it might still be considered as recreation.

S: (wistfully) Oh . . . that's easy, it's the gemball game. Many souls come to a space where we sit in a great circle. Then each of us creates an energy ball the size of a tennis ball, which looks like a crystalline gemstone.

Dr. N: Do the balls have any particular meaning?

S: Of course, the energy colors represent individual expression.

Dr. N: Okay, what happens next in this game?

S: Each person holds their ball until someone says, "GO!" Then, we all gently push our balls to the center of the ring.

Dr. N: Do they all bang against each other, as in marbles?

S: I guess . . . in a way. The gemballs carom off each other with radiating colors splashing in all directions . . . but they don't quite stop . . . we keep them moving.

Dr. N: I'm not sure I understand . . . (subject breaks in and continues)

S: Finally, one comes to you. During each series of play, a corresponding player will receive my ball if there is a magnetic attraction.

Dr. N: What if you don't receive a ball from another player?

S: It happens quite often. We play rounds with large groups of different players—eventually a ball will roll into my lap.

Dr. N: Do two players have to receive a ball from each other?

S: No, gemball is not a programmed game. Anything can happen.

Dr. N: What does receiving a ball from someone else mean?

S: This tells you that you might be linked to the owner in some fashion. Gemball is an intimate game of expectation and trust because you never know where your ball is going or what you will receive back.

Dr. N: After you receive a ball, then what do you do?

S: (laughs) You pick up the ball that comes to you in the palms of your hands. The gemball gives you the means to learn about the private aspects of a soul which could relate to you in a special way. I have made many future life decisions to be with certain people based upon this game.

During my early research, I had no idea of the many ramifications of spiritual games. They all have their own distinctions that give pleasure. As I became knowledgeable with spiritual recreation, my subjects felt more comfortable in providing me with details about their favorite pastimes. I learned that certain games appeal to the particular character of the souls who play them. Eventually, I realized some games could escalate into training exercises and that individual souls from many groups gravitated to this activity. One game stands out in my mind in this respect.

I find the hide-and-seek game to have significant implications for future traveler souls whom I will be discussing in the next chapter. The execution of this game offers a variety of proficiency levels in teaching spatial frames of reference to interested souls. I began to take notice of this particular game after I heard about the appearance of coaches when the game became more complex. My clients call them the Gamekeepers. These are the specialist trainers who will expose those adventuresome beings who show talent to trips into different dimensions. Here is a quote from a highly advanced soul who wishes to specialize as a traveler:

> Hide-and-seek in the spirit world begins as an exercise between light and darkness. With the younger souls we charge up our energy from a distance and then wink it out when the kids come in our direction. We block and then open up our telepathic energy at the same time to mix up the visual and mental signals. In the beginning we create doorways of light within structured columns of energy which are employed as shadowed panels which may be arranged in parallel or horizontal lines. Later we make them random geometric patterns. Most young ones have a terrible time learning to detect and find us as we

dart between the doorways, but they have fun because at this stage they still consider this playing a game.

Some become so good we can't trick them anymore. In time these souls—those that want to continue—become trainees and are ready to be ushered into our playground of interdimensional zones, which are divided by energy barriers and vibrational pulse rates. This is tough because the trainees must learn to adapt to different wave configurations which exist within each dimension and match their energy quickly to pass through. We lose many souls at this point who don't wish to continue. The work is like being in a hall of mirrors. The souls like me, who refuse to quit because we love the work, must now master the mental dimensions without structure or form. They exist as vacuums between the physical dimensions. Part of me still considers this training as recreation. It is so captivating I can't wait to get back home and engage in this exercise again with my friends.

Four General Types of Souls

Before moving on to a discussion of the more advanced souls in the next chapter, I should list the major types of souls I have encountered within the community of spiritual life. There must be many more than these four categories of souls, however, I am limited by the memories of my clients concerning other possible soul types in the spirit world.

1. Souls who are either unable or unwilling to function individually. These souls usually work within collectives and never seem to leave the spirit world. Even so, I am told all souls are given the opportunity to experiment with existing in both physical and mental universes.

2. Souls who do not wish to incarnate in physical form. Also, they may not possess the requisite properties of light energy to engage in this activity. They seem to work only in mental worlds and appear to move easily between different dimensions. Most of their talents are beyond the comprehension of my clients.

3. Souls who incarnate only on physical worlds. I sense that some
   have the capability for training in mental spheres between lives,
   but are not inclined to do so. They are not attracted to interdimensional travel, even during recreation. Quite a number of my
   clients are in this category.

4. Souls who have both the ability and desire to function in all
   types of physical and mental environments. This does not necessarily give them more enlightenment than other soul types. Yet,
   their wide range of practical experience and capabilities position
   them for many specialization opportunities involving varied
   assignments of responsibility.

~8

The Advancing Soul

Graduation

There comes that time in a soul's existence when it is ready to move away from its primary soul group. My next case comes from a soul who recently attained level III after thousands of years of incarnating on Earth. This subject became very excited by the images in her mind of this recent event in the spirit world. The symbolic descriptions involving analogies to educational settings by now are very familiar to the reader. In her current life she is a teacher of children with learning disabilities.

Case 54

Dr. N: You seem very blissful about appearing in front of your council.

S: Yes, I have scrubbed off the last of my body armor.

Dr. N: Body armor?

S: Yes, my protective armor—to avoid being hurt. It took me centuries to learn to trust and be open with people inclined to hurt me as an outgrowth of their own anger. This was my last major hurdle.

Dr. N: Why was this so difficult for you?

S: I identified too much with my emotions rather than my spiritual strength. This created self-doubt in my relations with others whom I perceived to be stronger and more knowledgeable than myself—but they were not.

Dr. N: If this last major hurdle involved self-identity, how do you see yourself at present?

S: Finally, I used a rope of flowers to swing over the abyss of pain and hurt. I no longer give away too much of my energy unnecessarily. (pause) Physical and mental hardship has to do with self-definition. In the last 1,000 years, I have improved upon maintaining my identity in each life . . . under adverse circumstances, and to honor myself as a human being who could not be superseded by others. I no longer need body armor to achieve this.

Dr. N: What does your council say to you about your positive actions involving self-definition?

S: They are satisfied that I have passed this difficult test—that I did not let the adverse circumstances of these many lives dictate my vision of myself—who I really am. They are very pleased that I have reached a higher level of my potential through patience and diligence.

Dr. N: Why do you think you had to go through so much in your lives on Earth?

S: How can I teach others unless I have gone through fire myself to become strong?

Dr. N: Well . . . (subject interrupts me with something which has appeared in her mind as a result of my last question)

S: Oh . . . they have a surprise for me. Oh, I'm so HAPPY!

Note: At this moment my subject breaks down with tears of joy and anticipation of the scene unfolding in her mind. I pull out my trusty box of tissues and we continue.

Dr. N: Move forward and tell me what the surprise is all about.

S: (bubbling) It's graduation time! We are gathering in the temple. Aru, my guide, is here along with the chairman of my council. Master teachers and students are assembling from everywhere.

Dr. N: Can you break this down a little for me? How many teachers and students do you see?

S: (hurriedly) Ah . . . some twelve teachers and . . . maybe forty students.

Dr. N: Are some of the students from your own primary group?

S: (pause) There are three of us. Students have been brought from other groups who are ready. I don't know most of them.

Dr. N: I notice some hesitation on your part. Where are the others of your own group?

S: (with regret) They are not yet ready.

Dr. N: What is the core color of all these students around you?

S: Bright, solid yellow. Oh, you have no idea how long it has taken us to arrive here.

Dr. N: Perhaps I do. Why don't you describe the proceedings for me?

S: (takes a deep breath) Everyone is in a festive mood, like a coming-out party. We all line up and float in . . . and I'm going to sit up front. Aru is smiling proudly at me. A few words are spoken by the masters who acknowledge how hard we have worked. Then our names are called.

Dr. N: Individually?

S: Yes . . . I hear my name, "Iri" . . . I float forward to receive a scroll with my name printed on the front.

Dr. N: What else do these scrolls have on them?

S: (modestly) It's rather private . . . about those achievements which took me the longest . . . and how I overcame them.

Dr. N: So, in a way, this is more than a diploma. It's a testimonial record of your work.

S: (softly) Yes.

Dr. N: Is everyone wearing cap and gowns?

S: (quickly) No! (then smiling) Oh . . . I see . . . you are teasing me.

Dr. N: Well, maybe a little. Tell me, Iri, what takes place after the ceremonies?

S: We gather around to talk about our new assignments and I have the opportunity to meet with some of the souls who are in my specialty area. We will meet again in new classes that will make the best use of our abilities.

Dr. N: What will be your first assignment, Iri?

S: I will be nurturing the youngest souls. It's as if we will be raising flowers from the seedlings. You feed them with tenderness and understanding.

Dr. N: And where do you think these newer souls come from?

S: (pause) From the divine egg—the womb of creation—spun out like silken thread . . . and then taken to the nursery mothers . . . and then to us. It's very exciting. The responsibility will be so challenging.

Movement to the Intermediate Levels

When I work with a subject who is transitioning into a level III group, there may be some initial confusion as to why they see themselves leaving and returning to their primary cluster group on a regular basis. During hypnosis, not everyone is able to see a scene in their mind and then quickly integrate this frame into the entire movie of their spiritual life. The task of a facilitator is to proceed slowly and let the scene unfold naturally. A client who had not yet graduated from his group but had begun the process of pulling away told me, "I am starting to feel a little cut off from my family. There are new souls around me that I have not worked with before."

The integrity of a soul's original cluster group remains intact in a timeless way. Regardless of who is graduating, they never lose their bond to old companions. Primary cluster groups began their existence together and remain closely associated through hundreds of incarnations. I have had souls who were with their primary groups for some 50,000 years before they were ready to move on to the intermediate levels, while a much smaller percentage have achieved this state of development within 5,000 years. Once reaching level III, I find that souls begin to rise much more rapidly into the advanced levels. Souls develop at different rates while displaying a variety of talents along the way. I notice that when souls start to spend less time in recreation and socializing they are working harder and becoming more focused on perfecting certain skills that will contribute to the forces of cosmic consciousness.

With the attaining of level III there is a change in soul behavior. These souls have now begun to expand their vistas away from their primary groups. The advancing souls don't disregard all they have known before, it's just that they are now so engrossed in their training it has become an all-consuming goal. These souls are fascinated by what they can do and want to become even more proficient. By the time they approach a level IV range of development, the transition is complete.

In the course of their transition, recent level IIIs soon recognize that they are no longer limited to one classroom. Their old friends are aware of what is going on, but it seems to be mutually understood that not too many questions should be asked about these absences. I refer readers back to the experience of the soul Lavani in case 32. The transition is a slow one, in keeping with the practice of infinite care that is so evident in all spiritual training. The assignments to new specialty groups are formed with other like-minded souls based upon a number of considerations. The three principal elements I am most aware of for soul specialty selection are talent, past performance and personal desire. I would expect needs of the spirit world to be another important element, but this information is denied me.

I suppose it could be said that when a soul is elevated into the intermediate levels of training they are being initiated into a guild of sorts. However, I would not equate this with the historic craft guilds of the Middle Ages, which were called Mystery Schools of training. These were exclusive and rather secret organizations for members only. Although there are elements of privacy accorded to souls selected for specialized training, it is by no means elitist. Aspiring new arrivals are always welcomed to groups of specialists.

These assemblages of more specialized souls are rather loosely knit at first. I have defined them as independent study groups. The training begins slowly on a periodic basis with different specialized teachers. This allows for an evaluation period for souls by their trainers. Souls who are testing the waters may leave these specialty groups while other promising candidates can be added. This practice is in opposition to the formation of long-term primary soul groups. The instruction becomes more intense as these new groups demonstrate they can handle assignments. In these early stages, while souls are being weaned from their original groups, they still retain their regular guides and attend primary group functions. Independent study has a greater emphasis on self-direction by the soul in their tasks, which becomes even more pronounced as they develop into level IV and V proficiency.

A number of soul specializations have been listed in preceding chapters. In order of presentation, they have been described as the Dreammasters, Redeemers of Lost Souls, Keepers of Neutrality, Restoration Masters, Incubator Mothers, Archivist Souls, Animal Caretaker Souls, Musical Directors, and Gamekeepers. There seems to be an overlapping of certain specialties. For instance, Gamekeepers who train others in travel may also be Explorer Souls for new sites useful in R & R and the more serious planetary aspects of energy training. In this chapter, I will cite further examples of soul specialties. I am sure readers will recognize what specialty area might fit their own inclinations.

There does not appear to be a certain path that would ultimately lead souls to a seat on a council. The Elders seem to come from a background of many specializations. I think most people feel the teacher-guides probably have an inside track to such positions. Of course, it is natural guides would appear to the average client to be the premier profession. Yet I know this perception is colored by the fact that while all my subjects have guides, many have little contact with advanced souls in other specialties. I can only imagine what other specializations souls are offered that no subject is able to describe.

When I discuss the topic of specialty areas during my lectures, a lot of people say they thought all souls were being groomed to be teacher-guides. I had the same idea in the early phases of my research. Eventually, I learned that while teaching is a leading specialty in the spirit world, this does not mean that most souls make great teachers. Because teaching is so vital to souls, I will begin with a category of this field I haven't covered before.

Specializations

Nursery Teachers

In *Journey of Souls* I discussed the activities of junior and senior teaching guides, and my subjects have documented the activities of their guides in this book. However, not much information has been offered about advanced souls who are brand-new teachers in training. They are called the Nursery Teachers, or caretakers of children, because the young souls they work with have not yet begun their incarnations.

Following case 26 in chapter 5, I quoted the recent memories of a very young soul on Earth who explained that once a new soul is created they are not immediately thrown into a physical incarnation. Earth is such a difficult school for training it is best that many new souls are allowed time in adjusting to planetary life as discarnates. This is illustrated by the following report from a subject:

> I remember when I was a very young soul and came to Earth for the first time with a couple of friends. As spirits we floated around to check our capacity and adaptability to this place while accompanied by our teacher. We were shown how to collect the magnetic vibrations of this planet and blend them with our own. We needed to feel what it would take for us to be in physical form here.

It is my belief a large majority of my clients are inclined toward teacher training to be guides. This is because they venerate their own guides, who have such a strong influence on their current development, and wish to emulate them. Of course, a soul's current aspirations and eventual specialization assignments may not coincide. Teachers must be good communicators. Yet a skilled communicator who is able to motivate, for example, might not have the ability to work with a soul mind trying to integrate with many human egos in all their host bodies.

Nursery Teachers who work with very young souls may not choose to become guides for the general population of souls for many reasons. Working with the child soul is challenging because many young souls do not seem to be able to move on with their reincarnations and will require remedial studies. Case 28 told us something about the spiritual setting of teachers and the elementary souls, which I will expand upon in case 55.

I have to keep on my toes with advanced clients, and questioning them about soul colors in their descriptions of settings is a big help. The man in case 55 is entering a level IV proficiency and had just finished telling me about the variety of yellow-blue lights in his own specialty group composed of three souls. I was ready to move on to something else when I thought of one more question, which opened up a whole new line of inquiry.

Case 55

Dr. N: Is that all the colors you see in this vicinity?

S: No, there are eleven kids—white lights—bunched together off to the left of us. Their energy is smaller, with a shorter energy pattern, and rather scattered. The young ones are very exuberant.

Note: At this point my subject became very excited when he recognized one of these souls as his child today. I let him enjoy this moment and then we continued.

Dr. N: Do you see any differences in light intensity from these eleven souls?

S: Not much. The very innocent and timid kids have dim lights. We don't have one of those right now.

Dr. N: What relationship do you have with these eleven souls?

S: I'm being assisted in their training by two colleagues whom I haven't known for very long because they come from other groups.

Dr. N: Did the three of you have a common background on Earth to prepare you for this initial teaching assignment?

S: Well, we were teachers, holy men, healers . . . that kind of thing in our past lives. One must have sensitivity and great patience for this sort of work. (stops, then adds as an afterthought) You know, teachers can learn from students.

Dr. N: I'm sure that's true. Why don't you give me a sense of where you and these children are right now in the spirit world.

S: We are sent to neutral areas for training because it would be too inhibiting for these kids to be near the regular teaching classrooms.

Dr. N: What's going on at the moment?

S: (laughs) They are whizzing about in all directions, more interested in pulling pranks on each other than learning anything. Things will change when they start to incarnate.

My next quote is a condensation from the case of a woman who is working with souls that have just begun to incarnate:

> I have my hands full right now with seven goof-offs. They like being playboys and playgirls during their incarnations. They just want to stay as children and not take life seriously. They are overly fond of earthly pleasures and don't want to deal with the hard stuff. Their major interest is looking beautiful in the next life. Ulant, my senior guide, has left them with me and I don't see him very much. I'll admit my style is extremely lenient. I use lots of gentleness and love. Some of the other teachers say I spoil them outrageously. I know of teachers who express a lot of frustration and become stern with their young students, especially those with potential. The council is interested in my teaching methods. They want to test my theories of permissiveness rather than giving this class a mental spanking. My concept of teaching is that once these child souls do start to develop, the leap they will take into maturity will be more rapid because they won't have had their self-confidence shaken by too many hard lessons and setbacks too soon.

Ethicists

For a long time I considered the instruction of ethics to be part of all teaching rather than a specialty by itself. The next case is that of a twenty-six-year-old man from Detroit, a level V, whose spiritual name is Andarado. Initially, I tried to dissuade him from coming to see me. I normally do not take clients under the age of thirty. This is because I don't think the average young person has passed that many major forks in the road of life. Their amnesia blocks may be too firmly in place. There is also the increased possibility of obstructions by their spirit guides during hypnosis who might feel it is too early for their student to see certain karmic pathways. Andarado was an exception and I'm glad he overruled my concerns.

This client had sent me a letter stating, "I am anxious to experience my immortal identity because I have long felt I know things and have skills beyond what I should for my age." I hear these declarations from many young people and, more often than not, their stage of development is not what they imagined after a session with me. This was not true with this client. When I met Andarado, I was struck by his intensity, alertness and self-containment, which I found unusual for someone his age.

As his session progressed, I found that Andarado first came to Earth during the rise of Babylon, which I thought was rather late in Earth time for a blue light. He told me his incarnations began on a dark, quiet world with intelligent, although unemotional, life forms who were dying as a race. This was a world devoted to reason and logic. Eventually, Andarado asked for a transfer to a brighter world where he could incarnate into a more sensitive being. He was given Earth.

While reviewing his past experiences in a spiritual classroom, I learned of Andarado's interest in how planetary magnetic energy affects intelligent behavior on certain worlds. His latest assignment was creating brain tissue for a small feline creature. Andarado explained, "I set up a lattice of energy to screen and study patterns of behavior responses. I have to be careful not to hook up a 12-volt battery into a 6-volt system." I assumed he was studying to be a Master of Design. I was in for a surprise.

Case 56

Dr. N: Andarado, we have talked about your work in the spirit world with teaching students. You have also explained a little about your energy creation studies with the thought processes of lower forms of life. This leads me to conclude you are preparing to be a specialist in either teaching or design.

S: (laughs) Neither is true. I am training to be an Ethicist.

Dr. N: Oh? How about these two areas of your early studies we have just talked about?

S: They have been offered to me as prerequisites so I will be more effective as an Ethicist. This is my passion, working with the moral codes of intelligent beings.

Dr. N: But isn't the reviewing of morality, values and the standards of conduct basic to the work of all teaching guides?

S: Yes, but moral principles as they relate to objective values are so essential to human development one can specialize in that field. There is usually an Ethicist on every council.

Dr. N: Why did you spend so much time on another world before coming to Earth?

S: Being versed in the morality of other intelligent societies is good training for any Ethicist.

Dr. N: Okay, Andarado, tell me—how many student souls from Earth did they give you when you began working between lives on your true vocation?

S: Only a couple at first.

Dr. N: I suppose they were very young souls?

S: Yes, but then that changed and I now have eighteen middle-level souls.

Dr. N: Why are you allowed to be working with level IIIs when you have not finished incarnating on Earth yourself?

S: This is exactly the reason for my current assignment. I'm not experienced enough to be helping the very troubled, less-developed souls. Because I am still unseasoned, they don't give me the really difficult cases. I can give advice to souls with more maturity because I was in their shoes not so long ago.

Dr. N: Do you work with your students both in the spirit world and while they are on Earth?

S: (firmly) Not during the periods when they are incarnating on Earth. That is the prerogative of their teaching guides. I work with them only in the spirit world.

Dr. N: How do you see ethics as a test for human society?

S: Primarily because it is so easy for human beings to drift away from moral behavior and to rationalize their actions.

Dr. N: Would you say this is because the average person is pragmatic in believing the end justifies the means in being perceived as individually successful?

S: Yes, and this appears to people to be in opposition to universalism.

Dr. N: Do you see any resolution in the conflict between universalism and rugged individualism in human attitudes?

S: Working for world betterment would eventually do away with intolerance against those who are different from us. The need for personal status and elitism is the conflict because it is equated with happiness.

Dr. N: So you see our dilemma as the conflict between placing a desire for personal happiness and individual goals above the alleviation of suffering among the human population?

S: For many on this planet that is the dilemma of selfishness.

Dr. N: Could you take this a bit further? Are you saying that humans by nature are not a race of egalitarian and charitable people?

S: The average human has this dilemma, although many do not think being self-centered is a problem for them. This is the great test for coming to Earth and why my work is so difficult here. The lesson of Earth, as far as morality and ethics are concerned, is for the soul to be encased in the body of a being whose instincts—whose very nature—cry out for personal survival. The plight of others is secondary.

Dr. N: You do not find a natural good in humans which is linked to the conscience of a soul?

S: Of course, that is a major part of my specialty, to develop this element of goodness so that eventually it will be a natural reaction to difficult circumstances on Earth.

Dr. N: Does the need for self-reliance have to be in opposition to a consideration for others on this planet?

S: Personal ideals and values can result in general happiness for society as a whole, if we become fully engaged with the righteousness of the soul mind as the core power of Self.

Dr. N: What is the most helpful advice you give your students before they come back to Earth?

S: (grins) They are like race horses, so I caution them to be patient and pace themselves. The energy that goes into controlling the human body must be parceled out carefully. They are at the stage of learning the fine balance of ethical behavior. When they live in a physical world as dense as Earth, they must guard against being absorbed by it in order to be effective.

After I finished with this client, I reflected on how many physiologists believe the human sensory system is overdeveloped as an outgrowth of our primitive origins. Aggression and avoidance behavior has been a means of survival for humans since the Stone Age. In our evolutionary process, we have a brain which does not yet have complete control over our bodily responses. Under high emotional stress, we tend to lose rationality. Jung tells us, "The rational and irrational exist side by side and healthy people recognize the workings of both forces within themselves. We should look to our mental neuroses and physical ailments as unconscious value patterns."

Most of us start off making a lot of dumb mistakes and by the end of our life we become smarter. The idea of coming back in repeated incarnations is that eventually we will get it right early on and lead productive lives from the beginning. In this quest we are often ego-driven and we forget that what is good for us is generally good for other people. Unfortunately the philosopher Kant was right when he said, "If we believe in the immortality of the soul created by a divine source, this presupposes free will which may not include moral behavior."

There is a great need for Ethicist Souls. It can be said that there are reasons for the actions of some people turning out badly because of an underdeveloped soul co-existing with a disturbed human brain. Because of these conditions, our free will toward making good choices could be more inhibited. I have tried to show that in the spirit world souls do not use this argument as a valid excuse for the lack of control over emotions in a host body.

The solution for all of us to improve is staying with the process of continuing evolution to become better than we are. Our spirit guides were once just like us before they attained their current status. We are given many host bodies and all of them are imperfect. Rather than being obsessive about a body which will only last one lifetime, concentrate on the evolution of your soul Self and rely on your spiritual power. As we do this our capability for connecting with others will evolve and eventually cut through the dilemma of moral distinctions that were articulated by the soul Andarado.

Harmonizer Souls

This specialty represents a broad classification of souls with many subgroups. Nevertheless, while I access the minds of so many people, I do see an interdependence and connection behind all soul specialties. Souls in the general category of Harmonizers often incarnate as communicators working in a variety of capacities. When they are discarnated beings, I am told they work as restorers of disrupted energy on the face of the Earth. Incarnating Harmonizer Souls might be statesmen, prophets, inspirational messengers, negotiators, artists, musicians and writers. Typically, they are souls who balance the energy of planetary events involving human relationships. They may be public or private figures who operate behind the stage of world events. These souls are not healers in the traditional mode of working with individuals because Harmonizers function on a larger scale in attempting to diffuse negative energy.

In my first book, I wrote about the Sages, who are highly advanced souls that are still incarnating on Earth even though it is unnecessary for their own personal development. I am told they are skilled linguists with the ability to phrase words in vibrational tones that deeply touch people. These wise beings are here because it is their mission to help humanity in a direct physical way. They are unobtrusive and may wish for no public attention. From what I can gather, they are not large in number. These highly evolved old souls among us are considered to be active observers of events. They report on human trends that they feel require special attention. For this reason, I place them under Harmonizer Souls.

It is evident to my subjects that the Sages are somehow connected to another group of Harmonizer specialists in the spirit world whom they call the Watchers. These beings do not incarnate but receive information from many sources about conditions on Earth and other worlds as well. I have precious little data about them. What I do have comes from a few clients who know of them only through their own training to be Harmonizer Souls. Presumably, a Watcher provides information to other Harmonizers, who will act to moderate the affects of social and physical forces creating havoc on Earth. The case which follows is from a level V called Larian who is in training to be a Harmonizer.

Case 57

Dr. N: Larian, could you explain something about being in the specialty of harmonizing and what you do?

S: I am a raw recruit, but I will try. I am learning about harmonizing Earth's discordant energy to help people.

Dr. N: Do you mean with the geophysical elements of Earth, such as high winds, fire, earthquakes—that sort of thing?

S: I have friends in that pursuit, but this is not my area of study.

Dr. N: Well all right, then—before we get to your tasks, what are your friends learning?

S: These planetary restorers soften the destructive aftermath of natural physical forces, which cause large amounts of negative energy.

Dr. N: Why don't the powers that exist in the spirit world just prevent these natural disasters from happening in the first place and save people a lot of grief?

S: (shakes head) Then they wouldn't be natural catastrophes, which are intended to be part of the conditions of life on Earth. A planetary harmonizer would not interfere with these forces, even if they had the capability—which I don't think they do.

Dr. N: Then what is their function?

S: Spread the seeds of coherent energy into the disturbed, to neutralize large concentrations of negative energy. They work with polarity and magnetic force to assist in human recovery. (grins) We call them the vacuum cleaners.

Dr. N: Okay, Larian, where does your own work fit into the scheme of things?

S: I hope to make a contribution with catastrophic events directly created by people.

Dr. N: How many other trainees are in your section?

S: Four.

Dr. N: Do you and your associates plan to stop wars?

S: (perturbed) I don't think I am getting across to you. Our training is not designed to tamper with the minds of people who cause human suffering.

Dr. N: Why not? Are you saying as a Harmonizer Soul you would not want to intercede in some way with a Hitlerian psychopath bent on destruction?

S: The mind of the psychopath is closed to reason. I am in training to maintain positive energy around calmer heads who can make a difference in world events.

Dr. N: Isn't that tampering with free will, cause and effect, and the whole issue of natural karmic influences?

S: (pause) The conditions are already in place for the unfolding of cause and effect. We wish to allow for more rational thinking by sending waves of positive energy to the right people. We do not orchestrate resolutions. We offer a quiet atmosphere for dialogue.

Dr. N: You know, Larian, it seems to me you are fence-straddling between tampering and not doing so.

S: Then I am not getting through to you. Maybe if I explain more what I am doing at present you will see the difference. I am learning to adjust my energy beam to diffuse and rearrange the forces of negative human energy generated each day on Earth. It is like opening a dam to provide needed water to make the valley below fertile.

Dr. N: I don't know if I am convinced yet, but please continue.

S: (patiently) I go to a huge dome to practice with my small group. Arlett is there, she is our instructor—very accomplished— catches our mistakes at once. It is here we practice the art of balancing vibrational disharmony. Eventually, we hope to smooth out large masses of disruptive energy patterns on Earth.

Dr. N: What happens in the dome?

S: It provides a geometric base for certain oscillations and intervals to simulate erratic waves of human thought from large groups. It is deliberately stirred up for us. We are supposed to smooth it out.

Dr. N: Mmm . . . to foster expressions of harmonic thought?

S: Yes, thought and communication. We also study vocal tones and analyze their meanings—anything which influences negative thought. We want to help people who wish to help themselves. This is not direct interference.

Dr. N: All right, Larian, but when you become proficient at being a Harmonizer Soul, what power will you possess?

S: We will become senders of recovering energy to combat mass disillusionment. The melody of a Harmonizer whispers through the corridors of Earth of better things to come. We are messengers of hope.

After listening to the explanations of a number of Harmonizer Souls, I have come to believe that those spiritual masters who designed this laboratory of chaos we call Earth did not set things in motion and then walk away. There are superior beings who care enough about our survival to watch over us. Frankly, for much of my life I did not believe this could be true. There is a common theme I hear among Harmonizer Souls. They wish to give people the means to help themselves where they can, but they are not the conscience of human beings and they do not interfere with our free will. We were created and sent to Earth to problem-solve within the matrix of an intelligent life form living in a difficult environment which involves suffering but also great beauty and promise. It is this balance we must recognize in our day-to-day reality. There is an old Chinese proverb that states "We count our miseries carefully and accept our blessings without much thought."

Masters of Design

While this specialization is also multifaceted, to me it represents two major subdivisions of souls. Within a geophysical environment, there are purely structural specialists and those who create living things within these settings. The Master of Design trainees of my limited experience are assigned to work in a physical universe, frequently with uninhabited planets in the process of cooling after being formed out of stars. Those souls who are involved with the creation of life forms are engaged with worlds where new life is evolving.

I will begin by reviewing the activities of the structural souls who are in training to use energy for the designing of planetary geology. I think of them as architect-builders of topography who work with the component parts making up planetary surface features. This would include mountains, bodies of water, atmosphere and climate. Although structural specialists are associated with souls dedicated to landscaping with plants, trees and living creatures, that work is considered to be a separate classification of design. Structurally oriented souls are likely to begin their craft by constructing, in the spirit world, objects they knew in life.

Case 58

Dr. N: How many souls were in your original cluster group?

S: There were twenty-one . . . most of us have been split up now.

Dr. N: Does that mean you don't see much of the original group?

S: (reflectively) No . . . that's not it . . . just that we are scattered around. Most of us don't work together anymore. (brightening) I do see my old friends at other times.

Dr. N: Did any members of the old group come with you?

S: Three . . . and two stayed.

Dr. N: How many souls have been assigned to your new group?

S: Eight right now, and we hear one more is coming.

Dr. N: I am curious how this change in your endeavors came about. Can you explain what the transition out of your original group was like for you?

S: (long pause) Well, in the beginning I noticed another guide began dropping in on our study sessions. We learned his name was Baatak. He had been invited by my guide Eirow to observe us for a while.

Dr. N: Did Baatak drop in at random during all phases of your work activities at that time?

S: No, he came only during the structural periods.

Dr. N: And what was the nature of your structural work then?

S: Oh, you know, the use of energy in structural composition. I like to sculpt matter into utilitarian designs.

Dr. N: I see . . . well, I'll come back to that. Tell me, did Baatak participate in your group activities during his visits to the old cluster?

S: No, he was an observer. He watched each of us carefully during the structural periods. Occasionally, he would ask one of us specific questions about how the work we were engaged in was coming along and if we felt an . . . affinity toward the work.

Dr. N: Give me an idea of your feelings about Baatak at this time and his attitude toward you.

S: I took to him right away. I think he saw that I really enjoyed what we were doing.

Dr. N: Then what happened with you and Baatak?

S: After a while (three more lifetimes), a few of us were invited to go with him for short periods to a new group that was being formed. I remember wanting Hyanth to come . . . so we could be together.

Dr. N: Is Hyanth someone important to you?

S: Yes, my soulmate.

Dr. N: And did she come with you into your new group?

S: No, Hyanth did not take to this concentrated structural work all that much . . . and so she went to another group that was being formed.

Dr. N: What did Hyanth object to about your new group?

S: Let me put it this way. I enjoy carving and shaping energy, experimenting with the relationships between planes and geometrical solids as building blocks of matter.

Dr. N: And Hyanth?

S: (with pride) Hyanth is attracted to designing the beautiful aspects of environmental settings suitable for life. She is wonderful with scenery. While I might construct a fitting series of interconnecting mountains she would be more interested in the plants and trees growing on the mountain.

Dr. N: Let me understand something. Do you just go to a physical world and build a mountain, with someone like Hyanth concentrating on life forms such as the trees?

S: No, we work with physical worlds which are forming and set in motion the geologic forces which will build the mountain. My structural projects don't have to have life. Also, Hyanth doesn't create a forest of adult trees on worlds suitable for life. Her people would design the cells which might eventually grow into the trees they want.

Dr. N: Does this mean your group and Hyanth's are separated?

S: (deep sigh) No, she is working nearby.

Dr. N: What is it like being in a newly formed group?

S: I don't think I will ever be totally apart from my old bunch. We complemented one another in so many ways. For thousands of years we helped each other in all our lives. Now . . . well, the mixture of new people is strange. We all feel the same way about our old groups. We come from different backgrounds and experiences, it takes some getting use to.

Dr. N: Would you go so far as to say there is rivalry between the members of your new soul group?

S: (grins) Nooo . . . not really . . . we all have the same motives to help each other make a contribution. The teasing and joking in our original groups is mostly gone. Everyone is serious. We each have our own talent, ideas and ways of doing things. We can see that Baatak is in the process of unifying us and we are learning to pay close attention to the abilities of each other. It is an honor to be here, but we still have weaknesses.

Dr. N: What is yours?

S: I am afraid of experimenting with my power. I like working in comfortable situations where I know I can design something perfectly. One of my new friends is just the opposite. He produces some good planetary stuff and then just jumps in and comes up with something wacky like screwing up the atmosphere so no life of any kind can breathe. He gets all tangled up with complex plans that are beyond his capabilities.

Dr. N: Can you explain to me how you personally start with a structural design project in class?

S: By first visualizing what I want. I carefully put it together in my mind to get a clear blueprint. With my new group we are learning how to use the proper quality of energy in proper composition to a large scale. With Eirow I worked in parts, while Baatak wants everything to be an interconnecting whole.

Dr. N: So the interrelation of energy elements is important to both the form and balance of your work?

S: Absolutely! Light energy begins the process but there must be a harmony to the design, and it should have practical applications. (bursts out laughing)

Dr. N: Why are you laughing?

S: I was thinking about a construction project with Hyanth. It was in our off time. Hyanth and I were kidding each other about being too self-important. She challenged me to build a small version of the elegant church where we were married in one of our lives. I was a stone cutter in that life. (in Medieval France)

Dr. N: Did you accept her challenge?

S: (still laughing) Yes, on the condition she would help me.

Dr. N: Was that fair? I mean, she is not a specialist in structure.

S: She isn't. Hyanth agreed to try and reproduce the stained glass windows and sculptures that she had loved. She wanted beauty and I wanted function. What a mess! I started by using flat beams of energy for the walls and was doing fairly well with the connecting arches, but the vaults and dome were a disaster. I called for Baatak and he fixed everything.

Dr. N: (an often-asked question) But this is all an illusion?

S: (laughing) Are you so sure of that? This building will stand for as long as we wish it to be here for us.

Dr. N: And then what?

S: It will disappear.

Dr. N: So where are you in your planetary studies?

S: I am involved with creating particles of energy for rock shapes on a full planetary scale.

Dr. N: Is this where most of your attention is directed now?

S: No, mostly I must still experiment alone with many smaller models of topography to learn how to integrate all the elements of matter. So many mistakes happen but I enjoy the training. It's just very slow.

Who gives souls the power to do what they do with matter? My subjects say they have the undeveloped capabilities, which are nurtured by teachers as their immediate source. They believe these masters receive the power they have from something higher. Yet ordinary souls themselves demonstrate smaller aspects of this greater power. I have spent years debating with myself about creation while trying to incorporate fragments of information about the cosmos from the designer souls. I have come to the conclusion that intelligent energy waves create subatomic particles of matter and it is the vibrational frequency of these waves that causes matter to react in desired ways.

Astronomers are mystified by the fact there is some unknown form of energy contributing to the total density of our universe acting against gravity to expand empty space. I have reported that a musical resonance of intelligent energy waves appears to play a role in cosmology. Many people in my cases explain that harmonics are associated with "rhythmic values of energy notes which have ratios and proportions." My subjects who are Structural Souls say these designs relate to the formation of "geometric shapes that float as elastic patterns," which contribute to the building blocks of a living universe. The geometry of space was exemplified by a client quote on page 135 and in case 44.

The Masters of Design have enormous influence on creation. I'm told they are capable of bridging universes that seem not to have a beginning or end, exacting their purposes among countless environmental settings. Carried to its logical conclusion, this would mean these masters—or grandmasters—would be capable of creating the spinning gas clouds of galactic matter which started the process of stars, planets and eventual life in our universe.

I am certain there is intelligent thought behind the formation of all animate and inanimate objects. This observation comes from souls who use their light energy for conceiving, designing, and then manipulating the molecules and cell structure of living matter which possess the physical properties they want in finished form. In my last case, I learned that the artistic designer soul of Hyanth formed full-grown trees in the spirit world to see if the finished product was appropriate, and then worked backward down to the seedlings and finally to the tree cells. This is one process of creating matter for functional use. I also indicated an example of this sort of energy training in case 35, with the creation and alteration of mice.

My next case is another illustration of those souls who work with living organisms. These designer souls are the biologists and botanists of the spirit world and they say that extraterrestrial life exists on billions of planets. I have an extensive file on souls who have incarnated on other worlds and souls who have traveled to a variety of strange worlds for both study and recreation between their lives on Earth.

Case 59

This is a distinctive case concerning a designer soul called Kala. As our session progressed, my subject spoke to me about a recent planetary assignment involving the need to adjust a problem with the ecosystem that was not going to be corrected by evolutionary adaptation. Before this case, I had not expected that souls would return to a planetary site for modifications of an existing environment since that would mean their designs were fallible. It was revealing for me to learn Kala's experience involved the altering of the molecular chemistry of an existing creature in a controlled experiment.

When clients describe their soul experiences with life on other worlds, I try to learn about the galactic location, the planet's size, orbit, the distance it lies from its star, atmospheric composition, gravitation and topography. I suppose my background as an amateur astronomer gives me an additional incentive to learn these details. Nonetheless, many clients find it annoying to try and answer astronomy questions they consider distracting and irrelevant. In our physical universe we know of 100 billion galaxies. Each of these silvery islands, separated by vast distances in light years, moves within the dark sea of space and contains countless billions of suns with the likelihood of life-supporting planets. Because my celestial references have little meaning to most subjects in hypnosis, and the worlds they talk about are so far away from Earth's quadrant in space, I frequently just move on rather than impede the session.

Kala tried to explain to me that her creation design training class went to a planet "nowhere near Earth." She called this world Jaspear and said it was in a double (binary) star system orbiting a "hot yellow star nearby, with a dull red larger star much farther away." I was also told Jaspear was a little larger than Earth but had smaller oceans. She added this world was semi-tropical with four moons. After a little encouragement, Kala was willing to discuss her work involving a strange creature that has certain odd similarities to animals on Earth.

The average client with experience on an alien planet has feelings of reluctance about giving me information they consider to be privileged. I have mentioned this fact before in other areas of my spiritual research. Subjects clam up when they feel they should not be revealing knowledge entrusted to them, or that they are not intended to uncover in their current lives. This is particularly true with alien civilizations. It is frustrating for me to hear such statements as, "Neither you nor I are supposed to know about such places." With Kala, I explained how important it was for both of us to know her capabilities as a soul, rather than my simply being an inquisitive investigator. Another effective hypnosis technique I might use to get around client blocks toward speaking about other worlds is to ask, "Have you known any fascinating alien life forms you care a great deal about?" This approach is irresistible to many souls who travel for work or play.

Dr. N: Kala, I would like to further explore what you have told me about your assignment to Jaspear. I think this would help me understand your specialty. Why don't you begin with your training class and how the project on Jaspear was presented.

S: The six of us have been assigned to work with some seniors (Design Masters) to deal with this world where runaway vegetation has threatened the food supply of the small land animals.

Dr. N: So, basically the problem on Jaspear involves the ecosystem?

S: Yes, the thick vines . . . a voracious vinelike bush. It grows so fast it kills those plants needed for the food supply. There is little space left for the land creatures of Jaspear to graze.

Dr. N: And they can't eat the vines?

S: No, and that's why we went to Jaspear on this assignment.

Dr. N: (reacting too quickly) Oh, to rid the planet of these vines?

S: No, they are indigenous to the planet and its soil.

Dr. N: Well, then, what is the assignment?

S: To create a animal which will eat the vines—to control the spreading of this bush which chokes off so much other vegetation.

Dr. N: What animal?

S: (laughing) It is the Rinucula.

Dr. N: How are you going to do that with an animal that is not indigenous to Jaspear?

S: By creating a mutation from an existing small four-footed animal and accelerating its growth.

Dr. N: Kala, you can change the DNA genetic codes of one animal to create another?

S: I could not do this by myself. We have the combined energy of my training class, plus the skillful manipulation of the two seniors who have accompanied us on this field trip.

Dr. N: You use your energy to alter the molecular chemistry of an organism in order to circumvent natural selection?

S: Yes, to radiate the cells of a group of the small animals. We mutate the existing species and make it much larger so it will survive. Since we don't have the time to wait for natural selection, we will also accelerate growth of the four-legged animal.

Dr. N: Do you accelerate the growth of the mutation so that the Rinucula appears right away, or do you accelerate the size of the creature itself?

S: Both—we want the Rinucula to be big and we want this evolutionary change to take place in one generation.

Dr. N: How many Earth years will this take?

S: (pause) Oh . . . fifty years or so . . . to us it seems like a day.

Dr. N: What did you do to the small animal who will become a Rinucula?

S: We keep the legs and hairy torso—but it all will be larger.

Dr. N: Tell me about the finished product. What does a Rinucula look like?

S: (laughing) A . . . large curving nose down around the mouth . . . big lips . . . huge jaws . . . massive forehead . . . walks on four legs with hooves. About the size of a horse.

Dr. N: You said you kept the hair of the original animal?

S: Yes, it's all over the Rinucula—long reddish-brown hair.

Dr. N: What about the brain of this animal—is it greater or less than a horse?

S: The Rinucula is smarter than a horse.

Dr. N: He sounds like something out of a Dr. Seuss children's book.

S: (grins) That's why it's so much fun to think about him.

Dr. N: Has the Rinucula made a difference on Jaspear?

S: Yes, because he is many times the size of the original animal, and has other alterations—such as his huge jaw and body strength— he is really eating up the vines. The Rinucula is a docile creature with no natural predators and a voracious eater, like the original animal. That's what the seniors wanted.

Dr. N: What about his reproduction on this planet? Do the Rinucula multiply quickly?

S: No, they reproduce slowly—that is why we had to create quite a number of Rinuculas after we programmed the desired genetic characteristics.

Dr. N: Do you know how this experiment ended?

S: Jaspear is now a more balanced world of plant eaters. We wanted the other animals to thrive as well. The vines are now under control.

Dr. N: Do you plan eventually to have highly intelligent life on Jaspear—is that what this is all about?

S: (vaguely) Perhaps the seniors do . . . I have no way of knowing.

Explorers

I consider most people who gain experience in different environments outside the spirit world between lives to be a type of Explorer Soul. They may be souls whose personal development requires in-depth experience on different worlds or simply recreational travelers. I also have clients who engage in temporary work assignments between lives that involve travel. Explorer Souls in training travel to physical and mental worlds in our universe and even into other dimensions. From the accounts I hear about, I picture a full-fledged Explorer Soul as a highly specialized, non-incarnating being who seeks out suitable training sites for the less-experienced souls and then eventually leads them to these regions. Their work ethic is one of reconnaissance.

When souls who are still incarnating on Earth move from the spirit world to other locations, these trips seem to be from point to point with no stops along the way. My clients say that in their travels to other places they do not perceive the trips to be long or short. This is illustrated by the following two quotes:

> From the spirit world to a physical world it is like a door opens and you see the walls, of what appears to be a hallway, a tube, whirling past on either side. Then another portal-type doorway opens and you are there.

> When I pass into another dimension to a mental world I am like a piece of static flowing through a TV screen into magnetic zones structured by pure thought. The voids are composed of large, pulsating fields of energy. I feel the power of this energy more than when I go to a material universe because we must adapt our wave resonance to existing conditions in order to easily pass through. I want to keep my energy tight, so I don't get lost. These trips are not instantaneous, but almost.

Most of the souls I work with who explore other worlds are led by instructors. Also, I find those subjects who travel interdimensionally are not limited to souls in an advanced state of development. We saw this in the hide-and-seek game. They seem to be adventuresome souls who relish travel, the challenges of different environments, and new forms of self-expression. I have been told of existences where intelligent beings reside within blocks of matter so dense it is described as resembling the composition of silver and lead. Others tell me about realms appearing as shining glass surfaces amid towers of crystal. There are physical worlds consisting of fire, water, ice or gas where all manner of intelligent life thrives. These spheres within which Explorer Souls move have light, pastel or dark environments. However, the dark habitats do not bear the sinister connotations that people associate with regions of foreboding.

The Explorer Souls do not emphasize a polarity of light and darkness in their travels as much as other elements. These could include a restless or serene environment, thin or heavy density, physical or mental domains, and conditions lending themselves to what has been described as "purified or coarse intelligence." Traveler souls who move into different realms of cosmic consciousness must learn to align their energy with symmetry to local conditions within these demarcations. Explorer guides can take souls on brief visits to higher dimensional levels to raise their consciousness. In the minds of many subjects, these trips don't last long and this is probably to avoid overwhelming younger souls.

In the last chapter, under recreational activities in the spirit world, I said that soul travel often involves working vacations. These visits are usually to physical worlds for souls from Earth and can last from a few days up to hundreds of years in Earth time. I receive a great deal of information about other worlds from discussions of a client's R & R periods between lives. My hypnosis subjects are usually more relaxed about giving me details of their recreational travel to other worlds, as demonstrated by the next case.

Case 60

Dr. N: What activity are you most engaged in between lives when you are not reviewing karmic lessons with your soul group?

S: Well . . . I do take trips . . . ah . . . but they are rather personal. I don't think I should talk about this sort of thing . . .

Dr. N: I don't wish to make you uncomfortable with telling me things which you feel you shouldn't. (pause) Just let me ask if there is some exotic place you travel to between lives which gives you fond memories?

S: (reacts quickly with a broad smile) Oh, yes—to Brooel.

Dr. N: (lowering my voice) Is this a world where you incarnate?

S: No, I remain as a soul because I only go to Brooel to rejuvenate my spirit . . . and it's fun to take trips here because it is like Earth with no people.

Dr. N: (in a reassuring tone) I see, so you mostly go for rest and recreation. Why don't you tell me about the physical aspects of Brooel compared to Earth.

S: It is smaller than Earth and colder because the sun is further away. It has mountains, trees, flowers and fresh water but no oceans.

Dr. N: Who brings you to Brooel?

S: Uh . . . a Master Navigator by the name of Jhumu.

Dr. N: Would this be the same type of soul as an Explorer who is a specialist in travel, or someone like your own guide?

S: Jhumu is an Explorer all right, we call them navigators. (pause) But our guides can come with us too if they want.

Dr. N: I understand completely. Tell me, do you usually go alone or with other members of your soul group?

S: We could come alone but the navigators usually bring a few members of different groups.

Dr. N: What do you think of Jhumu?

S: (more relaxed) Jhumu likes being a tour director for those of us who are taking breaks from our normal activities. He says it gives us perspective.

Dr. N: That sounds interesting. I know you are anxious to explain why Brooel is great fun, so why don't we begin by my asking you about the animal life on this planet.

S: Ah . . . no fish, frogs, snakes—no amphibians.

Dr. N: Oh? Why is that, do you think?

S: (pause and a little confused) I don't know, except those of us who come here want to be involved with a special land animal . . . who is—. (stops)

Dr. N: (coaxing) An animal you remember?

S: (laughs) Our favorite . . . the Arder. They are like a small bear with cat features all rolled into one. (wrapping her arms around her sides) The Arder is a wonderful, furry, cuddly, peaceful animal which is really not an animal as we know it.

Dr. N: What does this mean?

S: The Arder is very intelligent and affectionate.

Dr. N: How does their intelligence compare to humans?

S: That's difficult to say. It is not higher or lower than humans . . . just different.

Dr. N: What is most different?

S: They have absolutely no need for conflict or competition among their kind. This is why we are brought to this peaceful setting—it gives us hope for a better future on Earth—what Earth could become if we all got our act together.

Dr. N: What do you and your friends do on Brooel?

S: We come and play with these gentle creatures, who seem to have a connection for souls from Earth needing rest. We materialize our energy in a minor way to interact with the Arders.

Dr. N: Can you be more specific about this process?

S: Well . . . we assume transparent human shapes to hug them. We float into their minds . . . so unearthly and subtle. After life on a hard physical world such as Earth, they heal us in this setting.

The Arder is a soothing creature which motivates us to see what is possible with the human body.

The setting for R & R is as much of a factor on these trips of exploration by souls as the attributes of the alien life forms they find there. While in trance, my subjects have great empathy for the unspoiled planets which are similar to Earth but with no people. They look upon these places as their own special playgrounds. I don't see nearly as many clients with memories of going to mental worlds. This is natural. We are beings used to bright light and physical dimensions. The following quote is another example of interaction with a life form purely for recreation.

> We are taken by the travelers to the place of the Quigleys. They are the size of a muskrat, fat and fluffy with a forehead similar to a bull-nosed dolphin. The Quigley has big, rounded ears and straight-out whiskers. They have the IQ of perhaps a smart dog. They are devoted and happy animals who love us. Their planet is an ancient, mystical land of gently rolling hills and valleys carpeted with flowers and small, delicate trees. It is very bright here and there is an inland body of fresh water. We relax and play in this world of perfect peace.

If we have dreams of being tall giants, very short elfin-appearing beings, or having the bodies of water and air creatures, this could mean these dreams reflect unconscious memories of a prior incarnation on another world. However, it is also just as likely we were associated with this type of entity on R & R visits to some exotic world. Much of our mythology about strange creatures may also stem from these memories. I should add that most people have dreams of being able to fly. This probably relates more to our memories of floating around as a soul in a disembodied state than being a flying creature in a former life.

In order to appreciate the symbiotic relationship between an earthly soul who has had associations with other forms of life, let's examine the next excerpt from one of my cases who is a hybrid soul. I refer the reader to my comments about hybrids on page 100. In the quote below of a fond memory, my client became very nostalgic. Sometimes a hybrid soul will tell me about being taken by an Explorer Soul between lives to a world similar to that of their first physical incarnations.

Between my lives on Earth, I visit a water world called
Anturium, which is so restful after a difficult life on land.
Anturium has only one land mass, the size of Iceland. I
come with a few of my friends who also have an affinity to
water. We are brought by an Explorer-guide who is familiar with this region. Here we join the Kratens, who look a
little like whales. They are telepathic and a long-lived race
who do not mind our coming and mentally connecting
with them for a while. Occasionally, they gather at certain
locations to telepathically communicate with intelligent
aquatic life forms who exist on two other planets (around
stars in the galactic vicinity of Anturium). What I love
about this place is the unity and harmony of thought with
the Kratens which rejuvenates my mind and reminds me
of my original planet.

Apparently, the Kratens have the ability to project their minds as
beacons of unified thought away from Anturium to other worlds by
knowing the points of confluence in the magnetic energy belt around
their planet. These vortex areas, similar to the ley lines of Earth discussed in chapter 4, seem to give the Kraten's telepathic power a boost
and serve as conduits to better interstellar communication. From this
case and hundreds of others, I have come to the conclusion that everything on Earth and in the universe is apparently connected by thought
waves to and from the spirit world. This may also be true for other
dimensions near us as well. The multiple progression of intelligence
with all elements of matter represents a symphony of order and direction based upon a plan of universal consciousness.

In the last chapter, I explained how some recreational games are used
as training vehicles for the souls attracted to exploration. The more
adept engage in interdimensional travel. One of my Explorer-trainee
clients said to me, "I was told that to become an Explorer I would have
to experience many realities by beginning my travels to physical worlds,
and then escalating to the mental existences and interdimensional
travel." In order to acquaint the reader with interdimensional life, I have
chosen the strange case of a client from Japan who told me in deep
hypnosis that his soul was originally from another dimension. His spiritual name is Kanno.

Case 61

Kanno is a Japanese scientist who, years ago, came to the U.S. for his advanced education. Today he prefers a life of relative isolation in laboratories. He suffers from a poor immune system, a common complaint among hybrid soul clients. These people are negatively influenced by too-little experience with the human body and too many alien imprints carried over from their former existences. As I have said, it may take the hybrid soul many generations of earthly incarnations before a complete memory cleansing of old body energy patterns will take place.

I began our session in my customary fashion, by regressing Kanno to the time when he was inside his mother's womb. This is a good place for a spiritual regressionist to start interacting with a client's soul. While inside his mother, my subject reported that he had trepidations about his coming birth stemming from his one prior life on Earth some 300 years ago in India. I continued the regression to Kanno's death scene in India and then we crossed into the spirit world. I will pick up the dialogue with Kanno when he meets his guide, Phinus.

Dr. N: What does Phinus say to you?

S: She says, "Welcome back, how did you like the ride?"

Dr. N: And what is your response?

S: Did it have to be so terrible?

Dr. N: Does she agree with your assessment of life in India?

S: Phinus reminds me that I volunteered to have a difficult opening life on Earth because I wanted to receive the full impact of a disruptive planet. I was the poorest of the poor in India and lived in squalor.

Dr. N: Did you want to suffer this much in your initial life?

S: The life was terrible and I didn't handle it well. When a childless family took my daughter against my will by paying the owner of the shack where I lived, I became so distraught I could not function. (Kanno jerks in his chair and emotionally relives the moments after his last death) WHAT KIND OF A PLANET IS THIS ANYWAY? PEOPLE SELLING CHILDREN!

Dr. N: (at this point I do not yet know about Kanno's hybrid origins and I make a wrong assumption) This does seem as though it was a very difficult first incarnation for a new soul on Earth.

S: Who said I was a new soul?

Dr. N: I'm sorry, Kanno. I just assumed that right now you are only in your second incarnation on Earth.

S: That's true, but I'm from another dimension.

Dr. N: (startled) Oh, then what can you tell me about this other dimension?

S: We had no physical worlds as you have in this dimension. My incarnations were on a mental world.

Dr. N: What did you look like on this world?

S: I had an elongated, flowing body—spongy, with no skeletal structure. We were rather transparent forms of silvery light.

Dr. N: Did you prefer a certain type of gender?

S: We were all hermaphrodites.

Dr. N: Kanno, please explain the difference between traveling to the dimension of your origins from the spirit world as opposed to coming into our universe.

S: In my dimension movement is like going through soft, translucent filaments of light. Coming into your universe is like plowing through thick, heavy, moisture-laden fog.

Dr. N: And being on Earth for the first time—what was that like compared to your home world?

S: Having concrete tied to your feet. The first thing you notice is the heavy weight of the dense energy here compared to a mental world. (pause) It isn't just heavy—it's coarse . . . severe . . . I was really jolted in that life in India.

Dr. N: Is all this a little better now—are you becoming acclimatized?

S: (without confidence) To some extent. It's still pretty difficult . . .

Dr. N: I can see that. Kanno, what is the most troubling aspect about the human brain for you?

S: (abruptly) Ahh—it's the impulsive behavior—the physical reaction to things—without analytical thought. There is danger in connecting with the wrong kind of human being, too . . . treachery . . . I can't deal with this.

Dr. N: (Kanno is sweating profusely and I quiet him now a bit before continuing) Tell me about your mental world. Does it have a name?

S: (pause) It's a sound which I can't re-create with my voice. (begins reminiscing) We float in a sea of gentle mental currents . . . soft . . . playful . . . so unlike Earth.

Dr. N: Then why come here?

S: (with a deep sigh) I am studying to be an Explorer-teacher. Most of my associates are satisfied to confine their efforts to one dimension. I finally told Phinus I wanted broader experience with a hard world in a completely different zone of existence. She told me she had a senior colleague who recommended another dimension with a strenuous physical world that had a reputation for producing vigorous, insightful souls (with a gallows laugh)— once you survive the lessons. This was Earth.

Dr. N: Did you get the impression there were other choices open to you?

S: (shrugs) Guides don't give you many choices in such situations. Phinus said that when I completed my work on Earth I would be strengthened in ways my friends who refused such assignments would not be. She said Earth would also be quite interesting and I accepted that.

Dr. N: Did any of your friends come with you into our dimension?

S: No, I was the only one who elected to go and I almost refused to return again in this life. My associates think I am very brave. They know if I make it, I'm going to be an effective traveler.

Dr. N: Let's talk about travel, Kanno. As an interdimensional traveler, you probably know if there is a finite number of dimensions around our physical universe.

S: (flatly) I do not know.

Dr. N: (cautiously) Well, is your home dimension next to ours?

S: No, I must pass through three other dimensions to get here.

Dr. N: Kanno, it would be helpful if you would try and describe what you see as you pass through these dimensions you are familiar with in your travels.

S: The first dimension is a sphere full of colors and violent explosions of light, sound and energy . . . I think it is still forming. The next is black and empty—we call it the unused sphere. Then there is a beautiful dimension which has both physical and mental worlds composed of gentle emotion, tender elements and keen thought. This dimension is superior to my original dimension and your universe as well.

Dr. N: It's now your universe too, Kanno. Tell me, does the trip through the total of four dimensions take long?

S: No, quickly—like air particles passing through a filter.

Dr. N: Can you give me a sense of the structural design between these dimensions in relation to the spirit world? You described the dimensions as spheres. Why don't we start with that.

S: (long pause) I can't tell you much. Everything is . . . in a circle around the center of the spirit world. Each of these universes appears to me to be an interlocking sphere with the next, as in a chain.

Dr. N: (after failing to gain more information) How are you getting on in our universe now, Kanno?

S: (rubbing his hand on his forehead) Better. I am learning how to discharge my energy in a steady, positive stream without depleting my reserve. It helps me to be away from people for long periods. I expect to really improve after a few more lives, but I am looking forward to completing my time here on Earth.

Before leaving the realm of the Explorer Soul, I should add that this sort of training involves learning about the texture of intelligent energy. I am frustrated in not being able to discover more about the properties of this energy in motion on mental worlds. Some information comes to me from those souls who have had experience on physical worlds which are also considered mental, as demonstrated by the following condensed quote:

> We visit the volcanic gas world of Crion to learn by assimilation. It is a mental world with outward physical attributes. Our group of Explorers float as blobs of fluid energy in a sea of gaseous substances. We are metamorphic and able to change shape and form into the tiny beings whose life is centered around pure thought. There is absolute vibrational uniformity here, unlike Earth.

Souls who travel interdimensionally explain that their movements appear to be in and out of curved spheres connected by zones that are opened and closed by converging vibrational attunement. Explorer trainees have to learn this skill. From the accounts I have heard, the interdimensional travelers must also learn about the surface boundaries of zones connecting universes as hikers locating trailheads between mountain ranges. Souls speak of points, lines and surfaces in multi-space which indicate larger structural solids, at least for the physical universes. I would think dimensions having geometric designs need hyperspace to hold them. Yet Explorer Souls travel so fast in some sort of hyperspace it seems to me the essence of speed, time and direction of travel is hardly definitive. Training to be an Explorer must indeed be formidable, as indicated by this quote from a client who travels through five dimensions between her lives:

> These dimensions are meshed with one another so that I have no sense of boundaries except for two elements, sound and color. With sound, I must learn to attune my energy to the vibrational frequency of each dimension, and some are so complex I can not yet go to them. With color, the purples, blues, yellows, reds and whites are manifestations of light and density for those energy particles in the dimensions where I travel.

∽9

The Ring of Destiny

The Screening Room of Future Lives

The place of future life selection is seen as a sphere containing highly concentrated force fields of glowing energy screens. As I mentioned in the section on spiritual libraries, the place of life selection has been characterized as the Ring of Destiny, where we first behold our next body. Most subjects see the Ring as a circular, domed theater with floor-to-ceiling panoramic screens which surround them completely while they are situated in a shadowed viewing area. Some people see the screens as being on two or three sides while they stand or sit on a raised deck. From this observation deck, souls can look up, straight ahead or down at the screens that are huge compared to what is seen in the other learning centers of the spirit world. The Ring displays futuristic scenes of events and people the soul will encounter in the life to come. Some clients have commented that each screen reflects scenes of childhood, adolescence, adulthood, and old age of the bodies they are reviewing, while others say that all the screens show them the same scene at one time.

The whole spiritual structure of the screening room is designed to give the viewer an ability either to observe or participate in the action, just as in libraries. It does seem to me that more people elect to enter the screens of the Ring during life selection than with the screens in the other learning centers. They want to actually experience snippets of future events in certain bodies before making any final decisions. The preference to enter a scene or just observe is always left up to the individual soul. As with the smaller consoles, the Ring also has what appears to be control panels or lever bars to monitor the action. People call this procedure scanning the timelines, and the more advanced tell me they can control the array of events in front of them with their minds. The sequence of events can, to some extent, be regulated in stop action for parts of a future life the soul may wish to consider more carefully.

I cannot stress too much that all my subjects feel what they are seeing has been edited for their benefit and that they have less control over what they can watch than, say, in the library. Moreover, I have the impression that when looking into the future, they see more of an early life than later. This may be due to bias in reporting since those years are already over by the time I see the client. The key viewing years of a new life seem to be between eight and twenty, when the first major forks in life begin to emerge. Many people tell me they are shown certain years in great detail while other parts of their future life are completely left out. The control panels seem to be of no use here, yet this never bothers my subjects. I believe their current amnesia also plays a part. As one forty-nine-year-old man explained, "I was shown my current body at ages four, sixteen, and twenty-eight, but I think I am now being blocked from recalling what I saw afterwards."

During viewing, the screens ebb and flow like a film of water. One woman used a suitable metaphor to represent her feelings about the experience when she said:

> As the screens come alive they resemble a three-dimensional underwater aquarium. When I look at a life it's like taking a deep breath and going underwater. People, places, events—everything floats by you in a flash before your eyes as if you are drowning. Then you come back to the surface. When you are actually sampling a scene from the life they show you, it reflects the time a person is able to stay underwater.

In many ways, uncovering the memories my subjects have about their last experience in the life selection room and their interpretations as to body choice is one of the most therapeutic and informative aspects of my hypnosis sessions. My clinical work is greatly enhanced when a client returns to the Ring because of the relevancy to their current life. By offering the reader a more comprehensive picture of this process, I hope to bring a greater appreciation of the importance of each life we select in our cycle of lives.

This chapter contains one final soul specialty that I will add to my list. These are the Timemasters, who are coordinators engaged with past, present and future timelines of people and events. Timemasters are the highly adroit experts who give the impression of actually directing the presentations in our theater-in-the-round. These master souls are members of an entire fellowship of planners that include guides, Archivists and council Elders, who are involved with designing our future.

A large percentage of my subjects never see Timemasters in the screening room. Some clients feel they are alone in the Ring except for a "projectionist." Others will enter the Ring with a personal guide, or perhaps an Elder, who is the only advisor they are aware of helping them during life selection. In terms of our own input, many souls have already organized their thoughts about the next reincarnation. Our guides and council members have helped refine these thoughts with questions about what we think our next life should be about and the type of human being that might best suit us. Still, we are not really prepared for the choices offered to us once we enter the life selection room. There is a sense of wonder and even some apprehension for the average soul.

The Timemasters of the Ring seem to be shadowy figures in the background who may be consulted by those guides who accompany us to the viewing areas. Even if they are seen, my clients are not inclined to communicate with them during observations. This is why my next case is atypical.

Case 62

Dr. N: Please give me a picture of what takes place as you enter the sphere of life selection.

S: There are two beings who come forward to work with my guide, Fyum. He seems to know them well.

Dr. N: Do you see them in this place before every new life?

S: No, only when the next life is going to be particularly difficult— which means a number of hard body choices.

Dr. N: Do you mean more body choices than usual, or more complex individual bodies?

S: Mmm ... usually I get only a couple of body choices and that makes it easier for me.

Dr. N: Do you know the names of these two specialists who talk to Fyum?

S: (jerks in chair) Never! That's just not something I would know. There isn't any ... easy familiarity here with these masters of time ... that's why Fyum is with me.

Dr. N: I understand. So do your best to give me an idea of what these Timemasters of your life offerings are like.

S: (more relaxed now) Okay, number 1 is masculine-appearing and he is rigorous in his demeanor. I know he is inclined toward having me choose a certain body—the one which will be the most useful. This body will give me the maximum experience I need in my future life.

Dr. N: Oh ... from all I have heard, the Ring directors are rather quiet, unobtrusive beings.

S: Well ... yes, that's true, but during the choosing, there is always a preferred body choice that the planners feel is best. This body is given a prominent presentation. (pause) Everyone knows this is the first time I have seen these choices—and they want my choice to be fruitful.

Dr. N: So I have heard. Why don't you tell me about number 2?

S: (smiling) She is feminine and softer ... more flexible. She wants me to accept the body which will be pleasurable to be inside. She leans to moderation and turns to 1 and says there is plenty of time to learn my lessons. I have the feeling there is a deliberate juxtaposition between them for my benefit.

Dr. N: Sort of like the good cop, bad cop routine during an interrogation?

S: (laughs) Yeah, maybe, so I will have an advocate in both camps with Fyum taking the middle road.

Dr. N: So Fyum is kind of a referee?

S: Mmm . . . no, that's not true. Fyum is neither lenient nor severe in attitude as I deliberate my choices. It is made clear to me that the body choice is mine alone because I am going to have to live with it. (a burst of laughter) Hey, I made a pun!

Dr. N: I think you did. We really do have to live with our choices. Why don't you explain what choosing the body you had in your last life was all about before we go further.

S: In my last life, I chose a difficult path with the body of a woman who would die within two years of marriage. My husband in that life needed to feel the loss of someone he loved deeply for a karmic debt from the life before.

Dr. N: So there was a high probability that this particular body was going to die young and the main question was would you be the soul who would elect to choose that body?

S: Yes, that's about it.

Dr. N: Well, please go on and tell me the circumstances surrounding your death as a young woman in that life.

S: In the screening room I saw I had three choices of death during a narrow time span involving my life on a ranch near Amarillo, Texas. I could die quickly from a stray bullet during a gunfight between two drunken men. I could die more slowly after a fall from a bucking horse. And I could die by drowning in a river.

Dr. N: Was there any chance you might live?

S: (pause) A slight one, but that would defeat the purpose of my joining with that body.

Dr. N: Which was what?

S: My soulmate and I chose to be husband and wife on this ranch because he needed the lesson. I rejected the other body choices. I came to help him.

Dr. N: Tell me what was on your mind as you looked at the three choices in the screening room.

S: I chose the bullet, naturally. The manner of my death was not about these choices as much as the meaning behind my dying young.

The reader may wonder about the connection of the laws of karma to future possibilities and probabilities. Karma does not only pertain to our deeds, it is internal as well, reflecting our thoughts, feelings and impulses—all relating to cause and effect. Karma is more than taking proper actions toward others, it is also having the intention to do so. While the timeline for the Amarillo woman had a high probability of being short, her early death was not chiseled in stone. One of the variables here was the type of soul that would occupy that particular body. Even with the soul who elected to take this body anticipating a short life, there were elements of free will to be considered. I learned that it was not 100 percent ordained that this woman would die young by the stray bullet that hit her while she was standing across the street from the saloon where the gunfight took place. When I asked if she might have avoided going into Amarillo for supplies that day my, client said, "Yes, but something impelled me to go into town right when I did, and I almost didn't go without knowing why." Another soul might not have gone at the last minute without knowing why either.

Timelines and Body Choices

Although time has little relevance outside our physical universe, we see ourselves and everything around us aging each day. We live on a planet around a star, which is also constantly aging in chronological time. The cycle of life involves movement of time and the timelines of our dimensional reality appear to be influenced by advanced beings who allow reincarnating souls to study the past and see into the future. In libraries and spiritual learning centers we can view other possible actions we might have taken in former lives to explore the "what ifs" of our past. Under the doctrine of free will, the events of the past were not inevitable any more than our actions within those events. Fate does not decree that a certain situation has to come out a particular way. We are not puppets on a string. In our universe, when the past is over, these events and the people involved with them become eternal and are forever preserved in spiritual libraries. Since past, present and future in chronological time represent *now* time in the spirit world, how is future time treated in the Ring of life selection?

In chapter 5, following case 30, I postulated on the many possibilities for the same event existing in parallel universes. In physical universes, this hypothesis means planets such as Earth could be duplicated within the same time frames and exist simultaneously as moving particle waves of light energy. Universes might be parallel, superimposed co-existing realities within the same dimension, or something else inconceivable. Regardless of the spatial layout, from the true reality of the spirit world, time and events are tracked, stopped, and moved forward and backward by examiners of Earth. The major trunk lines, which I call base lines, are the probabilities of future events in certain bodies presented as possibilities for our examination in the Ring.

The waves of past events still indelibly exist, as in spiritual libraries, but if the present and future also exist in *now* time, how can the future be changed when the past is not? Is this an impossible paradox? In quantum mechanics, particles of light seem to vanish at one point and reappear instantaneously in another place. If each event in time exists along wavelike ripples of probabilities and possibilities, is it likely that a past event is given certain eternal properties where future events are still fluid and open to change? My strong feeling is yes.

However, after years of listening to people explain about their life choices, I do not believe future alternatives are unlimited in number. There is no need for our choices in life to be infinite. These possibilities only have to be varied enough for us to learn from the lessons. For example, in case 29, Amy indicated to me from a past life review in the library that her alternative choices to suicide began to fall off the chart of possibilities after a while.

The planners deal in the "what ifs" of our lives. Events which have not yet taken place in the grand scheme of things are known by Timemasters and others for their greater or lesser potential of happening. We do not simply study alternate timelines of future events in the Ring. Rather, we examine the alternative bodies offered us that will exist within those events. These bodies will be born into roughly the same time frames. Watching the most probable series of events linked to those bodies under consideration is like previewing advance promotional scenes from a movie.

As they view specific scenes of what the Timemasters want them to see, some souls feel they are playing a chess game where they don't yet know all the possible moves available for a desired ending. Usually, souls look at parts of a future life on a base line, or Ring Line, as some clients call it. The Ring Line represents the greatest probable course of a life for each body examined. The soul preparing for incarnation knows that one chess move, one minute change in the game they are watching, could alter the outcome. I find it intriguing that most of the time souls are not shown any in-depth probable future outcomes. They know there are many other possible moves on the chessboard of life which can change at any moment of play. Frankly, this is what makes the game interesting for most souls. Changes in life are conditional on our free will toward a certain action. This causality is part of the laws of karma. Karma is opportunity but it also involves fortitude and endurance because the game will bring setbacks and losses along with personal victories.

Reports of what goes on in these screening rooms are very consistent between hypnosis subjects. Their affirmations of what they all see boggle the mind. Still, while in the Ring, people are not able to view events into the future beyond the next immediate life span of the bodies presented to them. Evidently, this might cloud the way souls see the lives they are viewing. Taking my cue from this spirit world practice, I prefer not to work with progression in hypnosis except in spiritual screening rooms. Once in a while, in conjunction with something else under discussion out of the Ring, a subject will get brief flashes of scenes where they are participating in a future event, such as being on a starship. I usually don't push for more information here. Moreover, these flashes of future existences are mercurial since people may only see a single possibility that could change when the time actually arrives, owing to a whole host of new circumstances and decisions based upon the time-lines of history leading up to these events.

The screening rooms are helpful to those souls with reservations about accepting a covenant for the next life. For many, observing certain aspects of their future gives them confidence. Nevertheless, some apprehensive souls have said they refuse to enter the screens to directly sample bodies for fear they might lose their nerve in accepting a difficult life contract. The more intrepid souls feel the screening room is designed to foster just the opposite reaction because you are allowed to test the waters before jumping in.

A poignant example of someone preparing for a trial is the selection of a homosexual body. Since a predisposition to being a gay or lesbian person is essentially biological and not the result of social learning or environment, these bodies are picked by souls for two basic reasons. As I have said before, at levels I and II many souls choose bodies of one particular gender around 75 percent of the time because they are comfortable being male or female. I find that my gay and lesbian clients have started the process of alternating gender choices in their lives, which is reflective of the more developed soul. Choosing to be a gay male or lesbian female is one means of affecting that transition in a particular life. Thus, their current sex may not be as familiar to them as the body of the opposite sex, such as a gay male feeling as if he is actually in the body of a female.

The second and far more important factor is souls choosing a gay or lesbian orientation in advance of the life they are now living because they deliberately chose to exist in a society that would be prejudiced against them. My gay and lesbian clients are usually not young, inexperienced souls. If they go public, this means these people have decided to live a life where they will be swimming upstream in a culture with rigid gender role stereotypes. They must try and rise above public abuse in order to find self-esteem and self-identity. This takes daring and resolve, which I see when I take these clients back to the life selection room when these decisions were made.

To illustrate all this, I had a gay male client who was once an Empress in China. After a long wait, he was in his first incarnation since that life of luxury and power. This soul, known as Jamona, explained that as an Empress he was in the body of a strikingly beautiful woman who wore a fortune in jewels and was waited on hand and foot, befitting her rank. It was a life of self-indulgence, lack of trust in everyone around her due to court intrigue, and adulation by her subjects. In the life selection room, just before Jamona's current life, there were three body choices. This is what my client had to say about his decision:

> Of my three choices, two were women and one was a handsome young man who, I was told, "was feminine inside." One woman was very thin, almost frail-looking, who was to live a quiet life of a devoted wife and mother. The other woman was chic, kind of flashy, and destined to be a society gadfly. She was also emotionally cold. I chose the man because I would have to cope with a life of homosexuality. I knew if I could overcome the shame of society it would offset my life of adulation as an Empress.

These selections were in keeping with the usual spread of body choices. The attractive society woman would simply have been an extension of my client's former life as a public figure who was self-absorbed and envied. The housewife would not have been a poor choice. Here was a middle-of-the-road offering where Jamona would have learned to be humble and accept life's trials in poor circumstances. Even so, the candidate was another woman and Jamona wanted to break a long cycle of being in female bodies.

Choosing the life of a gay man, according to Jamona, was the hardest one, although he has been much more financially secure than the woman of ordinary means. We are not coached during these selections but the older souls know there is often one tempting choice which would not test us very much. Jamona knew this was the society woman. He made his choice not because he was pushed into selecting the leading candidate of the gay male but because the trial was clearly the hardest. My client told me, "There have been many people in my life who have treated me with disgust and even loathing. I needed to experience this discrimination—to feel unsafe and vulnerable."

One thing I have noticed in the selection of bodies is that the more advanced souls are able to make insightful comparisons between the bodies offered them within the time periods that are presented. I also see many less-advanced souls accept the body they know they ought to choose as the best course of action. They trust the selection process more than themselves. A client said, "For me, getting a new body is like trying on a new suit of clothes off the rack which you want to buy and hope it won't need alterations."

Timemasters

Only once every few years does a Timemaster in training come my way. When I recognize one, they are a resource to be treasured. Since there are other specialties associated with timelines I must guard against making early presumptions in the hypnosis session. For instance, the Archivist Souls assist souls in searching out their past histories and alternative timelines to those events. Thus, they function more as historians and chroniclers than as Timemasters who would track timelines of the immediate future for bodies under consideration in the life selection room. As with the other soul specialties, I'm sure there is overlapping here, too, with many masters working on time coordination for souls in need of their services. This is why my clients often lump them all together in their minds with the label of planners.

There is much the Timemaster trainees don't know yet, or so they say. As I probe the esoteric aspects of any soul specialty, there is the necessity of sorting out the usual blockages of details I am not supposed to know as opposed to what my advanced subject really doesn't know. Readers may wonder why I didn't ask other relevant questions in the cases presented in this book. The chances are I did, but received no response. Sometimes, both the trainee in a specialty area and I bring forth information which starts off as being inadvertent and then snowballs. Such was the case with a soul called Obidom, who is an engineer in his current life. I will begin the dialogue at a memorable point in our session.

Case 63

Dr. N: Obidom, can you tell me what you do between lives that represents your greatest challenge as a soul?

S: I study time on the planet Earth.

Dr. N: To what end?

S: I wish to be a master of this art . . . traveling the timelines . . . understanding the sequences with people living in a physical world. To help the planners assist souls in their life selections.

Dr. N: How is your program progressing?

S: (sighs) Very slowly, I'm such a beginner I need many mentors.

Dr. N: Why were you chosen for this training?

S: It is very difficult for me to tell you because I don't think I am very worthy of this art. I suppose it all began because I enjoy manipulating energy and became rather good at it in my classes.

Dr. N: Well, isn't this true of many souls who make things by energy manipulation in their creation classes?

S: (beginning to warm to my questions) This is different, we don't create . . . in the same way.

Dr. N: What is different about your work?

S: To work with time, you must learn spatial manipulation. You start with models and then go to the real thing.

Dr. N: What sort of models?

S: (dreamily) Oh . . . a huge vaporized pool . . . of swirling liquid energy . . . thinning in those gaps where scenes are simulated for us in mini-bites . . . the gaps open . . . you see neon tubes of fluctuating light . . . ready for entry. (stops) It's really hard to explain.

Dr. N: That's all right, Obidom. I would like to discuss where you are now working, who teaches you, and something about the practical art of becoming a Timemaster.

S: (quietly) Time training is conducted at a temple. (grins) We call it the Temple of Time—where teachers instruct us in the application of energy sequences for events.

Dr. N: What are sequences?

S: Timelines exist as energy sequences of events which move.

Dr. N: Tell me how you manipulate energy in the timelines.

S: Time is manipulated by compressing and stretching energy particles within a unified field and to regulate its flow . . . like playing
with rubber bands.

Dr. N: Can you change events in the past, present and future? Is that
what you mean by manipulation?

S: (long pause) No, I can only monitor the energy sequences. We
operate as . . . highwaymen who enter and exit the sequences—
which we consider roads—by speeding up and slowing down.
Condensing our energy speeds us up and expansion slows us
down. It's the same thing with events and people who appear on
the sequences as points in the roads. We don't create anything.
We intersect as observers.

Dr. N: Then who created the time sequences in the first place?

S: (exasperated) How can I know that? At my stage I am only trying
to function within the system.

Dr. N: Just asking, Obidom. You're being very helpful. Tell me, to
what purpose do you function as a Timemaster in training?

S: We are given one-event assignments . . . the human choices
around that event all have meaning. The practical applications of
what we do involve human streams of thought and actions that
join in a river of time.

Dr. N: I would call these occurrences passages of action and
memory of that action.

S: I would agree. Particles of energy do involve memory.

Dr. N: How?

S: Energy is the carrier of thought and memory within the
sequences and these never pass into oblivion. The conduit by
which time is perceived begins with thought—the shaping of
an idea—then the event and finally the memory of the event.

Dr. N: How is all this recorded into the sequences?

S: By the vibrational tone of each recorded particle of energy. This is what we recover.

Dr. N: Can the sequences exist in all sorts of alternate realities?

S: (pause) Yes . . . overlapping and interlaced . . . this is what makes the search interesting if one has the skill to find them. All things can be observed and retrieved for study.

Dr. N: I need more direction here, Obidom.

S: There is a lot I can't tell you. The particles of energy which are part of the causation for the setting up of events in time involve vibrational patterns with many alternatives. We view all this human history as useful for future incarnations of people.

Dr. N: Tell me how you feel about alternate possibilities to events.

S: (long pause) We study what is productive. Events—poor, better, best—are played out until they cease to be productive. (sighs deeply) Anyway, I'm still very new at that. I study the past scenes of what has taken place.

Dr. N: So are you saying everything that can exist in time does not necessarily exist if there is nothing for human beings to learn from its existence?

S: (pause) Ah . . . yes, similar situations of decision-making call for slightly different solutions and after a while the differences are so small they would be nonproductive as lessons.

Dr. N: From all you have told me, Obidom, I have the feeling you are not much engaged in future time just yet. So how do you see yourself?

S: I think of myself more as an archeologist in time. My assignments are studying people and events of the past and present. The future is murky . . . the sequences unclear . . . no, I'm an archeologist with time right now.

Dr. N: Where did your studies really begin in this field?

S: When my class was assembled for training at the temple.

Dr. N: How many souls are in your class?

S: There are six of us ... (pause, adding) I didn't know anyone before we got there.

Dr. N: Obidom, tell me about your initial training. Certainly, this must be clear in your mind.

S: I was sent to the world of Galath. It is a physical world similar to the geography of Earth. This world once had a great civilization, highly technical, and the Galathians were able to travel to other planets, which led to their undoing. Galath now has no highly intelligent life forms.

Dr. N: I don't understand why you were sent to a dead world?

S: It's not dead as much as vacant. When we arrived for training we assumed a transparent form which resembled the humanoid appearance of the old Galathians. (laughs)

Dr. N: Tell me about them.

S: I was just thinking ... they were yellowish-green people, very tall and willowy, without apparent joints ... they had large, multi-faceted insect eyes ...

Dr. N: What were they like as a people?

S: The Galathians were wise but foolish—like the rest of us. They came to believe in their invincibility.

Dr. N: But what is the purpose of coming here? Isn't everything gone?

S: Don't you see? Their timelines still exist. We are here to practice intersecting with the old history of this place. This is kind of an exotic world with beat-up space platforms still circling the planet. On the ground there are huge spheres of habitation which are now empty and falling apart ... plants growing in their ancient halls of learning, decaying vestiges of this once-great civilization are scattered about ...

Dr. N: Just what do you and your five classmates do, Obidom?

S: We beam out our energy . . . and float through the corridors of their past time. One of the teachers helps us adjust our vibrations to intersect with certain periods of Galathian history. It is fragmentary because of our lack of skill . . . but certain scenes of their power are vivid.

Dr. N: So nothing of the past is ever really lost?

S: No, although the Galathians are gone, everything they did, in a sense, still lives . . . their triumphs . . . their decline . . . we can study their mistakes. I can retrieve people talking at certain moments . . . what they were thinking before they were conquered by another race and assimilated into their culture away from here. The Galathians had a musical language which flows around their broken ships of space and deserted streets.

Dr. N: What is your ultimate goal, Obidom?

S: When I become proficient I will serve as an advisor for the planners who wish to design certain situations for people . . . help the library researchers . . . assist in coordinating selections in the sphere of life (i.e., the Ring)—that sort of thing.

Dr. N: Obidom, I have a personal question for you. If I was a soul with some time off between lives, could I come back to my hometown as it existed when I was a boy and see myself again with my family and friends in scenes from the past? I don't mean re-creating all this in the spirit world, but actually coming back to Earth in a disembodied state, as you did on Galath.

S: (smiles) Sure . . . although you might need some help with a talented teacher before you got the hang of it. Just don't expect to do any tinkering around with the original to make alterations. (sardonically) Remember, you would be a ghost.

Free Will

At one of my lectures in Vancouver, B.C., a distraught woman rose and cried out loudly, "You New Age gurus tell us on one hand we have free will to make choices in our life and on the other that we are predestined to follow a certain plan because of past life karma. Which is it? I have no free will in my life because I am at the mercy of forces over which I have no control. My life is one of sorrow." After my talk I sat down next to this woman for a few minutes and learned that her nineteen-year-old son had recently been killed on a motorcycle.

People have the idea that free will and destiny are opposing forces. They do not realize that destiny represents the sum of our deeds over thousands of years in a multitude of incarnations. In all these lives we had freedom of choice. Our current life represents all past experiences both pleasant and unpleasant, and so we are the product of all our former choices. Add to this the fact that we may have deliberately placed ourselves in situations that test how we will react to events in our current life, which are not perceived by the conscious mind. This too involves personal choices. We occupy a particular body for many reasons. The young motorcycle rider, by his mother's own admission, lived for speed and essentially got a high from the dangers of his obsession.

Because my last section on time opened the door to future probabilities and possibilities, it is appropriate to examine the ramifications of free will a little further. Reincarnation would mean nothing if all life was predetermined. In my remarks about timelines, I suggested that the future may exist in many realities. People who have premonitions about the future may be right or wrong. If someone saw themselves being killed in a certain place and time and it didn't happen, this potential causality could mean it was only the most dire of alternative possibilities.

An argument for determinism, as opposed to free will, is that one Source, or a collective group of lesser divinities, is responsible for planet Earth being populated with humans who suffer from disease, pain, hunger and fear. We live in a world of earthquakes, hurricanes, floods, fires, and other natural disasters over which we have no control. I have often said that Earth is considered by souls to be a very difficult school. The great lesson of Earth is to overcome both planetary and private destructive forces in life, grow strong from the effort, and move on.

To a great extent we come equipped with what we need to take care of ourselves. Karma may at times seem punitive, but there is justice and balance which we may not recognize in our sorrow. Fear arises when we separate ourselves from our spiritual power. We knew many of the challenges in advance of our life and chose them for good reasons. Accidents involving our bodies are not considered to be accidental by the soul, as I have tried to show in many cases, such as case 62 with the woman from Amarillo who was shot to death. The sheer will of our true Self has the power to rise in opposition to our weakness in character, especially during adversity. We have the freedom to remake our lives after any catastrophe if we are willing to take the responsibility to do so.

More important than the events that test us in life is our reaction to these events and how we handle the consequences. This is the primary reason for conscious amnesia. I have indicated that the soul is not usually shown all the alternatives to probable future events in the life to come. There are good reasons for this practice despite spontaneous spiritual memory recall, which exists with some people. Amnesia allows for free will and self-determination without the constraints of unconscious flashback memories about what we viewed in the screening room. While the scenes presented to us covering our next life are selective, my cases have shown we will be given the opportunity to review all the major alternatives after the life is over. I have a short but very graphic example of free will that reveals how even discarnate souls can be surprised by a sudden decision which can change the probable outcome in life.

I had a client who was killed at the Battle of Gettysburg in 1863 as a newly recruited Union soldier. His name was John and he lived in a small community near Gettysburg. Although just sixteen, John and his sweetheart, Rose, had begun to talk of marriage in the future. The night before the three-day battle began, a Union officer rode into John's area looking for a young non-combatant who could ride a horse well to deliver dispatches. John had no plans to enlist in the war because of his age and the fact he was needed on his mother's farm. The Union officer found John and hurriedly explained his urgency, promising that John's enlistment would end when the battle ended. John was a fine horseman and he impulsively agreed to ride for the Union because "I did not want to miss out on a chance for the grand adventure." He had to leave immediately without saying goodbye to anyone. John was killed the next day.

Even as he floated above his body, John could not believe he was seeing himself lying on the ground dead. Upon returning to his spirit group, John was met by Rose—that portion of her essence she had not taken to Earth. At the moment Rose saw John she cried out, "Why are you back here? We were supposed to be married!" These soulmates quickly realized that John had abruptly chosen a path that deviated from his probable life. Even so, each path has karmic benefits of some sort, as was the case with John's brief Army experience.

I asked this client if he had been shown scenes in the screening room of what was going to happen at Gettysburg. He replied, "No, I accepted what they showed me up to the age of sixteen because I knew they had good reasons to reveal only what I needed to know before that life. I have faith in the decisions of my guides." John, the boy soldier, was not shown the possibility of his death at Gettysburg and this is very typical with such cases. Yet what about those cases where an untimely death is such a high probability in life that there is a necessity for the planners to give us the opportunity to volunteer for these bodies as a matter of personal benefit from the experience?

I know past life regressionists who have had numerous cases of heroic souls who volunteered to participate in the holocaust in Nazi Germany. I certainly have. Perhaps this is because so many of these souls from the death camps are now living new lives in America. There are options for all kinds of disasters. For the bad ones, sometimes souls are prepared for what lies ahead for them by attending pre-life rehearsals, as illustrated by this statement from a client:

> I remember passing by a large group of souls in a preparation class who were gathered in an amphitheater structure. They were all listening to a speaker tell them about the value of life even though they were only going to Earth for a short time. They had all volunteered to be in some sort of disaster where they would be killed together. They were told to get mentally prepared and to make the most out of the time they had and that if they wished their next lives could be much longer.

Case 64

This is a case of euthanasia involving a subject named Sandy. She provided me with another example of an instance where a death scene was shown to the principals of a future life. As is so often true with souls who must witness their death in advance of a life, volunteering is part of the contract. During my intake interview, I learned that Sandy was closely bonded to her brother, Keith, and that they were members of a large family. As his older sister, she had taken care of him like a mother while they were growing up. Keith was hot-headed and in his teenage years he lived on the ragged edge, driving fast cars and getting into numerous scrapes with the law. Sandy told me Keith lived as though he had a death wish. She added that Keith had hurt some people along the way with a capricious life style, but he had a good heart and his zest for living each day to its fullest was contagious.

Sandy always had a premonition her brother would die young. Keith was diagnosed with Amyotrophic Lateral Sclerosis (ALS) at age twenty-seven and died two years later. ALS is a degenerative disease of motor movements that progresses into muscle atrophy within a couple of years. Toward the end, many patients must be on a respirator to breathe and they receive large doses of morphine to combat agonizing pain.

When Sandy reached her spirit group during our session, we discovered brother and sister were companion souls. Keith was the fun-loving prankster in their group and over many previous centuries he had been rather careless of others' feelings. In consultations with his guide and members of the group, Keith recognized it was essential that he learn humility in order to advance. Being a soul of temerity, Keith asked for a life where he would be given a potent challenge toward acquiring humility rather than have this lesson strung out over many lives. He was warned that accelerated lives can be very rough. Keith said he was ready. It was a bitter pill in the Ring to discover he would have to volunteer for an athletic body which would be immobilized by ALS. Sandy said that there was a point in the life selection room where her brother almost backed out. I will pick up her narrative at this place in our session.

> **Dr. N:** Please tell me as much as you can about Keith's reaction to the body he was offered.

S: (solemnly) He was shown the worst—his body before and after the illness struck. How his independence would be taken away to make him dependent upon us. They kept nothing from him. Keith saw in the beginning of the disease there would be much self-pity and remorse, then terrible anger, but if he fought he would learn.

Dr. N: (switching back and forth from current time to the spirit world with Sandy) And did he learn?

S: Oh, yes. Near the end Keith grew calm, accepting and appreciative of what we did for him.

Dr. N: Do you have anything you would like to explain about how Keith prepared for this life with you?

S: (after a long pause my client's face takes on a look of acquiescence) I will tell you. It will be good to talk about this . . . I have told no one before. (begins to cry and I work on keeping her in focus)

Dr. N: We don't have to do this if it is too painful.

S: No, I want to. (takes a deep breath) As we prepared to come forward into this life, I was to be the oldest child in our family so I came first. We had a long discussion just before my time. Keith said he was prepared to suffer but when he reached the point where he was totally incapacitated—when he couldn't take any more—I was to shut off his life support system and free him.

Dr. N: You were going to do this in a hospital?

S: We planned for that in the spirit world but then, thank God, he was sent home during his last seven weeks and that made our plan easier.

Dr. N: Is this about pain? Certainly Keith must have had pain killers.

S: Morphine can only do so much. The last seven weeks were terrible even with the respirator and pain killers. His lungs were so affected he could not move or talk near the end.

Dr. N: I understand. Tell me about the plan you and Keith devised in the spirit world before your lives began.

S: (sighs) We began our drill by creating a bed and the life support system Keith saw in the screening room. He had every detail in his mind. Then we practiced because I thought I would be dodging doctors and nurses. I worked with the machine and studied the advance warning signs of his illness. In the drill, we went over the signals Keith would give me which would show he was ready to be released from his suffering. Finally, he asked for my promise to stay strong and let nothing deter me in the final moments. I gave him this promise willingly.

After Sandy regained full consciousness we discussed her role in the death of her brother. She said when there was a particular smell, or "death odor," from Keith's throat area, she knew it was time to get ready. I should add that this body sign did not necessarily mean Keith was going to die right away. Almost without thinking, Sandy spoke in her brother's ear, "Keith, are you ready to go?" Then came the prearranged signal. At this moment Keith squeezed his eyes open and shut three times for the "yes" response. Calmly, she detached Keith's life support system. The doctor came to the house later, found the life support system reattached, and pronounced Keith dead.

For the rest of the day, she felt no guilt. That night, lying in bed, a doubt crept into Sandy's mind about her automatic reactions, and she questioned herself. After tossing and turning she finally fell into a fitful sleep. Soon Keith came to her in a dream. Smiling with gratitude, he conveyed to Sandy that she had done everything perfectly and that he loved her. A few weeks later Sandy was meditating and had a vision of her brother sitting on a bench talking with "two monks dressed in robes." Keith turned, laughed at her, and said, "Hang in there, Sis!"

To a devout religionist, this man's life did not belong to himself, but to God. While it is true that we are given our bodies by an act of divine creation, everyone's life belongs ultimately to them. The right to die is a hotly debated topic in legal circles today, especially as it pertains to doctor-assisted suicide with the terminally ill. It has been said that if death is the final act of life's drama, and we want that last act to reflect our own convictions during life, we should have that right regardless of the religious or moral convictions of a majority. The opposing view is that if life is a gift, of which we are the custodians, we have certain moral duties despite our own feelings. Knowing what I do about how our souls choose life, with the free will to make changes during that life, I believe we clearly have the right to choose death when no quality of life remains and there is no possibility of recovery. It is not intended that a degradation of our humanity be prolonged. The next case provides a more conventional representation of free will in terms of a full life.

Case 65

Emily was a woman in her late forties who came to see me because she was troubled by her purpose in life. During the years she was raising her children, Emily worked as a part-time secretary. Dissatisfied with this role, she returned to school and qualified as a nurse with an interest in geriatrics. During training, she discovered she liked treating the elderly because they were more inclined to talk about their faith. Emily had been attracted to spirituality all her life. She told me that her upbringing by a strict, rather cruel and overly pious father had turned her toward less-structured avenues of spirituality.

Although she had become a registered nurse some two years before our meeting, Emily had not worked in her new profession because of self-doubts about her competence. Due to her happy marriage with a supportive husband it had been easy just to slip into volunteer work without pay, pressure or responsibility.

As I moved Emily rapidly through her most immediate past life in the early stages of our session we discovered her name had been Sister Grace, a nun for the Sisters of Mercy in New England. The Order wanted her to accept the position of Mother Superior but she refused due to her fears of leadership and feelings of unworthiness. Indeed, a later overview from the spirit world of Emily's other recent past lives attested to a pattern of lives as priests and nuns in cloistered environments. She remarked, "I was able to serve God without getting too involved with the troubles of outside society."

I am often asked if the planners force certain lives on us for particular reasons. This case is a good example of just how indulgent our guides can be until we are finally ready for greater challenges. In the past 500 years, all of Emily's lives had been in religious orders in one form or another. She was comfortable with these lives and unwilling to make major changes. This past behavior represents a defining element of her confusion about life today.

The dialogue for this case opens at the second council meeting after Emily's life as Sister Grace, which means she was in preparation for her current life. If I discover there is to be a second council meeting between lives, it will usually take place just before we go to the Ring, and I know the life to come is likely to involve an opportunity for significant change. Both the type and number of Elders who appear at these second meetings depend on the kinds of lives and bodies to be presented.

Dr. N: When you are at this second council meeting is the makeup of the panel the same as the first one?

S: No, only two appear—my chairperson and a member who seems to have taken a special interest in what I will be offered in the next life.

Dr. N: Well, since we have already talked about your first council meeting following the life as Sister Grace, just give me a sense of what is now going on before you go to the place of life selection.

S: They want to know if I have thought long and hard about being in such a rut over the last 500 years and if I am ready to get involved with mainstream society.

Dr. N: Would they be upset with you if you returned to a religious life once again?

S: No, they are too wise for this sort of thing. They would just know I wasn't ready for a new undertaking yet. They are very gentle with me. I am reminded that my self-discipline and faith are to be admired and I learned a great deal, but that too much repetition over many lives can hold me back.

Dr. N: Did you take lots of risks before the last 500 years—before all those religious lives?

S: (laughs) I had been on a different path for a long time. I was . . . excessive . . . let's say celibacy was not on my agenda.

Dr. N: So, after being Sister Grace, it was time to bring the next series of life choices back to some sort of center—to bring balance into your existence on Earth?

S: Yes, and I tell them I am ready for a change.

Note: My use of time shifts at council meetings was discussed in chapter 6. With this case, I now shift forward to scenes in the life selection room to obtain a better therapeutic framework to help Emily. What follows is a portion of the cognitive reframing I used, which began with the venting and identification of personal conflicts. It is my intention that this hypnosis subject will recognize the opportunity her spiritual planners have given her to move forward into new ventures with greater self-awareness.

Dr. N: We are now in the place where you are reviewing your current body as Emily for the first time. Are you alone or with someone?

S: That second council member is with me and I feel the presence of another . . . who I can't see. (probably a coordinating Timemaster)

Dr. N: (after briefly discussing other body choices) Why are you attracted to the body of Emily?

S: I go inside a screen to feel the wavelengths of this brain . . . and how our mutual vibrations will blend. It is a good meld . . . between us . . . her talents and sensitivity are very compatible with me.

Dr. N: (reinforcement) So you can see the planners have your best interests at heart.

S: Oh, yes.

Dr. N: What do you see as the most significant aspect of your future life as Emily?

S: (long pause) This is hard for me to answer. I see her conflicts—they are my own—being torn between doing one thing and wanting another kind of career. I do not see myself as a nurse.

Dr. N: Since you are qualified now to be a nurse, could it be that you are shown more but at this moment your spiritual memory of these details is not revealed because the planners don't want to interfere with your free will to make a decision at such an important crossroad?

S: Maybe, I'm not sure. (pause) Ah . . . we don't have to be shown occupations . . . one can see . . . moods . . . attitudes and feelings at different times in the sphere of life with a particular body.

Dr. N: Good, I want you to ride with those feelings about this body you occupy and tell me how you can thrive as a person.

S: (another long pause) By nurturing people.

Dr. N: And what does that tell you?

S: (thinking, but no response)

Dr. N: And in the sphere of life selection, do you think the insight you now have about Emily is sufficient for you to accept this person and move forward to make a contribution in life?

S: Yes.

At this juncture in our session, Emily realized that there were elements of synchronicity in reviewing these past events in the Ring with me at this time and having free will to change her life. Some trips to the Ring give us more detail about a future life than others. Emily saw it was no accident she was assigned to an overly strict religious household as a child, which would drive her away from old, conditioned behavior patterns into new paths of thought. She saw that her freedom to make new choices and rely on her gut feelings gave her permission to undertake the search.

Uncertainty in life is frequently an outgrowth of former life patterns and obsessions. Emily's old inner fear of not wanting to accept responsible positions within the church because she felt unworthy surfaced again in her current professional life. While the door was opening to her in the field of medicine in a profound way, it also left her confused. Why did it seem both right and wrong at the same time? Emily had become mired in her plans for a midlife course correction over unconscious self-doubts which had peaked in her last life as Sister Grace.

Within six months of our meeting I received a letter from Emily explaining that she had taken a job with a nursing home and loved it. This particular facility wanted nurses who would not shy away from spiritual counseling to assist patients in dealing with feelings of helplessness, loneliness and depression. Emily wrote that she felt spiritually fulfilled. I don't deserve much credit for shedding light on this situation because Emily had already started on her quest before our session. She just needed a nudge to keep going. Today, nearing age fifty, she has broken free.

This case is not presented to denigrate traditional religion or religious orders by implying that Emily's soul had somehow wasted 500 years of incarnation time by taking roles of priests and nuns. Those were beneficial years of acting on her spiritual calling. Today those same callings are satisfied on a different road. Change is a hallmark of karma through the use of free will in making course corrections into unfamiliar waters. Searching for who you really are is getting in touch with your inner Self and bringing passion and meaning into what you do in life.

Souls of the Young
The Loss of a Child

The Ring represents a cycle of life, death and rebirth. For the soul, children play a vital role in their regeneration of life. What are the spiritual implications when this highly functional organism dies before it hardly got started? There have been grieving parents who have written me inquiring about the meanings surrounding the untimely death of their children and these letters are always difficult to answer. Those of us who have not gone through the agony of losing a child can only imagine the pain suffered by these parents. Some people who lose a child jump to the wrong conclusion that their terrible loss is the result of a karmic debt they must pay because of some transgression in a former life involving child abuse.

If the lost child was a teenager, or older, the karmic forces that led to the death customarily relate directly to the young person and not so much to the parent. Moreover, even when the death of a younger child does karmically involve the parent, this lesson does not automatically mean the parent was a perpetrator of mistreatment to children in a former life. The lesson could have been the result of many other elements, including that of indirect action. One of my clients who came to me about a year after the death of her eight-year-old daughter related the following story to me during her session.

> I was a wealthy matron in London in the nineteenth century. I paid little attention to the suffering of the young waifs on the street around my townhouse. I callously disregarded their plight because they were not my children; to my mind they were the responsibility of their parents or the state and had nothing to do with me. I looked the other way even though I had plenty of money to support an orphanage and a safe house for young unwed mothers nearby. I knew these services were struggling to make ends meet and I did nothing. Between lives I decided to correct my superficial ways. I agreed to experience the anguish of loving my own child and having her taken away. God, what pain, but I am learning compassion.

Information about the soul and infant mortality has come to me over many years which may provide some solace to mothers who feel remorse over both voluntary and involuntary actions involving the loss of an unborn child. This would include both issues of abortion and miscarriages. Please keep in mind during my review of this material that the karmic cause and effect relating to earlier past life incidents are particular to each parent-child relationship. My intent is to give the reader some general interpretations about the young that I have acquired from the reports of many subjects.

I will begin by stating that I have never had a single case where a soul joined the fetus in the first trimester. The reason that souls do not begin their complex merger with a fetus under three months is quite simply because there is not enough brain tissue for them to work with at this stage. I have a dear friend who is an obstetric nurse at a major hospital in Oregon. When she heard me make this statement on a national radio show she called to say, "Michael, why won't you let these little ones have their souls?" She was clearly upset with me over the question of who does and who does not have a soul in place if a baby is not going to term. I began by saying something to the effect that I don't make the rules, so please don't kill the messenger. I suspect this caregiver of babies, who has seen many who did not survive and leave her hospital, felt that from the moment of conception a fetus with a soul identity would somehow receive more spiritual comforting than otherwise.

I told my friend there is a universal consciousness of love surrounding all unborn babies. The creative force of existence is never separated from any form of living energy. A fetus can be alive as an individual entity without yet having an immortal soul identity. If a mother aborts her child in the first trimester, there are loving spiritual forces hovering nearby to comfort this mother and watch over the child. I have been told that even in cases of miscarriages and abortions between four and nine months, souls can be in place to support both the child and mother in a more direct physical manner with energy. Souls know in advance the probabilities of the baby going to term.

For example, if a pregnant woman loses her child because she fell down a stairway, say in the seventh month, it was not absolutely preordained she would take this fall. There was also the possibility on that particular day, at a certain moment in time, she might have decided at the last minute not to descend the stairway. However, if a young, unmarried girl becomes pregnant and decides to abort her child because it is unwanted, the chances are high this was a significant probable event of choice. These two interpretations of causality are, of course, hypothetical. Nevertheless, various scenarios of significant events in our life are known in advance when we choose certain bodies in the Ring. All have karmic implications and purpose for us.

Souls are not assigned to babies at random. When a mother loses her child for whatever reason, I have found the odds are quite high that the soul of this baby will return again to the same mother with her next child. If this mother does not bear another child, the soul may return to another close member of the family because that was the original intent. When a life is short, souls call these filler lives and they too have purpose for the parent. Here is an illustration:

> I joined a fetus at four months for a three-month exis-
> tence. During this time my mother needed to feel my
> soul energy to know that giving and losing life is very
> profound. I did not wish to let the sadness of losing me
> prevent her from having the courage to try again. We
> knew this fetus was not going to term, but there was a
> good probability of a second child after me and I wanted
> that partnership with her. She doesn't realize that I was
> once her son and now I am her daughter. I think I was
> able to soften her bitterness and grief by sending my
> mother comforting thoughts in the stillness of all the
> nights between her two pregnancies.

As I mentioned in the section on soulmates in chapter 7, when babies and young children die their souls typically do not rise into the spirit world alone. Spirit guides, caretakers of the young, or a member of the child's soul group are frequently involved with meeting these souls right at ground level. If a parent is killed at the same time as their small child, they stay together, as the following quote demonstrates:

> After my son and I were killed by bandits (Sweden, 1842),
> I comforted him as we rose together. Because he was so
> young, he was disoriented and confused at first. I held my
> son close and told him how much I loved him and that
> we were going home. As we rose together, I said that we
> would soon be met by our friends and then parted for a
> while, before being reunited once again.

New Body-Soul Partnerships

The process of a soul joining with an unborn child is an appropriate end to the case histories I have presented in this book. The soul is now ready to embark on another reincarnation adventure with hopes and expectations for a fresh new role in life. The partnership between the physical and etheric minds that usher a whole human being into the world can be smooth or rocky in the early adjustment stages of childhood. Even so, it is the end result and how we finish the course we traveled that counts the most.

During our lifetime, the soul and the body are so intertwined that the duality of expression may confuse us as to who we really are. The complexities of this association between body and soul represent an alliance of long evolutionary development going back perhaps to the late Pleistocene era when hominoids on this planet were originally considered suitable for soul colonization. The oldest divisions of our modern brain still remain in place as survival mechanisms. Some people, such as the soul Kliday in case 36, acknowledge touching primitive sections of the brain when they enter a fetus. These are the areas that control our visceral, physical reactions, which are instinctual and emotional rather than intellectual. Some of my clients have said that a few brains they have joined seemed more primitive than all the others.

Ego has been defined as Self, conceived as a spiritual substance upon which experience is superimposed. This psyche would define the soul, but there is an ego of a kind relegated to the brain which experiences the external world through the senses governing action and reaction. It is this functional organism—created before the soul arrived—that the soul must join in a mother. In a sense, there are two egos at work here and this is most evident to me during regressions when I take my subjects to the Ring and later when they join a fetus. It is in the fetus where the body-soul partnership really begins.

The soul and brain of a new baby appear to begin their association as two separate and distinct entities and become one mind. Some people are bothered that my two-entity position, or duality of body and spirit, means that while the immortal character of the soul lives on, the temporary personality of the body dies. Yet it was the soul, in concert with the mind of a body, which created a unique personality of a single Self. Although the physical organism of the body will die, the soul who occupied that body never forgets the host which allowed them to experience Earth in a particular time and place. We have seen how souls can remember and re-create who they were in certain timelines.

Every physical body has its own unique design and the concepts, ideas and judgments of any human mind are directly related to the soul who is occupying that body. I endeavored to show in chapters 3 and 4 how some body-soul combinations work more efficiently than others. Physiologists do not know why intense emotion may cause irrational behavior in one person and logical coping actions in another. For me, the answer lies in the soul. When the body-soul partnership is underway in the fetus of a client's current body, I do hear evaluations from many of them about brain circuitry being fine-tuned or a bit jumbled in the new baby. The remarks from a level V soul about entering a body are instructive in terms of attachments:

> No two brains are constructed in precisely the same way. When I initially enter the womb of my mother, I touch the brain gently. I flow in . . . seeking . . . probing . . . searching. It is like osmosis. I know immediately if this brain is going to be smooth or rough sailing for our mutual communication. I will receive my mother's emotional feelings during pregnancy more than her clear thoughts. That's how I know if the baby is wanted or not, and this makes a difference in the baby getting a good or bad start.
>
> When I enter the fetus of an unwanted baby, I can make a positive difference by energy engagement with this child. When I was a young soul, I would get caught up with the alienation of a parent and both the child and I felt a separation. I have been working with babies for thousands of years and I can handle whatever sort of child they give me so we are both fulfilled by coming together. I have too much work to do in life to be slowed down by a body match which does not happen to be perfect for me.

When a soul reaches level III, most are able to make rapid adjustments once inside a fetus. A subject told me bluntly, "When a complex, highly advanced soul combines with a sluggish brain, it is like hitching a race horse to a plow horse." Usually my clients express this sentiment about bodies in a more deferential manner. There are karmic reasons for all body-soul matches. Also, a high IQ is no indication of an advanced soul. It is not a low IQ but the disturbed, irrational mind that poses problems for the less-experienced souls.

As for body matches with the soul, our options are offered to us in good faith for a variety of life designs. Body choices in the Ring are never used to trap us into something unsuitable for our development. The sphere of life selection is not a department store fire sale of merchandise. The planners have no interest in sandbagging some unsuspecting soul with a "poor-quality" body. There is purpose for both egos behind every body-soul match. While the body delights the soul as a means of both physical and mental expression, it is capable of bringing great pain. The lesson of this merger is to forge a harmonious unification of body and soul so that they function as one unit. I have two perspectives that illustrate this collaboration:

> I am a volatile soul with hasty inclinations and I prefer aggressive bodies with temperaments which complement my own inclinations. We call this sort of combination of mirror images a double-double. I can never slow down. I must admit the quiet bodies with noncombative minds do calm me, but then I tend to become very lazy and complacent.

> I am comfortable with emotionally cold hosts. I also love analytical minds so we can take our time before committing to things. Inside Jane it's as though I'm on a rollercoaster ride. She is so reckless, jumping into situations—I mean I try to drag her back—but she gets so out of control she brings us a lot of pain. Yet, there is much joy too—it's all overwhelming, but what a wild ride!

Certain body matches do produce lives of frustration and very difficult challenges. However, only a couple of times in my entire career have I ever had a soul who admitted they asked to be replaced in a fetus it found impossible to adjust to in any way. In both cases, another soul took its place before the eighth month. A prenatal exchange due to incompatibility is an extremely rare occurrence because this is what the life selection room is all about.

In chapter 3, where I discussed people who engage in wrongdoing, I explained how our inner soul Self might not be in harmony with our body. I also said that no soul is innately evil when it joins a fetus. Still, the soul does not enter with a blank slate either. A soul's immortal character is influenced by all the attributes and temperament of the brain, which challenges the soul's maturity. I have said there are souls who are more susceptible than others in falling prey to negative influences in life. Most of the cases in this book reflect souls who struggle in opposition or work in harmonious conjunction with their bodies. Souls combating the need to control may not blend well with a body ego disposed to confrontation. On the other hand, a cautious, low-energy soul could choose a rather passive, introverted body temperament in order to institute boldness in concert with its host.

When a soul joins with a new baby, I can be fairly sure the partnership will address both the soul's shortcomings and a body-mind who needs this particular soul. The planners choose bodies for us which are intended to combine our character defects with certain body temperaments to produce specific personality combinations. From clients who are medical doctors and physiologists, I have been given brief anatomical glimpses about souls entering the developing brain of a fetus. Case 66 is an example. Posthypnotic suggestions have enabled subjects in these professions to sketch out simplified diagrams of what they were trying to say about these linkages while under hypnosis. This has helped my understanding.

Case 66

Dr. N: I would like to know if the initial transition into the fetus is always about the same for you?

S: No, it is not. Even though I might have had x-ray vision into the mind of the child during life selection, my entry can still be ragged.

Dr. N: Give me your most recent example of a difficult entry.

S: Three lives ago, I joined with a very stiff, unreceptive brain. It felt my presence was invasive. This was unusual because most of my host bodies accept my presence. I'm ordinarily considered to be a new roommate.

Dr. N: Are you saying this particular host body felt you were an alien presence that it should reject?

S: No, it was a dull mind of dense energy pockets. My arrival was an intrusion on its lack of mental activity ... there was ... isolation between compartments of the brain . . . creating resistance to . . . communication. Lethargic minds require more effort on my part. They resist change.

Dr. N: Change of what?

S: Of my being in its space, requiring some reaction to deal with this fact. I caused this mind to think and it was not a curious mind. I began pushing buttons and found it did not want to be summoned by me.

Dr. N: What did you expect?

S: From my review in the sphere (the Ring), I saw the end result of an adult mind but I didn't see all the difficulties with the baby's mind . . . when it was new.

Dr. N: I see, and you are saying this mind considered your intrusion as a threat?

S: No, only a nuisance. Eventually, I was accepted and the child and I adapted to each other.

Dr. N: Let's go back to your statement about pushing buttons. Please explain to me what this means to you with a standard entry into the fetus of your choice?

S: When I enter a developing brain I am accustomed to joining around the fourth month—our guides give us some latitude here—but I never enter after the sixth month. When I enter the womb of the mother I create a red light of tight energy and direct it up and down the spinal column of the baby—following a network of neurons to the brain.

Dr. N: Why do you do that?

S: This tells me about the efficiency of thought transmission—the sensory relays . . .

Dr. N: Then, what do you do?

S: Play my red light around the dura mater—the outer layer of the brain . . . gently . . .

Dr. N: Why red light?

S: This allows me to be . . . especially sensitive to the physical feel-ings of this new person. I meld my energy warmth to the gray-blues of brain matter. Before I get there, the brain is simply gray. What I am doing is turning on the lights in a dark room with a tree in the middle.

Dr. N: You lost me. Explain about the tree.

S: (intensely) The tree is the stem. I park myself between the two hemispheres of the brain to get a ringside seat as to how this sys-tem will function. Then I move around the branches of the tree to investigate the circuitry. I want to know how dense the energy is in the fibers around the wheel of the cerebral cortex folding around the thalamus . . . I want to learn how this brain thinks and senses things.

Dr. N: How important is energy density or the lack of it in the brain?

S: A mind that has excessive density in certain areas means there are blockages which inhibit the bridges between efficient neuron activity. I want to make some adjustments in these road blocks with my energy if I can—you know—while the brain is still forming.

Dr. N: You can make a difference in how the brain develops?

S: (laughs at me) Of course! Did you think souls are passengers on a train? I stimulate these areas ever so slightly.

Dr. N: (deliberately obtuse) Well, I thought you and the baby . . . are both in miniature by the way you exhibit intelligence in the beginning.

S: (laughs) Not until birth.

Dr. N: Are you saying that you can improve brain wave function with all these activities you have described?

S: That is our expectation. The whole idea is matching your vibra-tional levels and capabilities with that of the natural rhythms of the child's brain waves—their electrical flow. (with exuberance) I think my host bodies are grateful for my assistance in improving the speed of thought over bridges. (stops and then adds) Maybe this is wishful thinking.

Dr. N: What do you see in the future for the brain with continued evolution and the influence of souls as a stimulus?

S: Mental telepathy.

Certainly, I have had younger souls who appear to be more inactive after body entry than case 66. This is a far sight better than agitating the child by ineptness from overzealous, inexperienced souls. The average soul probes their new host for information but in a way that has been described as "tickling the child to give it pleasure." Essentially, this is an important time for integration between body and soul with the mother also mentally entering into this process of getting acquainted. By no means is the seat of the soul limited to the brain. Soul energy radiates throughout the whole body of the child.

Case 66 is a medical doctor. My next case comes from a non-medically oriented client about the union of two entities to form one whole as a new life begins. Each soul has its own preferences about when and how they wish to enter the fetus. The following case gives us an indication of the procedures used by a very considerate, evolved soul.

Case 67

Dr. N: Tell me what it is like to enter the mind of a baby and when you usually enter.

S: In the beginning I think of it as a betrothal. I entered my current body in the eighth month. I prefer to enter on the late side when the brain is larger so I have more to work with during the coupling.

Dr. N: Isn't there a downside to entering late? I mean, you are then dealing with a more independent individual.

S: Some of my friends feel that way, I don't. I want to be able to talk with the child when there is more mutual awareness.

Dr. N: (being dense to elicit a response) Talk—talk to a fetus—what are you saying . . . ?

S: (laughs at me) Of course we interact with the child.

Dr. N: Take me through this slowly. Who says what first?

S: The child may say, "Who are you?" I answer, "A friend who has come to play and be a part of you."

Dr. N: (with deliberate provocation) Isn't that deceitful? You haven't come to play. You have come to occupy this mind.

S: Oh, please! Who have you been talking to? This mind and my soul were created to be together. Do you think I am some sort of foreign intruder on Earth? I have joined with babies who welcomed me as if I were expected.

Dr. N: There are souls who have had a different experience.

S: Look, I know souls who are clumsy. They go in like bulls in a china shop with their over-eagerness to get started with an agenda. Too much frontal energy all at once sets up resistance.

Dr. N: In your current lifetime, was the child at all anxious about your entry?

S: No, they don't know enough yet to be anxious. I begin by caressing the brain. I am able to immediately project warm thoughts of love and companionship. Most of the babies just accept me as being part of themselves. A few hold back—like my current body.

Dr. N: Oh, really? What was unusual about this fetus?

S: It wasn't a big deal. Its thoughts were, "Now that you are here, who am I going to be?"

Dr. N: I think that's a very big deal. Essentially, the child is acknowledging that its identity depends on you.

S: (patiently) The child has begun to ask itself, "Who am I?" Some children are more aware of this than others. A few are resistant because, to them, we are an irritation to their inert beginnings— like a pearl in an oyster.

Dr. N: So you don't feel the child senses it is being forced to give up something of its individuality?

S: No, we have come as souls to give the child . . . depth of personality. Its being is enhanced by our presence. Without us they would largely function as unripened fruit.

Dr. N: But does the child understand any of this before birth?

S: It only knows that I want to be friends so we can do things together. We begin by communicating with each other with simple things such as an uncomfortable body position in the mother's womb. There have been times when the umbilical chord was wrapped around the neck of the baby and I have calmed the child where otherwise it might have squirmed and made things worse.

Dr. N: Please continue with how you assist the baby.

S: I prepare the child for birth, which is going to be a shock when it happens. Imagine being forced out of a warm, comfortable, secure womb into the bright lights of a hospital room . . . the noise . . . having to breathe air . . . being handled. The child appreciates my help because my primary goal now is to combat fear by soothing the brain with assurances that everything will be fine.

Dr. N: I wonder what it was like for children before souls came to help them?

S: The brain was too primitive then to conceptualize the trauma of birthing. There was little awareness. (Laughs) Of course I wasn't around in those days.

Dr. N: Are you able to calm anxious mothers in any way?

S: We must be proficient. During much of my existence I had little or no effect on my mothers if they were frightened, sad or angry during pregnancy. You must be able to align your energy vibrations with both the child and the mother's natural body rhythms. You have to harmonize three sets of wave levels—which includes your own—to soothe the mother. I might even have the baby kick the mother to let her know we are all right.

Dr. N: Then at birth, I supposed the hard work of the merger is over?

S: To be honest, the merger isn't complete yet for me. I talk to my body as a second entity up to the age of six. It is better not to force a full meld right away. We play games as two people for a while.

Dr. N: I have noticed a lot of young children talk to themselves as if they were with an imaginary playmate. Is that their soul?

S: (grinning) That's right, although our guides enjoy playing with us as young children too. And have you also noticed the elderly talking to themselves a lot? They are preparing for separation at the other end in their own way.

Dr. N: In general how do you feel about coming back to Earth in life after life?

S: As a gift. This is such a multifaceted planet. Sure, this place brings heartache, but it is delightful too and incredibly beautiful. The human body is a marvel of form and structure. I never cease to be awed by each new body, the many different ways I can express myself in them, especially in the most important way—love.

~10

Our Spiritual Path

The concept of our resurrection into beings who belong in a kingdom of eternity goes far back into human antiquity. From our early origins, we have believed that life and afterlife are sustained by divine intelligence as a single, unified whole. These sentiments come from the memories of many people I have regressed to the Stone Age. For ages since then, we thought of the soul world as another state of consciousness rather than an abstract place. The afterlife was considered to be only an extension of our physical life. I believe the world is returning to those concepts, which were beautifully expressed by Spinoza, who said, "All the cosmos is a single substance of which we are a part. God is not an external manifestation, but everything that is."

I consider such legends as Atlantis and Shangri-La as having their origins in the eternal longing we feel for recapturing a Utopia that once existed but is now lost. In the superconscious mind of every person I have ever placed in deep hypnosis lies the memory of a Utopian home. Originally, the concept of Utopia was intended to illustrate ideas, not a society. My subjects see the spirit world as a community of ideas. In this sense, the afterlife involves self-purification of thought. Beings who are still incarnating are far from perfect, as demonstrated by my cases. Nevertheless, we can justifiably think of our existence in the spirit world as Utopian because there is a universal harmony of spirit. Righteousness, honesty, humor and love are the primary foundations of our life after life.

After reading the information contained in this book, I know it must seem cruel that the Utopia of our dreams does exist within all of us but is blocked from conscious memory by amnesia. When some of these blocks are overcome through hypnosis, meditation, prayer, channeling, yoga, imagination and dreams, or a mental state reached through physical exertion, there is a sense of personal empowerment. Some 2,400 years ago, Plato wrote about reincarnation and said that souls must travel over Lethe, the River of Forgetfulness, whose waters produce a loss of memory from our true nature.

The sacred truths of our etheric history can be recovered today because we are able to circumvent the conscious mind and reach the unconscious, which was not immersed in the River of Forgetfulness. Our higher Self remembers our past triumphs and transgressions in a selective way, whispering to us across time and space. Our personal spirit guides endeavor to give us the best from both worlds, the ethereal and material. Each new baby is given a fresh start with an open future. Our spiritual masters wish to produce karmic opportunity without the constraints of our knowing those pitfalls we experienced in former lives. They become more lenient in a selective way with amnesia as we engage in self-discovery. This is our best route to wisdom.

The question has been fairly asked as to why amnesia blocks about our spiritual life have been loosened to permit research into the spirit world. I think about this issue a great deal because now in the twenty-first century I expect younger hypnotherapists to go far beyond what my generation has been able to accomplish in unlocking the spiritual mind. I feel the reasons for our ability to discover more of the mysteries about life on the other side is a direct outgrowth of living in the twentieth century.

The advancement of innovative techniques in hypnosis would have to be listed as a consideration. However, I believe there are more compelling reasons why our amnesia has become less constrictive over the last thirty years. Never before has such a variety of drugs been so pervasive in the human population. These mind-altering chemicals imprison the soul within a body encumbered by a mental fog. The soul's essence is unable to express itself through a chemically addicted mind. I feel the planners on the other side have lost patience with this aspect of human society. There are other reasons as well. As the twentieth century draws to a close we live in a frantic, rage-filled, overpopulated, environmentally degraded world. The mass destruction of our planet in the last hundred years from all sources is unequaled in human experience.

I do not have a dark vision of the future, despite my comments. It may be true that to the people who are living in an era, their time seems more decadent than the last. Yet we have made great advancements culturally, politically and economically in the last hundred years. In many ways the world is a far safer place than it was in 1950. Internationally, nations have more social conscience and commitments to work for peace than ever before in our long history of monarchies and dictatorships, which were still very much in evidence at the start of the twentieth century. What we face in the twenty-first century is the eroding of individualism and human dignity in an overcrowded society dominated by materialism. Globalization, urban sprawl and bigness is a formula for loneliness and disassociation. Many people believe in nothing but survival.

I believe the spiritual door has been opened to our immortality because to deny us this knowledge has proven to be counterproductive. In the spirit world of my experience, if something on Earth isn't working it can be changed. Amnesiac blocks were set in place with human beings to prevent preconditioned responses to certain karmic events. However, the benefits of amnesia may no longer outweigh the drawbacks of lives existing within a vacuum of chemically-induced apathy. There are too many people trying to escape from reality because they do not see their identity as having purpose or meaning. Drugs and alcohol aside, in overcrowded, high-tech societies around the world, people have an emptiness of spirit because they are ruled by their body-ego senses. They have little or no connection to their real Self.

Because each of us is a unique being, different from all others, it is incumbent upon those who desire internal peace to find their own spirituality. When we totally align ourselves to belief systems based upon the experience of other people, I feel we lose something of our individuality in the process. The road to self-discovery and shaping a personal philosophy not designed by the doctrines of organizations takes effort but the rewards are great. There are many routes to this goal which begins by trusting in yourself. Camus tells us, "Both the rational and irrational lead to the same understanding. Truly, the path traveled matters little; the will to arrive is enough."

Visions of the afterlife lie within each of us as a sanctuary while we travel the maze of Earth's pathways. The difficulty in uncovering fragments of our eternal home is due in no small part to life's distractions. It is not a bad thing to accept life as it is, asking no questions and assuming that in the end what is supposed to happen will happen. However, for those with a longing to know more, simple acceptance of life is totally unsatisfying. For some travelers, life's mysteries cry out for attention, if being alive is to have any meaning.

In the search for our own path of spirituality it is wise to ask, "What sort of behavioral code do I believe in?" Some theologians suggest that nonreligious people are attempting to cut loose from moral and ethical responsibility dictated to us in scripture from a higher authority. However, we are not evaluated after death by our religious associations but rather by our conduct and values. In the spirit world I am familiar with, we are measured more by what we do for others rather than ourselves. If traditional religious activity serves your purpose and provides you with spiritual sustenance, you are probably motivated by a belief in scripture and perhaps the desire for comradeship in worship. The same attractions are true with people who join metaphysical groups and derive satisfaction from following the ideas of prescribed spiritual texts with like-minded people. While such practices may be comforting and edifying for your spiritual growth, it must be recognized that these pathways do not suit everyone.

If there is no inner peace, it does not matter what sort of spiritual affiliation you have. Disengagement in life arises when we separate ourselves from our inner power by taking the position that we are all alone, without spiritual guidance, because no one upstairs is listening. I have great respect for people with abiding faith in something since for a large part of my life I had no solid foundation of spirituality, despite my searching. There are atheists and agnostics who take the position that since religious and spiritual knowledge cannot be based upon natural or proven evidence, it is unacceptable. Simply having faith is not truly revealed knowledge to the skeptic. I identify with these people because I was one of them. My faith in the hereafter slowly began as an outgrowth of my participation with subjects in hypnosis. This is a discipline I believed in professionally before my research discoveries. Nevertheless, my own spiritual awareness was also the result of years of personal meditation and introspection about this research.

Spiritual perception must be an individual quest or it has no meaning. We are greatly influenced by our own immediate reality, and we can act on that reality one step at a time without the necessity of seeing too far into the distance. Even steps in the wrong direction give us insight into the many paths designed to teach us. To bring the soul Self into harmony with our physical environment, we are given freedom of choice to exercise free will in the search for the reasons why we are here. On the road of life we must take responsibility for all our decisions without blaming other people for life's setbacks that bring unhappiness.

As I mentioned, to be effective in our mission we are expected to help others on their paths whenever possible. By helping others we help ourselves. Reaching out to others is inhibited when we nurture our own uniqueness to such an extent that we become totally self-absorbed. However, being an absentee landlord in your own house makes you ineffective as a person as well. You were not given your body by a chance of nature. It was selected for you by spiritual advisors and after previewing their offerings of other host bodies, you agreed to accept the body you now have. Thus, you are not a victim of circumstance. You are entrusted with your body to be an active participant in life, not a bystander. We must not lose sight of the idea that we accepted this sacred contract of life and this means the roles we play on Earth are actually greater than ourselves.

Our soul energy was created by a higher authority than we can know in our present state of development. Consequently, we must focus on who we are as a person to find that fragment of divinity within us. The only limitations to personal insight are self-imposed. If the spiritual paths of others have no relevance to you, this does not mean the way designed for your needs is nonexistent. The reason for our being who we are is a major truth in life. Where one person may find an aspect of that truth manifested to them, it will not be in the same place for another.

Essentially, we are alone with our soul, yet people who feel lonely haven't quite found themselves. Self-discovery of the soul has to do with self-possession. The capturing of our individual essence is like falling in love. Something within you lying dormant is awakened at a point in your life by a stimulus. The soul flirts with you at first, tempting you to go further with delights that are only seen from a distance. The initial attraction of self-discovery begins with an almost playful touching of the conscious by the unconscious mind. As the intensity of wanting to fully possess our inner Self grows, we are drawn irresistibly into a more intimate connection. Knowing our soul becomes a marriage of fidelity to one's Self. The fascinating aspect about self-discovery is that when you hear that inner voice you instantly recognize it. Based on my practice, I am convinced that everyone on this planet has a personal spiritual guide. Spirit guides speak to our inner mind if we are receptive. While some guides are more easily reached than others, each of us has the ability to call upon and be heard by these guides.

There are no accidents in life, yet people get confused by what they perceive to be randomness. It is this philosophy that works against thoughts of spiritual order. It becomes an easy next step to feel we have no control in our lives and trying to find ourselves is pointless since nothing we do matters anyway. Believing in the randomness of events negatively influences our reaction to situations and allows us to avoid thinking about explanations for them. Having a fatalistic outlook on life by saying "It's God's will" or even "It's my karma" contributes to inaction and lack of purpose.

That which is meaningful in life comes in small pieces or large chunks all at one time. Self-awareness can take us beyond what we thought was our original destination. Karma is the setting in motion of those conditions on our path that foster learning. The concept of a Source orchestrating all of this need not be pretentious. The spiritual externalist waits for reunification with a Creator after death, while the internalist feels part of a Oneness each day. Spiritual insight comes to us in quiet, introspective, subtle moments which are manifested by the power of a single thought.

Life is a matter of constant change toward fulfillment. Our place in the world today may be different tomorrow. We must learn to adapt to these different perspectives in life because that, too, is part of the plan for our development. In so doing, there is a transcendence of Self from the masking process of a temporary outer shell to that which lies deep within our permanent soul mind. To uplift the human mind from feelings of disenchantment, we must expand our consciousness while forgiving ourselves for mistakes. I believe it is vital to our mental health that we laugh at ourselves and the foolish predicaments we get into along the road. Life is full of conflicts and the struggle, pain and happiness we experience are all reasons for our being here. Each day is a new beginning.

I have a final quote that came from a subject who was preparing for another departure from the spirit world into a new incarnation on Earth. I think his statement offers a fitting conclusion to this book:

> Coming to Earth is about traveling away from our home to a foreign land. Some things seem familiar but most are strange until we get used to them, especially conditions which are unforgiving. Our real home is a place of absolute peace, total acceptance and complete love. As souls separated from our home we can no longer assume these beautiful features will be present around us. On Earth we must learn to cope with intolerance, anger and sadness while searching for joy and love. We must not lose our integrity along the way, sacrificing goodness for survival and acquiring attitudes either superior or inferior to those around us. We know that living in an imperfect world will help us to appreciate the true meaning of perfection. We ask for courage and humility before our journey into another life. As we grow in awareness so will the quality of our existence. This is how we are tested. Passing this test is our destiny.

Index

Spirit Guides & Angel Guardians
Contact Your Invisible Helpers

RICHARD WEBSTER

They come to our aid when we least expect it, and they disappear as soon as their work is done. Invisible helpers are available to all of us; in fact, we all regularly receive messages from our guardian angels and spirit guides but usually fail to recognize them. This book will help you to realize when this occurs. And when you carry out the exercises provided, you will be able to communicate freely with both your guardian angels and spirit guides.

You will see your spiritual and personal growth take a huge leap forward as soon as you welcome your angels and guides into your life. This book contains numerous case studies that show how angels have touched the lives of others, just like yourself. Experience more fun, happiness, and fulfillment than ever before. Other people will also notice the difference as you become calmer, more relaxed, and more loving than ever before.

- Learn the important differences between a guardian angel and a spirit guide
- Invoke the Archangels for help in achieving your goals
- Discover the different ways your guardian angel speaks to you
- Create your own guardian angel from within
- Use your guardian angel to aid in healing yourself and others
- Find your life's purpose through your guardian angel

1-56718-795-1
368 pp., 5 ³/₁₆ x 8 $9.95

To order, call 1-877-NEW WRLD
Prices subject to change without notice

How to Meet & Work with Spirit Guides

TED ANDREWS

We often experience spirit contact in our lives but fail to recognize it for what it is. Now you can learn to access and attune to beings such as guardian angels, nature spirits and elementals, spirit totems, archangels, gods and goddesses—as well as family and friends after their physical death.Karma is a simple law of consequence, not of moralistic retribution and penalty. It's a way of viewing existence that results in increased mental health and self-responsibility.

Contact with higher soul energies strengthens the will and enlightens the mind. Through a series of simple exercises, you can safely and gradually increase your awareness of spirits and your ability to identify them. You will learn to develop an intentional and directed contact with any number of spirit beings. Discover meditations to open up your subconscious. Learn which acupressure points effectively stimulate your intuitive faculties. Find out how to form a group for spirit work, use crystal balls, perform automatic writing, attune your aura for spirit contact, use sigils to contact the great archangels, and much more! Read *How to Meet and Work with Spirit Guides* and take your first steps through the corridors of life beyond the physical.

0-87542-008-7
192 pp., mass market $5.99

Death: Beginning or End?
Methods for Immortality

DR. JONN MUMFORD (SWAMI ANANDAKAPILA SARASWATI)

This book is an exhilarating celebration of life—and death. It is a thought-provoking and interactive tool that will alter your perceptions about death and prepare you for reincarnation. Explore the history of death rituals and attitudes from other ages and cultures. Uncover surprising facts about this inevitable life event. Moreover, discover the ultimate truth about death, knowledge that is guaranteed to have a profound impact on how you live the rest of your life!

Learn how your experience of life after birth will impact your experience of life after death. Personally engage in five "alchemical laboratories"—five of the most crucial "stocktaking" exercises you will ever do. Learn a traditional Hindu meditation that will provide a psychic and mental refuge as well as deep physical relaxation. Practice a mantra that can liberate you from the endless wheel of blind incarnation. Use the tools provided in the book and avoid the death's biggest tragedy: to not ever discover who you are in life.

1-56718-476-6
224 pp., 5³⁄₁₆ x 6

$9.95

How to Uncover Your Past Lives

TED ANDREWS

Knowledge of your past lives can be extremely rewarding. It can assist you in opening to new depths within your own psychological makeup. It can provide greater insight into present circumstances with loved ones, career and health. It is also a lot of fun.

Now Ted Andrews shares with you nine different techniques that you can use to access your past lives. Between techniques, Andrews discusses issues such as karma and how it is expressed in your present life, the source of past life information, soul mates and twin souls, proving past lives, the mysteries of birth and death, animals and reincarnation, abortion and premature death, and the role of reincarnation in Christianity.

To explore your past lives, you need only use one or more of the techniques offered. Complete instructions are provided for a safe and easy regression. Learn to dowse to pinpoint the years and places of your lives with great accuracy, make your own self-hypnosis tape, attune to the incoming child during pregnancy, use the tarot and the cabala in past life meditations, keep a past life journal, and more.

0-87542-022-2
240 pp., mass market $4.99

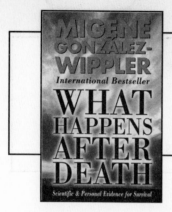

What Happens After Death
Scientific & Personal Evidence for Survival

MIGENE GONZÁLEZ-WIPPLER

What does science tell us about life after death? How do the different religions explain the mystery? What is the answer given by the strange mystical science known as Spiritism? These and other questions about the life beyond are explored in *What Happens After Death*.

The first part of the book is an objective study of the research about life after death. The second part is a personal narrative by a spirit guide named Kirkudian about his various incarnations. While the two sections could be considered two separate books, they simply express the same concepts in uniquely different ways.

Experience for yourself one soul's journey through the afterlife, and discover the ultimate truth: that every soul is created in union with all other souls, and that we are all manifestations of one purpose.

1-56718-327-1
256 pp., 5³⁄₁₆ x 8

$7.95

How to Communicate with Spirits
ELIZABETH OWEN

Spiritualist mediums share their fascinating experiences with the "other side" . . .

No where else will you find such a wealth of anecdotes from noted professional mediums residing within a Spiritualist community. These real-life psychics shed light on spirit entities, spirit guides, relatives who are in spirit, and communication with all of those on the spirit side of life.

You will explore the different categories of spirit guidance, and you will hear from the mediums themselves about their first contacts with the spirit world, as well as the various phenomena they have encountered.

- Noted mediums residing within a Spiritualist community share their innermost experiences, opinions, and advice regarding spirit communication
- Includes instructions for table tipping, automatic writing, and meditating to make contact with spirits
- For anyone interested in developing and understanding spiritual gifts

1-56718-530-4
5 ³⁄₁₆ x 8 • 240 pp. glossary • bibliog. $9.95

To order, call 1-877-NEW WRLD
Prices subject to change without notice